# Integrations of Technology Utilization and Social Dynamics in Organizations

Dawn Medlin
*Appalachian State University, USA*

| | |
|---|---|
| Managing Director: | Lindsay Johnston |
| Senior Editorial Director: | Heather A. Probst |
| Book Production Manager: | Sean Woznicki |
| Development Manager: | Joel Gamon |
| Assistant Acquisitions Editor: | Kayla Wolfe |
| Typesetter: | Lisandro Gonzalez |
| Cover Design: | Nick Newcomer |

Published in the United States of America by
Information Science Reference (an imprint of IGI Global)
701 E. Chocolate Avenue
Hershey PA 17033
Tel: 717-533-8845
Fax: 717-533-8661
E-mail: cust@igi-global.com
Web site: http://www.igi-global.com

Library of Congress Cataloging-in-Publication Data

Integrations of technology utilization and social dynamics in organizations / Dawn Medlin, editor.
    p. cm.
  Includes bibliographical references and index.
   ISBN 978-1-4666-1948-7 (hbk.) -- ISBN 978-1-4666-1949-4 (ebook) -- ISBN 978-1-4666-1950-0 (print & perpetual access) 1. Information technology. 2. Information technology--Social aspects. I. Medlin, Dawn, 1957-
  T58.5.I56486 2013
  658.4'038011--dc23
                        2012009913

British Cataloguing in Publication Data
A Cataloguing in Publication record for this book is available from the British Library.

The views expressed in this book are those of the authors, but not necessarily of the publisher.

# Table of Contents

**Section 1**
**Workforce Issues**

**Section 2**
**Organizational Issues**

## Section 3
## Virtual and Software Issues

# Detailed Table of Contents

## Section 1
## Workforce Issues

**Chapter 1**

*Salem Al-Agtash, Yarmouk University, Jordan*

This paper provides an assessment of workforce need in the Jordanian ICT industry. The results have shown that there is a growing workforce gap in the ICT sector. The technical skills of graduates are not satisfactory, and there is an increasing demand for skilled graduates. In addition to the technical skills required, communication skills, creative thinking, and English language skills were seen as important "soft skill elements" across all job categories and are missing in the current ICT workforce. The skills and competencies identified in this study can be used to motivate a design of an effective, flexible and relevant ICT program that can contribute to building a skillful workforce focusing on specialized and hands-on practices in ICT domains.

**Chapter 2**

*Damien Joseph, Nanyang Technological University, Singapore*
*Mei Ling Tan, Nanyang Technological University, Singapore*
*Soon Ang, Nanyang Technological University, Singapore*

This study proposes that IT professionals' behavioral orientation towards IT knowledge and skills updating demands can take on two contrasting forms: updating-as-play or updating-as-work. Drawing on threat-rigidity theory (Staw, Sandelands, & Dutton, 1981), the authors hypothesize that IT professionals who feel threatened by professional obsolescence are more likely to approach updating-as-work more than as play. Results from a sample of IT professionals are consistent with threat-rigidity theory (Staw et al., 1981) in that the threat of professional obsolescence is negatively related to updating-as-play and is positively related to updating-as-work. The authors also find that updating-as-play is negatively related to turnaway intentions and that updating-as-work is positively related to turnover intentions; these findings are consistent with IT theories of job mobility. The authors conclude this study with a discussion of these results and propose future research directions.

**Chapter 3**

George Nezlek, Grand Valley State University, USA
Gerald DeHondt, Grand Valley State University, USA

This paper investigates trends and changes in the gender earnings gap for individuals employed in clerical and professional level information systems positions in the U.S. labor market for the period of 1991 through 2008. It examines changes in the earnings gap for IS workers, specifically considering changes relative to the so-called "Internet bubble" observed primarily during the late 1990s. Quantitative analysis of changes in the wage gap, adjusted for key determinants, is based on data from the Current Population Survey (CPS). Examination of these data suggests that the gender earnings gap is persistent despite frequent claims to the contrary from industry surveys and that the gap is narrower for professional level positions. Furthermore, the data suggest that female IS workers, particularly in professional level occupations, may have experienced a beneficial effect from the internet bubble, but it is unclear whether or not that beneficial effect may be fading in the post-bubble internet bust of the early 21st century.

**Chapter 4**

Jo Ellen Moore, Southern Illinois University Edwardsville, USA
Mary Sue Love, Southern Illinois University Edwardsville, USA

This paper examines "technology geek" through the social psychological lens of stigma. The research expands on an aspect of stigma that can materialize in work settings but has not been fully explicated in prior stigma theory, namely, prestige. The authors argue that a stigma may be worn with pride rather than shame, typified by the case of the technology geek, called "prestigious stigma." The theory building focuses on interactions between the technology geek and others in the organization, positing that prestigiously stigmatized individuals behave in ways that differ from what social psychologists have generally posited for the stigmatized. This effort culminates in a model of mixed interaction involving the technology geek, which extends prior stigma theory and provides insights for practice and future research regarding technology professionals in organizations.

**Chapter 5**

Jukka-Pekka Kauppinen, Oy International Business Machines Ab, Finland
Hannu Kivijärvi, Aalto University School of Economics, Finland
Jari Talvinen, Aalto University School of Economics, Finland

In the current competitive environment, managing organizational change successfully requires comprehensive understanding of change management concepts and processes as well as the implied drivers behind them. Information technology (IT) field is not an exception; growing interest exists for understanding organizational change and change management in the IT industry. Fast-paced changes in today's IT and business environments are inevitable and the challenges associated with organizational changes are becoming more complex. This study aims to find at least partial answers to the question how employees' commitment to change and the implementation quality of a change process affect achieving the goals and succeeding in an organizational change initiative. The study is conducted in two parts in a Finnish IT company providing complex IT solutions and services. The first part, the pilot study, identifies factors hindering employees' commitment to change. The pilot study is followed by a quantitative main study, which investigates the relationships between employees' level of commitment during the different phases of a change project, the change process quality, the importance and realization level of the different goals set for the change project, and the final success of the change initiative. The results indicate that a strong, positive relationship exists between the change process quality and the level of employees' commitment to change.

**Chapter 6**

*Amit V. Deokar, Dakota State University, USA*

*Thomas O. Meservy, University of Memphis, USA*

*Joel Helquist, Utah Valley University, USA*

*John Kruse, MITRE Corporation, USA*

Collaboration and the success of collaborative efforts has been the focus of much information systems research. Recent measures of collaboration success include effectiveness, efficiency, productivity, commitment, satisfaction with the process, and satisfaction with the outcome. While the possible antecedents of collaboration success are varied, this paper suggests that constructs from the e-learning literature that evolved independently from the information systems collaboration literature can be used to explain differences in perceived collaboration success. Results from a recent exploratory study demonstrate that cognitive presence and social presence explain a large amount of the variance of different collaboration success metrics.

**Chapter 7**

*Victoria Badura, Chadron State College, USA*

*Aaron Read, University of Nebraska at Omaha, USA*

*Robert O. Briggs, University of Nebraska at Omaha, USA*

*Gert-Jan de Vreede, University of Nebraska at Omaha, USA & Delft University of Technology,*
*    The Netherlands*

Groups can generate so many ideas during a decision making process involving brainstorming that they become an impediment to group processes. Convergence activities reduce the number of ideas generated by the group and clarify those ideas, allowing the group to move forward with a set of ideas worthy of further attention. Research about convergence and its affect on collaboration is in the early stages. To further this research, measures of convergence are developed in this study as part of an assessment of the effects of convergence on an ideation artifact produced by managers attempting to solve an actual business problem. This paper presents a method for quantifying the reduction and clarification that has occurred through convergence using an assessment of a pre- and post-convergence artifact. This study expands upon understanding of collaboration by presenting the method of characterizing the convergence artifacts.

**Section 2**
**Organizational Issues**

**Chapter 8**

*Philip Raeth, EBS Universität für Wirtschaft und Recht, Germany*

*Stefan Smolnik, EBS Universität für Wirtschaft und Recht, Germany*

The recent rise of Web 2.0 ideas, principles, and applications has significantly affected the communication and interaction in social networks. While Web 2.0's Internet usage and benefits have been investigated, certain questions are still unanswered: whether benefits such as enhanced collaboration and knowledge sharing also apply in an organizational context and whether there are more, still uncovered, benefits. Since research on the corporate adoption and use of Web 2.0 technologies is still in its early stages, neither qualitative nor quantitative models that could provide answers have been proposed. As a starting point for further developing this research stream, the authors collected and reviewed the literature on internal corporate blogging. Then the framework by Ives et al. (1980) was chosen to categorize the identified 25 articles for further analysis. The paper describes building a conceptual model and identifying the antecedents and consequences of employee weblog usage within corporations. The findings of the review suggest that employee blogging in corporations is a social and an organizational phenomenon. Individual perceptions and attitudes, peers, and cultures have a crucial influence on weblog usage, while the organization and its culture provide a framework.

# Chapter 9

Knowledge management strives for effective capture and application of organizational knowledge, a resource imperative in sustaining organizations. To better achieve knowledge management initiatives, examination of factors influencing adoption and usage of knowledge management systems (KMS) are of great interest. Implementation of technological solutions considered organizational innovation is subject to potential problems of resistance, implying analysis of social factors equally important to technological factors. With Innovation Diffusion Theory as a foundation, this research examines factors influencing adoption and usage of KMS. The model is extended to include Reciprocity Expectation, an important factor affecting knowledge management processes. Results indicate that some factors are important in determining adoption while others are important for continued usage. This research emphasizes careful consideration and re-evaluation of both social and technological factors throughout all stages of technology implementation; more specifically, Reciprocity Expectation may be an important factor affecting length of adoption, but insignificant in determining continued usage.

# Chapter 10

The reliance on information technology (IT) keeps increasing and rapidly as technology advances. Information technology has become so significant that it is critical to the success or failure of many organisations. Hence the organisations emphasises on strategy for IT, to enable and support their processes and activities, periodically. The IT strategy is influenced by many factors at both development and implementation levels. These factors enable and at the same time constraint during the development and implementation of the IT strategy in the organisation. The research examines the types of factors which exist during the development and implementation of IT strategy. This includes the roles of the factors and how they manifest to influence IT strategy. In achieving this object of the research, a case study method was employed and Structuration Theory was applied to examine the factors which emerge and how they impact the development and implementation of IT strategy in the organisation.

# Chapter 11

Although virtual organizations and networks have been studied, there is still need for research regarding their inner dynamics and the mechanisms of leadership and governance. This paper investigates micro-political processes i.e. informal actions of individual actors to gain power and exert influence, which is a well-researched concept in traditional organizations with respect to inter-organizational networks. This study investigates structures and strategies of power within virtual networks. Results show that micro-political tactics known from research in traditional organizations are used in inter-organizational settings. Additional micro-political tactics, specific to virtual networks, are identified. The latter are related to the use of information and communication technology (ICT). A second quantitative study surveyed 359 members of inter-organizational networks on their use of micro-political tactics. Results confirm that micro-political strategies are widely used in virtual networks. The degree of virtuality was associated with the use of certain tactics. Possible implications for the structure and governance of virtual networks and the design of the technology that is used to support virtual cooperation are discussed.

## Section 3
## Virtual and Software Issues

### Chapter 12

*Sean P. Goggins, Drexel University, USA*
*Matthew Schmidt, University of Missouri, USA*
*Jesus Guajardo, University of Texas Health Science Center, USA*
*Joi L. Moore, University of Missouri, USA*

Teams meet in 3D virtual worlds more frequently than ever before, yet the tools for evaluating 3D collaboration environments are underdeveloped. To close the 3D collaboration tool evaluation gap, the authors integrate lessons from the gaming industry and distributed work research. They develop two complementary approaches. First, the individual user's perspective using eye-tracking (ET) is addressed, and second, the collaborative experience of the group using a technique called All-Views-Qualitative-Analysis (AVQA) is evaluated. The latter integrates the points-of-view of all subjects in a small group collaborating on a creative work task in a 3 dimensional virtual world. The authors show how these techniques enable evaluation of 3D environment design from the perspective of human computer interaction theory and theories related to distributed work. The paper discusses why designers should seek ways to leverage the advantages of 3D collaboration technologies and avoid recreating mirrors of physical space in these environments.

### Chapter 13

*Bruce A. Reinig, San Diego State University, USA*
*Robert K. Plice, San Diego State University, USA*

The software industry loses billions of dollars annually to software piracy and has raised awareness of the high software piracy rates worldwide, particularly in emerging economies. In this paper, the authors build a general model of software piracy that includes three economic and social factors suggested by the literature, including per capita GNI, the relative size of a country's IT market, and government corruption. The paper demonstrates that the relationship between national software piracy and per capita GNI is nonlinear, with additional gains in per capita GNI, producing marginally smaller reductions in software piracy. No structural variation is found in the model with respect to whether an economy is developed or emerging, using the OECD membership as a proxy. However, a structural break did exist with respect to the relative size of a country's IT market. The analysis suggests that the classification of an economy as developed or emerging does not necessarily advance the understanding of the causal mechanisms that give rise to software piracy. Findings suggest that more insight can be gained by focusing on strategies that take into account the relative size of a country's IT market.

The importance of the labyrinth as a trope in the Western tradition can hardly be overstated. Far from being a metaphor that describes just anything, it is a sign whose meaning appears in specific contexts. This article argues how the labyrinth's triple function as visual, verbal and spatial sign—as well as its paradoxical function as unicursal and multicursal structure—makes it flexible enough to represent the paradoxical and complex nature of the modern workplace, the city, the mall and the individual subject's position within an ever burgeoning network of relationships brought about by consumerism, capitalism, and commodification. Understanding the labyrinth trope helps people to understand the subject's relationship to power and the very technology that we have created and in which we are trapped.

The link between "Going Green" in research practices and Information and Communication Technologies (ICTs) is studied using general ethics and social psychology literature. This paper investigates and concludes that a researcher's ethical judgment is the strongest factor influencing their intention to follow green research practices (GRP). Their ethical judgment is molded indirectly by the researcher's attitude towards environmental awareness. Their intention towards GRP is influenced by existing research practices and experience in using a technology touted as a greening enabler, Web 2.0. The strength of the relationship suggests there is no pivotal turning point in the research practices to become green. This paper concludes that GRP represent a smaller, albeit important, paradigm shift affecting the conduct and dissemination of research with positive spillover effects for the environment.

# Preface

This handbook introduces to the reader current research articles that address the different areas of information technology usage and adoption within organizations, studies that address new software development in relation to organizations and end-users, as well as the social issues that are either impacted or created by the use of new systems. Additionally, the handbook aims to provide academicians and practitioners scholarly value in the field of social and organizational dynamics within in the field of information technology. Articles in this handbook will provide one comprehensive source of the latest trends and research in the field of social and organizational issues as they relate to information technologies and information systems. The book provides high quality research chapters on various topics that range from workforce issues to the development, adoption, and identification of new technologies. Industry professionals can use the handbook to identify timely topics within the area of social and organization issues in relation to information technologies and systems which may guide them in gaining knowledge that will and can affect organizational change.

## SOCIAL AND ORGANIZATIONAL ISSUES

There are many social and organizations issues arising from the use of information technology use and systems. Historically, as well as currently, information technology and systems is comprised of people, technology, and knowledge processes. In addition, all of the components of information systems are mutually connected and cannot exist individually to perform the role of informing. Therefore social and organizational issues are inherent with the use of information technology and information systems.

Currently, through the Internet and other technological innovations, organizations have seen an increase in the collecting, storing, processing, transmission, and presentation of information that has not only transformed the information technology sector itself into a highly dynamic and expanding field of activity, but has also created new markets, generated new global investment opportunities, and offered new job openings. In response to these new opportunities, organizations have had to rapidly and efficiently change in order to remain competitive, thus affecting their organizational cultures. Organizational culture consists of the major understanding and assumption that a business must plan for, implement, and handle change. Change can be created by several factors, especially by social factors.

As the professional work world has changed dramatically over the past decade, organizations are more global, and employee groups are much more likely to be culturally diverse. Therefore, being in such a culturally diverse workforce means employees will need to be able to enter a new culturally fluent context where mastering the norms, and feeling comfortable in doing so, allows for individuals to become either highly successful or woefully ill-prepared. In addition, changes in society as a result of increased international trade and cultural exchange continue to have a significant impact on organizations and their information systems, as well as the humans involved with those systems.

Organizational structures have also changed, and have become less hierarchical and more collaborative with today's networked offices around the world. In addition, these new work worlds are full of technological distractions that would have been unimaginable to the 20th-century manager. Modern organizations must deal with the introduction of new information technology systems and technologies, and in so doing, must deal with the human aspects related to this activity.

In his book *The World is Flat,* Thomas Friedman describes three areas of globalization. The most current of these areas is Globalization 3.0, dated from 2000 until today, which is characterized by individuals from around the world who can compete and influence other people, corporations, and countries by using the Internet and other powerful technology tools. Workers in this era are from around the world with differing cultures, lifestyles, and tasks. These opportunities offer several advantages, from the use of combining work that can be accomplished in subtasks to applying the smartest workers to the task. At the same time, there are obstacles that can be introduced such as cultural differences that include work issues, language differences, and others.

The area of social and organizational issues in relation to information technology has been and continues to be an increasing field that encompasses various areas such as building relationships between the information systems area and other academic disciplines; addressing cultural issues in the area of social barriers and digital divides; assimilation of emerging technologies into an organization; looking at diversity within the workforce in areas related to gender, race, age, education, and socio-economic differences in IT (information technology), as well as diversity in virtual work teams; ethical and human reactions issues surrounding codes of conduct; human interaction issues related to leadership, motivation, and social presence; and information technology security issues including the misuse of data and the social, legal, and ethical issues of IS (information systems) security.

Within the past decade the world has gone from a total of 12 billion e-mails a day to 247 billion, from 400,000 text messages to 4.5 billion, from an individual average of 2.7 hours a week online to 18 hours. Therefore, in some form or fashion, a computer or an information system keeps end users connected to colleagues, customers, clients, family, community, entertainment, and hobbies; to everything we know we should be doing and everything we know we shouldn't. The dynamic use and introduction of IT introduces the aforementioned issues surrounding the area of social and organizational issues in relation to the adoption and use of information systems.

This handbook aims to answer the question, "Why should you understand the social and organizational issues surrounding IT?" The answer is simple. Despite a wealth of knowledge in this area, the answer forms another question: "Don't you want to be the most informed user; that is, a person who is knowledgeable about information systems and information technology and its effects on the individuals who are involved with these systems and technologies?" In general, informed and educated individuals tend to get more value from the technologies that they are using. Therefore, if an end user can understand the many benefits from technology use then they can better understand why it is needed.

## CHAPTERS IN THE HANDBOOK

The handbook consists of 14 chapters organized into three sections, which address workforce issues, organizational issues, and virtual and software issues. Each section contains chapters relevant to the section, which are related in topical areas to the other chapters.

In each of the aforementioned articles, new research is presented that addresses the human and social factors in relation to information technology and information systems. As the roles of both humans and computers change, so do the opportunities.

Beginning with Section 1, *Workforce Issues*, seven chapters are introduced that focus on issues related to topic areas, such as the lack of technical skills of graduates to enter the IT workforce, earnings in relation to gender, the stigma of being a technology geek, collaboration and collaboration efforts, and lastly, the management of organizational change.

A brief description of each chapter follows.

Chapter 1, "Workforce Assessment in the Jordanian ICT Industry," is presented first to introduce the view that there is a growing workforce gap in the ICT sector within Jordan. But the case of non-qualified workers for IT positions has also affected other countries such as the United States, where there is a rising and identified need for qualified and skilled graduates, but a decline in their apparent skills. Therefore, a contrast is acknowledged that highlights the fact that what is produced at the university level (the graduate) and what is needed within the ICT industry (the skills and knowledge) are at a crossroads of defining what technical skills and knowledge are required to be successful within the IT field. The author presents several key factors: 1) in Jordan, the need for qualified IT workers is quickly growing; 2) very little empirical research has been conducted to assess the quality and the relevance of the ICT curriculum; 3) how can a comprehensive ICT program be built and a model developed to motivate the development of a curriculum that challenges students be a part of a successful workforce? The results of this study found that there is a lack in technical skills among graduates of the higher education system, and the results of the study can be used to identify curricular areas that can be improved upon.

Chapter 2 discusses how remaining relevant in the workplace is a persistent concern for people in all professions, especially in today's economy. The information technology industry is no exception, where the relevance of knowledge and skills must be continuously maintained in order to meet the demands of the profession. The article titled "Is Updating Play or Work? The Mediating Role of Updating Orientation in Linking Threat of Professional Obsolescence to Turnover/Turnaway Intentions" is a study that examines the behavior of IT professionals in the face of constant threat of obsolescence. Specifically, the study looks at updating skills as play or work and the relationship of that attitude towards turnover and turnaway intentions. Additionally, and according to the authors, IT professionals hold one of two forms of updating orientations, where some regard updating as work, while others tend to view updating as play. Patterns of job mobility intentions associated with each of the two forms of updating orientation were also examined. In summary, the authors found that the results indicated a negative relationship exists between the threat of obsolescence and updating as play, and a positive relationship with updating as work.

Chapter 3, "Gender Wage Differentials in Information Systems: 1991-2008 A Quantitative Analysis," analyzes the salary disparity between men and women to determine if the compensation gap has changed over time. The study uses data compiled by the Current Population Survey (CPS) and evaluates the salaries of men and women across industries and professions. The study focused primarily on (1) whether the gender wage gap diminished in IS professions since 1990, (2) how the Internet bubble and the high demand of skilled IS workers affected the disparity, and (3) what impacts the "new economy" had on wages after the dot com bust. The research found that in professional level occupations there was a narrower wage gap and that the higher demand for IS professionals in the 1990s was inversely related to salary disparity as the gap once again increased after the dot com bust. In summary, their findings were concluded by stating that "it still seems to be a man's world when it comes to the bottom line of compensation."

Chapter 4 describes how social stigma has traditionally had negative effects on people who have occupations that are considered undesirable, like garbage men and gravediggers. The unspoken perception is a "devaluing of the stigmatized individual and the view that they are less than…" except in the case of the technology geek as described in the paper "An Examination of Prestigious Stigma: The Case of the Technology Geek." According to Goffman (1963), "A stigma is fundamentally different from a conventional stereotype due to its global nature. Stereotyping assigns a particular characteristic (positive or negative) to an individual, but assigning a stigma leaves one's whole identity discredited." The article further describes how a geek exerts a position of prestigious stigma and discusses the value of better integrating their expertise within the organization.

Chapter 5 discusses the process of managing organizational change, or change management, which requires well-defined processes and plans for deployment. This practice is especially true within the information technology industry, where the changes include employees learning new ways of executing tasks. "Committing to Organizational Change in IT Industry" is a study that evaluates the relationship between employees' commitment to change and the quality of the transition. The study further identifies factors that hinder employees' willingness to change behaviors such as negative perceptions and low expectations that may result from a change within the organization. The study results indicate that better planning, communication, and commitment by management is a key factor in a quality organizational change effort.

Chapter 6 shows how new technologies and collaboration tools on the Internet have injected enthusiasm among end users and have created collaboration efforts among those who interact and learn from one another. Though more recent technologies implemented within organizations have the capability to be effective collaboration tools, many of the knowledge management systems and Web 2.0 technologies end up functioning more as places to post information rather than as collaboration tools, as were intended for use by the organizations. "Understanding Collaboration Success in Context of Cognitive and Social Presence" looks at how cognitive and social presences have a bigger role in collaborative success than does the technology used. The study looks at the constructs of e-learning literature to demonstrate this point, which was developed independently of the information systems collaboration literature.

In Chapter 7, the authors show how organizations are actively pursuing tools and methods that best allow their employees to collaborate and solve business problems. Brainstorming is a part of the collaborative and problem solving process. However, a refinement to brainstorming called convergence is discussed in "Coding for Unique Ideas and Ambiguity: A Method for Measuring the Effect of Convergence on the Artifact of an Ideation Activity," and offers a simplified approach to the same idea, according to the study. The main idea is to adopt a standardized approach to brainstorming and to submit ideas so that the ideas are useful and have clarity to all participants. The study refers to this method as a coding scheme.

Section 2, titled *Organizational Issues*, addresses topics related to the usage, ideas, and principles surrounding the topic of Web 2.0 and knowledge management systems, the influencing factors that affect and influence technology adoption, the alignment of IT strategy to business strategy, and finally the inner dynamics and the mechanisms of leadership and governance surrounding the virtual organizations topic and who is really in control of the individual players.

Chapter 8, "Towards a Model of Employee Weblog Usage: A Process-Oriented Analysis of Antecedents and Consequences," is a study on Web 2.0 technologies and the impact that they have exerted on communication within organizations. The study researches whether collaboration and social networking tools in a work setting are beneficial and whether there are any uncovered benefits. Employee blogging is one part of the study to determine antecedents and consequences of its use. The study did not yield conclusive results because the adoption of Web 2.0 ideas and principles has happened so recently, but the researchers have provided a framework as a result of this study for future research.

Chapter 9 discusses how knowledge management systems (KMS) try to provide a platform where business experiences within a company can be researched and shared. "Examining the Varying Influence of Social and Technical Aspects on Adoption" researches factors of user adoption and continued usage of such technology. As organizations operate globally with teams communicating remotely, the ability to remain effective and efficient has become increasingly important. The study evaluates social and technological factors and concludes that a key factor in the success of KMS implementations is the fostering of a "reciprocity expectation" within an organization, which usually occurs in the form of a shared domain knowledge database.

Chapter 10 shows that as IT reliance increases, so does the importance of having a well thought-out development and implementation strategy. IT strategy is one of the ways that companies compete and create distinction in the market. "A Model for Operationalising Influencing Factors in IT Strategy Deployment" examines externalities and the role of those factors and how they influence an organization's IT strategy. The approach this study takes is to examine Structuration Theory, which looks at elements such as cultural diversity as an indicator to determine the effectiveness of a company's IT strategy.

Chapter 11, "Playing Virtual Power Games: Micro-Political Processes in Inter-Organizational Networks" is a study that looks at the virtual work environment and investigates the micro-political processes that individuals use to assert their own governance or leadership within a non-traditional network. Globalization and virtual technology has made way for this new type of virtual organization, consisting of contractors and small business networks. The results from this study suggest that each network develops its own culture, which allows individuals to join and conform or find a network that fits their culture and ideals. There is an element of self-selection (or low barriers to entry) that does not exist in the traditional sense, as it does virtually.

Section 3 of this handbook deals with the topic of *Virtual and Software Issues*. This section is devoted to several different important topics such as the nuances surrounding virtual communications and working within a virtual world, understanding the trends and trendsetting related to the topic of software piracy in emerging and developed countries, and how people might look at their work lives in relation to a labyrinth. Finally, research is presented that investigates the linkage between "going green," ICTs, and researcher's attitudes towards environmental awareness.

Chapter 12 shows that through the ability to create dynamic learning environments, collaborative business applications, or interactive, multi-user simulations, virtual collaboration has increasingly become a part of how organizations may work on tasks together. "3D Virtual Worlds: Assessing the Experience and Informing Design" brainstorms the possibility of using 3D technology to increase the effectiveness of virtual collaboration tools. The study uses the gaming world as an example of how 3D environments already capture a level of immersion and emotion that is currently not realized in a conventional user interface. This article provides tools to evaluate the level of user engagement to determine the feasibility for work collaboration. The study does find that virtual worlds do not replace physical presence and people recreate as much of the physical world as is possible within the 3D environment, therefore finding that collaboration tools may be quite effective in the work tasks area.

In Chapter 13, the authors describe how the software industry loses billions of dollars to piracy every year and is undertaking initiatives to understand this trend. "Toward an Understanding of Software Piracy in Developed and Emerging Economies" is a study where researchers address the trends of software piracy and study the tendencies of developed versus emerging economies to identify piracy indicators. Three economic and social factors that the paper looked at were (1) per capita GNI, (2) the relative size of a country's IT market, and (3) government corruption. In analyzing these three factors, the study suggests that there is no correlation between software piracy and whether a country is developed or emerging. However, there is a slight relationship between the relative size of a country's IT market and corruption with software piracy.

In Chapter 14, technology, the number of product choices, shopping, and the network of real and virtual relationships people now have are scenarios described in "Getting Lost in the Labyrinth: Information and Technology in the Marketplace." According to the article and suggested by the author John Conway, "The labyrinth is a complicated trope that fits the paradoxical complexity of how we experience our modern lives." Further, he found that leveraging the labyrinth as a resource can add a new dimension of understanding and meaning in our own lives, which will further enhance how we can view technology and our working lives within the marketplace as labyrinths.

Chapter 15, "Using an Ethical Framework to Examine Linkages Between "Going Green" in Research Practices and Information and Communication Technologies," examines the factors determining whether a researcher uses green research practices (GRP). GRP refers to the transition of researchers who traditionally relied on travel and paper to work that can be facilitated through the use of information and communication technologies. Much of the paper refers to Kuhn's study on paradigm shifts, but the conclusion is that the strongest influence on GRP is the researcher's ethical judgment and, indirectly, from their attitude towards the environment.

## SUMMARY

In summary, this handbook is written to provide an overview of the integration of technology utilization and social dynamics in organizations. What have been noted throughout these aforementioned chapters are the following observations for mangers, researchers, scholars and end users of information technologies and information systems. Probably only a fraction of the benefits derived from information technology-based innovations have so far been reaped; the rest remain to be acquired in the next decades. The shift towards systems integration to capitalize the full potential benefits of information technology requires considerable adaptations, learning processes, and structural changes in existing socioeconomic institutions and organizational systems. The tradition in most current organizations is still to operate in a largely "disintegrated" fashion, reminiscent of the Ford-Taylorist management approaches that dominated the fourth Kondratiev cycle. These approaches consisted of a high division of labor, increasing functional specialization/differentiation and de-skilling of many tasks, rigid manufacturing procedures and controls, long management hierarchies with bureaucratic decision-making procedures and a "mechanistic" approach to performance. Under these conditions, the adoption and uses of information technologies are found to be restricted to piecemeal technology improvements. By contrast, information technology-based systems offer organizations the opportunity of functional integration, multi-skilled staff, rapid and flexible decision-making structures with greater delegation of responsibilities and greater autonomy of operating units, and a more flexible and "organic" approach enabling a quick adjustment to changing environmental conditions (Piore and Sabel, 1984).

In the case of developing countries, information technologies have a significant impact on the growth and success of organizations. Issues surrounding technology adoption and adequate staffing are two large issues that developing countries are most currently facing. Although the socio-economic structure of these countries sometimes resists organizational or institutional changes, the complex interrelations between these changes and information technologies have significant implications for the way information technology does and will affect the societies and economies of developing countries. As a matter of fact, the negative and positive potential impacts of IT on these countries are a matter of great controversy among economists and politicians. The main short-term issues usually discussed are the potential erosion of the comparative advantages of low labor costs, and the effects of automation, particularly on international competitiveness. Implications of information technology usage for those countries hold great importance.

It is anticipated that this handbook, which offers a comprehensive and diverse look at the integration of technology utilization and social dynamics in organizations, will contribute to a better understanding of this field of study. Additionally, this handbook is written for the academician and professional researcher to offer an opportunity to be introduced to timely topics in this area. The handbook is also written with managers in mind, who can use the frameworks and models provided to serve as a guide in decision making processes. Lastly, it is presumed that this handbook will serve as an inspiration for future researchers to explore the current and emerging topics in this immense field of study.

## REFERENCE

Piore, M., & Sabel, C. (1984). *The second industrial divide*. New York, NY: Basic Books.

*Dawn Medlin*
*Appalachian State University, USA*

# Section 1
# Workforce Issues

# Chapter 1
# Workforce Assessment in the Jordanian ICT Industry

**Salem Al-Agtash**
*Yarmouk University, Jordan*

## ABSTRACT

*This paper provides an assessment of workforce need in the Jordanian ICT industry. The results have shown that there is a growing workforce gap in the ICT sector. The technical skills of graduates are not satisfactory, and there is an increasing demand for skilled graduates. In addition to the technical skills required, communication skills, creative thinking, and English language skills were seen as important "soft skill elements" across all job categories and are missing in the current ICT workforce. The skills and competencies identified in this study can be used to motivate a design of an effective, flexible and relevant ICT program that can contribute to building a skillful workforce focusing on specialized and hands-on practices in ICT domains.*

## 1. INTRODUCTION

Emerging global knowledge economies have created a demand for highly skilled ICT workforce in all industries. As a result, ICT labor markets have become highly competitive. With the tremendous wealth recently generated in the Gulf States and subsequent industrial booms, such markets in the region became highly attractive to many Jordanian ICT workers. A large number of experienced ICT professionals leave the country every year. Faced with such conditions, the demand for a highly skilled ICT workforce has increased tremen-

dously. As the result of workforce migration, the ICT workforce in Jordan comprise of graduates who are young and possess little experiences and knowledge.

In Jordan, current trends indicate that the skill set composition of the ICT workforce is changing. With a growing pool of 19,000 ICT related labor force and steadily inflowing 6,000 ICT graduates yearly, Jordan has a potential to become a regional leader in the ICT sector (JIB, 2006). Jordan ranked 14th out of 110 countries for the number of engineers and scientists according to the Global Competitiveness Report 2004- 2005 (Porter *et al.*, 2005).

DOI: 10.4018/978-1-4666-1948-7.ch001

In spite of the growing importance of ICT workforce, very little empirical research has been done to assess quality and relevance in Jordan ICT education. The need for better quality and relevance of workforce skills has been identified by the Information Technology Association - Jordan as one of the challenges facing the ICT sector and affecting its growth, development and effectiveness.

While considerable effort has been made to achieve remarkable growth in the Jordanian ICT sector and to devise improvement directions, the only information available for the ICT industry in Jordan are the statistics of Jordanian IT industry (Int@J, 2007). The available evidence confirms that the current quality of ICT education cannot meet the labor market requirements, neither can it cope with the evolution of ICT technologies. However, in-depth analysis of the sector and scientific evaluation of the workforce gap in Jordan have not yet been adequately dealt with. Meanwhile, available studies on workforce assessment exist for ICT industries elsewhere. Of these studies, reference (Sri Lanka ICT Association, 2007) gives in depth analysis of the IT workforce in Siri Lanka. Reference (Hu *et al.*, 2007) provides an evaluation of issues relating to ICT workforce in Taiwan with focus on planning, supply, and recruitment and retention of ICT skills among multinational companies. In reference by (Holm *et al.*, 2002), the authors present best practices of ICT workforce management in Finland. A framework for Queensland government ICT skills are given in Queensland government office (2009). Reference (Stephen *et al.*, 2009) gives analysis on the ICT skills readiness for the emerging global digital economy in Botswana. These references provide assessment models for ICT workforce skills and productivity under different sets of assumptions and issues. This study uses the references as a guideline for the articulation of ICT curricula design and skill development to enable young Jordanian graduates to compete internationally.

The Jordanian ICT educational institutions fall short of providing levels of the ICT skills required in the job market. Large numbers of ICT graduates have no immediate employment, and would need intensive professional training, often 1-2 years on-job training to successfully compete for jobs. The gap is growing between the ability of the ICT educational systems in Jordan to provide skillful graduates and the requirements of the ICT sector. This gap has grown even wider than ever, and calls for rapid adjustments and improvements in relevant ICT programs offered.

This study has been conducted in collaboration with the USAID/Jordan Economic Growth Program (SABEQ) and European (EU) Commission/ TEMPUS with EU funding. The study sought to (1) assess the workforce gap on the basis of competencies required by the Job market; (2) provide a significant contribution to the development of a new vision for ICT education, which is centered, first and foremost, on a commitment to build ICT workforce qualified for the local and regional ICT and knowledge intensive industries; and (3) provide a framework for ICT skills development strategies at the government level that can enable Jordan to participate competitively in the emerging digital economy.

The results of the study which covered 53 ICT companies in Jordan have shown that the dominant educational level of employees (81%) in the ICT sector is university education. Their technical skills, however, are not satisfactory and there seems to be a huge demand for skillful graduates. The technical competencies and skills mostly needed are on Oracle and MS-SQL in the domain of database systems; creative thinking skills and graphic design in the domain of digital media and animations; Microsoft Engineering in the domain of system administration; system analysis and business analysis in the domain of systems integration; network design and internet security in the domain of system and network administration; .NET programming, C++, system design, and team work skills in the domain of programming and software engineering; project management, communication skills, and writing skills in the project/program management domain. In addition to the technical skills required, communication skills, creative thinking, and English language skills were seen as important "soft skill elements" across all job categories and are missing in the current ICT workforce.

The skills and competencies identified in this study can be used to motivate a design of a new ICT educational model, which accommodates flexible curricula, enhances student internship mobility, and fosters student technical skills, through capstone projects with industry involvement, experiential learning, and professional excellence. The skills not only can complement the knowledge areas of the guidelines of the final IEEE/ACM computing curricula of 2010, (ACM, 2010), but also can be integrated to expand their practical requirements in the vendor specific ICT technologies. The design of such an educational model can then be characterized with relevance, orientation towards market and industry needs, and quality assured to meet international standards.

The technology implications of this study can also be compared to the results of the capability studies that have been mainly conducted in other national contexts, such as the 2009 and 2010 surveys carried out by (Luftman & Ben-Zvi, 2010). In the 2010 survey, the top five technologies and applications identified are: Business Intelligence, Virtualization, Enterprise Resource Planning (ERP) systems, Continuity Planning, and Cloud Computing. These technologies require highly skillful ICT workforce, which Jordan ICT education and industry sectors would need to align in their strategies in order to keep in pace with evolving technology trends. The remaining sections of this paper give more details on the results of the study, the specific competencies needed, and guidelines for ICT curricula design. The paper is concluded with discussions and implications of the survey results and recommendations for better alignment between ICT education and industry needs.

## 2. SURVEY CONTEXT

A questionnaire was designed to conduct a comprehensive survey on the ICT industry, in coordination with academic institutions, Int@j (information technology association - Jordan) and MoICT (Ministry of information & communication technology). It has been revised by EU and USAID partners. The role of Int@j in particular was more consultative to avoid bias in shaping the results of the study. The survey focused on several technical and non-technical domains, including information management, networking and infrastructure, software development, web applications, embedded systems, technology architecture, ERP systems and more. The design of the survey emphasized more specific insights regarding the competencies and skills required in a wide range of ICT technologies. One of the important strengths of the survey analysis is in its ability to identify important technology trends in the Jordanian ICT sector, technical and non-technical skill set requirements, and curricula implications for effective study programs in ICT. The survey results represent in-depth view of the Jordanian ICT industry, provide an industry profile, and highlight the competencies required in the ICT job market.

The questionnaire was distributed to a total of 120 ICT companies by email, followed by phone calls and interviews by teams from the German-Jordanian University and Int@j. The team collected full data from 53 companies. The main respondents to the survey were the active board members of Int@j. The sample size under study represents about 44% of the ICT sector (Int@j members) responsible for major ICT activities in Jordan with an overall sampling variability of ±5% at the 90% confidence level.

The survey findings give relative insights into the ICT industry and its technology requirements, workforce needs, competitiveness, and possible improvement directions. The survey items are categorized into four levels:

- Company profile data covering details on the ICT industry, its size, business sector, market orientation, ownership, sales distribution, graduate demographics, and development/ implementation strategies.
- Development/implementation level information covering details on the development/implementation processes, methodology, international benchmarks and standards, and market research methods.
- Education level information covering the educational level of employees, required qualifications, R&D facilities, recruitment of professionals - degree requirements, lack of skills, theoretical know-how, practical skills, continuing training requirements, and turn-over rates.
- Technical level information covering details on IT technologies, tools, skills, and platforms in use: IDEs, DB tools, programming/SE, project management, quality assurance, technical support, web tools, management information systems, ERP systems, archiving systems, Data warehousing, networking, technical architecture, digital media, and soft skill elements.

The following sections give more detailed evaluations in these four categories.

## 3. COMPANY PROFILE DATA

The data on the profiles of companies included in the sample provides insight on the size of ICT firms in Jordan and an in-depth understanding of employability patterns including gender distribution, primary/secondary business focus, market orientation, and customer base. The implications of these findings can guide policies for further improvements in building a more solid indigenous ICT Industry as a major contributor to Jordan's economy. It will highlight how realistically the set and time bound ICT strategic goals can be in

terms of doubling the sector's revenues and employment. The data represent 14 different items grouped into employment, ownership and market orientation, and business domains.

## A. Employment

Results reveal that the number of employees in ICT companies is in different ranges. Zero percent of companies employ less than 2 or more than 500 people, 2% of companies employ 2-9, 32% of companies employ 10-25, 30% employ 26-50, 15% employ 51-100, and 21% employ 100-500 people, as shown in Figure 1. The gender distribution in these numbers is 69% male and 31% female in the primary business workforce and 79% male and 21% female in the overall workforce. The results show that Jordan ICT firms are small-to-medium enterprises (SMEs) and may have difficulty gaining a competitive advantage in the global ICT market. Females in the overall ICT workforce represent 21%, while in non-IT companies, the percentage drops to 15%.

On the basis of these finding, a suggested policy direction is to foster collaboration and consortia of Jordanian ICT companies to more efficiently compete in the international market and encourage investments. SMEs are considered the main drivers of the Jordan ICT sector and are the effective employing power, but may need to consolidate and form consortia to compete globally.

## B. Company Ownership and Market Orientation

The results demonstrate that 62% of companies are nationally owned, 23% are internationally owned, and 15% are owned by national and international shareholders. This indicates that Jordan has nurtured a good portion of international investments in ICT, and there is an opportunity for this portion to grow.

*Figure 1. Percentage of companies for different ranges of employees*

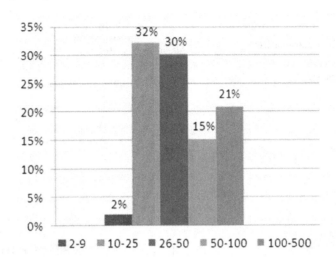

The market orientation is equal to 20% for local markets and 80% for regional and international markets broken down as follow: 20% of shares are in North America, 18% in Europe, 27% in the Gulf – GCC, 18% in non – GCC countries, and 10% in east Asia. Of the sales and IT services, 27% are distributed by direct sales to customers and clients, 44% to businesses, and 29% to governments, NGOs, and donors.

This suggests that the Gulf is a strong market for direct sales and ICT sales to businesses. More efforts need to be devoted to establish a stronger presence in the booming ICT markets of the Gulf States, which resulted from the tremendous wealth generated by the continuing boosts of the Oil prices.

## C. Primary and Secondary Business

In the primary business sector, the main focus of companies included in the sample is on programming (11%), Data Base systems (8%), Web development (8%), with the least focus is on Digital media and animation (2%). These results are presented in Figure 2. Companies do not seem to have a secondary business focus. The area of programming and software engineering ranked the highest and digital media and animation ranked the lowest in the business domains of companies under investigation. The convergence phenomenon presents a huge business opportunity in the global scope of sales and services, as evidenced by the tremendous growth of broadband; increases in mobile penetration, digital TV and Internet protocol (IP) connectivity; and the widespread of online social interaction and creative collaboration. This reveals that programming/ software engineering will continue to be an area of focus in the industry. Yet, the business domain of digital media and animation needs to be nurtured and given more focus as convergence began to mark a crucial period in the evolution of media and communication industries.

## 4. DEVELOPMENT/ IMPLEMENTATION LEVEL INFORMATION

The data presented in this section gives solid information on the development/implementation processes of ICT firms, methodology, benchmarks and standards, and practices in market research. This information sheds light on the compliance

*Figure 2. Primary business sector*

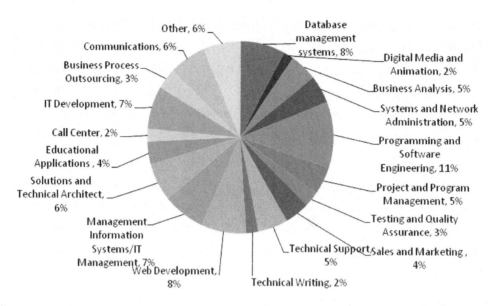

of ICT firms to international standards, hence revealing the level of competitiveness of ICT firms in the global market.

Seventy percent – 70% of surveyed companies use SDLC (Software development life cycle) development methodology, and 30% use an ad hoc JAD (Joint application development). This demonstrates compliance to a uniform development cycle that requires knowledge of requirement elicitation, design patterns, implementation, and testing procedures. These practices need to be embedded in the teaching processes of ICT programs, mainly in student capstone projects.

Forty nine percent – 49% of companies included in the sample use in-house development on a pure coding basis, while 35% use off-the-shelf development, and 16% use code generation tools for development and implementation. This information is consistent with the findings that more focus of the sector is on programming/software engineering business domain. As a matter of fact, recent advances in software technologies have spurred an increasing interest in component integration and service oriented architecture domains, which are given less attention in the Jordanian

ICT sector. This calls for action to adopt effective market research methods to continuously monitor technology trends and avoid being left out of the global market.

Survey results show that 57% of companies develop customized products; 20% fully implement their own products; and 12% of companies are product resellers. Of these companies, 68% implement and deliver on a pure order bases. This information is consistent, since similar percentages of customized products and component integration/off-shelf development.

Only 57% of companies apply market research methods to monitor technological trends in the market, leading to less dynamic and less vibrant ICT industry. Only 14% of companies use CMMI development standards. Policies should encourage CMMI benchmarks as it has become the de facto standard in the software industry, and thus gain a competitive advantage in the global market.

## 5. EDUCATIONAL LEVEL INFORMATION

The data presented in this section provides a better understanding of the educational requirements of the ICT workforce, recruitment problems, levels of existing theoretical and practical skills, staff training, and internship trends. The information clarifies the existing mismatch between supply and demand of ICT workforce.

### A. Degree Requirements

The results demonstrate that 81% of employees hold university degrees (Bachelor degree: 52%, and Master/Doctorate: 29%), 11% hold vocational degrees, and 9% hold high school degrees. Respondents indicated that 94% of the new recruits must hold at least a university degree, of which 67% should be at the level of Bachelor's degree and 21% at the postgraduate level. This shows that there is a tremendous demand for more highly educated workers and it is therefore important that educational institutions adequately prepare their graduates for the ICT job market demands.

About 55% of the companies surveyed have R&D departments, of which 56% employ technical staff, 24% employ scientists and 21% employ people from interdisciplinary backgrounds. Even though this result is interesting as a strong indicator of R&D activities, still very little has been generated in innovation and IP products and patents from the Jordanian ICT industry.

### B. Level of Satisfaction

Since most of the companies are expanding, there is a need for well-educated and highly skilled professionals. 90% of the respondents said that they had trouble recruiting ICT workers. There is a real concern in finding skillful and well-educated graduates. These findings confirm what is already expected. In general, companies complain about the skills and theoretical know-how of graduates and evaluate their level as 'not good'.

On the satisfaction level of know-how of the graduates, only 5% of companies rated them as 'very good', 27% as 'good', 40% as 'acceptable', 18% as 'not bad' and 10% as 'not good'. Similarly, the interviewees rated the skills of the graduates as follows: 6% rated them as 'very good', 21% as 'good', 23% as 'acceptable', 34% as 'not bad' and 16% as 'not good'. Figure 3 demonstrates the level of satisfaction of employees, from the perspective of both practical skills and theoretical know-how.

Overall employers are satisfied with the theoretical know-how but not with the practical skills of graduates. These results shed some light on the nature of mismatch between supply and demand of the ICT workforce.

### C. Job Conditions

The results of the survey reveal that 56% of the companies provide industrial placement to students. This can be considered as a preparation stage for students to be ready for the job market. In a fast changing field of technology, keeping abreast of new developments is vital for success. Training opportunities to further develop knowledge is important for ICT workers as much as their employers. For developing further skills of their employees, companies provide on-the-job training (68%), and external short-term courses (90%). External training was found to be conducted in the Gulf (28%), Europe (24%), and North America (13%). It is interesting that more than two-thirds of employers offer on-the-job training. These results may be interpreted as a reflection of the lack of preparation of workers for their Jobs or employers are keen to bring their workers up to the tasks they must perform. Therefore, educational institutions need to seriously consider the perceptions of industry on how well their graduates are qualified for the job market. They must introduce

7

*Figure 3. Satisfied with theoretical know-how/ practical skills of university graduates*

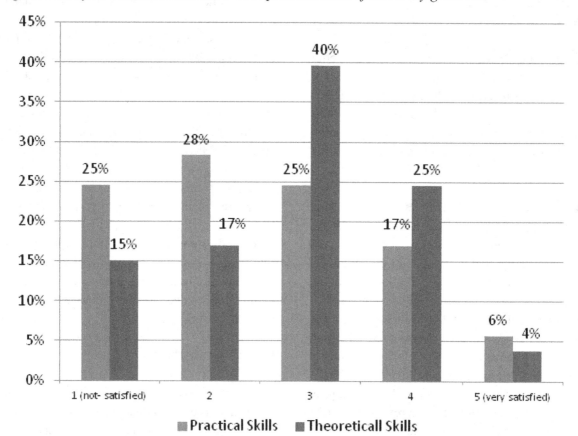

flexible ICT programs that can accommodate the constantly changing technological requirements of the industry.

While training employees adds value to the organizations, it also increases the value and employability of ICT professionals. In an environment where supply is short this may result in higher turnover rates. The data showed an average of 33% turnover of employees with less than two years of experience; 45% turnover of employees of two years to less than four years of experience; 14% turnover of employees of four years to less than six years of experience; and 8% turnover of employees of eight year to less than ten years of experience. These results demonstrate that there are more turnovers at the lower end of the experience scale. Discussions revealed that employees

travel to the Gulf States after building sufficient years of experience and get higher paying jobs.

Salaries for ICT workers are probably among the highest of all industries in Jordan. A junior business/ technical professional can expect a salary of about 650 USD per month. A mid level business/ technical professional can expect a salary of about 1130 USD per month. A senior business technical/ professional can a salary in the range of 2140 – 2530 USD per month. As employees gain more experience, salaries go up faster in the ICT sector.

These findings show that the demand for workers means that there are opportunities for advancement in the field – and that people leave for other jobs, mainly to the Gulf States as salaries in ICT double or often triple.

## 6. TECHNICAL LEVEL INFORMATION

The technical information revealed in this study gives an in-depth understanding of technological trends in ICT firms, skills and competencies required, and job categories in the domains of software development, system administration, information management, embedded systems, network administration, project management, sales and marketing, and graphic design and animations. The results may be used to guide educational institutions to build relevant ICT programs with curricula structures that are dynamic to meet changing technological requirements of the industry, and to build laboratories that give hands-on-experiences to students on state-of-the-art technologies as needed in the job market. More discussions are given next on technology frameworks and skill and competency requirements.

### A. Technology Framework

The results demonstrated in this section give more information on development/implementation tools, technologies, architecture, design patterns, and database systems. This information can be used to revamp ICT curricula in terms of theoretical content and practical skills to match the needs and requirements of the ICT industry. Figure 4 shows a distribution of knowledge areas/technology tools, where 76% of companies use development/implementation tools (DA), of which 55% focus on Microsoft .Net tools and 38% on J2EE tools. In this case, more focus should be given to introduce software architecture courses that give technological details on both Microsoft .NET and J2EE tools.

The figure demonstrates 69% of companies use software design tools (SD), of which 23% use COM objects, 18% use Java patterns, and 16% use EJB patterns. This demonstrates a necessity to introduce software design patterns with more focus on COM objects and EJB - Java design patterns.

Findings indicate 79% of companies use software IDE, of which 40% use .NET, 23% use Oracle, and 16% use Java development environment. This information give directions on the importance of introducing .NET integrated development environment in course work and practical labs. The technological trends in ICT firms follow Microsoft technologies in development, administration, and DB systems. It should be noted that

*Figure 4. Distribution of knowledge areas/ technology tools*

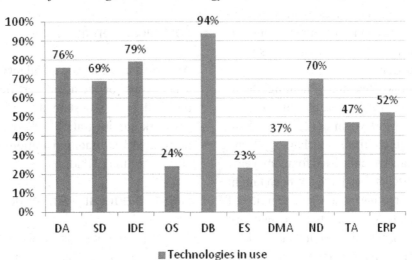

the other technologies are also important, but they are less needed in the local job market.

The distribution of use in operating system technologies (OS) is 24% of which: 50% of surveyed companies use Windows systems, 24% use Unix systems, and 25% use Linux systems. 54% of companies implement daily backup processes, 90% of companies maintain their own infrastructure with administration competencies required in MS Windows (27%), network (27%, of which 56% use Cisco systems), DB (22%), Linux (12%), and Unix (10%).

These findings can guide design of a curriculum for courses in operating systems and networking, where more focus may be given on windows technologies, Unix/Linux systems, support of infrastructure, as well as Cisco networking systems.

Ninety four - 94% of companies use DB tools, of which 40% use MS SQL, 31% use Oracle, 16% use MySQL, and 7% use IBM DB2. This information gives directions on what to embed as a technology in DB courses. More focus should be given to MS SQL, Oracle and possibly open source MySQL technologies.

Embedded technology (ES) is used in only 23% of companies, of which about 50% use PLC/PIC microcontroller technologies. Other embedded technologies in use are not clear, and respondents have not indicated the specific other technologies. This result is expected, since embedded system development and implementations in Jordanian major industrial sites and governmental institutions rely on foreign companies. More has to be done in this direction.

ERP (Enterprise Resource Planning) technologies in use constitute 51%, of which Oracle financials (41%), MS Dynamics (23%) and SAP (9%). This finding confirms a technology trend in Oracle financials which existed for many years in this domain. ERP topics have not been taught in Universities, creating as a result scarcity of skills. Other technologies in use are network design (ND): 69%, technical architecture (TA): 45%, and digital media and animation (DMA):

37%. Educational institutions can contribute to the industry by introducing advanced ERP courses with mixed technology focus.

## B. Technical Competencies and Skill Set Requirements

This section sheds more light on the specific technical competencies and skill set requirements in variety of technological domains. The findings can assist educational institutions to better identify learning outcomes in the specific domains that match different job categories. These competencies are illustrated in the following subsections.

### Database Systems and Applications

Table 1 is an excerpt of our findings. It shows that Oracle, MS-SQL, DB design and administration, creative thinking skills, and English language skills are seen necessary in the work environment in the domain of DB systems and applications with similar frequencies. The scale is from 1 (highest rate) to 10 (lowest rate). In this case, the learning outcomes of courses designed for Data Base systems and applications may take into account knowledge in Oracle, MS SQL, Data Base design while integrating soft skill elements: creative thinking, problem solving, decision making, and English language.

### Technical Certifications

As shown in Table 2, respondents have identified a necessity for technical certifications, mainly required in MS system administration (80%), Network administration (78%), DB administration (72%), Linux administration (30%), and Unix administration (21%).

### Digital Media and Animation

Creative thinking skills are needed in this domain with a rate of 42% compared to 37% graphic

*Table 1. Essential skills needed – data base systems and applications*

| Rate (1 highest) Domain | 1 | 2 | 3 | 4 | 5 | 6 | 7 | 8 | 9 | 10 |
|---|---|---|---|---|---|---|---|---|---|---|
| Oracle | 35% | 9% | 2% | 4% | 9% | 2% | 0% | 0% | 4% | 2% |
| MS-SQL Server | 35% | 15% | 4% | 4% | 4% | 2% | 7% | 2% | 2% | 0% |
| Database Design & Admin | 37% | 15% | 17% | 2% | 11% | 4% | 2% | 4% | 0% | 0% |
| Systems Analysis | 26% | 15% | 11% | 15% | 11% | 0% | 2% | 0% | 0% | 0% |
| Systems Application Admin | 15% | 17% | 9% | 9% | 2% | 7% | 4% | 4% | 2% | 0% |
| Systems Application Support | 11% | 11% | 20% | 2% | 13% | 9% | 4% | 0% | 2% | 4% |
| Systems Design | 24% | 22% | 11% | 9% | 9% | 2% | 2% | 4% | 0% | 2% |
| Programming | 35% | 11% | 7% | 15% | 7% | 2% | 0% | 2% | 2% | 0% |
| Creative Thinking Skills | 39% | 20% | 7% | 2% | 7% | 2% | 2% | 4% | 0% | 0% |
| English Language Skills | 22% | 13% | 17% | 0% | 7% | 2% | 4% | 2% | 7% | 2% |
| Others | 7% | 0% | 0% | 0% | 0% | 0% | 0% | 0% | 0% | 0% |

*Table 2. Essential skills needed – technical certifications*

| Rate (1 highest) Domain | 1 | 2 | 3 | 4 | 5 | 6 | 7 | 8 | 9 | 10 |
|---|---|---|---|---|---|---|---|---|---|---|
| System Administrator – MS | 80% | 0% | 0% | 0% | 0% | 0% | 0% | 0% | 0% | 0% |
| System Administrator –Linux | 30% | 0% | 0% | 0% | 0% | 0% | 0% | 0% | 0% | 0% |
| System Administrator – Unix | 21% | 0% | 0% | 0% | 0% | 0% | 0% | 0% | 0% | 0% |
| Network Administrator | 78% | 0% | 0% | 0% | 0% | 0% | 0% | 0% | 0% | 0% |
| DB Administrator | 72% | 0% | 0% | 0% | 0% | 0% | 0% | 0% | 0% | 0% |
| Others | 0% | 0% | 0% | 0% | 0% | 0% | 0% | 0% | 0% | 0% |

design, 30% XML and HTML technologies, and 32% business analysis (Table 3). Despite the fact that this domain represents only 2% of the primary business of companies under study (Figure 2), more focus may be given to building capacity and skills in the digital media and animation business, which is expected to flourish in the coming few years. Universities are encouraged to foster creative thinking skills in developing digital media and animation courses.

## System Analysis and Integration

Ranking of essential skills needed included system analysis, ranked highest by 49% of the respon-dents, business analysis and project management were identified by 43% of the companies with other skills identified by fewer companies (Table 4). Thus system/business analysis and project management concepts need to be introduced and expanded in ICT programs and experiences.

## Systems and Network Administration

The demand for essential skills in systems and network administration were identified as (Table 5): Network design as most important by 57% of the respondents, internet and systems security by 43% and network implementation by 34%. More emphasis has to be given to network design, imple-

*Table 3. Essential skills needed – digital media and animations*

| Rate (1 highest) | | | | | | | | | | |
| Domain | 1 | 2 | 3 | 4 | 5 | 6 | 7 | 8 | 9 | 10 |
|---|---|---|---|---|---|---|---|---|---|---|
| Graphic Design | 37% | 32% | 11% | 0% | 0% | 5% | 0% | 0% | 0% | 3% |
| Creative Thinking Skills | 42% | 21% | 21% | 5% | 0% | 0% | 0% | 6% | 0% | 0% |
| HCI Design | 21% | 16% | 5% | 0% | 5% | 5% | 0% | 3% | 0% | 0% |
| Html | 30% | 16% | 16% | 16% | 0% | 0% | 0% | 0% | 6% | 3% |
| XML | 30% | 11% | 11% | 21% | 5% | 0% | 0% | 0% | 3% | 0% |
| Business Analysis | 32% | 16% | 5% | 5% | 0% | 0% | 0% | 0% | 0% | 0% |
| Others | 0% | 0% | 0% | 0% | 11% | 0% | 0% | 0% | 3% | 3% |

*Table 4. Essential skills needed – system analysis and integration*

| Rate (1 highest) | | | | | | | | | | |
| Domain | 1 | 2 | 3 | 4 | 5 | 6 | 7 | 8 | 9 | 10 |
|---|---|---|---|---|---|---|---|---|---|---|
| Business Analysis | 43% | 11% | 17% | 6% | 3% | 3% | 0% | 0% | 0% | 0% |
| Systems Analysis | 49% | 20% | 11% | 3% | 3% | 0% | 0% | 0% | 0% | 0% |
| System Design | 31% | 20% | 14% | 6% | 3% | 6% | 0% | 0% | 0% | 0% |
| People & Change Management | 20% | 20% | 11% | 6% | 6% | 3% | 0% | 0% | 0% | 0% |
| Customer Services | 20% | 17% | 14% | 6% | 9% | 9% | 0% | 0% | 0% | 0% |
| Project Management | 43% | 20% | 9% | 6% | 3% | 3% | 0% | 0% | 0% | 0% |
| Other (please mention) | 6% | 0% | 0% | 0% | 0% | 0% | 0% | 0% | 0% | 0% |

mentation, and security concepts in developing courses in networking to meet industry demand. Table 5 gives the statistical data distribution of the technology elements needs in this category.

## Programming and Software Engineering

Essential skills in the domain of programming and software engineering are (Table 6): .Net (44%), programming skills (41%), system design (32%), business analysis (37%), team work (29%), and others are needed with similar rates. In this domain, team work skills have to be emphasized in the teaching processes of courses related to programming and software development, in addition to the technical skills.

These results indicate which certifications are most demanded in the job market. It should be noted that the Ministry of Higher Education in Jordan has recently urged Universities to accommodate technology certifications in ICT programs. Certifications in MS system and Data Base administration may need to be given more emphasis in institutions.

## Project/Program Management

The demand of essential skills in this domain includes (Table 7): project management skills at a rate of 74%, communication skills at a rate of 40%, writing skills (both technical and non-technical) at a rate of 35%. Project management with emphasis on communication skills, is another important domain that needs to be given much

*Table 5. Essential skills needed – systems and network administration*

| Rate (1 highest) | | | | | | | | | | |
|---|---|---|---|---|---|---|---|---|---|---|
| Domain | 1 | 2 | 3 | 4 | 5 | 6 | 7 | 8 | 9 | 10 |
| Network Implementation | 34% | 26% | 11% | 6% | 0% | 0% | 3% | 0% | 0% | 3% |
| Network Design | 57% | 9% | 11% | 0% | 0% | 0% | 0% | 6% | 0% | 0% |
| Systems Application Admin | 29% | 11% | 26% | 3% | 3% | 6% | 0% | 3% | 0% | 0% |
| Hardware Engineering | 14% | 17% | 6% | 6% | 3% | 0% | 3% | 0% | 6% | 3% |
| Internet and Systems Security | 43% | 14% | 11% | 17% | 3% | 0% | 3% | 0% | 3% | 0% |
| Systems Application Support | 23% | 20% | 3% | 6% | 0% | 0% | 0% | 0% | 0% | 0% |
| Systems Analysis | 20% | 23% | 11% | 3% | 3% | 3% | 0% | 0% | 3% | 3% |
| Router Configuration | 26% | 6% | 9% | 6% | 14% | 0% | 0% | 3% | 0% | 0% |
| Database Design & Admin | 20% | 6% | 20% | 11% | 3% | 3% | 3% | 0% | 0% | 0% |
| Linux | 11% | 9% | 9% | 0% | 3% | 0% | 0% | 0% | 0% | 6% |
| UNIX | 14% | 6% | 14% | 3% | 6% | 3% | 3% | 0% | 0% | 0% |
| Others | 6% | 0% | 0% | 0% | 0% | 0% | 0% | 0% | 0% | 0% |

*Table 6. Essential skills needed – programming and software engineering*

| Rate (1 highest) | | | | | | | | | | |
|---|---|---|---|---|---|---|---|---|---|---|
| Domain | 1 | 2 | 3 | 4 | 5 | 6 | 7 | 8 | 9 | 10 |
| Programming | 41% | 2% | 12% | 5% | 2% | 2% | 0% | 0% | 0% | 3% |
| Systems Design | 32% | 22% | 12% | 2% | 7% | 0% | 0% | 0% | 0% | 0% |
| .NET | 44% | 15% | 5% | 0% | 0% | 2% | 0% | 2% | 0% | 0% |
| Systems Analysis | 29% | 10% | 20% | 10% | 2% | 0% | 0% | 0% | 0% | 3% |
| Visual Basic | 15% | 2% | 15% | 0% | 5% | 0% | 0% | 0% | 0% | 0% |
| Java | 27% | 10% | 10% | 5% | 2% | 0% | 2% | 0% | 0% | 0% |
| Systems Testing | 32% | 5% | 7% | 5% | 12% | 5% | 0% | 0% | 2% | 3% |
| Business Analysis | 37% | 10% | 0% | 5% | 2% | 2% | 2% | 0% | 2% | 0% |
| Team Working | 29% | 12% | 7% | 2% | 0% | 5% | 2% | 5% | 0% | 0% |
| C++ | 20% | 5% | 5% | 2% | 0% | 0% | 2% | 2% | 0% | 6% |
| Others | 0% | 5% | 0% | 0% | 0% | 0% | 0% | 0% | 0% | 0% |

attention when identifying the learning outcomes of courses in project and program management.

## Sales and Marketing

When it comes to essential skills in this domain only 10% of surveyed companies consider the skills in this domain of a priority. This is not surprising due to the strong indication of the technical orientation of Jordanian ICT firms and a lack of focus on marketing and sales. As can be seen in Table 8, the highest rate of skills in this category is only 14%. Regular workshops and seminars may be given to ICT firms on the importance of marketing and sales as driving forces to entry in the global arena. Educational institutions can play a major role by preparing their graduates in technology as well as marketing and sales.

*Table 7. Essential skills needed – project / program management*

| Rate (1 highest) | | | | | | | | | | |
|---|---|---|---|---|---|---|---|---|---|---|
| **Domain** | **1** | **2** | **3** | **4** | **5** | **6** | **7** | **8** | **9** | **10** |
| Project Management | 74% | 5% | 5% | 5% | 0% | 2% | 0% | 2% | 0% | 0% |
| People & Change Management | 26% | 17% | 10% | 2% | 5% | 0% | 0% | 0% | 2% | 0% |
| Communication Skills | 40% | 19% | 7% | 2% | 0% | 0% | 2% | 2% | 2% | 0% |
| Interpersonal Skills | 24% | 14% | 7% | 2% | 0% | 2% | 2% | 2% | 0% | 2% |
| Business Analysis | 36% | 19% | 5% | 5% | 0% | 0% | 0% | 2% | 0% | 2% |
| Systems Analysis | 26% | 26% | 5% | 2% | 2% | 0% | 2% | 0% | 0% | 0% |
| Project Design | 33% | 12% | 10% | 2% | 2% | 7% | 2% | 0% | 0% | 2% |
| Project Monitoring & Evaluation | 38% | 5% | 7% | 10% | 10% | 5% | 2% | 0% | 0% | 0% |
| English Language Skills | 29% | 19% | 5% | 0% | 2% | 0% | 5% | 0% | 5% | 0% |
| Technical Writing Skills | 21% | 24% | 2% | 2% | 5% | 5% | 2% | 2% | 0% | 2% |
| Non-Technical Writing skills | 14% | 21% | 5% | 0% | 0% | 2% | 2% | 2% | 2% | 2% |
| Presentation Skills | 21% | 17% | 10% | 7% | 0% | 2% | 0% | 5% | 5% | 0% |
| Team Work | 29% | 19% | 7% | 0% | 7% | 0% | 5% | 0% | 5% | 2% |
| Customer Service | 31% | 12% | 5% | 5% | 5% | 2% | 0% | 0% | 0% | 2% |
| Others | 5% | 0% | 0% | 0% | 0% | 0% | 0% | 0% | 0% | 0% |

## Technical Support

As shown in Table 9, essential skills in this domain include customer service support at a rate of 66%, system application support and administration at a rate of 51%. Customer support and application support concepts are seen important in maintaining customer satisfaction and in guaranteeing continuity of developed products. Such concepts are encouraged to be part of what could be taught in Universities.

## Communications

Essential skills in the domain of communications include: wireless LAN at a rate of 89%, digital communications at a rate of 54%, and broadband techniques at a rate of 49% (Table 10). This reveals a widespread trend toward wireless technologies in ICT firms and other industries, and thus more emphasis must be given to wireless communication in the design of the communications body of knowledge of ICT curricula.

## 7. DISCUSSIONS AND IMPLICATIONS

The overall responses to the survey and the analysis of date provide specific insights and implications on the profile of the ICT industry in Jordan, identify the skill sets needed and implications for relevant curricula design, and finally discussions of recommendation to set up a policy framework for more effective ICT educational systems that are able to produce graduates with the skill set required by the job market and its dynamic nature in the ICT industry. The main findings are summarized as follows:

A.  The ICT industry in Jordan is mostly comprised of SMEs with 62% of companies having 50 employees or less. The total ICT workforce in the sample survey was 3,392 of which 31% are female. Available statistics indicate that the total Jordanian workforce in the ICT sector is about 17,000, and the overall ICT workforce in ICT, non-ICT, and other

*Table 8. Essential skills needed – sales and marketing*

| Rate (1 highest) | | | | | | | | | | |
|---|---|---|---|---|---|---|---|---|---|---|
| Domain | 1 | 2 | 3 | 4 | 5 | 6 | 7 | 8 | 9 | 10 |
| Sales/Marketing Analysis & Techniques | 14% | 3% | 10% | 17% | 59% | 0% | 0% | 0% | 0% | 0% |
| Communication Skills | 14% | 7% | 10% | 10% | 55% | 0% | 0% | 0% | 0% | 0% |
| Interpersonal Skills | 3% | 14% | 17% | 17% | 41% | 3% | 0% | 0% | 0% | 0% |
| Proficiency in English language | 10% | 3% | 24% | 24% | 38% | 0% | 0% | 0% | 0% | 0% |
| Customer Service | 14% | 3% | 10% | 24% | 48% | 0% | 0% | 3% | 0% | 0% |
| Creative Thinking Skills | 3% | 3% | 10% | 34% | 34% | 0% | 0% | 0% | 0% | 0% |
| Technical Writing | 0% | 10% | 31% | 21% | 24% | 0% | 3% | 0% | 0% | 0% |
| Personal/Time Management | 3% | 10% | 14% | 21% | 41% | 3% | 3% | 0% | 0% | 0% |
| Professional/Workplace Ethics | 3% | 7% | 3% | 28% | 52% | 0% | 0% | 3% | 0% | 0% |
| Proficiency in English Language | 7% | 0% | 14% | 17% | 38% | 0% | 0% | 0% | 3% | 0% |
| Other (please mention) | 3% | 0% | 0% | 0% | 3% | 3% | 0% | 0% | 0% | 0% |

*Table 9. Essential skills needed – technical support*

| Rate (1 highest) | | | | | | | | | | |
|---|---|---|---|---|---|---|---|---|---|---|
| Domain | 1 | 2 | 3 | 4 | 5 | 6 | 7 | 8 | 9 | 10 |
| Customer Service | 66% | 6% | 0% | 3% | 0% | 3% | 0% | 0% | 0% | 0% |
| Systems Application Support | 51% | 14% | 14% | 0% | 3% | 0% | 0% | 0% | 3% | 0% |
| Hardware Engineering | 17% | 20% | 11% | 3% | 11% | 0% | 0% | 3% | 0% | 0% |
| Communication Skills | 37% | 29% | 6% | 0% | 3% | 0% | 0% | 0% | 0% | 0% |
| Systems Application Admin | 46% | 20% | 6% | 6% | 0% | 3% | 3% | 0% | 0% | 0% |
| Training | 26% | 29% | 11% | 3% | 0% | 3% | 3% | 6% | 0% | 0% |
| Systems Testing | 26% | 14% | 17% | 6% | 3% | 6% | 0% | 3% | 3% | 0% |
| Technical Writing | 20% | 20% | 9% | 0% | 9% | 0% | 3% | 0% | 9% | 0% |
| Interpersonal Skills | 29% | 29% | 3% | 3% | 3% | 0% | 6% | 0% | 0% | 0% |
| Creative Thinking Skills | 40% | 11% | 11% | 3% | 6% | 3% | 0% | 3% | 0% | 0% |
| Others | 6% | 3% | 0% | 0% | 0% | 0% | 0% | 0% | 0% | 0% |

relevant sectors exceeding 60,000. Student enrolment in ICT programs in Jordanian universities is about 27,000 with approximately 6,000 graduates per year, while the number of new jobs is estimated at 5,000 per year. The Jordan ICT strategy estimated that the ICT industry would need a total ICT workforce of 35,000 by 2011. The current situation indicates there is a 2,000 over sup-

ply of new job entrants (graduates) but does not reflect the true nature of the labor force as large numbers of ICT workers leave the country for better job conditions in the Gulf States and some of the graduates will find work in other fields. As a result, this still puts additional pressure on the Jordanian ICT job market for a better quality workforce.

*Table 10. Essential skills needed – data base systems and applications*

| Rate (1 highest) Domain | 1 | 2 | 3 | 4 | 5 | 6 | 7 | 8 | 9 | 10 |
|---|---|---|---|---|---|---|---|---|---|---|
| Wireless LAN | 89% | 0% | 0% | 3% | 0% | 0% | 0% | 0% | 0% | 0% |
| Broadband Techniques | 49% | 9% | 3% | 0% | 0% | 0% | 0% | 0% | 0% | 0% |
| Radio Mechanics | 3% | 3% | 3% | 0% | 0% | 0% | 0% | 0% | 0% | 0% |
| Telecom Engineering | 26% | 0% | 3% | 0% | 3% | 0% | 0% | 0% | 0% | 0% |
| Broadcast Techniques | 14% | 3% | 0% | 3% | 0% | 0% | 0% | 0% | 0% | 0% |
| Digital Communications | 54% | 3% | 0% | 0% | 3% | 0% | 0% | 0% | 0% | 0% |
| Analog Communications | 29% | 6% | 0% | 0% | 0% | 0% | 0% | 0% | 0% | 0% |
| Others | 6% | 3% | 0% | 0% | 0% | 0% | 0% | 0% | 0% | 0% |

B.  Predominant ICT industry Job categories reported in the survey included: Programming/Software Engineering (11%), Web development (8%), Database management systems (8%), and others are ranging between 2-7%, of the workforce.

C.  Finding technically qualified employees is a major problem with 90% of the companies. The IT industry indicated in the survey that the professional skills of university graduates do not meet the job market requirements. Graduates often need to go through a process of re-training, adding additional recruitment and training costs for employers. The ICT industry provides on-the-job training (68% of companies) and external short-term training (90% of companies) to keep abreast of new developments. External short-term training is conducted in the Gulf (28%), Europe (24%), and North America (13%). Training opportunities to further develop knowledge is important for ICT workers as much as for their employers. While training employees adds value to the organizations it also increases the value and employability of IT professionals. In this job market where supply is short, the consequence is higher attrition with employers battling for fewer employees.

D.  In systems and network administration, database administration, and development job categories, there is a strong emphasis on the need for job applicants to have vendor certifications. However, this was considered to be less important than specific experience and academic qualifications. Technical competencies and skills mostly needed are on Oracle and MS-SQL in the domain of DB systems; creative thinking skills and graphic design in the domain of digital media and animations; MS administration in the domain of administration; system analysis and business analysis in the domain of systems integration; network design and internet security in the domain of system and network administration; .NET programming, system design, and team work skills in the domain of programming and software engineering; project management, communication skills, and writing skills in the project/program management domain.

E.  Communication skills and creative thinking skills were seen as important soft skills across all job categories. Employers feel that communication skills, proficiency in English language and creative thinking skills are missing in the ICT workforce, in university graduates, and new job entrants.

F.    Salaries for ICT workers are probably the best of all industries. The range is about 425 JD per month for junior level, 790 JD per month for mid level, and 1600 JD per month for senior level.

On the basis of these findings, concentrated efforts need to be made to create an institutionalized systematic and sustainable collaborative framework for professional and technical education that: links directly to the needs and requirements of the job market; promotes innovation within institutions, organizations, and companies; and enhances R&D activities through varieties of methods.

## A. Implications for Curricula Design

The IEEE/ACM computing curricula model (ACM, 2010) identifies core concepts for learning from many different knowledge areas in the fields of Computer Science and Engineering, Information Systems and Technology, and Software Engineering. The core areas identified are: Discrete structures, Human-Computer Interaction, Programming Fundamentals, Graphics and Visual Computing, Algorithms and Complexity, Intelligent Systems, Architecture and Organization, Information Management, Operating Systems, Social and Professional Issues, Net-Centric Computing, Software Engineering, Programming Languages, and Computational Science. Mapping these areas into ICT curricula has been a common practice in many Universities and ICT colleges worldwide.

The skills and competencies identified in this study related to these knowledge areas provide the specific technologies and practical experiences that the job market requires in Jordan. These skills can be used to motivate a design of an effective, flexible and relevant ICT educational model. Details of such a model will be investigated further in a future publication.

## B. Recommendations

On the basis of the survey findings and discussions with international educational experts and leaders of industry, the following are the specific recommendations to align ICT educational outcomes with the needs and requirements of the industry:

A.    Introducing a process of on-going university-industry coordination for the creation of dynamic curricula structure that is regularly reviewed and updated to ensure its relevance to the industrial sector;

B.    Adopt a holistic approach to enhance the quality of graduates through coordinating the curricula development process with staff development, practical student training programs, and industry-university collaboration;

C.    Create professional development plans to enhance the skills, knowledge, and teaching methodologies of university instructors and academics;

D.    Encourage teaching and R&D activities at universities that are linked to market needs;

E.    Encourage students to become aware of future opportunities for innovation by enrolling them in effective internship programs and capstone projects as a degree requirement; and

F.    Encourage and proactively design opportunities for industry experts to get involved in a variety of academic activities at universities, including joint research projects, teaching courses, participating on theses advisory committees, participating on advisory boards, taking part in short courses and seminars, and more.

## 8. CONCLUSION

This paper presents a workforce assessment in the Jordanian ICT industry. The assessment has been conducted on the basis of a sample survey which covered 53 ICT companies representing approximately 75% of the ICT sector. The results of the survey have an overall sampling variability of ±5% at the 90% confidence level. The results provide insights into the structure of the Jordanian ICT industry, its workforce fabrics, and the growing gap between its requirements and available ICT educational outcomes. The workforce gap in the ICT sector can best be managed through developing effective educational programs with specialized hands-on practices that can produce the right technical skills combined with abilities in English language, creative thinking, and other soft skill elements. The results and the implications of this study are intended to provide a platform for discussion between industry and academia to work collaboratively toward developing highly qualified ICT labor force for Jordan, the region, and the globe. The contributions can easily motive new ICT educational and industrial policies in Jordan and elsewhere to help maintain better Academia-Industry linkages and sustain development status at the forefront of higher education and at the leading edge of creating and disseminating new knowledge in the ICT domains.

## ACKNOWLEDGMENT

The author is grateful to the European Commission for the financial support of this study as part of the Tempus Project on Building Quality, Relevant, and Industry-Oriented IT Education. The author is also grateful to the German-Jordanian University, Ministry of ICT, USAID-SABEQ program, and INT@J for their contribution to the study, and to the anonymous reviewers of this paper for their valuable comments. This work has been supported as part of an EU Tempus Funded project for developing quality, relevant, and industry oriented IT education.

## REFERENCES

ACM. (2010). *Computing curricula.* Retrieved from http://www.acm.org/education/curricula-recommendations

Holm, J., Lahteenmaki, S., Salmela, H., Suomi, R., Suominen, A., & Viljanen, M. (2002). Best practices of ICT workforce management – a comparable research initiative in Finland. *Journal of European Industrial Training, 26*(7), 333–341. doi:10.1108/03090590210432688

Hu, M.-C., Zheng, C., & Lamond, D. (2007). Recruitment and retention of ICT skills among MNCs in Taiwan. *Chinese Management Studies, 1*(2), 78–92. doi:10.1108/17506140710757991

Int@J. (2007). Information Technology Association-Jordan. *IT Industry Statistics.* Retrieved from http://www.intaj.net/sites/default/files/IT_Industry_Statistics_2007.pdf

Jordan Investment Board (JIB). (2006). *Information communication technology sector.* Retrieved from http://www.jordaninvestment.com/

Luftman, J., & Ben-Zvi, T. (2010). Key issues for IT executives 2010: Judicious IT investments continue post-recession. *MIS Quarterly Executives, 9*(4).

Luftman, J., & Ben-Zvi, T. (2010). Key issues for IT executives 2009: Difficult economy's impact on IT. *MIS Quarterly Executives, 9*(1).

Mutula, S. M., & Van Brakel, P. (2007). ICT skills readiness for the emerging global digital economy among small businesses in developing countries - Case study of Botswana. *Library Hi Tech, 25*(2), 231–245. doi:10.1108/07378830710754992

Porter, M., Schwab, K., Martin, X., & Lopez-Claros, A. (2005). *The global competitiveness report 2004-2005.* Retrieved from https://members.weforum.org/pdf/Global_Competitiveness_Reports/GCR05_Video_Transcript.pdf

Queensland Government Chief Information Office. (2009). *Queensland government ICT skills framework*. Retrieved from http://www.psc.qld.gov.au

Sri Lanka, I. C. T. Association. (2007). *Rising demand: The increasing demand for IT workers spells a challenging opportunity for the IT industry*. Moratuwa, Sri Lanka: Author.

*This work was previously published in the International Journal of Social and Organizational Dynamics in IT, Volume 1, Issue 4, edited by Michael B. Knight, pp. 18-36, 2011 by IGI Publishing (an imprint of IGI Global).*

# Chapter 2
# Is Updating Play or Work?
## The Mediating Role of Updating Orientation in Linking Threat of Professional Obsolescence to Turnover/Turnaway Intentions

**Damien Joseph**
*Nanyang Technological University, Singapore*

**Mei Ling Tan**
*Nanyang Technological University, Singapore*

**Soon Ang**
*Nanyang Technological University, Singapore*

## ABSTRACT

*This study proposes that IT professionals' behavioral orientation towards IT knowledge and skills updating demands can take on two contrasting forms: updating-as-play or updating-as-work. Drawing on threat-rigidity theory (Staw, Sandelands, & Dutton, 1981), the authors hypothesize that IT professionals who feel threatened by professional obsolescence are more likely to approach updating-as-work more than as play. Results from a sample of IT professionals are consistent with threat-rigidity theory (Staw et al., 1981) in that the threat of professional obsolescence is negatively related to updating-as-play and is positively related to updating-as-work. The authors also find that updating-as-play is negatively related to turnaway intentions and that updating-as-work is positively related to turnover intentions; these findings are consistent with IT theories of job mobility. The authors conclude this study with a discussion of these results and propose future research directions.*

DOI: 10.4018/978-1-4666-1948-7.ch002

## INTRODUCTION

The threat of professional obsolescence remains an endemic challenge for IT professionals (Lee, Trauth, & Farwell, 1995; Nelson, 1991; Tsai, Compeau, & Haggerty, 2007). Unlike in other professions where knowledge and skills erode more slowly, the half-life of knowledge and skills in the IT profession is estimated at about two years (Ang & Slaughter, 2000; Dubin, 1990). The IT professional is therefore subjected to a continuous threat of professional obsolescence (Tsai et al., 2007), and must update their knowledge and skills continuously to remain productive in the IT profession. Otherwise, their IT careers may stagnate, or even decline, in terms of employability, promotability, and compensation.

Despite the importance of updating behaviors associated with the IT profession, limited theoretical and empirical research exists on updating behaviors – be it its ontology, etiology, structure, or consequences. Hence, we begin a program of research by asking: how do IT professionals perceive and approach updating?

We draw on the concept of play (Mainemelis & Ronson, 2006) to propose two distinct behavioral orientations towards updating: "updating-as-play" and "updating-as-work." We examine how each updating orientation is affected by the threat of professional obsolescence and how it subsequently affects job mobility intentions. In doing so, this study responds to a recent call by Joseph, Ng, Koh, and Ang (2007, p. 555) to examine antecedents of job mobility that are particularly germane to the IT discipline. As noted by Joseph et al. (2007), prior IT research on the job mobility intentions are limited in their contributions as the antecedents examined are similar to those that have been identified in the general organizational behavior literature. Therefore, this study contributes to the IT discipline by proposing that updating orientation is associated with job mobility intentions of IT professionals. The study also contributes to existing theory on updating by examining the consequences of updating orientation on job mobility intentions.

## THEORETICAL FOUNDATION AND HYPOTHESES DEVELOPMENT

Figure 1 presents the research model governing this study. It shows the hypotheses and the systems of relationships among the hypotheses.

### Threat of Professional Obsolescence and Updating Orientations

Professional obsolescence is defined as the erosion of professional knowledge and skills required for successful performance (e.g., Dubin, 1990; Ferdinand, 1966; Glass, 2000). To manage the threat of professional obsolescence, IT professionals are constantly required to learn and stay up-to-date with the latest technologies in the IT field (Tsai et al., 2007). How IT professionals view and approach updating is not well-understood. To address this gap, we draw on the concept of play orientation (Mainemelis & Ronson, 2006) to propose two distinct ways by which IT professionals approach updating: updating-as-play or updating-as-work.

Mainemelis and Ronson (2006, p. 85) define play as "a patterned behavioral orientation" (p. 85) towards performing any type of activity. A play orientation is characterized by five interdependent elements: positive affect; loose and flexible association between means and ends; freedom from external constraints; non-institutionalized boundaries of time and space; and a threshold experience. Updating-as-play is also expressive in nature in that updating is perceived as intrinsically rewarding. Because updating is seen as play with highly positive emotions such as "fun, relaxation, ecstatic joy, or emotional relief" (Mainemelis & Ronson, 2006, p. 91) updating is pursued as a goal

*Figure 1. Research model*

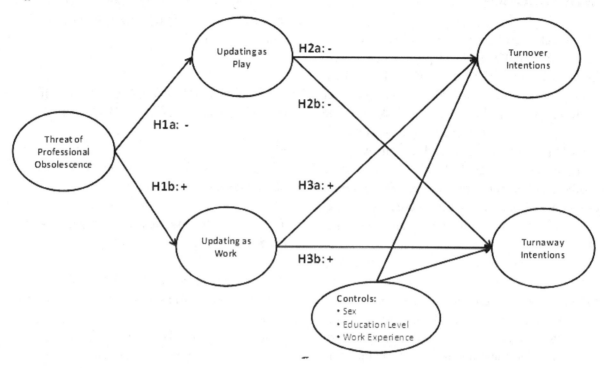

in and of itself. When updating is seen as play, updating behaviors are driven not by efficiency or by specific goals – they are free from job constraints and can be undertaken at any time or place. In support of the updating-as-play concept, Pazy (1996, p. 1195) found that some technology professionals regard updating as "fun," a break from routine, "rest and relaxation" and "a private pleasure" (p. 1195).

By contrast, updating-as-work is instrumental and efficiency-oriented (Glynn, 1994). When updating is seen as work, updating is tightly coupled with task performance and is undertaken only when it is absolutely required for task completion. Thus, updating-as-work is a task-focused and needs-based endeavor that is seldom accompanied by positive emotions. Evidence of the updating-as-work orientation can also be found in Pazy (1996, p. 1176), where it was reported that some technology professionals update only in areas "directly relevant to current tasks" (p. 1176).

The theory of threat-rigidity predicts how IT professionals would approach updating. The theory posits that a threat perceived by an individual elicits behavioral responses that tend to be less varied or more rigid (Staw et al., 1981). These responses are the result of restricting information processing and constricting control. In restricting information processing, individuals narrow their field of attention, reduce the sources of information, or depend on prior experiences. They narrow the scope of knowledge and information processing to their area of specialization at the expense of the broader scope of IT professional knowledge (Kozlowski & Farr, 1988; Pazy, 1994; Steiner & Farr, 1986). In constricting control, individuals shorten the time horizon to the present to alleviate the threat by perceiving a sense of security and protection within a temporarily unchanging bubble (Pazy, 1996).

Therefore, the more IT professionals regard professional obsolescence as a threat, the greater their tendency to narrow their field of attention to current tasks and divert away from exploratory and scanning activities (Joseph & Ang, 2001). Moreover, perceptions of threat trigger psychological stress and anxiety that inhibit positive affect. Thus, we expect that perceptions of the threat of professional obsolescence will trigger a work orientation towards updating and hinder a play orientation towards updating.

Hypothesis 1: The threat of professional obsolescence is H1(a) negatively related to updating-as-play; and H1(b) positively related to updating-as-work.

## Updating Orientation and their Consequent Job Mobility Intentions

There is limited research extending concepts of play and threat-rigidity theory to the consequences of updating orientation. Therefore, this study provides us the opportunity to contribute to extant literature by linking the updating orientation of IT professionals with their subsequent job mobility intentions. In this paper, we examine two forms of job mobility intentions: a) turnover intentions -- defined as individuals' intentions of holding the same or similar jobs in different organizations; and b) turnaway intentions -- defined as individuals' intentions of changing one's profession or occupation (Joseph, Boh, Ang, & Slaughter, in press).

Although updating-as-play is not goal-driven, it results in an improvement of domain-relevant skills (Mainemelis & Ronson, 2006). A play orientation towards updating broadens IT professionals' repertoire of knowledge and skills, enables them to discover unnoticed variables and opportunities, explore task-related behaviors, and achieve continuously higher levels of mastery (Mainemelis & Ronson, 2006). Thus, updating-as-play maintains IT professionals' currency of IT knowledge and skills. IT theories of job mobility (Joseph et al., 2007) have posited and concluded that skills development reduces turnover intentions by increasing IT professionals' job satisfaction and

embeddedness in the organization. In the same vein, we expect updating-as-play to reduce turnaway intentions by increasing IT professionals' embeddedness within the IT profession (Joseph et al., in press). Hence,

Hypothesis 2: Updating-as-play is negatively related to H2(a) turnover intentions; and H2(b) turnaway intentions.

Following the arguments based on the concept of play (Mainemelis & Ronson, 2006), we postulate that IT professionals who "update-as-play" would do so continually. On the other hand, IT professionals who "update-as-work" would update more intermittently and, therefore, are less likely to be up-to-date in their IT knowledge and skills. Human capital theory (Becker, 1975) suggests that the lack of up-to-date IT knowledge and skills would reduce levels of job performance. In turn, the lowered job performance of IT professionals has been related with reduced job satisfaction and thus, greater turnover intentions (Joseph et al., 2007).

The lack of up-to-date IT knowledge and skills would also narrow the range of job alternatives within the IT profession (Joseph et al., 2007). As alternative jobs within IT become limited, IT professionals may seek a career change as a response to the threat of professional obsolescence (Pazy, 1990; Tsai et al., 2007). A career change reduces subsequent professional obsolescence as occupation-specific knowledge and skills in other non-IT professions erode less rapidly (Dubin, 1990). In addition, IT professionals who have turned away from the IT profession to non-IT line positions become valued "power-users" in these line functions (Reich & Kaarst-Brown, 1999, 2003). Hence,

Hypothesis 3: Updating-as-work is positively related to H3(a) turnover intentions; and H3(b) turnaway intentions.

## METHOD

### Data Collection

The approach taken to test the hypotheses was a field study using survey methodology. We approached twenty-nine (29) organizations and gave ten questionnaires to each of the organizations to be distributed to their IT professionals. The 29 organizations were firms that employed IT professionals who attended an evening part time MBA program in a university situated in Singapore. Of the 290 questionnaires distributed, 181 usable questionnaires were returned, yielding a response rate of 62.4%.

### Sample

The respondents were on average 30.3 years old ($SD$ = 4.29 years) with an average working experience of 6.5 years ($SD$ = 4.34 years). Their average organization tenure was 3.10 years ($SD$ = 3.40 years). The sample comprised of 76.2% males and 23.8% females. Of the 181 IT professionals in the sample, 16.6% were non-graduates, 71.8% attained a Bachelor's degree and the remaining 11.6% possessed a post-graduate degree. The IT professionals surveyed held job roles in both systems development (e.g., applications development managers, systems analyst, and programmers) as well as IT infrastructure (e.g., data center managers, network managers, and database administrators).

### Measures

The questionnaire contained multiple measurement items relating to each of the constructs in the research model. Wherever possible, we used scales validated in previous studies. For the remaining constructs, we used sets of items generated based on reviews of prior relevant literature. For all items, respondents were asked to indicate the extent to which they agreed or disagreed with the statements on a seven-point Likert-type scale, anchored by "1" = "Strongly disagree" and "7" = "Strongly agree." A full list of items is provided in the Appendix.

The dependent variables of *Turnover Intentions* and *Turnaway Intentions* were measured with five items each adapted from Rusbult, Farrell, Rogers, and Mainouss (1988). Examples of items measuring *Turnover Intentions* include: "I have spent some time looking for another IT job" and "I will probably look for a new IT job outside my current company." Examples of items measuring *Turnaway Intentions* include: "I have spent some time looking for another *non*-IT job" and "I am considering quitting my current job for another *non*-IT job."

The independent variables are *Threat of Professional Obsolescence*, *Updating-as-play* and *Updating-as-work*. The *Threat of Professional Obsolescence* was measured with five items based on research by Pazy (1990, 1994, 1996). Examples of items measuring this construct include: "I feel the threat of professional obsolescence" and "I fear of technical obsolescence".

We developed the measures of *Updating-as-Play* and *Updating-as-Work* from the qualitative studies of coping with professional obsolescence by Pazy (1990) and Tsai et al. (2007). Examples of items measuring *Updating-as-play* include: "Updating is not tiring" and "Updating gives me tremendous pleasure". Examples of items measuring *Updating-as-work* include: "I feel that updating is not necessary unless it is relevant to my current job requirements" and "I am not at all concerned with updating unless developments are in my area of specialization."

The covariates in the model were Sex, Educational Level and Work Experience. *Sex* was measured with a dichotomous variable indicating Male as "0" and Female as "1". *Educational Level* was measured with a four level ordinal variable with "1" indicating High School Diploma, "2" indicating Bachelors degree and "3" indicating Postgraduate Degree. Finally, *Work Experience* was measured with a continuous variable indicating the total labor force experience held by an individual.

## Data Analysis

We used partial least squares (PLS) to analyze the measurement and structural models. PLS is suited for this study because it combines principal component analysis, path analysis, and regression to simultaneously evaluate theory and data (Chin, 1998; Hulland, 1999). Data analysis with PLS begins with the assessment of the measurement model followed by the assessment of the structural model. In assessing the measurement model, we examine the construct validity in terms of convergent and discriminant validities. The measurement model is also evaluated by examining the predictive and explanatory powers of the model (Gefen, Straub, & Boudreau, 2000). Finally, we conducted a bootstrapping test to compute estimates of standard errors for testing the statistical significance of path coefficients using t-tests.

## RESULTS

### Measurement Model

The acceptability of the measurement model is assessed by internal consistency between items and the model's convergent and discriminant validity. The composite reliability values of all constructs were close to or above 0.90, indicating high internal consistency (Bagozzi & Yi, 1988). Convergent and discriminant validities are assessed with the following criteria: (1) the square root of the average variance extracted (AVE) by a construct from its indicators should be at least 0.707, i.e., AVE itself should be greater than 0.5; (2) The square root of the AVE should be greater than the variance shared between the construct and other constructs in the model; and (3) standardized item loadings should be greater than 0.70 (Fornell & Larcker, 1981). The square root of AVE for each construct was greater than 0.707, all constructs shared more variance with their own indicators than with those of other constructs and that the items load highly, based on established guidelines (Hair, Anderson, Tatham, & Black, 1995), on respective constructs are above 0.80 and are statistically significant at the 0.001 level.

### Analysis of the Structural Model

Table 1 presents the descriptives and correlations of variables in the model. Figure 2 presents the results of the hypothesized structural model, which may be interpreted as standardized betas. In addition, the predictive strength of a hypothesized model can be assessed with its total explained variance. The model explained 6.04% of the total

*Table 1. Descriptives, inter-construct correlations and results of convergent and discriminant validities*

| | Mean | SD | N Items | CR[1] | AVE[2] | 1[3] | 2 | 3 | 4 | 5 | 6 | 7 |
|---|---|---|---|---|---|---|---|---|---|---|---|---|
| 1 Turnover Intentions | 3.441 | 1.439 | 4 | 0.894 | 0.631 | **0.794** | | | | | | |
| 2 Turnaway Intentions | 2.872 | 1.524 | 4 | 0.937 | 0.750 | 0.381 *** | **0.866** | | | | | |
| 3 Threat of Professional Obsolesence | 3.961 | 1.567 | 3 | 0.927 | 0.808 | 0.267 *** | 0.132 | **0.899** | | | | |
| 4 Updating as Play | 2.751 | 1.370 | 3 | 0.905 | 0.761 | 0.109 | 0.109 | 0.184 * | **0.872** | | | |
| 5 Updating as Work | 4.343 | 1.312 | 4 | 0.915 | 0.730 | 0.071 | -0.358 *** | -0.229 ** | -0.268 *** | **0.854** | | |
| 6 Sex | 1.238 | 0.427 | 1 | | | -0.083 | 0.096 | -0.042 | -0.031 | -0.032 | | |
| 7 Education Level | 2.939 | 0.559 | 1 | | | 0.001 | 0.023 | 0.004 | -0.046 | -0.074 | -0.125 | |
| 8 Work Experience | 6.465 | 4.339 | 1 | | | -0.151 * | -0.021 | -0.068 | 0.059 | -0.030 | -0.055 | -0.127 |

[1] Composite Reliability; [2] Average Variance Explained; [3] Emboldened numbers on the diagonal are the square root of AVE.
Off-diagonal elements are correlation among constructs.
* *p* < 0.05; ** *p* < 0.01; *** *p* < 0.001.

*Figure 2. Results*

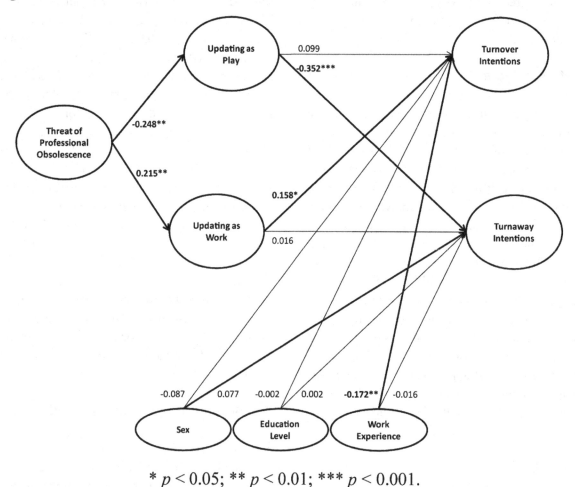

$* p < 0.05; ** p < 0.01; *** p < 0.001.$

variance in turnover intentions and 13.49% of the total variance in turnaway intentions. In turn, the threat of professional obsolescence explained 5.67% of the total variance in updating-as-play and 4.63% of the total variance in updating-as-work.

Hypothesis 1a posits that the threat of professional obsolescence is negatively related to updating-as-play and Hypothesis 1b posits that the threat of professional obsolescence is positively related to updating-as-work. Supportive of our hypothesis, we find that the threat of professional obsolescence is negatively related to updating-as-play ($\beta$ = -0.248, $t$ = 2.685, $p$ < 0.01). In addition, the threat of professional obsolescence is positively related to updating-as-work ($\beta$ =

0.215, $t$ = 3.021, $p$ < 0.01). Additional analysis of the difference between the estimated path coefficients of updating-as-play and updating-as-work indicates that IT professionals favor the latter over the former as a response to the threat of professional obsolescence ($t$ = -26.034, $df$ = 179, $p$ < 0.001).

Hypotheses 2a and 2b posit that updating-as-play is negatively related to both turnover intentions and turnaway intentions respectively. We find that updating-as-play is negatively related to turnaway intentions ($\beta$ = -0.352, $t$ = 4.367, $p$ < 0.001). However, we find that updating-as-play is not significantly related to turnover intentions ($\beta$ = 0.099, $t$ = 0.926, $ns$).

Hypothesis 3a and 3b posits that updating-as-work is positively related to both turnover intentions and turnaway intentions. In support of Hypothesis 3a, we find that updating-as-work is positively related to turnover intentions ($\beta = 0.158$, $t = 2.032$, $p < 0.05$). However, we find that updating-as-work is not significantly related to turnaway intentions ($\beta = 0.016$, $t = 0.184$, *ns*).

## DISCUSSION AND CONCLUSION

To date, there is scant research that has focused on how IT professionals respond to the threat of professional obsolescence (Pazy, 1990; Tsai et al., 2007). In this study, we introduce the idea that IT professionals respond to the threat of professional obsolescence by initiating updating behaviors. We propose that IT professionals hold one of two forms of updating orientations: some regard updating as work while others tend to view updating as play. Drawing on threat-rigidity theory (Staw et al., 1981), we find that IT professionals who feel threatened by professional obsolescence favor updating-as-work over updating-as-play.

We also took the opportunity in this study to examine the patterns of job mobility intentions associated with each of the two forms of updating orientation. Consistent with our hypotheses, we find that updating-as-work is positively related to turnover intentions while updating-as-play is negatively related to turnaway intentions.

Contrary to our expectations, we find that although updating-as-play deters turnaway intentions, it is not related to turnover intentions. Presumably turnover intentions are related to factors other than updating-as-play orientation. One possible factor could be the quality of the current employer's updating climate (Kozlowski & Farr, 1988; Kozlowski & Hults, 1987). Organization updating climate represents IT professionals' socially influenced perception of professional development support in terms of technologies, management policies, supervisor practices, and other salient work environment features (Kozlowski & Hults, 1987; Potosky & Ramakrishna, 2002). In essence, organization updating climate provides IT professionals with psychological support to acquire new and up-to-date IT knowledge and skiils (Schambach, 1994). We believe that the quality of an organization's updating climate could predict an IT professional's turnover intentions than updating orientations such as updating-as-play.

Our study also revealed that while updating-as-work is associated with higher turnover intentions, it is not related to turnaway intentions. A possible reason for this pattern of results might be that updating-as-work results in a targeted set of IT knowledge and skills that may be valued by other potential employers in the external labor market (Mithas & Krishnan, 2008). With organizations willing to pay a premium for IT experience in other firms, IT professionals, even those without up-to-date knowledge and skills, may be able to secure alternative employment; perhaps in organizations that have less demanding IT skills requirements. With available job alternatives in the external labor market, IT professionals may not be harboring thoughts about leaving the IT profession.

We would like to propose other areas for future research. First, one should examine more closely the role of organization updating climate in the updating-as-play to job mobility relationship. Specifically, future research could examine whether organization updating climate provides IT professionals with the latitude to experiment with the latest information technologies, and thereby, curbing their intentions to turnover or turnaway.

Second, future research could examine whether IT professionals with less up-to-date IT knowledge and skills do turnover to less demanding work environments. Extending this line of inquiry, future research could also estimate the financial returns to human capital (e.g., compensation packages) associated with possessing up-to-date IT knowledge and skills.

Finally, future research could examine other outcomes in addition to job mobility. Specifically, future research could determine whether job performance (in-role; helping; citizenship; counterproductive work behaviors) is related to updating orientations and perceived threat of professional obsolescence.

## APPENDIX

The following are the set of items utilized in this study.

## Turnover Intentions

1. I have spent some time looking for another IT job.
2. I will probably look for a new IT job outside my current company.
3. Where my employer does not keep his promises I think a lot about leaving the company for another IT job.
4. I often think about leaving the company for another IT job.
5. I am considering quitting my current job for another IT job.

## Turnaway Intentions

1. I have spent some time looking for another *non*-IT job.
2. I will probably look for a new *non*-IT job outside my current company.
3. Where my employer does not keep his promises I think a lot about leaving the company for a *non*-IT job.
4. I often think about leaving the company for a *non*-IT job.
5. I am considering quitting my current job for another *non*-IT job.

## Threat of Professional Obsolescence

When there are new developments in technology and knowledge in the IT field, …

1. … I fear of technical obsolescence.
2. … I feel intimidated.
3. … I feel the threat of obsolescence.

## Updating-as-Play

1. I update for fun.
2. Updating gives me tremendous pleasure.
3. Updating is not tiring.
4. Updating is a way to relieve myself from the routine of work.
5. Reading an IT journal is rest and relaxation.

## Updating-as-Work

When there are new developments in technology and knowledge in the IT field, …

1. … I feel that updating is not necessary unless it is relevant to my current job requirements.
2. … Updating can wait until I have time to devote solely to learning.
3. … I am not at all concerned with updating unless developments are in my area of specialization.

## REFERENCES

Ang, S., & Slaughter, S. (2000). The missing context of information technology personnel: A review and future directions for research. In Zmud, R. W. (Ed.), *Framing the domains of IT management: Projecting the future through the past* (pp. 305–327). Cincinnati, OH: Pinnaflex Educational Resources.

Bagozzi, R. P., & Yi, Y. (1988). On the evaluation of structural equation models. *Journal of the Academy of Marketing Science, 16*, 74–94. doi:10.1007/BF02723327

Becker, G. (1975). *Human capital*. Chicago, IL: University of Chicago Press.

Chin, W. W. (1998). Issues and opinion on structural equation modeling. *Management Information Systems Quarterly, 22*, 7–16.

Dubin, S. S. (1990). Maintaining competence through updating. In Willis, S. L., & Dubin, S. S. (Eds.), *Maintaining professional competence* (pp. 44–48). San Francisco, CA: Jossey-Bass.

Ferdinand, T. N. (1966). On the obsolescence of scientists and engineers. *American Scientist, 54*, 46–56.

Fornell, C., & Larcker, D. F. (1981). Evaluating structural equation models with observable variables and measurement error. *JMR, Journal of Marketing Research, 18*, 39–50. doi:10.2307/3151312

Gefen, D., Straub, D., & Boudreau, M. C. (2000). Structural equation modeling and regression: Guidelines for research practice. *Communications of the Association for Information Systems, 4*, 1–78.

Glass, R. (2000). On personal technical obsolescence. *Communications of the ACM, 43*, 15–17. doi:10.1145/341852.341872

Glynn, M. A. (1994). Effects of work task cues and play task cues on information-processing, judgment, and motivation. *The Journal of Applied Psychology, 79*, 34–45. doi:10.1037/0021-9010.79.1.34

Hair, J. F. Jr, Anderson, R. E., Tatham, R. L., & Black, W. C. (1995). *Multivariate data analysis with readings* (4th ed.). Upper Saddle River, NJ: Prentice Hall.

Hulland, J. (1999). Use of partial least squares (pls) in strategic management research: A review of four recent studies. *Strategic Management Journal, 20*, 195–204. doi:10.1002/(SICI)1097-0266(199902)20:2<195::AID-SMJ13>3.0.CO;2-7

Joseph, D., & Ang, S. (2001, December). The threat-rigidity model of professional obsolescence and its impact on occupational mobility of IT professionals. In *Proceedings of the Twenty-Second International Conference on Information Systems*, New Orleans, LA.

Joseph, D., Boh, W. F., Ang, S., & Slaughter, S. (Forthcoming). Careers of the information technology workforce: An analysis of career sequences, mobility and objective career success. *Management Information Systems Quarterly*.

Joseph, D., Ng, K. M., Koh, S. K. C., & Ang, S. (2007). Turnover of information technology professionals: A narrative review, meta-analytic structural equation modeling, and model development. *Management Information Systems Quarterly, 31*, 547–577.

Kozlowski, S. W. J., & Farr, J. L. (1988). An integrative model of updating and performance. *Human Performance, 1*, 5–29. doi:10.1207/s15327043hup0101_1

Kozlowski, S. W. J., & Hults, B. M. (1987). An exploration of climates for technical updating and performance. *Personnel Psychology, 40*, 539–563. doi:10.1111/j.1744-6570.1987.tb00614.x

Lacey, T. A., & Wright, B. (2009). Occupational employment projections to 2018. *Monthly Labor Review, 132*, 82–123.

Lee, D. M. S., Trauth, E. M., & Farwell, D. (1995). Critical skills and knowledge requirements of IS professionals - a joint academic-industry investigation. *Management Information Systems Quarterly, 19*, 313–340. doi:10.2307/249598

Mainemelis, C., & Ronson, S. (2006). Ideas are born in fields of play: Towards a theory of play and creativity in organizational settings. *Research in Organizational Behavior, 27*, 81–131. doi:10.1016/S0191-3085(06)27003-5

Mithas, S., & Krishnan, M. S. (2008). Human capital and institutional effects in the compensation of information technology professionals in the United States. *Management Science, 54*, 415–428. doi:10.1287/mnsc.1070.0778

Nelson, R. R. (1991). Educational needs as perceived by IS and end-user personnel: A survey of knowledge and skill requirements. *Management Information Systems Quarterly, 15*, 503–525. doi:10.2307/249454

Pazy, A. (1990). The threat of professional obsolescence - how do professionals at different career stages experience IT and cope with IT. *Human Resource Management, 29*, 251–269. doi:10.1002/hrm.3930290303

Pazy, A. (1994). Cognitive schemata of professional obsolescence. *Human Relations, 47*, 1167–1199. doi:10.1177/001872679404701002

Pazy, A. (1996). Concept and career-stage differentiation in obsolescence research. *Journal of Organizational Behavior, 17*, 59–78. doi:10.1002/(SICI)1099-1379(199601)17:1<59::AID-JOB735>3.0.CO;2-8

Potosky, D., & Ramakrishna, H. V. (2002). The moderating role of updating climate perceptions in the relationship between goal orientation, self-efficacy, and job performance. *Human Performance, 15*, 275–297. doi:10.1207/S15327043HUP1503_03

Reich, B. H., & Kaarst-Brown, M. L. (1999). Seeding the line: Understanding the transition from IT to non-IT careers. *Management Information Systems Quarterly, 23*, 337–364. doi:10.2307/249467

Reich, B. H., & Kaarst-Brown, M. L. (2003). Creating social and intellectual capital through IT career transitions. *The Journal of Strategic Information Systems, 12*, 91–109. doi:10.1016/S0963-8687(03)00017-9

Rusbult, C. E., Farrell, D., Rogers, G., & Mainouss, A. G. III. (1988). Impact of exchange variables on exit, voice, loyalty, and neglect: An integrative model of responses to declining job satisfaction. *Academy of Management Journal, 31*, 589–599. doi:10.2307/256461

Schambach, T. P. (1994). *Maintaining professional competence: An evaluation of factors affecting professional obsolescence of information technology professionals.* Unpublished manuscript, Tampa, FL.

Staw, B. M., Sandelands, L. E., & Dutton, J. E. (1981). Threat-rigidity effects in organizational behavior: A multilevel analysis. *Administrative Science Quarterly, 26*, 501–524. doi:10.2307/2392337

Steiner, D. D., & Farr, J. L. (1986). Career goals, organizational reward systems and technical updating in engineers. *Journal of Occupational Psychology, 59*, 13–24. doi:10.1111/j.2044-8325.1986.tb00209.x

Tsai, H. Y., Compeau, D., & Haggerty, N. (2007). Of races to run and battles to be won: Technical skill updating, stress, and coping of IT professionals. *Human Resource Management, 46*, 395–409. doi:10.1002/hrm.20170

*This work was previously published in the International Journal of Social and Organizational Dynamics in IT, Volume 1, Issue 4, edited by Michael B. Knight, pp. 37-47, 2011 by IGI Publishing (an imprint of IGI Global).*

# Chapter 3
# Gender Wage Differentials in Information Systems:
## 1991 – 2008 A Quantitative Analysis

**George Nezlek**
*Grand Valley State University, USA*

**Gerald DeHondt**
*Grand Valley State University, USA*

## ABSTRACT

*This paper investigates trends and changes in the gender earnings gap for individuals employed in clerical and professional level information systems positions in the U.S. labor market for the period of 1991 through 2008. It examines changes in the earnings gap for IS workers, specifically considering changes relative to the so-called "Internet bubble" observed primarily during the late 1990s. Quantitative analysis of changes in the wage gap, adjusted for key determinants, is based on data from the Current Population Survey (CPS). Examination of these data suggests that the gender earnings gap is persistent despite frequent claims to the contrary from industry surveys and that the gap is narrower for professional level positions. Furthermore, the data suggest that female IS workers, particularly in professional level occupations, may have experienced a beneficial effect from the internet bubble, but it is unclear whether or not that beneficial effect may be fading in the post-bubble internet bust of the early 21st century.*

## INTRODUCTION

Robust gender-based differences in earnings persist in the U.S. labor force, spanning industries, occupations, job levels, and economic climates. In spite of decades of legislation, diversity initiatives, significantly increased public awareness, sup-

port networks, and individual strategies, women have not achieved total salary parity with men. Researchers in a variety of academic disciplines have attempted to understand this phenomenon, in the hopes of contributing to the development of change strategies for public policy, educational institutions, business organizations, and individual women. These theoretical explanations have primarily emerged from the disciplinary frameworks

DOI: 10.4018/978-1-4666-1948-7.ch003

of economics, sociology and social/cognitive psychology (Baroudi & Igbaria, 1995; Truman & Baroudi, 1994).

The last half century has witnessed the rapid expansion and emergence of a dynamic occupational sector in Information Systems (IS), accompanied by the growth of a powerful mythology of a kind of sub-culture within the world of work. IS occupations include the programming, operation and maintenance of computers and other information systems technologies, management and administration of data processing operations, networks and databases, These well-documented (Truman & Baroudi, 1994) beliefs comprise a self-depicted saga of meritocracy, innovation, and individualism, largely freed from the baggage of the industrial heritage of the 20th Century. In the past, one widely held belief was that IS professionals were somehow different (Couger & Sawicki, 1980; Ginzberg & Baroudi, 1988), and that traditional rules did not apply. IS jobs were somehow different, and IS professionals possessed uniquely transferable job skills applicable across a very broad range of organizations and industries. Others have suggested that any differences that may have existed have diminished or disappeared as the Information Technology related sectors of the economy have matured and the use of such technologies has become ubiquitous (Kraft, 1984) It has also been suggested that gender wage discrepancies that persist in the US economy at large do not appear, or are vastly diminished, between men and women who work in IS. Finally, while there may be significant cultural and structural differences in IS occupations outside the U.S. economy, these differences are beyond the scope of this inquiry.

The purposes of the current study are to track the gender wage gap among domestic IS workers during the period from 1991 through 2008, using data from the Current Population Survey (CPS), with particular emphasis on the period commonly referred to as the "Internet Bubble" of the late 20th century. While a universally accepted time period for the Internet Bubble may not be agreed upon, it can generally be thought of as beginning in the early 1990's (with the advent of the Word Wide Web) and ending in the early 21st century, around the time of the collapse of the dot.com sector in approximately 2001. A previous study (Heywood & Nezlek, 1993) investigated the gender wage gap using samples taken from CPS data at five year intervals from 1975 through 1990, inclusive. The analysis here begins where that study left off. The authors' long-term intention is to integrate the findings from both of these studies in a future work. This study is designed to discover whether an enduring and significant wage gap actually remains, even after the typical sociological explanations (e.g., occupational segregation into "hard" and "soft" subfields) and economic explanations (e.g., differential human capital inputs) are accounted for, and how, if at all, the nature of that gap might have changed during a period of unprecedented demand for information technology professionals.

This research considers the following questions:

- Have IS occupations exhibited a diminishing gender wage gap since 1990?
- Did the "internet bubble" result in a smaller gender wage gap – suggesting that organizations might alter or abandon discriminatory practices when facing a relative scarcity of skilled IS workers?
- Did the collapse of the internet bubble have a disproportionate affect on female knowledge workers? As the so-called "new economy" contracted, was there a return to a higher level of gender wage inequity in IS occupations?

## Theoretical Foundation

Numerous studies have demonstrated the existence and persistence of the gender wage gap in the general US economy. Isaacs (1995) cites a finding from American Demographics that women employed full-time with two years or less experience earn 72% of the level for their male peers. A Wall Street Journal study of corporate managers found that women with the same credentials as their male peers earned approximately 82% of the wages for their male counterparts. Other studies (e.g., McDonald & Thornton, 2007) have found that after adjusting for college majors, starting salaries for male and female college graduates are approximately equivalent. It may appear that while both men and women begin their careers on equal footing, the gender wage gap can develop very quickly.

Many researchers distinguish among three explanatory frameworks - psychological, sociological, and economic - to provide an understanding of the persistence of this gender gap. A psychological framework may include actual individual differences in cognitive aptitude (Cawley & Heckman, 1999) but primarily considers stereotypes, expectations, and preferences of employers. It is also important to distinguish between a blatant bias that prevents equitable selection and compensation of women because of employers' distastes for hiring them, and a more subtle "statistical discrimination", in which employers act upon expectations of productivity differentials (Neumark, 1999). The latter generates group discrimination through self-fulfilling prophecies, and lower pay for high-performing group members based on an assumed lower average productivity of that group. There is a widely held belief that men are better at negotiations, better understanding the process, and are able to bring greater aggressiveness and confidence to the salary negotiating table (Crump, Logan, & McIlroy, 2007). This suggests that women may tend to believe this is the "male way", recognizing inherent gender differences in negotiating behavior.

In typically male-dominated disciplines such as science and engineering, research has pointed to conflicts between stereotypes of women and cultural stereotypes of professional success (He-

menway, 1995). A great deal of social/cognitive psychological research has looked at mechanisms such as implicit theories, perceptions of similarity and attraction, and schematic in-group/out-group categorization as explanations of barriers to mentoring and advancement for women.

The sociological framework explains the gap as a reflection of institutional barriers to full participation. This perspective holds that women face substantial barriers to acceptance and success. As an example, in academic institutions, women have been denied a level playing field due to such factors as issues in early education (inhibiting women from entering undergraduate programs in those fields), college and post-graduate education (Klawe & Leveson, 1995), lack of role models and mentors, inequitable distribution of resources and opportunities to women faculty, male-dominated cultures that perpetuate stereotypes, difficulty gaining credibility, and lack of institutional support for efforts to balance career and family demands (Rosser, 2003).

On a more macro level, the sociological perspective points to differences in industrial sectors, occupational categories, and types of firms to which men and women tend to be attracted (Baroudi & Igbaria, 1995). It is suggested that women are more often concentrated in lower-paying support and service occupations, and even when they hold line and management positions, these tend to be in lower paying, female-dominated industries (Ahuja, 2002). After nearly two decades of movement toward managerial integration, there remains no conclusive evidence that the entry of some women into the managerial ranks has brought material benefits to the majority who remain below (Cohen & Huffman, 2007).

The human capital framework holds that wages are largely determined by employees' long-term inputs into the labor process. Factors such as education, work experience, and job tenure explain much of the difference between men's and women's pay for nominally similar work. Specifically, human capital theory would predict that women would earn less than men, due to interrupted patterns of employment which result in less investment in training, education, or continuous job tenure (Baroudi & Igbaria, 1995; Igbaria & Chidambaram, 1997; Panteli, Stack, & Ramsay, 2001). The contention is that wage differences would disappear when human capital factors are held constant (Baroudi & Igbaria, 1995). Conversely, if the wage differences remain after controlling for human capital variables, one could conclude that investments in training, education, and experience yield different returns for men than for women (Igbaria & Chidambaram, 1997). Despite an apparent difference in education, women are able to better overcome this deficit, and maintain comparable productivity to men (Cameron & Butcher-Powell, 2006).

One study (Montgomery & Powell, 2003) did find that the salary gap was smaller for women who successfully completed an MBA than for matched peers who were accepted into MBA programs but chose not to enter or dropped out of the programs. The wage gap among matched non-MBAs was 14%, and 9% among MBAs. However, studies have also found significant wage gaps in advanced careers, including attorneys (Noonan, Corcoran, & Courant, 2005), Ph.D. economists (Singell & Stone, 1993), and Ph.D. computer scientists (Isaacs, 1995).

## The Current Study

The current study is based on the approach described in Heywood and Nezlek (1993), to test a human capital theory explanation for the gender wage gap among IS workers over time. A long running discussion in academic communities, and frequently the context for much of the research within the psychological and sociological frameworks, can be summarized in the recurrent theme of why more women don't pursue careers in IS-related fields (and numerous other technical occupations). The authors have chosen the human capital framework to consider what happens to the women who do.

According to human capital theory (Baroudi & Igbaria, 1995; Dattero, Galup, & Quan, 2005; Heywood & Nezlek, 1993; Igbaria & Chidambaram, 1997), true gender discrimination is demonstrated only if all variables that influence wages, other than gender, are controlled. While it is unlikely that any study can control for all such variables, the current study follows the choice of human capital and demographic variables that have been frequently cited in the literature (education, experience, marital status, race, job type, industrial sector, urban density, and geographic region). Wages of men and women in the IS related professions, controlled for these human capital and demographic variables, are tracked annually for the period of interest.

## Methodology

Data are drawn from the database of the Current Population Survey (CPS), a monthly survey which has been conducted for over 50 years by the U.S. Bureau of Labor Statistics and the Bureau of the Census (CPS Data Main Page, n.d.). CPS data are widely recognized as one of the standards for source data in demographic research. Each month, over 50,000 households are scientifically sampled and interviewed, providing employment data used by policymakers, legislators, academics, the press, and the general public. The CPS is widely regarded as a representative sample of the general population for research purposes. Data are accessed by use of Ferret (Federal Electronic Research and Review Extraction Tool), a web-based statistical and database extraction tool developed explicitly for this system by the Bureau of Labor Statistics and the Census Bureau (Data Ferret, n.d.).

For the current study, data are taken from the Annual Demographic Supplements (ADS) of the CPS (which are prepared in March of each year) for the years from 1991 to 2008. Samples are restricted to full-year, full-time, private sector workers in IS related occupations. Part-time workers are excluded, since annual earnings may be significantly affected by the duration of employment, and the nature of employment outside the domain of interest, and the data available do not pro-rate earnings for multiple occupational categories. While it might also be possible to extrapolate annual earnings for part-year workers, sample sizes for each year ranged from approximately 1,000 to 2,600 persons, which the authors believe are sufficient.

The samples are divided into cohorts based on gender and occupational class (professional or clerical). While the specific occupational categories that comprise the cohorts has changed over the period of this study, the motivation for distinguishing clerical versus managerial / professional level occupational classes remains the same. A major change in CPS occupational data classifications occurred in 2003, greatly expanding the number of IS-related positions. These changes reflect not only the growth in the overall IS-related sectors of the economy, but also the emergence of new occupational definitions as the field matures.

Analysis is conducted both on a combined sample of IS workers (professional and clerical), and separately for the professional and clerical occupations cohorts. If the analysis were conducted at the level of individual occupational categories, the classification changes in 2003 would have had a far more significant effect on the study, but this is minimized by conducting the analysis at the cohort level. Specifically, regression analysis is used to construct profiles and to compare the relative earnings of men and women in each of the relevant classes.

The occupations that make up the clerical and professional sub-groups are as follows:

CPS Occupational Categories 1991 – 2002
Professional Cohort
  ◦ Systems Analysts
  ◦ Computer Programmers
Clerical Cohort
  ◦ Computer Equipment Operators
  ◦ Peripheral Equipment Operators
  ◦ Data Entry Clerks

CPS Occupational Categories 2003 – present
Professional Cohort
  ◦ IS Managers
  ◦ Systems Analysts
  ◦ Computer Programmers
  ◦ Computer Engineers
  ◦ Database Administrators
  ◦ Support Specialists
  ◦ Network Administrators
  ◦ Network Analysts
  ◦ Hardware Engineers
Clerical Cohort
  ◦ Computer Operators
  ◦ Data Key System Operators
  ◦ Word Processor Operators
  ◦ Desktop Publishing Equipment Operators
  ◦ Computer Repairers

## Analysis

Analysis of the data is based on a technique known as the Oaxaca decomposition (Oaxaca, 1973), which has been widely used by labor economists (e.g., Montgomery & Powell, 2003; Neumark, 1999) to compare groups that are known to be subject to different regimes. The fact that men and women are subject to different earnings regimes is very well established in the literature.

The authors acknowledge that there may be alternatives to this approach, and that Oaxaca's technique is not without potential shortcomings. Discussion of two of the more commonly suggested issues with the method appear in Butler (1982) and Cotton (1988). Specifically, there are persistent questions about wage differentials based on demand versus supply side factors in the labor market, which Oaxaca's methodology does not distinguish. Another challenge results from the fact that the assortment of human capital variables used in the research may not represent all of the relevant factors. This type of analysis is based on otherwise unexplained residuals, so any inability to account for a significant source of variance would clearly be an issue of concern. However, this research specifically extends the work begun in Heywood and Nezlek (1993) and as a result, the variables chosen are the same set as explored in prior research, to allow for comparison of results across these studies.

Regression analysis is used to estimate coefficients for the human capital and other demographic factors cited above, to predict earnings for men and women. The regression analyses were conducted using Minitab, Microsoft Excel, and SPSS. While standard statistical (e.g., Chow) tests can assess the significance of the differences between cohorts, Oaxaca's technique allows for the consideration of questions that are much more interesting, such as: "How would men have fared if they had been treated the same way as women"? An illustration follows.

The present research recognizes that men and women are subject to different earnings regimes. Consider a standard regression model,

$$D = A + ax_1 + bx_2 + cx_3 + ... + e$$

in which D is the dependent variable, in this case the natural log of annual earnings reported by participants in the CPS. Although this measure may be limited, (e.g., quality of work and quality of life issues may be excluded), the variables chosen and analyses described here are typical throughout the labor economics and Human Resources literature (e.g., Butler, 1982; Cawley & Heckman, 1999; Cotton, 1988; Montgomery & Powell, 2003).

This research seeks to establish a basis for future comparisons between IS professions and other occupations. The measurements chosen also provide consistent estimates across the time period, which is a primary focus of the research. A is the constant term, $x_1...x_n$ are the independent variables. In this research, these will include traditional factors such as age, education, gender, marital status, experience, type of job, industry grouping, geographical category, etc. Finally, e

is the error term. All of the coefficient values are estimates, of course. It is well known that the coefficient estimates for male and female cohorts are often significantly different. Thus, dividing the sample into cohorts by gender yields the following two equations:

$$Dm = Am + amx_1m + bmx_2m + cmx_3m + ... + em$$

$$Df = Af + afx_1f + bfx_2f + cf x_3f + ... + ef$$

with the m and f suffixes referring to the male and female cohorts. The underlying assumption is that Am is potentially different from Af, etc. The difference (Dm - Df) provides us with one estimate of the earnings gap, but it is more interesting to see how men would have fared if they were subject to the same earnings regime as women. Consequently, we consider:

$$Dm,f = Af + afx_1m + bfx_2m + cfx_3m + ... + ef$$

and:

$$Df,m = Am + amx_1f + bmx_2f + cmx_3f + ... + em$$

which suggests how women would have fared if they were subject to the male earnings regime. From this, it is possible to construct two estimates of the gender gap:

$$Dm - Dm,f \text{ or } Df,m - Df$$

The following example applies the technique with sample data. Consider the group of men and women in the professional occupations cohort for 1999. Male average (log) earnings are 10.8396. Female average earnings are 10.6454. The simple estimate of the earnings gap would be 10.8396 – 10.6454; approximately .194 (19.4%). However, if males are treated according to the female earnings regime, estimated male log earnings fall to 10.6538, and if females are treated according to the male earnings regime, estimated female log earnings rise to 10.8119 So, when females are treated according to the male earnings regime, the estimated wage gap is 10.8396 – 10.8119, approximately 0.028 (2.8%). Correspondingly, when males are treated according to the female earnings regime, the estimate of the gap is 10.6538 – 10.6454; approximately 0.08 (0.8%).

These alternative estimates may be of far greater use than the simple comparison of the differences between male and female earnings, which will tend to exaggerate the extent of the gender earnings gap. It is also important to distinguish between the occupational cohorts, as women represent a greater proportion of the typically lower paying clerical group, and men a greater proportion of the typically higher paying professional group.

Using this approach, it is possible to more closely control for human capital and other demographic factors and to produce more realistic estimates of the extent of the gender earnings gap.

## Data Analysis & Interpretation

The data consist of a typical range of human capital factors for full-year, full-time, private-sector workers earning between 5,000 and 250,000 dollars and working at least 40 weeks in the year for which the earnings data pertain (to filter outliers due to coding anomalies in the data and to maintain consistency with data collected for a larger future study) in IS related occupations, as listed below:

Dependent Variable
- ◦ Annual Earnings (natural log)

Independent Variables
- ◦ Age
- ◦ Education
- ◦ Experience
- ◦ Gender
- ◦ Marital Status
- ◦ Race
- ◦ Occupation
- ◦ Industry Group
- ◦ Population Density
- ◦ Region

Prior research (Heywood & Nezlek, 1993) defines the set of independent variables of interest, both as appropriate with respect to similar studies in the literature, and for consistency across studies when comparing results.

Annual earnings are converted from an integer value to a natural log. This transformation is widely used in this type of research to facilitate easier estimation of the wage gap. Education is measured in terms of the highest grade level attained, as coded in the CPS data. Population Density is a three-level categorical variable to distinguish between rural, urban and large urban environments.

Occupations and industry groups are coded as series of categorical (dummy) variables for categories provided in the CPS data definitions. Experience is a proxy derived from age and educational attainment, and assumes that individuals have been continuously employed (in the categories specified) throughout the period of study. The authors readily acknowledge the potential shortcoming of this assumption, but no data are available upon which to propose a more credible alternative. There are also interesting questions that might be raised with respect to issues of organization size and relative job position (e.g., one might be a junior analyst versus a senior analyst) but these data unfortunately do not exist within the CPS data sets.

It is also readily acknowledged that effects of experience in the workforce are traditionally different for males and females. Women, historically, have tended to take greater and longer absences from the workplace for family-related reasons. There is a small but growing percentage of males who are beginning to assume what have traditionally been female roles (Shaver, 2007). Official estimates of the "stay at home Dad" population begin at roughly 2.7 percent of the stay-at-home workforce. Anecdotal evidence suggests this may actually be as high as 20 percent, but while this is a compelling topic for future discussion, the restriction of the data sampling to full-year, full-time, private sector workers removes most if not all of these individuals from the sample populations regardless of gender.

Briefly, some of these factors have persistent and significant effects, while others have little to none. Age, education, experience and gender are invariably significant across all years and cohorts. Marital status and race are not. Occupation has more of an effect in the combined samples, and less once the distinction is made between the professional and clerical cohorts – as would be expected. Industry groups are occasionally significant, but clearly this interacts with other variables. In a given year, it might seem to matter if an individual worked in manufacturing or professional services, but in other years this factor would be statistically insignificant. Population density and region exhibit similar intermittent and inconsistent individual effects. In some years,

it might be worth noting if an individual is from a large urban area, or from the Northeast rather than the Midwest, etc., but these effects are also sporadic.

R-Squared values for the individual regression models are in the range of 45-55% for the combined samples and fall to 15–25% when the samples are confined to the professional occupation cohorts. Readers are encouraged to contact the authors if more information regarding specific aspects of the regression analysis results is desired. In essence, the estimates of the gender earnings gap are based on the unexplained residuals.

## Combined Samples Data

Interpretation of the results begins with an assessment of the overall extent of the gender earnings gap. Three estimates of the gap are available from the data used. The data are presented in Table 1 and Figure 1 that follow.

*Table 1. Gender wage gap estimates 1991-2008 (combined cohorts)*

| Year | Traditional | Male-based | Female-based |
|---|---|---|---|
| 1991 | 42.6% | 22.8% | 24.3% |
| 1992 | 42.7% | 29.9% | 32.1% |
| 1993 | 44.7% | 24.3% | 30.3% |
| 1994 | 46.1% | 23.3% | 26.7% |
| 1995 | 46.2% | 28.4% | 31.2% |
| 1996 | 45.6% | 38.1% | 33.0% |
| 1997 | 45.2% | 17.3% | 25.1% |
| 1998 | 40.3% | 24.3% | 23.3% |
| 1999 | 51.5% | 30.8% | 31.9% |
| 2000 | 40.0% | 24.6% | 30.7% |
| 2001 | 44.7% | 32.4% | 31.9% |
| 2002 | 44.1% | 31.8% | 31.0% |
| 2003 | 67.3% | 57.5% | 58.3% |
| 2004 | 76.9% | 56.8% | 59.9% |
| 2005 | 61.2% | 46.3% | 49.2% |
| 2006 | 52.4% | 37.6% | 27.0% |
| 2007 | 46.4% | 24.9% | 32.8% |
| 2008 | 69.8% | 54.3% | 57.1% |

*Figure 1. Gender wage gap estimates 1991-2008 (combined cohorts)*

The first, which might be termed the "traditional" estimate, is obtained by taking the difference between men's and women's earnings for each of the years in question. The second, which is referred to as "male based", is computed based on the difference between men's earnings and the estimate of what men's earnings would have been had men been treated according to the female earnings regime. Finally, the "female based" estimate considers the converse scenario of the difference between women's earnings and the estimate of what women would have earned if treated according to the male earnings regime.

Although it would be appealing to jump to the conclusion that there was a dramatic increase in the size of the wage gap in 2003, the reader is reminded that there was a significant change in the recording of occupational category data within the CPS, as well as a dramatic increase in the size of the sample populations, as shown in Table 2.

The sizes and composition of the sample groups, as shown in Table 2, provide a great deal of insight into the difficulty of accurately assessing the gender earnings gap. It is clear that, in terms of sheer numbers, males dominate the (higher paying) professional cohorts to a greater extent, without exception (Igbaria, Parasuraman, & Greenhaus, 1997; Trauth & Quesenberry, 2006).

However, there is a steady increase in the proportion of females in professional level positions, reflecting changes in the nature of IS occupations on a general level, and the role of women in the field as well. Conversely, the lower paying clerical occupations, which are diminishing over time, are female dominated. Keeping in mind that the CPS is designed to try and reflect these demographic properties, if males dominate higher paying jobs, it is important to distinguish between a more legitimate wage differential between occupations versus a wage differential within occupations. While the existence of either type of differential

*Table 2. Sample population sizes from CPS Data 1991 - 2008*

| Sample Sizes | | | | | | |
|---|---|---|---|---|---|---|
| Year | Male | Prof | % | Fem | Prof | % |
| 1991 | 453 | 329 | 73 | 543 | 182 | 34 |
| 1992 | 481 | 360 | 75 | 507 | 147 | 29 |
| 1993 | 524 | 363 | 69 | 545 | 157 | 29 |
| 1994 | 499 | 378 | 76 | 398 | 153 | 38 |
| 1995 | 506 | 394 | 78 | 412 | 144 | 35 |
| 1996 | 434 | 358 | 82 | 366 | 146 | 40 |
| 1997 | 512 | 419 | 82 | 359 | 162 | 45 |
| 1998 | 589 | 472 | 80 | 410 | 184 | 45 |
| 1999 | 614 | 530 | 86 | 469 | 201 | 43 |
| 2000 | 672 | 578 | 86 | 460 | 225 | 49 |
| 2001 | 936 | 815 | 87 | 514 | 265 | 52 |
| 2002 | 965 | 838 | 87 | 550 | 282 | 51 |
| 2003 | 1362 | 1192 | 88 | 771 | 397 | 51 |
| 2004 | 1275 | 1167 | 92 | 688 | 394 | 57 |
| 2005 | 1439 | 1188 | 83 | 734 | 424 | 58 |
| 2006 | 1534 | 1268 | 83 | 713 | 443 | 62 |
| 2007 | 1512 | 1281 | 85 | 710 | 419 | 59 |
| 2008 | 1668 | 1458 | 87 | 680 | 467 | 69 |

might suggest discriminatory practices, the latter makes a far more compelling case when the argument concerns equal pay for equal work.

## Earnings Gaps in Professional Cohorts

Consistent with prior research and expectations, the picture is different in the professional cohorts when they are considered separately. Although an earnings differential exists and is persistent over time, it is considerably smaller. Once again, there is a sharp drop-off in female earnings in 2003, concurrent with the change in occupation coding, and therefore it is difficult to consider causality. There is also a second peculiar and seemingly inconsistent set of values for female earnings for 2008, and the unknown reasons for this are under investigation. This may indicate a change in the

trend, or consequences of the global economic turmoil of recent years. More data are required to make this determination, and these data simply do not exist at the time of this writing.

However, once again there is little evidence under the traditional model to support a contention that the earnings gap diminished during the internet bubble, or that it has increased in the recent past, unless the 2008 data are interpreted as a departure point for a new trend. Of greater interest is the relationship of the adjusted earnings curves, as shown in Figure 2.

In the combined samples, the adjusted earnings were closer to their original values, while in the professional cohorts, adjusted earnings are closer to the alternative groups. For example, when women are treated according to the male regime, in professional cohorts, the adjusted earnings are closer to men's earnings versus the combined

*Figure 2. Gender wage gap estimates 1991-2008 (professional cohorts)*

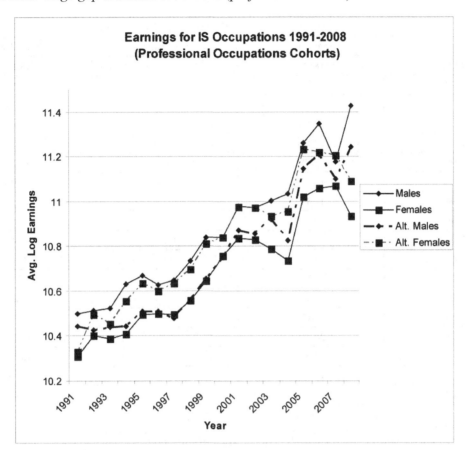

samples, where they would be closer to women's. One hypothesis is that there may be a greater degree of gender wage discrimination in the clerical level positions.

These data suggest that in the professional occupations cohorts, the gender wage gap may be much narrower than is often asserted by those who adopt the traditional view. Some studies have even reported a differential that might be the inverse (Leonard, 2001), although at some point it is important to note that some degree of statistical variance is inevitable. Parity does not need to imply perfect equality.

The visual evidence, shown in Figure 1, clearly suggests that some form of persistent gender wage gap exists and that it has certainly not diminished to any great extent over the period of this study.

The professional cohort, shown in Figure 2 and Table 3, does show a diminished earnings gap during the internet "bubble" years, but it may be returning in full force.

## Earnings Gaps in Clerical Cohorts

Figure 3 shows the trend in the earnings gap for the clerical occupations cohort. As with the professional cohort, the gap remains persistent throughout the period, and suggests a similar pattern with respect to the internet bubble time period.

The authors recommend caution in interpreting the data, and note the peculiar patterns in the data around the time of the change in occupational classifications within the CPS data sets. It is not clear to what extent aberrations in the data may

*Table 3. Gender wage gap estimates 1991-2008 (professional cohorts)*

| | Gender Wage Gap Estimates | | |
|---|---|---|---|
| Year | Traditional | Male based | Female based |
| 1991 | 18.9% | 16.9% | 13.3% |
| 1992 | 11.2% | 1.7% | 2.5% |
| 1993 | 13.4% | 6.7% | 5.3% |
| 1994 | 22.1% | 7.6% | 3.5% |
| 1995 | 17.1% | 3.5% | 1.2% |
| 1996 | 12.9% | 3.0% | 0.9% |
| 1997 | 15.5% | 1.5% | -1.5% |
| 1998 | 17.8% | 4.1% | 0.3% |
| 1999 | 19.4% | 2.8% | 0.8% |
| 2000 | 8.3% | 0.1% | -0.4% |
| 2001 | 14.4% | 0.5% | 3.5% |
| 2002 | 14.0% | 0.0% | 2.7% |
| 2003 | 21.6% | 7.2% | 13.2% |
| 2004 | 30.1% | 8.0% | 9.0% |
| 2005 | 24.0% | 2.7% | 12.5% |
| 2006 | 28.9% | 13.0% | 15.0% |
| 2007 | 10.6% | -2.8% | 3.0% |
| 2008 | 49.2% | 33.5% | 31.0% |

*Figure 3. Gender wage gap estimates 1991-2008 (clerical cohorts)*

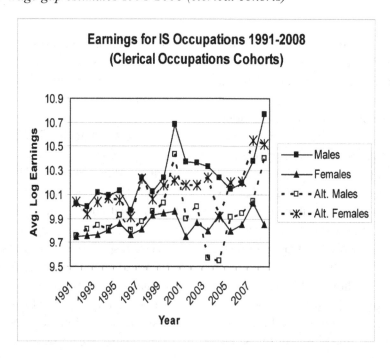

result from classification changes and / or errors in the data that may have arisen as a consequence of the changes in the occupational classification schemes, and this is an issue under investigation as this research continues. One of the known challenges to using the approach to estimating the earnings gap employed in this research is that the earnings gap estimates are based on unexplained residuals from analyses of variance in earnings. Despite the risks and imperfections inherent in this approach, the technique is used repeatedly in the literature, since there may be no other way to conduct the analysis. After all, employers engaged in illegal discriminatory practices are probably less likely to assist in quantifying their consequences precisely!

While micro-level interpretations of the data should be conducted cautiously, the broader trends in the data for the clerical cohorts are similar. There appears to be a narrower gap between male and female earnings during the late 1990's, with the gap widening again in the early 21st century.

Of equal if not greater interest are larger scale demographic changes. Since the CPS is designed and intended to reflect the total labor force, changes in the relative proportions of males and females in cohorts are also worthy of consideration. During the time frame considered in this research, it is no surprise that the overall sample populations have grown considerably – the explosive proliferation of IS professions during the latter 20th century is self-evident. The authors' interest is in the growth in the proportions of women in professional level occupations versus clerical level occupations, as shown in Table 2. While a traditional view of gender inequity would hold that males dominate the higher paying professional level occupations while women dominate the lower paying clerical ranks, the data suggest that women are making significant progress with respect to participation in the professional ranks. To express it in more vernacular terms, while the playing field may not yet be level, men and women appear to be starting to play on the same field.

## CONCLUSION

This study provides a significant contrast to prior studies of wage differences among IS workers that are often anecdotal in nature, frequently relying primarily on self-report surveys, typically limited to single samples in single time periods, and often conducted by trade organizations and journals (e.g., Anonymous, 1995; Baroudi & Igbaria, 1995; Beasley, Lomo-David, & Seubert, 2001; Bort, 2003; Cohen, 2001; Cole-Gomolski, 1998; Earls, 1995; Isaacs, 1995; Liu & Wilson, 2001; MacInnis, 2003; Menezes, 1999). There is also no lack of interest in the issue of why women choose to not enter the IS professions, but this study focuses exclusively on what happens to those women who do.

Specifically, this research has considered three issues related to the gender wage gap. The first issue is whether or not IS occupations have exhibited a diminishing gender wage gap since 1990. There is some limited evidence to suggest that the overall wage gap might have diminished over this period, but to the authors it seems far from compelling. However, there does seem to be a significantly narrower wage gap in the professional level occupations.

The second topic of interest concerns the so-called Internet "bubble" period of 1990's through the early 21st century. While it does not appear that the overall estimates of the wage gap are significantly narrower for these years than for the preceding years, professional level occupations do show a narrowing of the gap. This may be attributable to the higher total level of demand for IS professionals during that period, and is theoretically consistent with the notion that demand inelasticity in a labor market will inversely affect the ability of employers to discriminate (Heywood, 1987; Jacobsen, 2007).

Finally, the data are analyzed to consider whether or not the collapse of the internet bubble had a disproportionate affect on female knowledge workers. Once again, the data suggest that overall gender wage inequity remained somewhat consistent over the period of interest, economic conditions notwithstanding, and that if women in professional level IS occupations enjoyed a narrowing of the wage gap during the Internet bubble years, the collapse of the bubble has been accompanied by a return to higher levels of wage differentials. This observation is also consistent with the theoretical relationship between demand elasticity and gender wage discrimination. As demand has fallen, the gender wage gap has increased.

Many claims of gender-based wage differentials will depend on how one chooses to estimate them. By applying an acknowledged unbiased data source that has employed essentially consistent data collection techniques over several decades, many of the challenges of self-reporting bias, generalizability of results, and short-term effects are avoided. A well-recognized statistical technique for assessing differences between groups known to be subject to different regimes is employed, and three estimates of the gender wage gap have been constructed. Rather than run the risk of over or understating the nature of the earnings gap by the choice of a reference point, results from the perspectives of the three common reference points have been included and differentiated, and the reader can compare and contrast the results from their preferred perspective. The traditional estimate looks at differences between male and female earnings but does not factor in structural issues, such as the relative proportions of males and females in professional and clerical level positions. As such, it may provide a useful measure of structural differences in the economy at large, but is of less value when examining differences within occupational categories. The data gathered for this study clearly suggest that these structural issues are significant and need to be considered.

The Oaxaca Decomposition technique was applied to the data to estimate how male and female earnings might have been affected if males and females were subject to their respective alternative earnings regimes. This approach suggests that if

males were subject to the female earnings regime, or vice versa, the resulting estimates of the wage differential would be more appropriate than the traditional estimate. Despite the acknowledged potential shortcomings of this approach, it still seems to be a man's world when it comes to the bottom line of compensation.

The data clearly suggest that there is a persistent earnings differential between men and women for the period from 1991 through 2008, as reported by CPS data. This differential is noticeably smaller in professional level occupations.

## Implications for Future Research

One of the frequent counter arguments to the traditional view is that the gender earnings gap is in large measure a statistical aberration (Roth & Stolba, 1999). Women are clearly subject to a different set of criteria when assessing their career choices and outcomes. Many women deliberately choose alternative lifestyles and career paths. Women frequently take protracted amounts of time away from their career paths for family issues, etc. While changes in the economy, the workforce, and job roles are causing a growing percentage of males to pursue these non-traditional (for males) career paths (Shaver, 2007) there are not yet sufficient numbers of individuals in the sample populations nor available data to provide a basis for a quantitatively meaningful analysis. It may well be that, when these factors are taken into account, the nature and extent of gender based wage discrimination is far less than is typically argued. Still, the authors contend that any level of artificial wage discrimination is not desirable.

There has been a relentless and growing demand for qualified IS professionals, and IS positions usually rank at or near the top of the list in occupational studies for the economy at large. Given the perpetually high level of demand and the chronic relative scarcity of qualified individuals, it is a simple application of economics to assert that significant discrimination against half of the population is not going to be well tolerated, and the data from this study support that notion. It would appear that, at least at the professional level, one interpretation of the data is that women in IS positions enjoy less gender-based inequity than women in other occupational categories. The relative participation of women in professional-level IS positions has clearly moved in the direction of gender equity, even if data suggest that progress in compensation may still be lagging. The gender gap has not been eliminated, but at the least it appears to be diminishing. One intriguing implication of this is the potential for greater numbers of women to be drawn to IS careers if there is widespread awareness of the fact that the gender wage gap is lower in IS than for other professions.

Also of future interest is a comparison of the domestic IS job market with that of other countries – such as in the European Union or the Pacific Rim. There would be significant cultural differences to be considered, and the availability of data is unknown.

The demographic profiles of IS careers in the domestic market often exhibit a significant presence of imported labor. It is also a very popular practice to outsource systems development and support activities to offshore vendors. A compelling future research topic is consideration of the extent to which this offshoring outside the domestic labor market might be affecting returns to human capital investments within it.

This study has continued and expanded on the research from Heywood and Nezlek (1993), and while the methodologies are similar, the data from the two studies have not been formally linked. The previous work suggested a more significant earnings gap than was found in this research. A longer-term goal of this research is to create a data set appropriate for a wide range of possible longitudinal studies for the period from 1975 to the present. This will also require additional data collection for the years not included in Heywood and Nezlek (1993), where data were observed at five-year intervals. The 2003 changes in CPS oc-cupational classification coding pose a significant but not insurmountable challenge to that goal.

## ACKNOWLEDGMENT

A previous version of this manuscript appeared in the proceedings of the 43rd Hawaii Int'l Conference on System Sciences (HICSS). The authors wish to acknowledge the reviewers of that version of this manuscript as well as the current reviewers. Incorporating their suggestions has led to a more comprehensive and coherent presentation of the fundamental themes of this research.

## REFERENCES

Ahuja, M. K. (2002). Women in the Information Technology Profession: A literature review, synthesis and research agenda. *European Journal of Information Systems*, *11*(1), 20–34. doi:10.1057/palgrave/ejis/3000417

Anonymous,. (1995). Equal pay for equal work? Not yet. *Business Communications Review*, *25*(5), 29.

Baroudi, J. J., & Igbaria, M. (1995). An Examination of Gender Effects on Career Success of Information Systems Employees. *Journal of Management Information Systems*, *11*(3), 181–201.

Beasley, R. E., Lomo-David, E., & Seubert, V. R. (2001). Telework and Gender: Implications for the Management of Information Technology Professionals. *Industrial Management & Data Systems*, *101*(8/9), 477–482. doi:10.1108/02635570110410663

Bort, J. (2003). Women in Networking. *Network World*. Retrieved from www.nwfusion.com/you/2003/0721salaryside.html

Butler, R. J. (1982). Estimating Wage Discrimination in the Labor Market. *The Journal of Human Resources*, *17*, 606–621. doi:10.2307/145618

Cameron, B., & Butcher-Powell, L. (2006). Gender Differences Among IT Professionals in Dealing with Change and Skill Set Maintenance. *Interdisciplinary Journal of Information, Knowledge, and Management, 1*, 152–157.

Cawley, J., & Heckman, J. (1999). Meritocracy in America: Wages Within and Across Occupations. *Industrial Relations, 38*(3), 250–206. doi:10.1111/0019-8676.00130

Cohen, P., & Huffman, M. (2007). Working for the Woman? Female Managers and the Gender Wage Gap. *American Sociological Review, 72*, 681–704. doi:10.1177/000312240707200502

Cohen, S. (2001). Welcome to the Girls Club. *InfoWorld, 23*(17), 55–58.

Cole-Gomolski, B. (1998). More Opportunity, Fewer Women in IT. *Computerworld, 32*(45), 4.

Cotton, J. (1988). On the Decomposition of Wage Differentials. *The Review of Economics and Statistics, 70*(2), 236–243. doi:10.2307/1928307

Couger, J., & Sawicki, R. (1980). *Motivating and Managing Computer Personnel*. New York: Wiley & Sons.

Crump, B., Logan, K., & McIlroy, A. (2007). Does Gender Still Matter? A Study of the Views of Women in the ICT Industry in New Zealand. *Gender, Work and Organization, 14*(4), 349–370. doi:10.1111/j.1468-0432.2007.00348.x

Cukier, W., Shortt, D., & Devine, I. (2002). Gender and Information Technology: Implications of Definitions. *SIGCSE Bulletin, 34*(4), 142. doi:10.1145/820127.820188

*Data Ferret*. (n.d.). Retrieved from http://ferret.bls.census.gov/cgi-bin/ferret

Data Main Page, C. P. S. (n.d.). *Current Population Survey*. Retrieved from http://www.bls.census.gov/cps/cpsmain.htm

Dattero, R., Galup, S., & Quan, J. (2005). Assessing Gender Differences in Software Developers Using the Human Capital Model. *Information Resources Management Journal, 18*(3), 68–87.

Earls, A. R. (1995). Unequal Opportunity. *Computerworld, 29*(36), 70.

Ginzberg, M., & Baroudi, J. (1988). MIS Careers - A Theoretical Perspective. *Communications of the ACM, 31*(5), 586–594. doi:10.1145/42411.42422

Hemenway, K. (1995). Human Nature and the Glass Ceiling in Industry. *Communications of the ACM, 38*(1), 55–62. doi:10.1145/204865.204878

Heywood, J. (1987). Wage Discrimination and Market Structure. *Journal of Post Keynesian Economics, 9*(4), 617–628.

Heywood, J. S., & Nezlek, G. (1993). The Gender Wage Gap among Software Workers: Trends over the Last Two Decades. *Social Science Quarterly, 74*(3), 603–613.

Igbaria, M., & Chidambaram, L. (1997). The Impact of Gender on Career Success of Information Systems Professionals A Human Capital Perspective. *Information Technology & People, 10*(1), 63. doi:10.1108/09593849710166165

Igbaria, M., Parasuraman, S., & Greenhaus, J. H. (1997). Status Report on Women and Men in the IT Workplace. *Information Systems Management, 14*(3), 44–53. doi:10.1080/10580539708907059

Isaacs, E. (1995). Gender Discrimination in the Workplace: A Literature Review. *Communications of the ACM, 38*(1), 58–59. doi:10.1145/204865.384262

Jacobsen, J. (2007). *The Economics of Gender* (3rd ed.). Victoria, Australia: Blackwell Publishing.

Klawe, M., & Leveson, N. (1995). Women in Computing: Where are we now? *Communications of the ACM, 38*(1), 29–32. doi:10.1145/204865.204874

Kraft, P. (1984). *Programmers and Managers: The Routinization of Computer Programming in the United States.* New York: Springer Verlag.

Leonard, B. (2001). Female IT Contractors Earn More Than Male Counterparts. *HRMagazine, 46*(5), 29.

Liu, J., & Wilson, D. (2001). Developing Women in a Digital World. *Women in Management Review, 16*(7/8), 405–416. doi:10.1108/09649420110411701

MacInnis, P. (2003). The Gender Gap. *Computing Canada, 29*(11), 26.

McDonald, J., & Thornton, R. (2007). Do New Male and Female College Graduates Receive Unequal Pay? *The Journal of Human Resources, 42*(1), 32–48.

Menezes, J. (1999). Pay Rates Reveal IT's Gender Gap. *Computing Canada, 25*(31), 11–12.

Montgomery, M., & Powell, I. (2003). Does an Advanced Degree Reduce the Gender Wage Gap? Evidence From MBAs. *Industrial Relations, 42*(3), 396–418. doi:10.1111/1468-232X.00297

Neumark, D. (1999). Wage Differentials by Race and Sex: The roles of Taste Discrimination and Labor Market Information. *Industrial Relations, 38*(3), 414–445. doi:10.1111/0019-8676.00135

Noonan, M., Corcoran, M., & Courant, P. (2005). Pay Differences Among the Highly Trained: Cohort Differences in the Sex Gap in Lawyers' Earnings. *Social Forces, 84*(2), 853–872. doi:10.1353/sof.2006.0021

Oaxaca, R. (1973). Male-Female Wage Differentials in Urban Labor Markets. *International Economic Review, 14,* 693–709. doi:10.2307/2525981

Panteli, N., Stack, J., & Ramsay, H. (2001). Gender Patterns in Computing Work in the late 1990s. *New Technology, Work and Employment, 16*(1), 3. doi:10.1111/1468-005X.00073

Rosser, S. (2003). Women are Underrepresented in Science and Engineering Faculties. *Academe,* 25–28.

Roth, D. F., & Stolba, C. (1999). *Women's Figures.* Washington, DC: AEI Press.

Shaver, K. (2007). Stay-at-Home Dads Forge New Identities, Roles. *Washington Post,* A01.

Singell, L., & Stone, J. (1993). Gender Differences in PhD Economists' Careers. *Western Economic Association International, 11*(4), 95–106.

Trauth, E., & Quesenberry, J. (2006). Are Women an Underserved Community in the Information Technology Profession? In *Proceedings of the Twenty-Seventh International Conference on Information Systems (ICIS)*, Milwaukee, WI (pp. 1757-1770).

Truman, G. E., & Baroudi, J. J. (1994). Gender Differences in the Information Systems Managerial Ranks: an Assessment of Potential Discriminatory Practices. *Management Information Systems Quarterly, 18,* 129–141. doi:10.2307/249761

*This work was previously published in the International Journal of Social and Organizational Dynamics in IT, Volume 1, Issue 1, edited by Michael B. Knight, pp. 13-29, 2011 by IGI Publishing (an imprint of IGI Global).*

# Chapter 4

# An Examination of Prestigious Stigma:
## The Case of the Technology Geek

**Jo Ellen Moore**
*Southern Illinois University Edwardsville, USA*

**Mary Sue Love**
*Southern Illinois University Edwardsville, USA*

## ABSTRACT

*This paper examines "technology geek" through the social psychological lens of stigma. The research expands on an aspect of stigma that can materialize in work settings but has not been fully explicated in prior stigma theory, namely, prestige. The authors argue that a stigma may be worn with pride rather than shame, typified by the case of the technology geek, called "prestigious stigma." The theory building focuses on interactions between the technology geek and others in the organization, positing that prestigiously stigmatized individuals behave in ways that differ from what social psychologists have generally posited for the stigmatized. This effort culminates in a model of mixed interaction involving the technology geek, which extends prior stigma theory and provides insights for practice and future research regarding technology professionals in organizations.*

*"You can't live with 'em and you can't live without 'em.*

*No, I'm not talking about the opposite sex. I'm talking about geeks..."*

*Glen (2003: xv)*

Well researched in social psychology, stigma has traditionally considered the plight of individuals possessing an undesired differentness such as blindness or bodily deformity. More recently, organizational researchers have applied the stigma concept to less physical sources of non-normality (Cox, 1993). For example, Clair and her colleagues discussed the troubles of those bearing invisible stigmas in organizations (Clair, Beatty, & MacLean, 2005), while Ashforth and Kreiner (1999)

DOI: 10.4018/978-1-4666-1948-7.ch004

examined the stigma of "dirty work" experienced by those in occupations such as garbage collection and grave digging. What is the same in the social psychological and organizational formulations of the stigma concept is the devaluing of the stigmatized individual and the view that they are less than they should be (Goffman, 1963).

In extrapolating the social psychological conceptualization of stigma to organizational settings, an aspect of stigma emerges that has not been given sufficient attention in prior stigma theory. It is the property of prestige. A stigma may exist that is worn more with pride than shame, and we refer to this as a "prestigious stigma." Here, we focus on a particular manifestation of prestigious stigma that is commonly found in organizations, namely, the "technology geek." Our examination illuminates, among other things, the double-edged sword inherent in bearing this type of stigma, as displayed in the opening quotation.

We argue that, in organizations, the presence of prestige in conjunction with a stigma affects interactions between the stigmatized and non-stigmatized (in stigma terminology, this is called a "mixed interaction"). At an individual level, biases that arise within mixed interactions interfere with the career success of the stigmatized (Clair et al., 2005; Herek, 1996; Jones, Farina, Hastorf, Markus, Miller, & Scott, 1984; Leary, 1999; Reimann, 2001). These biases also affect organizational functioning by hindering the sharing of knowledge, and this in turn limits the effectiveness of decision-making and business processes. For these reasons, it is imperative that we understand, manage, and improve these interactions.

Toward this end, we explore the mixed interaction of the prestigiously stigmatized technology geek with others in the organization. In the pages to follow, we review the basic elements of the stigma concept from the social psychology literature and then introduce the stigma of technology geek, confirming that it does indeed qualify as a stigma. We next examine the special property of prestige that accompanies the technology geek stigma.

Then, we explore mixed interactions involving the prestigiously stigmatized, culminating in a theoretical model and propositions that extend prior stigma theory and can lead to research that will deepen our understanding of interactions between technology geeks and non-geeks in organizations. To conclude, we provide implications for practice and directions for future research.

## THE CONCEPT OF STIGMA

Social identity is at the core of the concept of stigma. Goffman (1963) contends that social settings lead to the establishment of categories of persons likely to be encountered consequently leading to normative expectations of the people we meet in a particular setting. These expectations include norms of appearance and behavior, making up the "virtual social identity" of an individual (i.e., what we anticipate the person will be like given the setting of the encounter). For example, in a work setting, we may expect a person we encounter to dress in a way that matches others in the organization and to communicate in the company vernacular (e.g., in an insurance company, to understand and be able to converse about insurance claims at some level).

But, what if, in the encounter, evidence arises that this person does not conform to the (virtual) social identity that we expect? In other words, what if the "actual social identity" (the set of attributes the individual actually possesses) runs counter to the anticipated identity? While the attributes the individual does possess might easily be well received in a different social setting where they match up with expectations, when the actual social identity presents *an undesired differentness* from what is expected, the person can be seen to possess a stigma.

According to Goffman (1963), when a person is stigmatized (i.e., when there is an undesired discrepancy between an individual's virtual and actual social identities) and this departure is known or apparent, it spoils his social identity in that setting and leaves him a discredited person. The non-stigmatized (in stigma terminology, these are the "normals") begin to construct an ideology, or mental picture, to explain the differentness, or inferiority, of the stigma bearer. This process consists of both automatic and controlled responses (Pryor, Reeder, Yeadon, & Hesson-McInnis, 2004), including avoidance (Pryor et al., 2004) and a predominance of negative stereotypes that devalue the whole person (Major & Crocker, 1993; Goffman, 1963). A stigma is fundamentally different from a conventional stereotype due to its global nature. Stereotyping assigns a particular characteristic (positive or negative) to an individual, but assigning a stigma leaves one's whole identity discredited (Goffman, 1963). The pervasive effects of stigmatization envelop not just the non-stigmatized view of the stigmatized, but color the stigmatized's view of themselves as well (Jones et al., 1984).

The major impact of stigmatization resides in social consequences or its effect on one's social identity (Dovidio, Major, & Crocker, 2000). And, since "a man's work is one of the most important parts of his social identity" (Hughes, 1994, p. 57), stigma is particularly tied to the social drama of work. Consequences of stigmatization are most evident in mixed interaction, to which we now turn.

## Mixed Interaction

Going forward, we use the term 'normal' to refer to the non-stigmatized, in keeping with the stigma literature. Mixed interaction refers to interactions between the stigmatized and normals and juxtaposes the expected and actual social identities of the stigmatized. An uncertain and uneasy situation, mixed contact is often tense and uncomfortable for each party and commonly results in alienation and discrimination (Crocker, Major, & Steele, 1998; Goffman, 1963; Link & Phelan, 2001). Prevailing theory holds that stigmatized individuals experience these situations more often than do normals and, as such, are likely to extend greater effort to smooth and manage the mixed interaction situations. In traditional stigma theory, the brunt of responsibility for managing mixed interactions is placed firmly on the bearer of the stigma (Goffman, 1963; Jones et al., 1984). Among his classic examples, Goffman (1963) describes an African American man adjusting his speech and tone to ease interactions with Caucasians.

Figure 1 summarizes present stigma theory regarding mixed interaction behaviors. The stigmatized individual is presumed to desire "normal interactions" and, because of that, is willing to work to get them (Jones et al., 1984). Efforts by the stigmatized to manage interactions with

*Figure 1. Stigmatized behavior in mixed interaction based on Goffman (1963)*

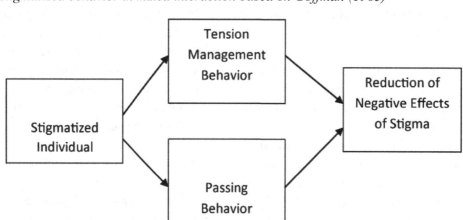

normals include gestures intended to ease tension between the parties (e.g., attempts to break the ice, and explicitly referring to one's own stigmatizing mark with nonchalance). Underlying these efforts is an alertness on the part of the stigmatized – an attentiveness to subtle and indirect clues to the normal's true beliefs and feelings about the stigma (Frable, Blackstone, & Sherbaum, 1990). Existing theory further suggests that stigmatized individuals may also make earnest attempts to "pass" as normals; that is, they try to conform and meet the expectations of the virtual social identity that is cast upon them by the non-stigmatized. These efforts are undertaken by the stigmatized because they seek to reduce the discomfort and other negative effects that the stigma tends to generate in mixed interaction (Kroeger, 2003).

By definition, a stigma is attributed to an individual by others. Others observe an undesirable differentness that causes them to devalue the person. Traditional stigma theory presumes that the differentness is also undesired by the stigmatized individual; i.e., the stigmatized would rather not possess the stigmatizing mark. This presumption is inherent in the existing theory represented in Figure 1: the stigmatized extends tension management efforts and tries to pass in an effort to remove the stigma from the mixed interaction, to the extent possible.

But what if this differentness, undesired by others, is *not* undesired by the stigmatized? Although not fully developed in his classic treatise, Goffman (1963) does touch upon certain types of stigmatizing conditions that individuals wear with pride rather than shame. Jones and his colleagues also allude to this element, stating "marked people (can) use their stigma to gain advantage over others and to define their own identity" (Jones et al., 1984, p. 98). Jones et al. (1984) suggest there are situations where stigmatized individuals may not want to conceal their stigma. In discussing such situations, they state that the stigmatized "may not find all false beliefs about them to be odious, and may very well find some false beliefs to be

flattering, advantageous, or benignly amusing" (Jones et al., 1984, p. 181). These researchers conclude that stigmatizing marks can meet a vastly different fate, "depending on whether they are associated with high or low social status—with wealth, prestige, and 'winners', or with poverty, ignorance, and 'losers'" (Jones et al., 1984, p. 303). Some preliminary studies have indeed found confirmation; that is, inviting others to perceive oneself as a member of a stigmatized group (Miller & Major, 2000) can accrue important advantages to the stigma bearer (Deaux & Major, 1987; Kaiser & Miller, 1999; Steele & Aronson, 1995; Von Baeyer, Sherk, & Zanna, 1981). Ashforth and Kreiner (1999) even go so far as to suggest that individuals with stigmatizing occupations "may actually elicit higher identification and collective esteem than many other occupations, precisely because the stigma may foster a strong culture with robust protective techniques for warding off the social threat" (p. 427).

While stigma theory has acknowledged that a person may embrace a stigma and wear it with pride rather than shame, there has been little focus on this situation. We explore such stigmas in the organizational setting of the technology geek and argue that, when prestige is present, a different mixed-interaction experience is likely to occur for both the stigmatized geeks and the normals.

## PRESTIGIOUS STIGMA AND THE TECHNOLOGY GEEK

Going forward, we use the term "prestigious stigma" to signify a stigma that is worn with pride rather than shame. Research confirms that the knowledge, skills, and intelligence required in a job are strongly correlated with occupational prestige ratings (Adler & Kraus, 1985; Sorokin, 1927; Villimez, 1974), and occupational prestige is typically associated with possession of an area of expertise that is highly valued by organizations. Prestigious stigma, like occupational prestige, represents expert power, one of the major sources of power firmly established by researchers over the years (Emerson, 1962; French & Raven, 1959; Mechanic, 1962; Mintzberg, 1983).

Simply put, prestige provides a "status shield" for the stigmatized individual – protection from difficulties and encumbrances that would otherwise be experienced (Ashforth & Kreiner, 1999; Hochschild, 1983; Stenross & Kleinman, 1989). Researchers note that when one possesses a status shield, others are less likely to challenge them and often feel too intimidated to complain directly to them face-to-face (Stenross & Kleinman, 1989) even though the tension may be chronic (Hughes, 1994).

When prestige accompanies a stigma, it does not remove the stigma. Normals perceive an undesired differentness that causes them to devalue the stigma bearer, and the stigmatized recognizes the differentness as well. But when prestige is present, an underlying assumption of traditional stigma theory is compromised: while the differentness is undesired by normals, the stigmatized may in fact desire their differentness.

## The Technology Geek

The American Heritage Dictionaries (2009) defines geek as "a person who is single-minded or accomplished in scientific or technical pursuits but is felt to be socially inept." Glen (2003) provides an example of technology geek behavior that illustrates the double-edged sword of technical expertise and social ineptness:

*The technical consultant had spent about a day looking at the client's systems to provide an initial impression of the work that would be required. At some point in the meeting, the Chief Technology Officer (CTO) turned to the consultant and asked what he thought of the new system. The consultant responded, "Well, you've got Windows NT 3.51 installed on a number of your systems. Only an idiot would put that in." The room fell silent. (Glen, 2003, p. 36)*

Anecdotal evidence of the technology geek abounds. Even school children have a vision of the geek identity. When asked to draw their image of a technology worker, middle school students showed a nerdy guy with thick glasses sleeping under a desk because the students said they thought technology workers work 24 hours a day (Manfred, 2000). An Information Technology Association of America (ITAA) task force examining the image of the information technology (IT) profession asked high school seniors "what do IT workers do?" and received this representation of solitary work: "Sit and work on the computer while drinking coffee and having conversations with custodians" (ITAA, 1998).

Research verifies these anecdotal views. Loogma, Umarik, and Vilu (2004) found strong evidence of the existence of the technology geek in a study of technology professionals in four European countries (Estonia, Germany, United Kingdom, and the Czech Republic). All four countries characterized a "geek" type of information technology (IT) specialist who identified strongly with technology, preferred to talk to a computer rather than interact with others, and was reluctant to develop broader communication skills. Their resulting spectrum of IT work identities ranged from "geek" to "techie" to "flexible specialist" to "translator" to "transgressor," and in this framework the "geek" was described as a technician with poor communication skills. It was along this communication dimension that these identities differed most, progressively increasing as identities moved toward "transgressor," with even the "techie" identity described as being open to advancing their communication skills.

The following scenario shows how the technical expertise of the geek, coupled with difficulties in social interaction, can affect organizational operations:

*An application development project is underway. The effort involves a few highly technical developers as well as a less technical integration team. Whenever the technical developers deliver modules to the integration team, some valuable information is inevitably overlooked and not included. This costs the integration group scores of person-hours trying to figure out the problem. To correct this loss of productivity and source of frustration, the integration group initiated a meeting with the technical developers for the purpose of creating a comprehensive checklist that developers can complete each time they send a new module to the integration team.*

*The meeting turned out to be rather brief. The technical developers began talking among themselves; acronyms were flying. When an integration team member asked for clarification of something being said, he was dismissed by a technical specialist with "you don't need to understand it." Another of the integration team members had prepared an initial draft of what the checklist might look like, based on what he understood from the integration perspective. When presented with this working document, the technical developers gave it a general "looks fine."*

*The first use of the checklist arrived and, unfortunately, the integration group spent an unexpected two full days trying to integrate the new module. Frustrated, they asked the developers for help. The developers quickly located the problem and said the integration team had not asked the right questions on the checklist, to which a member of the integration team snapped back, "But we asked for your input on that!"*

*Later, one technical developer said to another, "I know 10 times more about integration than that entire integration team. I see problems with their procedures that they don't even realize exist... are they ever going to get their act together?" (adapted from Whitten, 1995, p. 74)*

Not all technology professionals are geeks; indeed, members of the integration team in this scenario represent "normal" technology profes-

sionals. Remember that Loogma et al. (2004) discovered a total of five IT work identities, of which "geek" was the only one defined as deficient in communication and interaction and uninterested in improving in those areas. Most technology professionals communicate well and not only fulfill normative expectations of workplace interactions but also share them. Indeed, an experienced technology specialist observed that programmers who fit the lack-of-social-skills identity are present, but they are a smaller minority than most people think (Milton, 2003). Nevertheless, technology geeks do exist and their knowledge and skills are vital in organizational functioning.

To more thoroughly examine the stigma of technology geek, we first explore the stain that prompts it: social ineptness. Then, we look at the element of prestige that accompanies the stigma: technical expertise.

## Stigma: The Socially Inept Geek

A key element of the geek definition is social ineptitude. We argue this primarily manifests in the organizational setting as deficiencies in communication skills and practices, and this is what normals consider to be an undesired differentness. Normals commonly complain about problems in interacting with technology geeks, citing geek behaviors such as the use of unshared language (e.g., acronyms) and a seeming disinclination toward communication in general. Management consultant Glen (2003) observes that technology geeks have a tendency to believe communication ends with self-expression and that reception is someone else's problem. A normal in a large insurance company put it to one of the authors this way, "I have to listen more and filter more and figure out what questions to ask in order to understand... he doesn't meet me halfway" (Anonymous, personal communication, October 1, 2003).

Tschohl (2004) suggests the technology geek is much more comfortable dealing with things than with people, and Dugan (2001) speaks of a "techie/business gap," which he defines as the span that separates the technologist's mindset from that found in other areas of the business. Glen (2003) reports that he frequently hears clients complain that a geek is "too technical" but notes that the client is rarely if ever complaining that the person has too much technical expertise. Rather, what the client is really complaining about is the geek's inability, or disinclination, to communicate.

In the terminology of stigma, social ineptness is the blemish that stains the stigmatized and around which the spoiled identity is constructed. Normals in the organization expect individuals they encounter to display common interaction and communication practices that the technology geek by definition is unlikely to exhibit. This discrepancy between expected and actual social identities becomes apparent to normals when they attempt to interact with the technology geek. Normals, following traditional stigma theory, develop an ideology to explain the differentness, and they form a stigmatized identity they apply to the technology geek. What makes this stigma particularly interesting is the technical expertise the stigma bearer also possesses.

## Prestige: The Technical Expertise of the Geek

Although technology geeks are devalued by normals for their social ineptness, they possess an attribute that normals need, technical expertise. By definition the technology geek is single-minded or accomplished in technical pursuits. For the geek, working with technology provides continuous opportunities to exercise the mind and prove competence and expertise. Csikszentmihalyi (1997) describes the peak experience that geeks seek as experiencing flow or "being in the zone." When in a state of flow, high technical skills and high challenge meet and morph into an experience of effortless productivity and engagement that has elements of playfulness (Csikszentmihalyi, 1997;

Trevino & Webster, 1992; Webster, Trevino, & Ryan, 1993). Almost literally, time flies:

*"It's 2:00am. The only sound in the darkened room is the rapid, rhythmic click of a computer keyboard. Were it not for the bluish glow of the monitor, it would be impossible to see the desk cluttered with scraps of paper, piles of open manuals, and half-eaten food. The occupant, dressed only in a T-shirt and shorts, doesn't know what time it is, and he doesn't care. He is engrossed, completely submerged. And it's his day off" (Glen, 2003, p. 33).*

Hughes (1994) notes that differences in prestige ratings can exist within an occupational group; that is, prestige may be assigned to a particular fragment of an occupational group. Prestige, then, is likely to be attributed to the technology geek who possesses specialized knowledge and skills that are highly sought by the organization. Such expertise symbolizes status, adds to authority, and shapes relationships (Hogg & Terry, 2000; Wildavsky, 1974). The specialized knowledge and skills provide a strong base of expert power in organizations utilizing advanced technology. A *USA Today* article publicly proclaimed the prestige of the technology geek: "Knowledge is power, baby, and geek is chic" (Wloszczyna & Oldenburg, 2003).

Geeks perceive this prestige and take pride in their technical prowess. They are not offended by being called a geek; they view it as a badge of honor, a source of pride (Chapman, 1999). Pagers, business cell phones, being on call, being up all night to fix an emergency problem, use of technical jargon – these are things that call attention to the geeks' identity and they wear these with pride.

Goffman (1963) notes that those possessing a stigma often sponsor a publication of some kind that gives voice to shared feelings, consolidating and stabilizing for the reader his sense of the realness of "his" group and his attachment to it. These publications often form the ideology of the members of the group – their complaints, their aspirations, their politics – and may even include tales of atrocity involving mistreatment by normals. Such publications exist for geeks, including the slashdot.org website (the homepage is entitled "News for Nerds"), which is considered an online haven for hard-core computer geeks (Carroll, 2002). The prestigious community of the technology geek is further evidenced by: a proclaimed Geek Pride Day and geek manifesto that includes geek rights such as "The right to show off your geekiness" and "The right to have all the geeky friends that you want," as well as responsibilities like "Don't waste your time on anything not related to geekdom" (Twigg, 2010); a geek-to-geek online dating site (Geek 2 Geek, 2010); and, cruises such as Perl Whirl, a Geek Cruise that combined a seven-night trip to Alaska with intensive courses from Perl language experts (Fried, 2000).

When such a community exists, there is often pressure on the stigmatized to *not* conform, to not try to pass with normals: "… the member… should take pride in his illness and not seek to get well" (Goffman, 1963, p. 38). From the geek's perspective, the last thing we need is a 'cure' for geekness (Chapman, 1999).

## THE TECHNOLOGY GEEK AND MIXED INTERACTION

Before delving into mixed interaction with the prestigiously stigmatized technology geek, we wish to recognize one caveat: prestige may not be permanent. If the prestige associated with a stigma subsides and the stigmatized recognizes this, the stigma is no longer a prestigious one. The protective status shield is gone, and traditional stigma theory on mixed interaction would apply. In other words, if and when prestige falls away for a technology geek, we expect the geek to work to lose or hide the stigmatizing mark (social ineptness) and, in mixed interaction, to extend efforts to smooth and manage tension and exhibit passing behavior (Figure 1).

However when prestige accompanies a stigma, as it can with technology geeks, existing theory does not adequately capture the mixed interaction experience. We further draw upon theory and research in social psychology and organizational behavior to develop a model of mixed interaction involving a prestigiously stigmatized individual such as the technology geek. Figure 2 provides the overall framework of our propositions. We first consider behaviors the prestigiously stigmatized is posited to exhibit in mixed interaction. Then,

*Figure 2. The prestigiously stigmatized technology geek in mixed interaction*

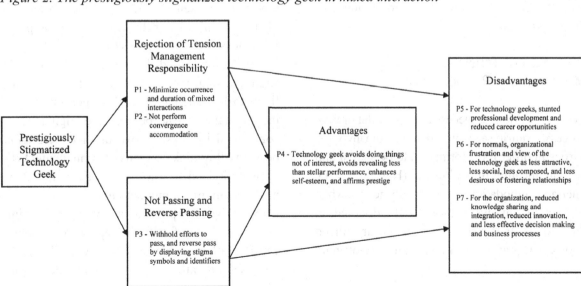

*Table 1. Five reasons to communicate with colleagues*

| Five Reasons to Communicate with Colleagues |
|---|
| 1. To tell them what to do |
| 2. To clarify understanding |
| 3. To see whether we have performed a task adequately |
| 4. To ensure that we are working towards a common goal |
| 5. To enjoy some social interaction |

Source: (Haslam, 2001; Mitchell, Dowling, Kabanoff, & Larson, 1988).

we examine potential outcomes of the behaviors, affecting the stigmatized, normals, and the organization.

## Behavior of the Prestigiously Stigmatized Technology Geek in Mixed Interaction

Traditional stigma theory presumes that the stigma bearer views his or her differentness as undesired and attempts to reduce tension and discomfort (Figure 1). In the case of a prestigious stigma, however, the stigmatized does not view his or her stigma as undesirable and so is less likely to try to atone for effects of the stigma on the interaction. Rather than make efforts to relieve the tension, we posit the prestigiously stigmatized will do the opposite: reject tension management responsibilities, make no efforts to pass, and even "reverse pass." In the sections to follow, we categorize behaviors for the prestigiously stigmatized in mixed interaction, shown in Figure 2, and now discussed in turn.

## Rejection of Tension Management Responsibility

Communication is necessarily a collaborative process, requiring accommodations from involved parties in order for information to be shared and become meaningful and useful (Haslam, 2001). Such accommodations are especially needed when interactions involve a stigmatized individual, in order to ease the tension caused by the unrealized norms that play upon the encounter (Goffman, 1963).

Speech accommodation theory provides a valuable lens by which to view tension management behavior in interactions (Giles, Coupland, & Coupland, 1991; Giles & Johnson, 1981; Giles, Mulac, Bradac, & Johnson, 1987). Speech accommodation examines the ways in which language use reflects and creates social structure, including the motivation of a person to communicate and pass on information. Researchers have identified five key reasons we communicate with work colleagues (Table 1). All of these motivations to communicate are contingent upon the communicator perceiving a shared social categorization with the communication recipient (Turner, 1991).

When a social identity is not shared, these motivations are expected to be much weaker (Daft, 1995; Wilensky, 1967) and, consequently, communication between the parties more sparse. Moreover, in interactions that involve transfer of knowledge, such as mixed interactions between the prestigiously stigmatized technology geek and a normal, Hansen (1999) argues the "intimacy" of the overall relationship between participants influences the effectiveness of the exchanges. Given the undesired differentness present in a stigma setting, it follows that the normal is unlikely to desire a shared social categorization with the stigmatized. And because the stigma is accompanied by prestige, we predict the stigma bearer will not take on tension management responsibility and will not feel motivated to communicate in mixed interactions.

Selective comparison, a cognitive framing mechanism, may fortify the separation of social categorizations for the technology geek. The prestigiously stigmatized geek may deliberately avoid comparisons with normals, selectively choosing comparisons with others who bear their stigma, thus providing more opportunity to compare favorably (Crocker & Major, 1989). For example, the technology geek has been characterized as believing that the only criterion of merit is technical knowledge – not productivity, not managerial skills, not communication skills (Glen, 2003). This is illustrated in one technical analyst's dismissal of the importance of the human element in getting the job done: "I have very little time for all this psychological stuff" (Hirschheim & Newman, 1991, p. 47). By selectively valuing technical expertise and devaluing communication and non-technical aspects of projects, the technology geek has no desire to interact effectively with normals and, correspondingly, little reason to manage or improve those interactions.

Ashforth and Kreiner (1999) take selective comparison a step further in their discussion of social weighting and differentiation of outsiders. By "condemning the condemner," the stigmatized not only chooses not to compare herself to normals but goes further, impugning the motives, character, knowledge, or authority of others (Sykes & Matza, 1957) and, in doing so, heightening the lack of shared social categorization. For example, the technology geek may belittle normals for their lack of technical knowledge, in effect denouncing the legitimacy of normals (e.g., the end of the scenario presented earlier: "I know 10 times more about integration than that entire integration team").

Taken together, a picture emerges of the prestigiously stigmatized technology geek who does not perceive a shared social categorization with others and, hence, is not motivated to communicate with them. As a result, the technology geek is expected to minimize interaction with normals, leading to our first proposition.

Proposition 1. The prestigiously stigmatized technology geek will seek to minimize the occurrence and duration of mixed interactions.

Speech accommodation theory, in addition to considering an individual's motivation to communicate, also identifies elements of communication style, including the practice of convergence. Convergence is an accommodation strategy wherein speakers modify their communication (e.g., vocabulary) so that its features are more similar to those perceived to be characteristic of the recipient. This practice contributes to the emergence of a shared perspective and the building of common meaning. The use of convergence signals a desire on the part of the communicator to break down intergroup boundaries and to be encompassed within a shared social categorization. On the other hand, eschewing convergence in communication implies a desire to maintain or enhance one's social distance from the other party (Haslam, 2001).

Simply put, when we see others as part of a shared social category (i.e., coworker), we are not only more likely to communicate but we are also more likely to align our communication style to match theirs. Persons possessing a prestigious stigma, however, focus on the lack of shared social categorization and are less likely to practice convergence. This is supported by research that indicates stigmatized individuals are more likely to conform to the expected identity when they view themselves as being of low relative status; but, when the stigmatized is high in self-certainty (as would accompany the element of prestige), they are less likely to decide to accept the normals' script (Neuberg, 1994; Swann & Ely, 1984).

In the case of the technology geek, shirking convergence responsibilities may be particularly appealing as it saves the geek from having to expend effort on things unrelated to the geek's primary drive (working with technology). Geeks are happy to stay within the ease of their own language of technical terms and acronyms. We posit that the prestigiously stigmatized technology geek is likely to shirk the practice of convergence and offer the following proposition to this effect.

Proposition 2. The prestigiously stigmatized technology geek will tend not to practice convergence accommodation in mixed interaction (i.e., not match their vocabulary and speech to that of normals).

## Not Passing and Reverse Passing

According to traditional stigma theory, the stigmatized wishes to be accepted as a normal and wants to meet the expectations of the virtual social identity (placed upon him by normals) as best he can. When possible, the stigmatized individual may seek to conceal the stigmatizing mark or deficiency, and Goffman (1963) refers to this as "passing."

We expect the prestigiously stigmatized to not extend the effort to pass in mixed interactions, however, because prestigiously stigmatized individuals do not view their differentness as undesired and are therefore less likely to conform to the virtual identity that normals expect of them (Neuberg, 1994; Swann & Ely, 1984). One explanation for such withholding of effort may stem from self-doubt. Self-doubt can lead an individual to invoke a type of self-protection strategy, namely self-handicapping (Arkin, 1981). Individuals invoke this behavior in hopes of concealing possible shortcomings. The self-handicapper withdraws effort as an alternative to accepting the risk of receiving feedback indicating a lack of ability or talent (Arkin & Oleson, 1998).

When the prestigiously stigmatized person possesses self-doubt regarding his or her ability to meet the expectations of normals, withdrawal of effort (or disengagement) is possible. Goffman (1963, p. 103) provides an example of a stigma bearer withholding effort because he wants to avoid calling attention to those failings most centrally identified with his stigma: "a near-blind person who knows that the persons present know about his differentness may yet hesitate to read, because to do this he would have to bring the book up to a few inches of his eyes, and this he

may feel expresses too glaringly (his stigma)." Similarly, the prestigiously stigmatized technology geek may withhold effort to communicate and document, preferring to be thought of as difficult or frustrating rather than risk a glaring revelation that he is not good at these things. Berglas and Jones (1978, p. 205) express the mindset of the self-handicapper in this way: "it is better to fail because one is lazy than because one is stupid." In other words, when faced with a possible threat to self-esteem, the individual is willing to compromise other personal qualities to avoid confirming an inability or incompetence.

Conversely, the prestigiously stigmatized may shirk efforts to pass simply because of disinterest. People generally regard things at which they are proficient to be more important than things at which they are not (Harter, 1986; Peterson, Major, Cozarelli, & Crocker, 1988; Taylor & Brown, 1988; Tesser & Campbell, 1980, 1983). Glen (2003) has characterized the technology geek as believing that the only criterion of merit is technical knowledge. Technology geeks therefore may view transfer-of-knowledge activities as annoying attempts to take them away from their main drive of working with technology. The knowledge-bearing technology geek may view such effort as a distraction from his or her primary mission, particularly when supporting the transfer means creating additional documentation and the like (Szulanski, 2000). One information technology manager put it this way, "If a project involves, say, developing a complex operating program and then writing the supporting documentation explaining it, you're likely to get the first part but not the second" (Parker, 2003, p. 32).

Crocker and Major (1989) report that people might be capable of performing competently in some domain and still not be motivated to do so if they do not value the domain. It is the prestige accompanying the technology geek stigma that can provide the status and freedom to ignore assignments or responsibilities involving communication and social exchange. In the end, whether spurred by self-doubt, disinterest or both, the prestigiously stigmatized technology geek is not expected to try to pass in mixed interactions.

We take this a step further in proposing that the prestigiously stigmatized technology geek will adopt behaviors that enhance the likelihood that others will attribute the geek stigma to them. We refer to these behaviors as "reverse passing," defined as efforts to make one's perceived differentness more noticeable. Traditional stigma theory provides a starting point for this discussion.

Goffman (1963) speaks of "stigma symbols," signs that draw attention to the stigma identity that the stigmatized wishes to hide, such as wrist markings that disclose that an individual has attempted suicide. Goffman (1963) acknowledges that it is possible for a stigma symbol to have a positive connotation to one group and a negative connotation to another. For example, shoulder patches that prison officials require escape-prone prisoners to wear mean one thing to prison guards (undesirable), while being a mark of pride for the wearer relative to fellow inmates.

Technology geeks have adopted myriad stigma symbols – such as carrying the latest technology gadgets, wearing clothes that are outside the general dress code of the organization, and speaking in techno-jargon – and they display these symbols proudly. These same stigma symbols, though, can carry a negative connotation to normals, e.g., bringing to mind experiences of frustration and difficulty they associate with the technology geek identity.

In addition to stigma signals, we expect the prestigiously stigmatized to reverse pass by using what we call "identifiers," conscious displays that *enforce* one's own stigmatized identity and further separate oneself from normals. This is in contrast to a concept from traditional stigma theory, disidentifiers, which are a means of passing used by stigmatized individuals in traditional mixed interaction. Goffman (1963, p. 44) describes disidentifers as behaviors and signs the stigmatized projects to "break up an otherwise coherent pic-

ture… (by) throwing severe doubt on the validity of the (stigma identity)." As an example, Goffman (1963) presented the situation wherein an African-American facing a racial stigmatization situation may make a conscious effort to refrain from using cultural slang and to speak with a minimal trace of accent or dialect.

In contrast, we define identifiers as behaviors and signs, the prestigiously stigmatized projects to call attention to and cement their differentness. One type of identifier we expect the prestigiously stigmatized technology geek to use in an organizational setting is speech divergence. Divergence is the tendency for speakers to modify their communication so that its features are more different from those perceived as characteristic of the recipient. Unlike convergence, which signifies the existence of, or desire for the recipient to be encompassed within, a shared social self-categorization, divergence reflects a desire on the part of the speaker to maintain a social self-categorization division (Haslam, 2001).

An example of speech divergence is found in a study regarding a technology design and implementation project: "Gary was concerned over Brian's monthly update reports. They contained no meaningful progress information… and were filled with meaningless technical jargon." (Franz & Robey, 1984, p. 1208). In this example, the technology professional's use of identifiers obscures the information and meaning sought by the recipient (i.e., the status of the communicator's work) and highlights the division between the social self-categorizations of the communicator and recipient.

Indeed, a common form of divergence involves the use of coded forms of communication, such as acronyms and specialized terminology (Levine & Moreland, 1991; Montgomery, 1986). When communicators use divergent language, they: demonstrate their own membership in a particular group; make recipients aware of their lack of membership in that group; and restrict access to the meaning of the communication (Haslam, 2001).

The technology geeks in the earlier scenario displayed divergence by using acronyms in the meeting and declining to explain to others what they meant. Ultimately, the prestigiously stigmatized technology geek wants to be recognized as such, and this leads to a propensity to reverse pass by displaying identifiers as well as stigma symbols.

Proposition 3. The prestigiously stigmatized technology geek will (a) withhold efforts to pass and (b) *reverse pass* by displaying stigma symbols and identifiers (such as speech divergence) in mixed interaction.

We have explored the component of prestige and put forth propositions suggesting that those bearing a prestigious stigma, such as that of the technology geek, will reject the standard responses of the stigmatized individual to manage the tension or to pass as normals in mixed interactions. Given the behaviors proposed to be exhibited by the prestigiously stigmatized in mixed interaction, we now examine potential effects of these behaviors.

## Advantages for the Technology Geek

For the many and varied reasons discussed above, we suggest that the bearer of a prestigious stigma realizes advantages that encourage the continuation of these behaviors. The advantages accrued by the prestigiously stigmatized are outlined in Figure 2.

Included are two advantages to the prestigiously stigmatized that were argued in conjunction with Proposition 3. By not passing, the prestigiously stigmatized technology geek avoids doing things not of interest and/or avoids revealing less than stellar performance on tasks with which the geek is not comfortable or not confident. For example, the technology geek has been characterized as skipping status meetings (Glen, 2003) and shirking requests to document (Parker, 2003).

We suggest two additional advantages to be gained by the technology geek through their mixed

interaction behavior: enhanced self-esteem and affirmation of prestige. In regard to self-esteem, when the prestigiously stigmatized geek rejects tension management responsibility, opts not to pass, and adopts reverse passing behaviors, he is in effect embracing the stigma. Accepting and embracing one's stigma enhances self-esteem (Crocker & Major, 1989, 1994). The behaviors exhibited by the prestigiously stigmatized in mixed interactions may also act to affirm the stigma holder's own perceptions of prestige. In rejecting tension management responsibility, choosing not to pass, and reverse passing, the technology geek exercises the status shield that prestige affords. Taken together, we propose the following in regard to advantages accrued by the technology geek in mixed interactions:

Proposition 4: Rejection of tension management responsibility, opting not to pass, and reverse passing in mixed interaction provide these advantages for the prestigiously stigmatized technology geek: (a) avoiding doing things not of interest, (b) avoiding revealing less than stellar performance, (c) enhancing self-esteem, and (d) affirming prestige.

Wearing a prestigious stigma, and its attendant rejection of behaviors of the traditionally stigmatized, offer significant advantages to the technology geek – but is there a concomitant price? Next, we examine potential negative outcomes for the prestigiously stigmatized and normals in mixed interaction.

## Disadvantages for the Technology Geek

We propose that prestigiously stigmatized technology geeks realize advantages through embracing their stigma, but not without a cost. We suggest these behaviors create significant disadvantages for the technology geek, as evidence exists that such behaviors can be self-limiting.

Earlier, in conjunction with Proposition 3, we suggested that self-doubt or disinterest (or both) lead to withholding effort. Crocker and Major (1989) argue that devaluing areas of performance and withdrawing effort from them actually reduce the motivation to improve. When individuals adopt lower goals, they receive relatively little useful feedback about their abilities and, correspondingly, little insight into what they do well and what they can do to improve (Baumeister, Heatherton, & Tice, 1993). Such strategies can lead to avoiding and overlooking negative performance feedback on dimensions that are amenable to learning and improvement, resulting in missed opportunities for professional development.

Evidence also suggests that self-handicapping strategies used to combat feelings of self-doubt tend to sustain it rather than reduce it, causing a negative spiral of self-doubt and self-handicapping that is further fueled by the outcomes of the process (Arkin, 1981). Altogether, the social psychological literature suggests that strategies used to immediate advantage by the technology geek end up limiting opportunities for improvement and professional growth.

In effect, when technology geeks reject tension management responsibilities and decline to meet the virtual social identity expected by normals, they hinder their own professional development (Tschohl, 2004). A study that followed a group of top technical performers at Bell Labs found that the most successful technical experts were the ones who took time to develop good interpersonal rapport with other members of their organization (Kelley & Caplan, 1993). Indeed, technical expertise alone has almost no relationship to trust (Krackhardt & Hanson, 1993), and trust plays an important role in collaboration, sustained coordination and cooperation in information systems and technology (Baba, 1999). In sum, behaviors of the prestigiously stigmatized technology geek in mixed interaction can become a barrier to their own professional development.

A stigma itself can generate biases in mixed interaction that interfere with the career success of a stigmatized individual (Clair et al., 2005; Herek, 1996; Jones et al., 1984; Leary, 1999; Reimann, 2001). And beyond that, for the prestigiously stigmatized, adoption of the self-limiting strategies previously discussed leads to performance and achievement levels that fall well below ability (Crocker & Major, 1989), which can further reduce advancement opportunities for the prestigiously stigmatized. Uncollaborative behavior in mixed interaction – such as the use of divergence accommodation and refusal to perform convergence accommodation – can be expected to limit promotional opportunities for the technology geek, as well as prospects for lateral, career-enhancing moves into areas heavily populated by normals. In their study of IT professionals, Loogma et al. (2004) noted reluctance on the part of technical specialists to assume more collaborative roles with communication components, and concluded that career paths are more restricted for IT professionals adopting a "geek" identity.

Ultimately, behaviors of the technology geek in mixed interaction can become a barrier to both their professional development and career advancement, which leads to the following proposition.

Proposition 5: Rejection of tension management responsibility, opting not to pass, and reverse passing in mixed interaction lead to (a) stunted professional development and (b) reduced career opportunities for the prestigiously stigmatized technology geek.

In sum, we have proposed that declining to put forth effort in mixed interactions has advantages and disadvantages for the technology geek. Yet, not only the stigma bearer is encumbered; there are disadvantages for normals, too. We consider these next.

## Disadvantages for Normals

It is not unusual, in a difficult transfer of knowledge, for the individual needing the knowledge to be stretched and to have to exercise non-routine skills and responses to affect the transfer (Szulanski, 2000). We expect such difficulties to occur in mixed interactions with the prestigiously stigmatized technology geek. In mixed interactions, the prestigiously stigmatized is considered unlikely to extend efforts to smooth and manage the exchanges; so if these interactions are to be managed, the responsibility is to be assumed by the normal (Fiske & Ruscher, 1993). To meet goals of a mixed interaction, the normal works harder to manage communication and arrive at a shared meaning – harder than would be necessary if interacting with another person, normal or non-prestigiously stigmatized. For example, a normal conveyed this description of interaction with a technology geek to one of the present authors: "He doesn't contribute to the collaboration that is needed; this makes me sort of resent him, makes me feel he is not doing his share to get the job done" (Anonymous, personal communication, October 1, 2003).

This sort of mixed-interaction experience is expected to create organizational frustration for the normal. Organizational frustration is comprised of negative feelings experienced when organizational events interfere with goal attainment and organizational maintenance (Fox & Spector, 1999; Spector, 1975, 1978), and it has been found to relate to aggression, complaints, and intention to quit (Chen & Spector, 1992; Neuberg, Smith, & Asher, 2000). From the perspective of the normal in mixed interaction, the prestigiously stigmatized technology geek is not doing what he should to contribute to effective collaboration and is likely perceived as interfering with the normal's effort to get things done and meet goals. In this way, the behavior of the prestigiously stigmatized technology geek in mixed interaction is proposed to generate organizational frustration for the normal.

According to traditional stigma theory, one of the most important questions normals must answer before they can sort through the emotions involved in mixed interaction is the question of origin or responsibility for the stigma or undesired differentness (Crandall, 2000; Crocker & Major, 1994; Jones et al., 1984). Stigmatizing conditions are considered differently based on this issue of controllability. For example, many consider obesity controllable and react differently to obese individuals than they do to individuals with a stigma deemed uncontrollable (e.g., blindness). Put simply, "when the individual is believed to be responsible for his deviance, some form of punishment is likely to be involved in the way others respond to it" (Freidson, 1966, p. 76; Farina, Holland, & Ring, 1966; Northcraft, 1981; Orcutt, 1976; Siller, Chipman, Ferguson, & Vann, 1967; Vann, 1976). Without question, perceived controllability of the stigma highly influences the normal's reaction to the stigmatized.

When normals conclude that the stigmatized individual has actually chosen the set of behaviors that create his stigma, punishment can be particularly harsh (Crandall & Moriarty, 1995; Jones et al., 1984; Weiner, Perry, &Magnusson, 1988) due to the belief that the condition could be altered with some effort and the stigmatized chooses not to engage in that effort (Hebl, Tickle, & Heatherton, 2000). Those so labeled are treated with less sympathy (Hebl, 1997; Farina et al., 1966; Levine & McBurney, 1977; Weiner et al., 1988) and elicit more anger than those whose stigmas are deemed uncontrollable (Crocker & Major, 1994).

We expect the effects of perceived controllability to apply for prestigious stigma as well. Specifically, we expect normals to attribute the prestigiously stigmatized's withholding of effort to disinterest, a controllable factor, rather than self-doubt. For the normal, the technology geek's rejection of tension management behavior conveys an unwillingness to communicate. "Willingness to communicate" (WTC) is a concept that refers to an individual's frequency and amount of talk (McCroskey & Richmond, 1987). High willingness to communicate is associated with increased frequency and amount of communication while low willingness to communicate is associated with decreased frequency and amount of communication (Richmond & Roach, 1992). Research reveals that individuals seen as willing to communicate (WTC) are perceived as more attractive and well-adjusted, more social and more composed than those seen as unwilling to communicate (Allgeier, 1974; McCroskey & Richmond, 1976).

At work, studies show that individuals with low WTC have more difficulty fostering relationships with their peers and supervisors (Daly & McCroskey, 1975; Daly, Richmond, & Leth, 1979) and indicate that even those low in WTC themselves seem to have negative perceptions of others who are low in WTC (Richmond & Roach, 1992). Such findings led Richmond and Roach (1992, p. 103) to conclude that "low willingness to communicate can interfere with interpersonal perceptions and will probably lead to negative perceptions on the part of others."

The research on WTC suggests that the prestigiously stigmatized technology geek will not be viewed by normals as unable to manage and smooth mixed interactions, but will be viewed as unwilling to. When geeks use divergent accommodation, for example, we posit they are likely viewed by normals as purposefully choosing this behavior. It follows from the WTC research, then, that behaviors the prestigiously stigmatized technology geek exhibits in mixed interaction will lead the normal to not only experience frustration but also to view the stigmatized as less attractive, less social, less composed and less desirous of fostering relationships. This is reflected in the following proposition.

Proposition 6: Rejection of tension management responsibility, opting not to pass, and reverse passing by the prestigiously stigmatized technology geek in mixed interaction lead to

(a) organizational frustration for the normal and (b) lead the normal to view the technology geek as less attractive, less social, less composed and less desirous of fostering relationships.

Finally, we explore the impact of the prestigiously stigmatized technology geek on the organization.

## Disadvantages for the Organization

Effective communication is crucial for organizations to function successfully in general (Lawrence & Lorsch, 1967; Richmond & Roach, 1992) and for positive and contributory interactions between technology personnel and others in the organization in particular (Barki & Hartwick, 2001; Bostrom, 1989; Dugan, 2001; Hirschheim & Newman, 1991; Keen, 1981; Nelson & Cooprider, 1996). Poor communication has been found to affect not only information systems development, but also productivity and innovation (Bostrom & Heinen, 1977; DaBrander & Edstrom, 1977; Lind & Zmud, 1991; Pinto & Millet, 1999). In fact, systems development is commonly recognized not only as a technical but also a social process, which highlights the importance of communicating shared meaning in organizations (Bostrom & Heinen, 1977).

Earlier, we posited that the prestigiously stigmatized technology geek minimizes contact with normals and declines to perform convergence accommodation in mixed interaction, and now we propose that such behavior limits knowledge integration, stunts innovation, and reduces effective decision making for the organization. The technology geek, by definition, views his purpose as the pursuit of technology, devaluing the need to communicate in mixed interactions and eschewing responsibility for the management of meaning. Glen (2003) reminds us that many geeks feel the job of communication often ends with self-expression, but the communication literature assures us that the transfer of information alone does not ensure effective communication (Halsam, 2001).

Current formulations of organizational competitive advantage and innovation turn increasingly to the importance of knowledge and its integration throughout the organization (Nordhaugh, 1993; Winch & Schneider, 1993). The crux of the issue of knowledge management is the organization's ability to integrate knowledge between and among levels within the organization (De Boer, Van Den Bosh, & Volberda, 1999; Grant, 1996a, 1996b). A general lack of information is often the cause of many faulty decisions:

*"Thus poor leadership, low motivation, faulty negotiation and under-performance are often seen to result from a 'failure to get a message across' or from a general paucity of information. 'No one knew what was going on,' 'Our wires were crossed,' 'I'm not sure we're speaking the same language,' 'Why wasn't I told?' – these are common complaints of exasperated employers and employees alike" (Haslam, 2001, p. 117).*

De Boer and his colleagues refer to combinative capabilities vital to knowledge management in organizations and discuss three: systems, coordination, and socialization. Systems capabilities relate to formal knowledge-sharing bases such as policy and procedure manuals and intranets. Coordination capabilities refer to integration of knowledge by interactions between members of a group, while socialization capabilities refer to the ability of the firm to produce a shared ideology (De Boer et al., 1996). IT professionals at the "transgressor" end of the IT identity spectrum (Loogma et al., 2004) may contribute to all three of these organizational capabilities; in contrast, prestigiously stigmatized technology geeks tend to reduce the coordination and socialization capabilities of the organization by rejecting the management of meaning in mixed interactions. Prestigiously stigmatized geeks often reduce systems capabilities as well by devaluing

the importance of procedures (Glen, 2003; Parker, 2003) leading to reduced knowledge integration.

In sum, the reverse passing and rejection of tension management behaviors that we posit to be exhibited by the prestigiously stigmatized technology geek in mixed interaction are expected to interfere with knowledge sharing and integration, which stunts innovation and leads to less effective decision making and business processes. This is captured in the following proposition.

Proposition 7: Rejection of tension management responsibility, opting not to pass, and reverse passing by the prestigiously stigmatized technology geek lead to reduced knowledge sharing and integration, reduced innovation, and less effective decision making and business processes in the organization.

## DISCUSSION

By examining the technology geek through the social psychological lens of stigma, we have modeled behaviors that the prestigiously stigmatized technology geek is likely to exhibit in interactions with normals, and we have identified several undesirable outcomes that can stem from those behaviors – outcomes that are undesirable for the technology geek, for those who interact with the geek, and for the organization as a whole. Here, we identify directions for future research regarding the prestigious stigma of technology geek, as well as practical implications that stem from our proposed theory.

### Directions for Future Research

Empirical efforts are needed to test the model and propositions, with the technology geek providing the starting point for investigation. Should the relationships hold for technology geeks, then future efforts should focus on identifying other prestigiously stigmatized roles in organizations.

Ashforth and Kreiner's (1999) concept of "dirty work" and their discussion of status shields in certain occupations may help to identify further organizational roles that possess both stigmatizing and prestigious elements.

In the organizational context it is common for stigmas to generally revolve around communication (e.g., the touch-feely HR professional, or the bean-counter accountant). For prestigious stigmas, this elucidates a need for research to investigate the potential for interaction between the nature of the stigma and the proposed behaviors of the prestigiously stigmatized in mixed interaction. Researchers also are encouraged to search for organizational stigmas in which the stigmatizing characteristic does not involve communication. Additional studies may delineate lack of communication skills from reluctance to develop them and examine consequences of each.

Gender differences should be considered in regard to the proposed behaviors of the prestigiously stigmatized. Knowing that men and women focus on different aspects of communication (women focus more on just the sort of relationship issues that we propose the prestigiously stigmatized eschew) (Tannen, 1994), future efforts should consider whether and how gender of the prestigiously stigmatized may affect mixed interaction.

Another direction for future research in regard to the technology geek stigma would be to examine whether a "geek personality" exists. Many publications outlining the technology geek suggest that he is a young, curious introverted male who is analytical, strives for rationality, and is judging in nature. His early technical prowess may have stunted the development of important social skills and his loyalty may lie more with his profession than with his employer (Glen, 2003; Rose, 1969). The employee engagement literature may provide a useful lens for research into this lay model.

Keeping with the theme of individual differences, Crocker and Major (1989), Crocker and Quinn (2000), and Crocker and Wolfe (2001), have determined that some stigmatized individu-

als seem to have higher levels of self-esteem than many normals. Further investigation is needed to examine the role of self-esteem for the prestigiously stigmatized and integrate what we know about self-protective strategies (including self-handicapping) and their role in either enhancing or inhibiting self-esteem (Arkin, 1981; Arkin & Oleson, 1998) for those holding a prestigious stigma. Baumeister and his colleagues concluded, "In short, ego threat appears to cause people with high self-esteem to abruptly develop an overriding concern with maximizing their esteem, and this overriding concern appears sufficient to influence their behavioral judgment – and not always in optimal or adaptive ways" (Baumeister et al., 1993, p. 143). If we first determine the extent to which prestigiously stigmatized technology geeks have high levels of self-esteem, we can increase our understanding of these types of esteem-enhancing behaviors, their implications and limitations.

Another area that warrants further clarification concerns the effects of perceived responsibility for the stigma. If, as we suggest, the prestigiously stigmatized technology geeks are perceived by normals as responsible for a controllable stigma, future investigation should tease out the effects this attribution has for normals and the geek. Furthermore, evidence suggests the stigmatized bases his reaction to normals on his own view of the controllability of his stigma (Crocker & Major, 1994; Crocker & Quinn, 2000), and that stigmatized individuals who believe their undesired differentness is within their control react more negatively toward normals (Major & Crocker, 1993). Clearly, the area of perceived controllability of the stigma is complex and merits further exploration.

Traditional stigma theory distinguishes a class of individuals known as the wise: "persons who are normal but whose special situation has made them intimately privy to the secret life of the stigmatized individual and sympathetic with it" (Goffman, 1963, p. 28). Members of the wise are compassionate toward the stigmatized and find themselves accorded a measure of acceptance, sort of a courtesy membership in the clan (Goffman, 1963). Research is needed to investigate the existence of the wise and the roles they play in regard to stigmatized and prestigiously stigmatized individuals in an organizational context. For example, we encourage studies to identify individuals anointed as wise by technology geeks to determine the nature of the experiences that carried them into the fold, and to investigate ways in which the wise can help improve interactions between the technology geek and (other) normals and ultimately enhance organizational performance.

Grant (1996b) contends that difficulties arising in the transmission or receipt of knowledge make knowledge transfer one of the most challenging components of knowledge management, and Turner and Makhija (2006) recognize that issues of knowledge transfer have generally received less attention by researchers than other aspects of knowledge management. Future efforts should focus on ways to ameliorate the inherent tension in mixed interactions between the prestigiously stigmatized and normals, and trust may prove to be an important variable to examine in regard to knowledge transfer between such parties. Techniques should be identified to be used by technology geeks and normals in mixed interactions to minimize potential negative consequences for all.

## Practical Implications

If the proposed dysfunctional mixed interactions are occurring in organizations, implications could be major. As discussed previously, knowledge integration between and among levels is an important way for organizations to gain competitive advantage (De Boer et al., 1999; Grant, 1996a; Nordhaugh, 1993; Winch & Schneider, 1993). And, quite simply, behaviors the prestigiously stigmatized technology geek is posited to exhibit in mixed interaction thwart knowledge integration. When the geek limits communication with normals and declines to perform convergence

accommodation, knowledge sharing and integration suffer. This is evidenced in the study of IT professionals by Loogma et al. (2004), in which the authors conclude that a shortage of technology specialists with good communication skills often resulted in inefficient team work, low quality of services, and inefficient project management.

For prestigiously stigmatized technology geeks and their managers, our theory may enlighten the geek to disadvantageous implications of their behavior. Experience can lead a person to discard certain self-presentation tactics, along with underlying facets of self-identity associated with those tactics (Ibarra, 1999). Insights gained from our social psychological model can aid managers in conveying to geeks the importance of meeting the normal halfway – and sometimes more – in mixed interactions.

For normals and their managers, investigative efforts associated with our proposed theory will offer understanding and opportunities to shape attitudes to be more conducive to managing a shared meaning in interaction with technology geeks. Doing so should reduce frustration for the normal and improve knowledge sharing in mixed interaction. To the degree that these relationships and communication channels are deepened and improved, organizations will benefit from better knowledge integration, better decision making and better processes.

## CONCLUSION

This article reflects an effort to better understand the technology geek and, in doing so, to improve the integration of geeks and their indispensable expertise within organizations. By illuminating the concept of prestige within stigma theory, we recognize how the prestigious stigma of technology geek can affect interactions between geeks and normals. Our model and propositions constitute a much needed step toward improving those interactions and work relationships, removing barriers in organizational knowledge integration, and improving the professional development of technology geeks.

## ACKNOWLEDGMENT

We would like to thank Anne O'Leary-Kelly for her encouragement and helpful comments on an earlier draft.

## REFERENCES

Adler, I., & Kraus, V. (1985). Components of occupational prestige evaluations. *Work & Organizations*, *12*, 23–39. doi:10.1177/0730888485012001002

Allgeier, A. R. (1974). *The effects of differential amounts of talkativeness on interpersonal judgments*. Unpublished doctoral dissertation, Purdue University, West Lafayette.

Arkin, R. M. (1981). Self-presentation styles. In Tedeschi, J. T. (Ed.), *Impression management theory and social psychology research* (pp. 311–333). New York, NY: Academic Press.

Arkin, R. M., & Oleson, K. C. (1998). Self-handicapping. In Darley, J. M., & Cooper, J. (Eds.), *Attribution and social interaction: The legacy of Edward E. Jones* (pp. 313–347). Washington, DC: American Psychological Association. doi:10.1037/10286-006

Ashforth, B. E., & Kreiner, G. E. (1999). How can you do it? Dirty work and the challenge of constructing a positive identity. *Academy of Management Review*, *24*(3), 413–434. doi:10.2307/259134

Baba, M. (1999). Dangerous liaisons: Trust, distrust, and information technology in American work organizations. *Human Organization*, *58*(3), 331–346.

Barki, H., & Hartwick, J. (2001). Interpersonal conflict and its management in information system development. *Management Information Systems Quarterly*, *25*(2), 195–228. doi:10.2307/3250929

Baumeister, R. F., Heatherton, T. F., & Tice, D. M. (1993). When ego threats lead to self-regulation failure: Negative consequences of high self-esteem. *Journal of Personality and Social Psychology*, *64*(1), 141–156. doi:10.1037/0022-3514.64.1.141

Berglas, S., & Jones, E. E. (1978). Drug choice as a self-handicapping strategy in response to noncontingent success. *Journal of Personality and Social Psychology*, *36*, 405–417. doi:10.1037/0022-3514.36.4.405

Bostrom, R. (1989). Successful application of communication techniques to improve the systems development process. *Information & Management*, *16*, 279–295. doi:10.1016/0378-7206(89)90005-0

Bostrom, R., & Heinen, S. (1977). MIS problems and failures: A socio-technical perspective part 1: The causes. *Management Information Systems Quarterly*, *1*, 17–32. doi:10.2307/248710

Carroll, J. (2002). Nurture the geek in you. *CA Magazine*, *135*(7), 18.

Chapman, G. (1999, September 27). Digital nation: Even if 'geekness' is a disorder, there's no rush to find a cure. *The Los Angeles Times*, p. 1.

Chen, P. Y., & Spector, P. E. (1992). Relationships of work stressor with aggression, withdrawal, theft and substance use: An exploratory study. *Journal of Occupational and Organizational Psychology*, *65*, 177–184.

Clair, J. A., Beatty, J. E., & MacLean, T. L. (2005). Out of sight but not out of mind: Managing invisible social identities in the workplace. *Academy of Management Review*, *30*, 78–95.

Cox, T. (1993). *Cultural diversity in organizations*. San Francisco, CA: Berrett-Kohler.

Crandall, C. S. (2000). Ideology and lay theories of stigma: The justification of stigmatization. In Heatherton, T. F., Kleck, R. E., Hebl, M. R., & Hull, J. G. (Eds.), *The social psychology of stigma* (pp. 126–150). New York, NY: The Guilford Press.

Crandall, C. S., & Moriarty, D. (1995). Physical illness stigma and social rejection. *The British Journal of Social Psychology, 34*, 67–83.

Crocker, J., & Major, B. (1989). Social stigma and self-esteem: The self-protective properties of stigma. *Psychological Review, 96*(4), 608–630. doi:10.1037/0033-295X.96.4.608

Crocker, J., & Major, B. (1994). Reactions to stigma: The moderating role of justifications. In M. P. Zanna & J. M. Olson (Eds.), *The Ontario symposium: Vol. 7. The psychology of prejudice* (pp. 289-314). Mahwah, NJ: Lawrence Erlbaum.

Crocker, J., Major, B., & Steele, C. (1998). Social stigma. In Gilbert, D. T., Fiske, S. T., & Lindzey, G. (Eds.), *The handbook of social psychology* (4th ed., *Vol. 2*, pp. 504–533). New York, NY: McGraw Hill.

Crocker, J., & Quinn, D. M. (2000). Social stigma and the self: Meanings, situations, and self-esteem. In Heatherton, T. F., Kleck, R. E., Hebl, M. R., & Hull, J. G. (Eds.), *The social psychology of stigma* (pp. 153–183). New York, NY: The Guilford Press.

Crocker, J., & Wolfe, C. T. (2001). Contingencies of self-worth. *Psychological Review, 108*(3), 593–623. doi:10.1037/0033-295X.108.3.593

Csikszentmihalyi, M. (1997). *Finding flow*. New York, NY: Basic Books.

Dabrander, B., & Edstrom, A. (1977). Successful information system development projects. *Management Science, 24*, 191–199. doi:10.1287/mnsc.24.2.191

Daft, R. L. (1995). *Organization theory and design* (5th ed.). Minneapolis, MN: West Publishing.

Daly, J. A., & McCroskey, J. C. (1975). Occupational choice and desirability as a function of communication apprehension. *Journal of Counseling Psychology, 22*, 309–313. doi:10.1037/h0076748

Daly, J. A., Richmond, V. P., & Leth, S. (1979). Social communicative anxiety and the personnel selection process: Testing the similarity effect in selection decisions. *Human Communication Research, 6*, 18–32. doi:10.1111/j.1468-2958.1979.tb00288.x

De Boer, M., Van Den Bosch, A. J., & Volberda, H. W. (1999). Managing organizational knowledge integration in the emerging multimedia complex. *Journal of Management Studies, 36*(3), 379–398. doi:10.1111/1467-6486.00141

Deaux, K., & Major, B. (1987). Putting gender into context: An integrative model of gender-related behavior. *Psychological Review, 94*, 369–389. doi:10.1037/0033-295X.94.3.369

Dovidio, J. F., Major, B., & Crocker, J. (2000). Stigma: Introduction and overview. In Heatherton, T. F., Kleck, R. E., Hebl, M. R., & Hull, J. G. (Eds.), *The social psychology of stigma* (pp. 1–28). New York, NY: The Guilford Press.

Dugan, S. (2001). Confronting the geek within. *InfoWorld, 23*(20), 66–68.

Emerson, R. E. (1962). Power-dependence relations. *American Sociological Review, 27*, 31–41. doi:10.2307/2089716

Farina, A., Holland, C. H., & Ring, K. (1966). The role of stigma and set in interpersonal attraction. *Journal of Abnormal Psychology, 71*, 421–428. doi:10.1037/h0020306

Fiske, S. T., & Ruscher, J. B. (1993). Negative interdependence and prejudice: Whence the affect? In Mackie, D. M., & Hamilton, D. L. (Eds.), *Affect, cognition, and stereotyping: Interactive processes in group perception* (pp. 239–268). San Diego, CA: Academic Press.

Fox, S., & Spector, P. E. (1999). A model of work frustration-aggression. *Journal of Organizational Behavior*, *20*, 915–931. doi:10.1002/(SICI)1099-1379(199911)20:6<915::AID-JOB918>3.0.CO;2-6

Frable, D., Blackstone, T., & Sherbaum, C. (1990). Marginal and mindful: Deviants in social interaction. *Journal of Personality and Social Psychology*, *59*, 140–149. doi:10.1037/0022-3514.59.1.140

Franz, C. R., & Robey, D. (1984). An investigation of user-led system design: Rational and political perspectives. *Communications of the ACM*, *27*, 1202–1209. doi:10.1145/2135.2138

Freidson, E. (1966). Disability as social deviance. In Sussam, M. B. (Ed.), *Sociology and rehabilitation*. Washington, DC: American Sociological Association.

French, J. R. P., & Raven, B. (1959). The bases of social power. In Cartwright, D. (Ed.), *Studies in social power*. Ann Arbor, MI: University of Michigan.

Fried, I. (2000). *Cruise line seeks geeks for Perl diving*. Retrieved from http://news.cnet.com/Cruise-line-seeks-geeks-for-Perl-diving/2100-1040_3-244435.html

Geek 2 Geek. (2010). *Welcome to Geek 2 Geek*. Retrieved from http://www.gk2gk.com

Giles, H., Coupland, J., & Coupland, N. (1991). *Contexts of accommodation: Developments in applied sociolinguistics. Studies in emotional and social interaction*. Cambridge, UK: Cambridge University Press. doi:10.1017/CBO9780511663673

Giles, H., & Johnson, P. (1981). The role of language in intergroup relations. In Turner, J. C., & Giles, H. (Eds.), *Intergroup behavior* (pp. 199–243). Oxford, UK: Blackwell.

Giles, H., Mulac, A., Bradac, J. J., & Johnson, P. (1987). Speech accommodation theory: The first decade and beyond. In Mclaughlin, C. M. (Ed.), *Communication yearbook* (*Vol. 10*, pp. 13–48). Newbury Park, CA: Sage.

Glen, P. (2003). *Leading geeks: How to manage and lead people who deliver technology*. San Francisco, CA: Jossey-Bass.

Goffman, E. (1963). *Stigma: Notes on the management of spoiled identity*. Upper Saddle River, NJ: Prentice Hall.

Grant, R. M. (1996a). Prospering in dynamically-competitive environments: Organizational capability as knowledge integration. *Organization Science*, *7*, 375–387. doi:10.1287/orsc.7.4.375

Grant, R. M.. (199b6). Toward a knowledge-based theory of the firm. *Strategic Management Journal*, *17*, 109–122.

Hansen, M. (1999). The search-transfer problem: The role of weak ties in sharing knowledge across organization subunits. *Administrative Science Quarterly*, *44*(1), 82–111. doi:10.2307/2667032

Harter, S. (1986). Processes underlying the construction, maintenance, and enhancement of the self-concept in children. In Suls, J., & Greenwald, A. G. (Eds.), *Psychological perspectives on the self* (*Vol. 3*, pp. 136–182). Mahwah, NJ: Lawrence Erlbaum.

Haslam, S. A. (2001). *Psychology in organizations: The social identity approach*. Thousand Oaks, CA: Sage.

Hebl, M. R. (1997). *Nonstigmatized individuals' reactions to the acknowledgment and valuation of a stigma by physically disabled and overweight individuals.* Unpublished doctoral dissertation, Dartmouth College, Hanover.

Hebl, M. R., Tickle, J., & Heatherton, T. F. (2000). Awkward moments in interactions between nonstigmatized and stigmatized individuals. In Heatherton, T. F., Kleck, R. E., Hebl, M. R., & Hull, J. G. (Eds.), *The social psychology of stigma* (pp. 275–306). New York, NY: The Guilford Press.

Herek, G. M. (1996). Why tell if you are not asked? Self disclosure, intergroup contact, and heterosexuals' attitudes toward lesbians and gay men. In Herek, G. M., Jobe, J. B., & Carney, R. M. (Eds.), *Out in force: Sexual orientation and the military* (pp. 197–225). Chicago, IL: The University of Chicago Press.

Hirschheim, R., & Newman, M. (1991). Symbolism and information systems development: Myth, metaphor, and magic. *Information Systems Research, 2*(1), 29–62. doi:10.1287/isre.2.1.29

Hochschild, A. R. (1983). *The managed heart: Commercialization of human feeling.* Berkeley, CA: University of California Press.

Hogg, M. A., & Terry, D. J. (2000). Social identity and self-categorization processes in organizational contexts. *Academy of Management Review, 25,* 121–140. doi:10.2307/259266

Hughes, E. C. (1994). *On work, race, and the sociological imagination.* Chicago, IL: The University of Chicago Press.

Ibarra, H. (1999). Provisional selves: Experimenting with image and identity in professional adaptation. *Administrative Science Quarterly, 44,* 764–791. doi:10.2307/2667055

Information Technology Association of America. (1998). Task force. Image of the information technology (IT) professions. *From myth to reality: Changing the image of information technology.* Retrieved from http://www.itaa.org/

Jones, E. E., Farina, A., Hastorf, A. H., Markus, H., Miller, D. T., & Scott, R. A. (1984). *Social stigma: The psychology of marked relationships.* New York, NY: Freeman.

Kaiser, C., & Miller, C. T. (2000). *Reacting to impending discriminations: Compensation for prejudice and attributions to discrimination.* Unpublished doctoral dissertation, University of Vermont, Burlington.

Keen, P. (1981). Information systems and organizational change. *Communications of the ACM, 24,* 24–33. doi:10.1145/358527.358543

Kelley, R., & Caplan, J. (1993). How bell labs creates start performers. *Harvard Business Review, 71,* 128–139.

Krackhardt, D., & Hanson, J. R. (1993). Informal networks: The company behind the charts. *Harvard Business Review, 71,* 104–111.

Kroeger, B. (2003). *Passing: When people can't be who they are.* New York, NY: Public Affairs.

Lawrence, P. R., & Lorsch, J. W. (1967). *Organization and environment: managing differentiation and integration.* Cambridge, MA: Harvard University Press.

Leary, K. (1999). Passing, posing, and "keeping it real.". *Constellations (Oxford, England), 6,* 85–96. doi:10.1111/1467-8675.00122

Levine, J. M., & McBurney, D. H. (1977). Causes and consequences of effluvia: Body odor awareness and controllability as determinants of interpersonal evaluation. *Personality and Social Psychology Bulletin, 3,* 442–445.

Levine, J. M., & Moreland, R. L. (1991). Culture and socialization in work groups. In Resnick, L. B., Levine, J. M., & Teasley, S. D. (Eds.), *Perspectives on socially shared cognition* (pp. 257–279). Washington, DC: American Psychological Association. doi:10.1037/10096-011

Lind, M., & Zmud, R. (1991). The influence of a convergence in understanding between technology providers and users on information technology innovativeness. *Organization Science, 2*, 195–217. doi:10.1287/orsc.2.2.195

Link, B. G., & Phelan, J. C. (2001). Conceptualizing stigma. *Annual Review of Psychology, 27*, 363–385.

Loogma, K., Umarik, M., & Vilu, R. (2004). Identification-flexibility dilemma of IT specialists. *Career Development International, 9*(3), 323–348. doi:10.1108/13620430410535878

Major, B., & Crocker, J. (1993). Social stigma: The consequences of attributional ambiguity. In Mackie, D. M., & Hamilton, D. L. (Eds.), *Affect, cognition, and stereotyping: Interactive processes in group perception* (pp. 345–370). San Diego, CA: Academic Press.

Manfred, E. (2000). Selling teens on IT. *Computerworld, 34*(46), 82–83.

McCroskey, J. C., & Richmond, V. P. (1976). The effects of communication apprehension on the perception of peers. *Western Speech Communication Journal, 40*, 14–21.

McCroskey, J. C., & Richmond, V. P. (1987). Willingness to communicate. In McCroskey, J. C., & Daly, J. A. (Eds.), *Personality and interpersonal communication* (pp. 129–156). Newbury Park, CA: Sage.

Mechanic, D. (1962). Source of power in lower participants in complex organizations. *Administrative Science Quarterly, 7*, 349–364. doi:10.2307/2390947

Miller, C. T., & Major, B. (2000). Coping with stigma and prejudice. In T. F. Heatherton, R. E. Kleck, M. R. Hebl, & J. G. Hull (Eds.), *The social psychology of stigma* (pp. 243-272). New York, NY: The Guilford Press. Milton, L. P. (2003). An identity perspective on the propensity of high-tech talent to unionize. *Journal of Labor Research, 24*, 31-53.

Mintzberg, H. (1983). *Power in and around organizations*. Upper Saddle River, NJ: Prentice Hall.

Mitchell, T. R., Dowling, P. J., Kabanoff, B. V., & Larson, J. R. (1988). *People in organizations: An introduction to organizational behaviour in Australia*. Sydney, Australia: McGraw-Hill.

Montgomery, M. (1986). *An introduction to language and society*. London, UK: Routledge. doi:10.4324/9780203312032

Nelson, K. M., & Cooprider, J. G. (1996). The contribution of shared knowledge to IS group performance. *Management Information Systems Quarterly, 20*(4), 409–432. doi:10.2307/249562

Neuberg, S. L. (1994). Expectancy-confirmation processes in stereotype-tinged social encounters: The moderating role of social goals. In Zanna, M. P., & Olson, J. M. (Eds.), *The psychology of prejudice: The Ontario symposium* (*Vol. 7*, pp. 103–130). Mahwah, NJ: Lawrence Erlbaum.

Neuberg, S. L., Smith, D. M., & Asher, T. (2000). Why people stigmatize: Toward a biocultural framework. In Heatherton, T. F., Kleck, R. E., Hebl, M. R., & Hull, J. G. (Eds.), *The social psychology of stigma* (pp. 31–61). New York, NY: The Guilford Press.

Nordhaugh, O. (1993). *Human capital in organizations: Competence, training and learning*. Oslo, Norway: Scandinavian University Press.

Northcraft, G. B. (1981). *The perception of disability*. Unpublished doctoral dissertation, Stanford University, Stanford.

Orcutt, J. D. (1976). Ideological variations in the structure of deviant types: A multivariate comparison of alcoholism and heroin addiction. *Social Forces, 55*, 419–437. doi:10.2307/2576233

Parker, D. (2003). Revenge of the nerds. *Australian CPA, 73*(4), 32.

Peterson, B., Major, B., Cozarelli, C., & Crocker, J. (1988). *The social construction of gender differences in values.* Paper presented at the Annual Meeting of the Eastern Psychological Association, Buffalo, NY.

Pinto, J. K., & Millet, I. (1999). *Successful information system implementation: The human side.* Newtown Square, PA: Project Management Institute.

Pryor, J. B., Reeder, G. D., Yeadon, C., & Hesson-McInnis, M. (2004). A dual-process model of reactions to perceived stigma. *Journal of Personality and Social Psychology, 87*(4), 436–452. doi:10.1037/0022-3514.87.4.436

Reimann, R. (2001). Lesbian mothers at work. In Bernstein, M., & Reimann, R. (Eds.), *Queer families, queer politics: Challenging culture and the state* (pp. 254–271). New York, NY: Columbia University Press.

Richmond, V. P., & Roach, K. D. (1992). Willingness to communicate and employee success in U.S. organizations. *Journal of Applied Communication Research*, 95–115. doi:10.1080/00909889209365321

Rose, M. (1969). *Computers, managers, and society.* New York, NY: Penguin.

Siller, J., Chipman, A., Ferguson, L., & Vann, D. H. (1967). *Attitudes of the nondisabled toward the physically disabled* (Tech. Rep. No. RD-707). New York, NY: New York University School of Education.

Sorokin, P. A. (1927). *Social mobility.* New York, NY: Harper.

Spector, P. E. (1975). Relationships of organizational frustration with reported behavioral reactions of employees. *The Journal of Applied Psychology, 60*, 635–637. doi:10.1037/h0077157

Spector, P. E. (1978). Organizational frustration: A model and review of the literature. *Personnel Psychology, 31*, 815–829. doi:10.1111/j.1744-6570.1978.tb02125.x

Steele, C. M., & Aronson, J. (1995). Stereotype threat and intellectual performance of African Americans. *Journal of Personality and Social Psychology, 69*, 797–811. doi:10.1037/0022-3514.69.5.797

Stenross, B., & Kleinman, S. (1989). The highs and lows of emotional labor. *Journal of Contemporary Ethnography, 17*(4), 435–452. doi:10.1177/089124189017004003

Swann, W. B. Jr, & Ely, R. J. (1984). A battle of wills: Self-verification versus behavioral confirmation. *Journal of Personality and Social Psychology, 46*, 1287–1302. doi:10.1037/0022-3514.46.6.1287

Sykes, G. M., & Matza, D. (1957). Techniques of neutralization: A theory of delinquency. *American Sociological Review, 22*, 664–670. doi:10.2307/2089195

Szulanski, G. (2000). The process of knowledge transfer: A diachronic analysis of stickiness. *Organizational Behavior and Human Decision Processes, 82*(1), 9–27. doi:10.1006/obhd.2000.2884

Tannen, D. (1994). *Talking from 9 to 5: How women's and men's conversational styles affect who gets heard, who gets credit, and what gets done at work.* New York, NY: William Morrow & Company.

Taylor, S. E., & Brown, J. (1988). Illusion and well-being: Some social psychological contributions to a theory of mental health. *Psychological Bulletin, 103*, 193–210. doi:10.1037/0033-2909.103.2.193

Tesser, A., & Campbell, J. (1980). Self-definition: The impact of relative performance and similarity of others. *Social Psychology Quarterly, 43,* 341–347. doi:10.2307/3033737

Tesser, A., & Campbell, J. (1983). Self-definition and self-evaluation maintenance. In Suls, J., & Greenwald, A. G. (Eds.), *Psychological perspectives on the self* (*Vol. 2*, pp. 1–31). Mahwah, NJ: Lawrence Erlbaum.

The American Heritage Dictionaries. (2000). *American heritage dictionary of the English language* (4th ed.). Boston, MA: Houghton Mifflin.

Trevino, L. K., & Webster, J. (1992). Flow in computer-mediated communication: Electronic mail and voice mail evaluation and impacts. *Communication Research, 19,* 539–573. doi:10.1177/009365092019005001

Tschohl, J. (2004). Geeks: Train and handle with care! *The Canadian Manager, 29*(3), 24.

Turner, J. C. (1991). *Social influence.* Berkshire, UK: Open University Press.

Turner, K. L., & Makhija, M. V. (2006). The role of organizational controls in managing knowledge. *Academy of Management Review, 31*(1), 197–217.

Twigg, N. (2010). *Celebrate Geek Pride Day 2010.* Retrieved on from http://www.forevergeek.com/2010/05/celebrate_geek_pride_day_2010/

Vann, D. H. (1976). *Personal responsibility, authoritarianism, and treatment of the obese.* Unpublished doctoral dissertation, New York University, New York.

Villimez, W. J. (1974). Ability vs. effort: Ideological correlates of occupational grading. *Social Forces, 53,* 45–52. doi:10.2307/2576836

Von Baeyer, C. L., Sherk, D. L., & Zanna, M. P. (1981). Impression management on the job interview: When the female applicant meets the male (chauvinist) interviewer. *Personality and Social Psychology Bulletin, 7,* 45–51. doi:10.1177/014616728171008

Webster, J., Trevino, L. K., & Ryan, L. (1993). The dimensionality and correlates of flow in human-computer interactions. *Computers in Human Behavior, 9,* 411–426. doi:10.1016/0747-5632(93)90032-N

Weiner, B., Perry, R., & Magnusson, J. (1988). An attributional analysis of reactions to stigmas. *Journal of Personality and Social Psychology, 55,* 738–748. doi:10.1037/0022-3514.55.5.738

Whitten, N. (1995). *Managing software development projects: Formula for success.* New York, NY: John Wiley & Sons.

Wildavsky, A. (1974). *The politics of the budgetary process* (2nd ed.). Boston, MA: Little, Brown.

Wilensky, H. L. (1967). The failure of intelligence: Knowledge and policy in government and industry. In *Proceedings of the Nineteenth Annual Winter Meeting of the Industrial Relations Research Association.*

Winch, G., & Schneider, E. (1993). Managing the knowledge-based organization: The case of architectural practice. *Journal of Management Studies, 6,* 923–937. doi:10.1111/j.1467-6486.1993.tb00472.x

Wloszczyna, S., & Oldenburg, A. (2003). *Fickle finger of fashion puts 'eek' in 'geek.* Retrieved from.http://www.usatoday.com/tech/news/2003-10-22-geek-chic_x.htm

*This work was previously published in the International Journal of Social and Organizational Dynamics in IT, Volume 1, Issue 2, edited by Michael B. Knight, pp. 1-25, 2011 by IGI Publishing (an imprint of IGI Global).*

# Chapter 5
# Committing to Organizational Change in IT Industry

**Jukka-Pekka Kauppinen**
*Oy International Business Machines Ab, Finland*

**Hannu Kivijärvi**
*Aalto University School of Economics, Finland*

**Jari Talvinen**
*Aalto University School of Economics, Finland*

## ABSTRACT

*In the current competitive environment, managing organizational change successfully requires comprehensive understanding of change management concepts and processes as well as the implied drivers behind them. Information technology (IT) field is not an exception; growing interest exists for understanding organizational change and change management in the IT industry. Fast-paced changes in today's IT and business environments are inevitable and the challenges associated with organizational changes are becoming more complex. This study aims to find at least partial answers to the question how employees' commitment to change and the implementation quality of a change process affect achieving the goals and succeeding in an organizational change initiative. The study is conducted in two parts in a Finnish IT company providing complex IT solutions and services. The first part, the pilot study, identifies factors hindering employees' commitment to change. The pilot study is followed by a quantitative main study, which investigates the relationships between employees' level of commitment during the different phases of a change project, the change process quality, the importance and realization level of the different goals set for the change project, and the final success of the change initiative. The results indicate that a strong, positive relationship exists between the change process quality and the level of employees' commitment to change.*

DOI: 10.4018/978-1-4666-1948-7.ch005

## INTRODUCTION

At present a large number of companies offering products and services in information technology (IT) field are struggling in the middle of a severe global financial crisis. Many of these companies are forced to change their organizational structures, business models and strategies as well as the technologies supporting the chosen strategies to maintain their competitiveness and to survive the harsh economic conditions. Consequently, there is a growing interest for understanding the key concepts of organizational change and change management in IT industry, too.

Organizational change and change management have been studied widely over the last decades (Beckhard, 1969; Daft, 1998; Kübler-Ross, 1969; Salancik, 1987). One of the reasons behind such a high interest and continuous enthusiasm for understanding organizational change and its management stems from the dynamic and unpredictable surrounding environment of modern companies. Constant changes in today's business and IT environments are inevitable and the challenges associated with organizational change are correspondingly becoming more complex. In the IT field, it is not only the companies' business models or strategies that are creating the urgent need for changing but also implementing new innovative technologies and architectural directions are driving organizational change too.

The existence of change in the surrounding environment of IT organizations is, however, widely known and the importance of studying organizational change from different perspectives has been well-understood in many organizations long before this exceptional financial crisis. The results of the IBM Global CEO Study 2008 indicated that as much as 83% of the 1500 interviewed global executives expected a substantial change to take place in the next three years. The high number illustrated an increase of 20% from the results of the same global study conducted two years earlier. At the same time, however, only 61% of those executives thought that they had the sufficient knowledge, skills and capabilities to manage the change successfully. This problematic situation has led to a phenomenon called the change gap. The change gap refers to a situation, where the challenges associated with organizational changes are expected to evolve faster than the knowledge and the skills to manage them (IBM, 2008).

Hence, studying the different aspects of organizational change as well as developing improved ways to manage changes successfully might not only help IT organizations in revising and implementing new business models, strategies and technologies, but in the present, exceptional circumstances, it might even determine their future and survival.

Organizational change research has been traditionally divided into two major theoretical branches, the theory of change and the theory of changing (Bennis, 1966). The theory of change concentrates on describing the change process and the dynamics by which a change takes place in an organization, whereas the theory of changing refers to how to get a change implemented in an organization. The well-known Lewin's (1951) model for organizational change and Schein's (1996) interpretation of Lewin's model represent the theory of change and are good examples of descriptive models of the organizational change process.

Lewin's model and Schein's interpretation for organizational change have been inspiring research also in the other theoretical branch, the theory of changing. Kotter (1995), for example, approached organizational change from the top management perspective and developed a normative model for organizational change utilizing both Schein's and Lewin's studies. He combined the most common change implementation mistakes into a high-level roadmap on how to transform an organization successfully. Another, rather similar and a widely cited normative model was developed by Cummings and Worley (1997).

As practical as these roadmap studies might be, they seem to cover the area concerning individual employees rather lightly. This area is often called the "soft stuff" in change management literature (Cummings & Worley, 1997; Kotter, 1995). While the high-level roadmap studies provide useful support for top management, they overlook micro level issues concerning the real people in the organizations. In fact, many of these popular change management studies recognize and even point out the high importance of challenges concerning individuals, but they often leave the subject outside more detailed discussion.

According to recent studies, ignoring change management at the individual level is a serious issue that might even lead to failing in organizational change initiatives. The IBM Global CEO Study 2008, for example, indicates that as much as 4 out of the 5 biggest reasons for failing in change initiatives can be traced back to poor management of the "soft stuff".

Another important area with limited focus in research is the employees' commitment to change. According to the various studies, employees' commitment has a significant role in successful change management (Herscovitch & Meyer, 2002). The problem is, however, that the concept of commitment to change is still somewhat unclear in current academic literature and there are only a few studies investigating the relationship between employees' commitment to change and organizational change. Especially in the IT field the number of studies focusing on organizational commitment and employees' commitment to change is very limited (Bashir & Ramay, 2008). Consequently, there are many uncovered and complex challenges still left to be solved within this field.

The main objective of this study is to investigate how employees' commitment to change and the implementation quality of different change process phases affect achieving the goals and succeeding in an organizational change initiative. The study aims at providing further and more in-depth

support for the few existing studies focusing on combining the areas of organizational change and the commitment to change.

This study is divided into five sections. After the theoretical background discussed, the study continues with a pilot study. The conceptual considerations and the main study are then presented, which is followed by a discussion and conclusions in the final section.

## THEORETICAL BACKGROUND

The theoretical background of this study stems mainly from organization and organizational behaviour theories. The focus within these areas is in organizational and individual change related theories as well as theories covering the areas of organizational commitment and employees' commitment to change.

## Organizational Change

The surrounding environment, opportunities and needs of organizations are constantly changing. Change can be driven by for example financial, technological and societal pressures. Consequently, responding to new challenges and adapting to the changes in the external environment requires organizations to change as well. The subject of organizational change can be, for example, organizational structures, strategies or business models.

Current organizational change theories break mainly into two branches. According to Bennis (1966), the field is divided into the theory of change and the theory of changing, while Porras and Robertson (1987) divide the theories into change process theories and change implementation theories. In general, the theories of changing and the change implementation theories describe how to get a change completed in an organization. The theories of change, or the change process theories, on the other hand refer to the dynamics by which a change takes place in an organization. In this study, the focus is in both theoretical branches. The borderline between these areas is wavering and describing organizational change and change management processes is difficult concentrating solely on either the theory of change or the theory of changing. Moreover, both branches have valuable aspects and theories to contribute to this study.

Depending on the theoretical approaching angle, organizational change has been defined in many different ways. In organization theory, it is defined simply as "the adoption of a new idea or behaviour by an organization" (Daft, 1998, p. 291). In organizational behaviour literature, on the other hand, organizational change is defined as "the act of varying or altering conventional ways of thinking or behaving" (Wagner & Hollenbeck, 1998, p. 345). Perhaps one of the most complete definitions that combines various perspectives is presented by Struckman and Yammarino (2003, p. 10): "Organizational change is a managed system, process, and/or behavioral response over time to a trigger event".

In the current literature (Daft, 1998; Poole & Van de Ven, 2004), different types of organizational change have been categorized by for example the scope and the depth as well as the planning state of the organizational change. McNamara (2006) classifies organizational change by the following four dichotomies:

1. Organization-wide versus subsystem change
2. Radical versus incremental change
3. Remedial versus developmental change
4. Unplanned versus planned change

In this study, the concept of organizational change refers to change initiatives that are closely comparable with the concept of organization development. These change initiatives are planned, organization wide, managed from the top and focus on increasing organizational effectiveness. This study limits the discussion to the for-profit organizations only. Hence, organizational change

in the public sector and not-for-profit organizations is outside the scope of this study.

Organizational change can be seen as a social theory punctuated equilibrium paradigm, which has its roots in evolutionary biology (Gould & Eldridge, 1977). In social sciences, the paradigm suggests that social systems, including all organizations and companies, spend extended periods of time in a stable state, i.e. in an *equilibrium*, which is shaken occasionally with transformation or *revolutionary and radical change* (Baumgartner & Jones, 1993; Gersick, 1991). During the equilibrium state, only incremental change is possible in an organization because of certain stabilizing forces. This phenomenon is called the *deep structure* and it is an essential part of the punctuated equilibrium theory. The deep structure refers to the chosen organizational practices, structures, internal processes and other activity patterns that hold a focal position in an organization and its organizational culture. Consequently, during the revolutionary periods, the stabilizing forces are shaken and the deep structure is broken down allowing change to take place (Gersick, 1991). Finally, the deep structure constitutes around the new equilibrium and freezes the occurred changes and new behaviour.

The theoretical background of organizational change process, on the other hand, stems from an assumption in organization theory claiming that individual members of an organization seek stability, and that change is perceived uncomfortable and risky (Lewin, 1946, 1951; Schein, 1996). Consequently, to enable organizational change, the perceived risk of the negative consequences of staying unchanged must be higher than the perceived risk of changing. Based on this assumption, organizational change literature has a wide variety of models in different shape and size depicting organizational change process.

One of the best known and earliest models describing organizational change process is social psychologist Lewin's *Unfreeze-Change-Freeze-*model (Lewin, 1946, 1951). The leading thought of his model is that all organizations, including companies, are systems, which are stabilized by certain internal forces. In order to change this system, the stabilizing forces must be first questioned and reduced. Only after shaking, or unfreezing, the stability, can organizational change take place. Consequently, after the change has taken place, the system stabilizes, or freezes, automatically around the new equilibrium.

Schein (1996) updated Lewin's (1951) model to address the challenges of modern organizational change. Schein took the Unfreeze-Change-Freeze –model as a basis for his studies and renamed the change process phases according to his own findings: becoming motivated to change, moving to a new state and making the change permanent. An important factor emphasized in Schein's interpretation of Lewin's model is the employees' motivation to change and how it affects the organizational change process.

## Individual Change

The organizational change theories and models presented above take an overarching and generalized approach to organizational change. In many organizational change initiatives, however, it is the individual employee who is required to change his/her behaviour above all. Kotter (1995) and Cummings and Worley (1997), for example, suggest that changes in employees' perceptions, attitudes, motivation and commitment are critical factors during an organizational change process. The same studies, however, give no detailed explanation on how change at the individual level actually takes place or how it might affect succeeding in organizational change initiatives.

In practice, the challenges associated with change at the individual level have been recognized at least to some extent. The IBM Global CEO Study 2008, for example, claimed that the majority of organizational change challenges are people and individual related.

While many individual level change studies rely on Lewin's theory and model for organizational change, there are also studies that approach the subject from a completely different angle and focus on the emotional changes of an individual during an organizational change process. Kübler-Ross (1969), for example, identifies and explains the five stages of grief during a radical change. The five stages identified by Kübler-Ross are: Denial - Anger - Bargaining - Depression - Acceptance.

Kübler-Ross's model has been widely utilized and modified to fit different purposes. Perlman and Takacs (Perlman & Takacs, 1990), for example, revised the model to fit organizational change process. They found out that the stages presented in the original stages of grief are closely similar to what employees encounter during an organizational change process over time. They extended the model to ten different phases and provided one of the most extensive models of organizational change at the individual level.

The key message of these individual change models and theories is that employees follow different emotional paths during an organizational change process and that individuals' emotional stages do not follow any particular order. This might become an additional challenge for change practitioners while planning and implementing organizational change initiatives.

## Commitment and Organizational Change

The last theoretical area of this study concentrates on organizational commitment and employees' commitment to change. The concept of employees' commitment is considered an important factor between success and failure in organizational change initiatives in a number of studies (Fedor et al., 2006; Herscovitch & Meyer, 2002; Iverson, 1996; Meyer & Allen, 1991). Some of these studies suggest that in successful change management special emphasis must be put in making the employees committed to change and committed to the outcome of the change effort (Cummings & Worley, 1997). The practical means to enhance the level of employees' commitment to change is, however, left often with very little emphasis.

In the current academic research, there are conflicting results concerning the linkage between employees' commitment and performance. Some studies claim that the research findings do not support any linkage between employees' performance and commitment (Mathieu & Zajac, 1990). There are, however, studies that strongly underline the positive correlation between the two factors (Mowday, 1998). In spite of the divided opinions, the linkage between other organizational consequences, such as protecting company assets, sharing company's beliefs, goals and values, investing freely in achieving the desired outcomes and even breaking the rules for the greater good of a company, has been illustrated in various studies (Conner & Patterson, 1982; Meyer & Allen, 1991; Senge, 1990).

Organizational commitment has divided researchers also by the approach into two schools of thought: the attitudinal and behavioural commitment (Mowday, 1998). Salancik (1987) defines commitment as a binding of an individual to behavioural acts. Mowday (1998) claims that there is no clear agreement on the nature of commitment, but concepts such as loyalty, attachment and allegiance are often used instead. Meyer and Allen (1991) suggest that commitment takes three different forms: Affective commitment, normative commitment and continuance commitment. Affective commitment refers to an employee's positive emotional attachment with, and involvement within an entity. This entity can be for example an organization, a supervisor, a project or a colleague in the same team. Normative commitment refers to the feelings of obligation to remain connected with an entity and it is also known as moral commitment. Meyer and Allen (1991) emphasize that due to the nature of moral commitment towards an entity it is only a temporary state and lost as soon

as the moral obligation -or the debt - is fulfilled. Continuance commitment refers to the awareness of the total costs derived from leaving an entity or an organization.

While the interest in understanding how change is experienced by an individual in an organization and how organizational commitment affects organizational change is constantly growing, lately also the importance of commitment to change has been emphasized by some studies (Herscovitch & Meyer, 2002; Turner et al., 2008). According to Herscovitch and Meyer (2002) and Turner et al. (2008), commitment to change is even a better predictor of behavioural support for organizational change than is organizational commitment.

Herscovitch and Meyer (2002, p. 476) define commitment to chance as "a force that binds an individual to a course of action deemed necessary for the successful implementation of a change initiative". They split commitment to change in three forms: *1) affective commitment to change, 2) normative commitment to change* and *3) continuance commitment to change.* These forms resemble the original three forms of organizational commitment identified by Meyer and Allen (1997).

The antecedents of commitment to change are somewhat lightly studied if compared with the antecedents of organizational commitment in general. Perhaps one of the most complete studies is conducted by Turner et al. (2008). In their study, Turner et al. combine the strategy and the role related antecedents found by Noble and Mokwa (1999) with employee-manager relationship and job motivation. Turner et al. also present affective commitment, normative commitment and continuance commitment to change in one, unified model, describing the development of the three forms of commitment through one set of antecedents. This approach seems more explicit and diversified than Meyer and Allen's (1997) separation of antecedents by the form of commitment. The antecedents for commitment to change, introduced by Turner et al. (2008), are:

- Fit of the organizational change with strategic vision
- Quality of relationship with manager
- Job motivation and
- Role autonomy.

The fit of the organizational change with strategic vision refers to a study by Noble and Mokwa (1999), who describe this antecedent as the degree to which the currently implemented strategy is seen as congruent with the overall direction of the organization. The quality of the relationship with the manager refers to satisfaction, commitment and trust in the relationship between an employee and a manager. The job motivation refers simply to positive perceptions and attitudes towards one's job and the role autonomy refers to employees' freedom of choice and initiation of their actions. According to Turner et al. (2008), the role autonomy has positive correlation only with the affective commitment to change.

In general, the studies on employees' commitment to change have a snapshot-type approach to commitment. Conner and Patterson (1982) argue that development of commitment to change can be illustrated as a causal model of phases that an organization must go through on the way to higher levels of commitment and in order to succeed in organizational change initiatives.

## PILOT STUDY

This section introduces the case company and the background of the case as well as presents the pilot study, its methods and results. The goal of the pilot study was to identify reasons hindering employees' commitment to change. The results were also utilized in the content validation in the conceptual model of the main study.

## Case Context

XYZ is a medium-sized Finnish information technology services and solutions provider concentrating on the local business-to-business markets. XYZ's business model combines information technology know-how with in-depth industry expertise from various business areas into complex solutions that create business benefits and value for its customers. Around 60% of the revenue comes from traditional IT services and the remaining 40% comes from IT product sales.

XYZ's Business Services Branch (later BSB) plans and executes complex business and application management transformation engagements. Through the wide range of consulting and technology services, BSB helps companies in developing new business models and strategies and in optimizing business performance to deliver higher value. The services offered by the BSB cover the whole life cycle of the change projects of business and data management. BSB conducts change initiatives as projects or outsourced services. At present, the unit employs a couple of hundred IT specialists and consultants.

Few years before the global financial crisis, the board of directors of XYZ decided to launch an internal program to improve the market position and the market share in IT services in Finland. The key objective of the program was to grow the net sales significantly over the next three years.

Two years after the launch, the program was considered a partial success. It exceeded the annual targets assigned for the program in three areas: improving profitability, improving customer satisfaction and improving employee satisfaction. The main objective, growing the net sales significantly, was not met to the planned extent. In 2008, the financial crisis influenced heavily companies' IT investments and it was very seldom that IT companies kept the growth targets at that time.

Consequently, by the end of 2008, the board of directors and the internal business development team decided that new, radical actions had to be taken immediately to re-direct the company back on the desired growth track. An important part of the organizational change program was an implementation project of a new sales and delivery method. The new method was designed to create better value for the customers by increasing the level of internal cooperation between sales and delivery personnel, changing the mindset from sales more towards design and delivery excellence and by revising the internal control processes throughout the life cycle of different projects. The difficult part of implementing and launching the new method was easily identified. The new method required more presales work from both sales and delivery personnel and it was expected to meet at least some resistance among the employees. Success in this change initiative was, however, very important for the company and the change project was planned to the smallest detail to minimize the resistance and to maximize employees' commitment and eventually the results of the change initiative.

## Results of the Pilot Study

The first part of the research process included conducting a pilot study to identify possible factors hindering employees' commitment to change. The empirical data of the pilot study was collected with focused interviews with several employees in different positions of the Business Services Branch. The interviewees were chosen using stratified random sampling and they represented different job roles ranging from sales and solution design to technical delivery areas. Approximately one fourth of the interviewees had managerial responsibilities.

All of the chosen employees were interviewed twice during the pilot study process. The first interviews were conducted during the spring 2009, right before the company-wide training campaign of the new method was launched. The objective of the first interviews was to identify possible reasons for not committing to the upcoming change, based

on the employees' current level of knowledge and understanding about the new method.

The second round of interviews took place two to three months later, after the first training sessions had finished. It was expected that the opinions, perceptions, attitudes and possible resistance to change would be stronger after the interviewees had been trained according to the new method and they had gained more knowledge of how the method would impact their daily duties. Hence, the objective for the second round of interviews was to find out the possible changes in perceptions, opinions and attitudes compared with the ones presented during the first round of interviews.

After the two rounds of interviews, the collected material was analyzed carefully to identify possible themes or patterns between the answers of the interviewees. According to the results of the interviews, there were multiple issues that might have affected the outcome of the change initiative by decreasing the level of employees' commitment to change and by affecting the organizational change process indirectly. These issues were increased stress level and work load, conflicting goals, lack of managers' commitment to change, lack of a clear continuation plan and a plan for sharing responsibilities clearly.

From employees' commitment to change -perspective, the possible factors affecting the level of commitment can be linked to the findings and the antecedents presented by Turner et al. (2008). It appeared that the presence of the continuance commitment to change was rather evident in comparison with the other forms of commitment. Almost one third of the interviewees mentioned monetary compensations and incentives as decisive factors affecting their level of commitment and support to the change initiative.

One of the first issues identified in the interviews was the conflict between employees' personal goals, operational business unit goals and the goals set for the whole change initiative. The personal goals were in line with the operational business unit goals, which, however, were set in a way that they did not support the main target of increasing the level of co-operation between sales and delivery personnel. This was perceived as the biggest reason hindering employees' commitment to change and affecting the change initiative in a harmful way.

Some of the answers were also closely linked to the job motivation. The conflicts between the personal goals and the goals set for the change initiative affected also employees' job motivation as the employees were told to do something else than what they were being measured and evaluated at.

The third antecedent, the quality of employee's relationship with the manager, was brought up through an issue identified during the second round of interviews: approximately half of the interviewees perceived that their supervisors or managers were not sufficiently committed to the change and they mainly acted compliant because of their position.

The conflict between employees' personal goals and the change vision could not be linked with the quality of employee's relationship with the manager, as the interviewees thought that their direct managers were more or less just messengers of the corporation policy and were not personally responsible for the conflicting goals.

The level of employees' commitment to change was not, however, the only area affected by the identified issues. These issues might have had an indirect impact on the change process quality, the goal realization level and eventually on the final success of the change initiative. As employees' commitment to change was affected by these issues, the low level of commitment might have decreased the change process quality and eventually affect reaching the goals set for the change initiative. In this case, this risk was rather significant as the identified issues were perceived very important.

## MAIN STUDY

The objective of the main study was to investigate the relationships between the employees' commitment to change, change process quality, goal realization level and the final success in the whole organizational change initiative.

To measure the correlation values and to analyze the success of the change initiative in the case company, a specific, web-based research tool was developed.

## A Framework for Success in Organizational Change

The theoretical framework used in this study combines the key elements from the studies of employees' commitment to change with the theories and models of organizational change and change management discussed in the earlier sections. The framework consists of four key elements, *the level of commitment, change process quality, realized goals* and *final success* (Figure 1). The framework describes how success in organizational change develops through these elements and how they are connected to each other. These elements and their connections are discussed next in more detail.

The first element, the level of commitment, refers to the employees' commitment to change in the different phases of the change initiative. The level of commitment in this framework covers and combines the three forms of commitment, the affective commitment to change, the normative commitment to change as well as the continuance commitment to change. This combination is supported by the empirical findings of Turner et al. (2008) reporting positive correlation between the three of the commitment types and the change process implementation.

In this framework, the level of commitment is connected to the process quality of each phase of the change process and eventually to the final success measure of the organizational change initiative through the goal realization levels. The

*Figure 1. Theoretical framework for success in organizational change*

| Concept | Commitment to Change | Quality Functions | Quality of Change Process | Realization Functions | Realized Goals | Success Function | Final Success |
|---|---|---|---|---|---|---|---|
| Content | Commitment to phase i | | Quality of phase i | | Realization level of goal i | | Single measure of Success |
| | | | Importance of phase i | | Importance of goal i | | |
| Back-ground | Pilot Study Cuninggs et al 1997 Hersccovitch et al 2002 Mowday 1998 Salancik 1977 | | Pilot Study Kotter 1995 Lewin 1951 Perlman et al 1990 Porras et al 1987 Schein 1996 | | Pilot study | | Pilot study |

framework has an assumption that the level of commitment affects the change process quality so that when the level of commitment is high in phase *i*, the process quality is also high in phase *i*, because the employees support the change activities more. Consequently, as the level of employees' commitment to change is low, the assumption is that it has a negative impact on the process quality.

The second element of the framework is the process quality. This element focuses on the implementation quality of each phase of the change process as well as on the perceived importance of these phases. The phases can be further divided into detailed change activities. Dividing the main phases into smaller activities enables collecting more accurate information about the quality of an individual change activity inside a phase. Comparing the quality and importance of a phase reveals, whether right things are made and whether there is a balance between the importance and the quality in the critical phases and activities.

The third element of the framework is the realized goals. This refers both to the realization level and the importance of the goals set for the change process. Similar to the process quality element, comparing the realization level and the importance of a goal set for the change process reveals whether

there is a balance between the goal importance and its realization level. For example, if a goal is realized fully, but its importance to the final success of the change initiative is very minimal, the change process is imbalanced emphasizing wrong issues and activities.

The last element in the theoretical framework is the final success measure of the organizational change initiative. This single measurement of success is connected to the realization level of the different goals set for the initiative.

## Research Hypotheses and Instrument

The hypotheses and the data collection instrument of this study were based on the theoretical framework illustrated in Figure 1. The framework required, however, to be concretized with the case and the results of the pilot study. In the concretized framework, the number of change process phases was set to three. This was in line with Schein's (1996) interpretation of Lewin's (1951) model for organizational change and also according to the change plan in the case company (Figure 2).

The different phases of the change process and the main activities planned inside them were:

*Figure 2. The change plan*

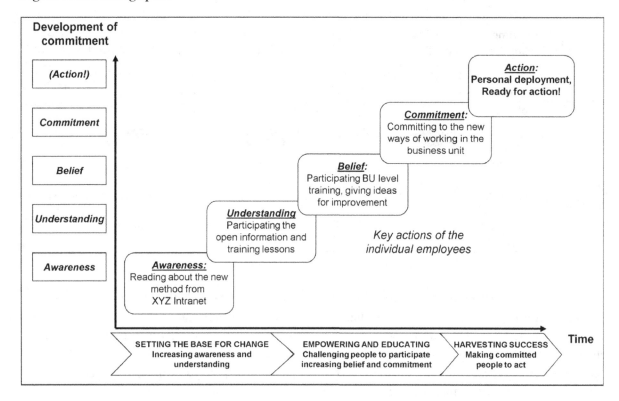

**Phase 1**: Setting the base for change
1. Increasing knowledge and awareness about the upcoming change through e.g. auditorium launch sessions and intranet newsletters.
2. Creating the vision for the change.
3. Communicating the reasons for the change.

**Phase 2**: Empowering and educating
1. Increasing the level of employees' commitment and acceptance through high-level and specialized training sessions.
2. Developing the method further to take the needs of different business units better into consideration.
3. Involving employees to identifying and lowering possible obstacles to change.

**Phase 3**: Expanding and harvesting success

1. Communicating constantly about the method – keeping the heat on.
2. Expanding success by publishing success stories about the method.
3. Encouraging people to start using the method.

There were three main goals for the change initiative in this model according to the change implementation plan within the case company. The goals for the change process were defined as follows:

**Goal 1:** Improving the co-operation between sales, solution design and delivery personnel.
**Goal 2:** Standardizing and simplifying internal sales processes.
**Goal 3:** Increasing the quality of proposals.

*Table 1. Key figures of the phases*

|  | Mean | Std.dev |
|---|---|---|
| **Phase 1** |  |  |
| Quality | 3.020 | 0.742 |
| Commitment | 3.080 | 0.877 |
| Importance | 4.080 | 0.778 |
| **Activities** |  |  |
| Stating the reason | 3.180 | 0.629 |
| Creating vision | 3.100 | 0.614 |
| Communicating credibility | 3.180 | 0.825 |
| **Phase 2** |  |  |
| Quality | 2.400 | 0.670 |
| Commitment | 2.660 | 0.798 |
| Importance | 4.140 | 0.808 |
| **Activities** |  |  |
| Training employees | 2.660 | 0.688 |
| Localizing the method | 2.400 | 0.639 |
| Removing obstacles | 2.320 | 0.819 |
| **Phase 3** |  |  |
| Quality | 2.380 | 0.697 |
| Commitment | 2.460 | 0.862 |
| Importance | 3.960 | 0.638 |
| **Activities** |  |  |
| Communicating continuously | 2.540 | 0.762 |
| Using managers as good examples | 2.300 | 0.814 |
| Encouraging change | 2.340 | 0.823 |

The single measurement of success stayed unchanged from the original framework.

Hypotheses:
H1: Higher commitment to change leads to better change process quality.
H2: Higher change process quality leads to a higher level of goal realization.
H3: Higher realization level of goals leads to a higher level of final success.

The actual research instrument was designed with a commercial web survey tool. The sample in the main study included 88 employees, who were chosen using the stratified random sampling method. Consequently, the survey was sent to 23 business consultants, 20 solution architects and specialists and the remaining 45 for IT specialists focusing on application and data management. The questionnaire had 25 main questions and a couple of background questions to verify for example the unit, position and service years.

## Results

The collected quantitative data was analyzed thoroughly using different statistical analysis methods including linear regression analysis. The key figures from the three phases are presented in Table 1. The results indicate that the perceived average quality of the first phase was 3,02 (on a scale from 1-5) whereas the quality of the other phases was significantly lower. Equally, the level of commitment to change was 3,08 during the first phase but significantly lower at the other phases of the change process. Generally, all phases were perceived important or very important.

The most important goal according to the perceptions of the respondents was improving the level of co-operation between sales and solution delivery personnel (Goal 1). This was also the main direct goal of the change initiative according to the change implementation plan. This goal was given an importance value of 4,56 out of five, which indicates that the respondents found this goal extremely important. The realization level of this goal was given a value of 2,30, which indicates that the change initiative did not succeed in increasing the level of co-operation significantly.

The second most important goal according to the perceptions of the respondents was simplifying and standardizing internal sales processes (Goal 2). This goal was given an importance value of 4,36, which is only slightly lower than the importance of the main goal indicating that the respondents considered that simplifying and standardizing internal processes was very important. The perceived realization level of this goal remained low at 2,32 indicating that the change initiative did not succeed in standardizing and simplifying the internal processes significantly.

The least important goal according to the results was improving the quality of business proposals. In spite of using the word "least", this goal was given an importance value of 4,3 on average, which indicates that the respondents found this goal very important as well. The realization level was slightly higher in comparison with the other goals with the value of 2,5. The value indicates, however, that the change initiative did not succeed in improving the quality of business proposals in

the BSB to the planned extent. The change initiative in XYZ was given a final success measure of 2,38 on average.

Next, the linear regression analysis was used in estimating the quality, realization and success functions.

## Quality Functions

The first regression analyses were related to the hypothesis H1. In this analysis, the level of commitment to change was the independent variable and the level of process quality was the dependent variable. The quality functions are:

$$Q_1 = 1.310 + 0.555 * C_1 \ (R^2 = 0.431)$$

$$Q_2 = 1.139 + 0.474 * C_2 \ (R^2 = 0.319)$$

$$Q_3 = 1.147 + 0.501 * C_3 \ (R^2 = 0.385)$$

where,

$Q_i$ = Quality of phase i, i = 1,2,3

$C_i$ = Commitment to phase i, i = 1,2,3

These results indicate that if the level of commitment increases in a phase, the process quality in the corresponding phase increases as well. This was also assumed in H1.

## Realization Functions

The second set of regression analyses were related to hypothesis H2. The results from the multivariate regression analysis are shown in the following three equations.

$$G_1 = -0.628 + 0.542*Q_3 + 0.435*Q_2 + 0.197*Q_1$$
$$(R^2 = 0.449)$$

$$(P = 0.283 \ 0.001 \ 0.008 \ 0.137)$$

$G_2 = 0.699+0.574*Q_3+0.263*Q_2-0.124*Q_1$ ($R^2 = 0.469$)

(P = 0.158 0.000 0.053 0.261)

$G_3 = 0.304+0.479*Q_3+0.199*Q_1+0.190*Q_2$ ($R^2 = 0.279$)

(P = 0.629 0.005 0.162 0.270)

where,

$G_j$ = Realization level of goal j, j = 1,2,3

$Q_i$ = Quality of phase i, i = 1,2,3

For the first realization function, the results of the multivariate regression analysis indicate that $Q_3$ was the most significant variable explaining almost 35% of the changes in the $G_1$. For the second function, the results indicate that almost 47% of the changes in goal realization level can be explained by the changes in the explanatory variables. The stepwise regression reveals that $Q_3$ was the most significant variable again explaining almost 40% of the changes in the $G_2$ whereas adding the variable $Q_2$ to the function increased the squared coefficient of multiple correlation by 5%. Adding $Q_1$ increased the $R^2$ only by 1,5% indicating that it had, once again, least impact on the realization level of Goal 2. For the third realization function the results of the multivariate regression analysis indicate that almost 28% of the changes in goal realization level can be explained by the changes in the explanatory variables. The stepwise regression reveals that $Q_3$ was again the most significant variable explaining almost 24% of the changes in the $G_3$ whereas adding the variables $Q_1$ and $Q_2$ to the function increased the squared coefficient of multiple correlation by only 4%.

Generally, the results indicate that there is a partially strong relationship between the change process quality and the goal realization level.

## Success Function

The final regression analysis was related to the hypothesis H3. In this analysis, the realization levels of different goals were independent factors and the final success measure was the dependent factor.

$S = 0.731+0.332*G_1+0.178*G_3+0.190*G_2$ ($R^2 = 0.580$)

(P = 0.004 0.006 0.036 0.149)

where,

S = Final success measure
$G_j$ = Realization level of goal j, j=1,2,3

The results from the multivariate regression analysis indicate that the squared coefficient of multiple correlation was very high indicating that 58% of the changes in the final success measure can be explained by the changes in the explanatory variables. The stepwise regression indicates that $G_1$ was the most significant variable explaining almost 52% of the changes in the S whereas adding the variable $G_3$ to the function increased the squared coefficient of multiple correlation by slightly less than 4,5%. Adding $G_2$ increased the $R^2$ only by 2% indicating that it had least impact on the realization level of S.

Unfortunately, the good quality values given to the first phase cannot be seen in the final success measure. It seems that the good beginning for the change faded away after the first phase was over. This is supported by the decreasing trend of employees' commitment to change and the findings of Conner and Patterson (1982) claiming that a change initiative can fail on any stage of the development of individual commitment to change, regardless of earlier success.

It seems that the significant part of the decrease in the level of employees' commitment to change and the change process quality took place between the first and the second phase. This was the same place, where the actual, concrete steps of change were supposed to be taken and the main responsibility of the change initiative was given to the business units. Perhaps some radical actions could still have turned the change initiative into success. Within the Business Service Branch, however, the decline in the level of commitment and in the change process quality continued throughout the change process resulting in a low final success measure.

## DISCUSSION AND CONCLUSION

The main objective of this study was to investigate how employees' commitment to change and the implementation quality of different change process phases affect achieving the goals and succeeding in an organizational change initiative and, consequently, to provide empirical support for the very few studies focusing on employees' commitment to change and organizational change. The secondary objective of this study was to identify factors hindering employees' commitment to change.

The interviews in the pilot study revealed that the employees in the case company had mostly negative perceptions and opinions about the upcoming change initiative and low expectations about the success of the implementation of the new method. Consequently, the level of commitment to change was hindered by multiple factors. First of all, one of the main issues hindering employees' commitment to change was a perceived conflict between the goals of the change initiative and the current operational objectives of the business unit and the personal goals set for the employees. Another important identified issue was the high workload and stress level. This hindered employees' commitment to change significantly, as the employees perceived that they had no time to participate in the activities supporting the change. The third critical identified factor was

the perception of the low level of commitment on the managerial level.

All the identified issues had high potential to cause serious harm for the final success of the change initiative. While the issues mainly affected the level of employees' commitment to change, they could have also affected the change process quality and the realization level of different goals set for the change initiative indirectly.

The results of the main study indicated that there was a strong, positive relationship between the change process quality and the level of employees' commitment to change. While the higher level of commitment to change led to higher change process quality, it could not be verified that it directly affected the success level of the whole change initiative. Instead, the results indicated that employees' commitment to a less relevant change process phase hardly had any correlation with the final success measure.

The results concerning the realization level of different goals indicated that there was a partially strong and positive relationship between the change process quality and the realization level of different goals. The results illustrated high correlation between the process quality in the second and the third change process phase and the realization level of different goals.

There could have been many different reasons behind these results. First of all, even though the first phase, creating a vision and defining the reasons to change was emphasized in the majority of the organizational change management literature presented in this study (Cummings & Worley, 1997; Schein, 1996), these actions might have been relevant only in order to advance to the next phase of the change initiative. However, in this study, the more concrete phases of change had significantly higher coefficients of determination perhaps, because the actual change was being made within those phases.

Another reason might be that during the first phase the employees were only required to commit to the change on the abstract level. On the second phase, however, the commitment to change became more concrete and the employees were expected to start working together to reach the shared goal of improved co-operation and the new, modified sales processes.

Finally, the results of the study indicated that there was a strong relationship between the goal realization level and the final success measure. Improving the co-operation between the sales, solution design and delivery personnel was perceived very important among the employees, whereas the other two goals were perceived less important. The high coefficient of determination of the first goal indicated that this was also perceived as the main goal of the change initiative.

Unfortunately, the realization levels of different goals and the final success measure remained at a low level. In spite of a good beginning, as the change process continued, the level of employees' commitment, change process quality as well as the goal realization levels decreased. One of the reasons for this could be related to the change of responsibility from the business development team to the business units after the first phase.

This case study underlined also the importance of committed management in organizational change initiatives. While this study concentrated mainly on the commitment to change on the regular employees' level excluding the top management, a corresponding study investigating the relationship between top management's commitment to change and succeeding in organizational change initiatives would be very interesting.

## REFERENCES

Bashir, S., & Ramay, M. I. (2008). Determinants of Organizational Commitment: A Study of Information Technology Professionals in Pakistan. *Journal of Behavioral and Applied Management*, *9*(1), 226–238.

Baumgartner, F., & Jones, B. (1993). *Agendas and Instability in American Politics*. Chicago, IL: The University of Chicago Press.

Beckhard, R. (1969). *Organization Development: Strategies and Models*. Reading, MA: Addison-Wesley.

Bennis, W. (1966). *Changing organizations*. New York, NY: McGraw-Hill.

Conner, D., & Patterson, R. (1982). Building Commitment to Organizational Change. *Training and Development Journal*, *36*(4), 18–30.

Cummings, T. G., & Worley, C. G. (1997). *Organization Development & Change*. Cincinnati, OH: South-Western College Publishing.

Daft, R. L. (1998). *Organization theory and design*. Cincinnati, OH: South-Western College Publishing.

Fedor, D. B., Caldwell, S., & Herold, D. M. (2006). The effects of organizational changes on employee commitment: A multilevel investigation. *Personnel Psychology*, *59*(1), 1–29. doi:10.1111/j.1744-6570.2006.00852.x

Gersick, C. (1991). Revolutionary Change Theories: A Multilevel Exploration of the Punctuated Equilibrium Paradigm. *Academy of Management Review*, *16*(1), 10–36.

Gould, S., & Eldredge, N. (1977). Punctuated equilibria: the tempo and mode of evolution reconsidered. *Paleobiology*, *3*(2), 115–151.

Herscovitch, L., & Meyer, J. (2002). Commitment to organizational change: extension of a three-component model. *The Journal of Applied Psychology*, *87*(3), 474–487. doi:10.1037/0021-9010.87.3.474

International Business Machines Corporation. (2008). *IBM Global CEO Study 2008*. Retrieved June 15, 2009, from http://www.ibm.com/ibm/ideasfromibm/us/ceo/20080505/

Iverson, R. D. (1996). Employee acceptance of organizational change: the role of organizational commitment. *International Journal of Human Resource Management, 7*(1), 122–149. doi:10.1080/09585199600000121

Kotter, J. (1995). Leading Change: Why Transformation Efforts Fail. *Harvard Business Review, 73*(2), 59–67.

Kübler-Ross, E. (1969). *On Death and Dying*. New York, NY: Touchstone.

Lewin, K. (1946). Research on Minority Problems. *Technology Review, 48*(3), 163–190.

Lewin, K. (1951). *Field theory in social science: Selected theoretical papers*. New York, NY: Harper and Row.

Mathieu, J., & Zajac, D. (1990). A review and meta-analysis of the antecedents, correlates, and consequences of organizational commitment. *Psychological Bulletin, 108*(2), 171–194. doi:10.1037/0033-2909.108.2.171

McNamara, C. (2006). *Field Guide to Consulting and Organizational Development*. Minneapolis, MN: Authenticity Consulting LLC.

Meyer, J., & Allen, N. (1991). A three-component conceptualization of organizational commitment. *Human Resource Management Review, 1*(1), 61–89. doi:10.1016/1053-4822(91)90011-Z

Meyer, J., & Allen, N. (1997). *Commitment in the Workplace: Theory, Research, and Application*. Thousand Oaks, CA: Sage.

Mowday, R. (1998). Reflections on the study and relevance of organizational commitment. *Human Resource Management Review, 8*(4), 387–401. doi:10.1016/S1053-4822(99)00006-6

Noble, C., & Mokwa, M. (1999). Implementing marketing strategies: developing and testing a managerial theory. *Journal of Marketing, 63*(4), 57–73. doi:10.2307/1251974

Perlman, D., & Takacs, G. (1990). The ten stages of change. *Nursing Management, 21*(4), 33–38. doi:10.1097/00006247-199004000-00010

Poole, M., & Van de Ven, A. (2004). *Handbook of Organizational Change and Innovation*. New York, NY: Oxford University Press.

Porras, J., & Robertson, P. (1987). Organizational development theory: A typology and evaluation. In Woodman, R. W., & Pasmore, W. A. (Eds.), *Research in Organizational Change and Development* (*Vol. 1*, pp. 1–57). Greenwich, CT: JAI Press.

Salancik, G. (1977). Commitment and the control of organizational behavior and belief. In Staw, B., & Salancik, G. (Eds.), *New directions in organizational Behavior* (pp. 1–53). Chicago, IL: St. Clair Press.

Schein, E. (1996). Kurt Lewin's change theory in the field and in the classroom: Notes toward a model of managed learning. *Systems Practice, 9*(1), 27–47. doi:10.1007/BF02173417

Senge, P. (1990). *The Fifth Discipline*. Kent, UK: Century Business.

Struckman, C., & Yammarino, F. (2003). Organizational change: A categorization scheme and response model with readiness factors. *Research in Organizational Change and Development, 14*(1), 1–50. doi:10.1016/S0897-3016(03)14079-7

Turner Parish, J., Cadwallader, S., & Busch, P. (2008). Want to, need to, ought to: employee commitment to organizational change. *Journal of Organizational Change Management, 21*(1), 32–52. doi:10.1108/09534810810847020

Wagner, J. III, & Hollenbeck, J. (1998). *Organizational behavior: Securing competitive advantage* (3rd ed.). Upper Saddle River, NJ: Prentice Hall.

*This work was previously published in the International Journal of Social and Organizational Dynamics in IT, Volume 1, Issue 4, edited by Michael B. Knight, pp. 1-17, 2011 by IGI Publishing (an imprint of IGI Global).*

# Chapter 6
# Understanding Collaboration Success in Context of Cognitive and Social Presence

**Amit V. Deokar**
*Dakota State University, USA*

**Thomas O. Meservy**
*University of Memphis, USA*

**Joel Helquist**
*Utah Valley University, USA*

**John Kruse**
*MITRE Corporation, USA*

## ABSTRACT

*Collaboration and the success of collaborative efforts has been the focus of much information systems research. Recent measures of collaboration success include effectiveness, efficiency, productivity, commitment, satisfaction with the process, and satisfaction with the outcome. While the possible antecedents of collaboration success are varied, this paper suggests that constructs from the e-learning literature that evolved independently from the information systems collaboration literature can be used to explain differences in perceived collaboration success. Results from a recent exploratory study demonstrate that cognitive presence and social presence explain a large amount of the variance of different collaboration success metrics.*

## 1. INTRODUCTION

The emergence of new technologies and a convergence on the Internet as a productivity tool has given birth to a grass-roots collaboration effort that has spread into many organizations. This

DOI: 10.4018/978-1-4666-1948-7.ch006

form of collaboration looks very different from the collaboration efforts of the past. Previously, much of the information systems collaboration literature had focused on groupware facilitated, synchronous, face-to-face (FTF) environments (Fjermestad, 1998), with success often based on satisfaction with the collaborative process or the outcome of the collaborative effort (Reinig, 2003).

While collaboration as a research topic continues to enjoy significant coverage in the information systems literature (Sidorova, Evangelopoulos, Valacich, & Ramakrishnan, 2008), this specific form of collaboration has never broken out of its niche positioning to achieve widespread implementation in the day-to-day activities of many organizations (Briggs, de Vreede, & Nunamaker, 2003).

Instead, today's emerging collaborative systems often lack explicit process structure needed to create collaborative artifacts or reach collaborative solutions, or simply address a very narrow aspect of the collaborative endeavor. Several technologies (such as discussion groups, forums, instant messaging, and wikis (CyberSmart, 2009)) have emerged and have been adopted at organizations in order to share a wide variety of information between individuals and groups. While many tend to lump all collaboration technologies into a single grouping, more accurately these tools can be seen as lying on a continuum of complexity in terms of the collaboration supported (Denning & Yaholkovsky, 2008). Where the aforementioned groupware tools are designed to support complicated products and processes, these new tools tend to support unstructured use and generally excel in more simple information sharing tasks.

Indeed, most of the collaborative technologies that are being widely adopted are not structured in a way to support highly complex group collaboration. Thus, lessons from the information systems collaboration literature do not necessarily directly translate to these new technologies. However, insights may be drawn from other disciplines that are either related to collaboration or provide support for it. Two examples of these supporting disciplines are human communication and education. In education, for example, e-learning literature investigates how participants use analogous technologies to support distributed, asynchronous learning with minimal input from a facilitator/moderator (i.e., the instructor).

This paper outlines the investigation of constructs adapted from the e-learning literature with respect to collaboration. Specifically, we look at cognitive presence and social presence and their ability to explain a large amount of the variance in measures of collaborative success. Cognitive and social presence may provide an additional avenue for examining the success of collaborative efforts and tools. To achieve these ends, a collaborative system for e-learning was developed and deployed in an exploratory study in order to assess the system's impact on collaboration and e-learning success.

The paper is organized as follows. Section 2 discusses the related work from the collaboration literature as well as the e-learning literature. Section 3 presents the integrated collaboration research model. Section 4 discusses the methodology followed in conducting an exploratory study to test the integrated model; followed by results and discussion in Section 5. Section 6 concludes by summarizing the contributions of the paper, some limitations and prospects for future work.

## 2. RELATED WORK

### 2.1. Collaboration Success

Collaboration success factors have been extensively studied in the information systems collaboration literature. We propose that success factors are much richer than just satisfaction with the collaborative effort or satisfaction with whomever is facilitating the discussion. Success of a collaborative effort may be assessed from multiple dimensions. Duivenvoorde, Kolfschoten, Briggs, and de Vreede (2009) recently reported a meta-analysis of collaboration outcomes described in several research studies to propose the following key dimensions for measuring successful collaboration from a participant perspective: group effectiveness, group efficiency, group productivity, commitment of resources, and satisfaction with process and outcome.

Though these measures are still based on user perception, they attempt to quantify collaboration success in a more fine-grained and objective fashion. Effectiveness and efficiency are typical dimensions measured to assess a given process. In this case they are extended to the group in order to better align with the goals of collaboration. Group productivity, in this context, is closely related to effectiveness in that it is a measure of the balance between resources expended and the results achieved. The commitment of resources is intended to gauge the investment that the participants make to the collaborative effort. Finally, participant satisfaction is used, as with more traditional groupware studies, to evaluate the participants' emotional estimation of the value of the collaboration.

## 2.2. Antecedents of Collaboration Success

There are, of course, a number of factors that precede collaboration success. Considerable research has been conducted to examine the antecedents of success in both laboratory and field work studies. Substantial work has been performed to consolidate this research into one framework (Fjermestad, 1998; Fjermestad & Hiltz, 1999, 2001). This four-factor framework categorizes the antecedents of collaborative success into four areas: contextual factors, intervening factors, adaptation factors, and outcome factors. This framework provides a mechanism for categorizing and summarizing research on collaboration characteristics and success.

Contextual factors include elements such as the environment within which the collaborative effort is performed. For example, the mode of interaction, group size, and whether a facilitator is present are contextual factors.

As the collaborative engagement proceeds, additional factors influence the interaction (e.g., session length, order of activities, number of collaborative sessions). These intervening factors lead to adaptation of the collaborative process. Adaptation includes such things as procedures, norms, and resources the group develops during execution of the collaborative tasks.

Lastly, the outcome factors are the resultant goals or outputs from the collaborative process. Many collaboration success metrics attempt to assess these outcome factors.

Within these four factors, Fjermestad and Hiltz (2001) found several characteristics of successful and unsuccessful group support systems (GSS) implementations. The antecedents of successful collaborative work include the use of a facilitator (contextual factor), specific training on the collaborative technology (intervening), and high levels of trust among the group (outcome factor). These characteristics of the collaborative effort were found to correlate with collaboration success and come from different factors in the four factors model.

## 2.3. Distributed, Collaborative Learning

With distance and online learning environments becoming an integral part of educational systems, the use of information technologies in general, and collaboration technologies in particular has received significant attention from educators and tool developers (Hanover Research Council, 2009; Hiltz & Turoff, 2005). Research in the field of education has focused on distributed, computer-mediated communication (CMC)-based education. We posit that many similarities exist between CMC learning and collaborative efforts. For example, collaborative learning tools aid the participants in creating knowledge by enabling interaction and discourse with peers and instructors (Weasenforth, Biesenbach-Lucas, & Meloni, 2002). In this manner, "[l]earning will be seen as more socially shared, active, and interactive than in the past" (Bonk & Wisher, 2000). The online learning is executed by way of collaborative functions and features of the CMC technology.

*Figure 1. Community of Inquiry Model (adapted from Garrison, Anderson, & Archer, 1999)*

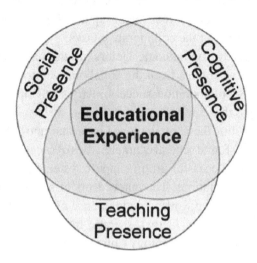

Garrison, Anderson, and Archer (1999) have proposed the community of inquiry model (Figure 1) as a way to characterize and investigate the online educational experience. This model posits that there are three requisite components of an educational experience that are shared by the students and the instructor: social, cognitive, and teaching presence. It is the interaction of these three elements that creates an effective learning environment (Garrison et al., 1999; Gilroy, 2001). We posit that these three presences are not only components of online learning environments but also of collaborative efforts.

Cognitive presence is arguably the most important of the three as it is the most fundamental to educational and collaborative success. Garrison et al. (1999) define this term as the participants being able "to construct meaning through sustained communication." Cognitive presence refers to the inquiry and dialogue that accompany the interactive learning and sharing processes. In a learning community, participants are able to ask questions, provide insights, and resolve unknown or unclear concepts as part of the learning process. Similar interaction is found in collaborative environments, where participants exchange and refine information critical to the task at hand. Indicators of cognitive presence include such things as identifying key issues, synthesizing ideas, resolving problems, and so forth.

Social presence refers to the participants projecting themselves socially and affectively in the community. Social presence provides the participants the ability to present themselves as unique individuals, enhancing the interpersonal dimensions of collaboration. This dimension provides support for the cognitive presences by enabling group cohesion. Social presence impacts the motivation of the participants to be actively involved in the collaborative processes. Indicators of social presence include such things as asking questions and sustaining discussion.

The last element in the community of inquiry model is teaching presence. This presence encompasses two main objectives. First, the subject matter and content to be discussed must be selected. Second, the discussion must be facilitated. Like social presence, teaching presence is a supportive mechanism that facilitates the cognitive processes involved with learning (Garrison et al., 1999). Our research model focuses on cognitive and social presence as antecedents of collaboration success. In certain situations, the process structure afforded by the collaborative feature set largely achieves the same goals as the facilitators' tailoring of the collaborative processes. Here we do not include teaching presence as a construct in our overall model because the subject matter and content for the experiment was selected by the researchers and no instructor was involved in facilitating the discussion between the participants. However, future research could examine the impact of teaching presence on collaboration success.

## 3. INTEGRATED COLLABORATION RESEARCH MODEL

In education research, the presences in the community of inquiry model constitute areas of focus that determine the success of an educational

*Figure 2. Integrated Collaboration E-learning Model*

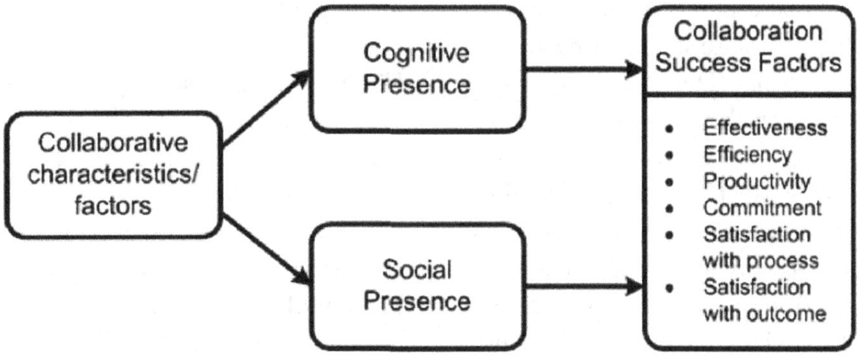

transaction. We posit that the cognitive and social presences also determine the success of other collaborative efforts. To examine the relationship between the presences and collaborative success, we propose a model that bridges the e-learning literature and the information systems collaboration literature.

A premise of past research is that certain collaborative characteristics or factors, if correctly appropriated, will lead to collaborative success. As previously outlined, the cognitive presence and social presence constructs encapsulate the critical components of an online, distributed environment. We posit that these constructs mediate the relationship between collaborative characteristics and success factors (Figure 2).

In this research paper, one premise is that the collaborative characteristics or factors impact cognitive presence. For example, Meservy, Helquist, Deokar, and Kruse (2009) argued that specific characteristics of the collaborative tool, such as the ability to rate, tag, and filter discourse of other participants, impacts perceptions of cognitive presence. Users are actively involved in evaluating concepts, enhancing the cognitive presence by focusing participants' attention on specific content.

Premise 1: Collaborative factors impact cognitive presence.

Another premise is that the choice of collaborative factors impacts social presence by either supporting or hindering discourse and interaction with collaborative peers. For example, certain collaborative tools enable participants to more easily evaluate, tag, filter, and identify relevant discourse and highlight comments and concepts that are valued by the collaborative group. This enhancement in supporting discourse is assumed to lead to an increased sense of community and ultimately improved ratings of social presence.

Premise 2: Collaborative factors impact social presence.

## 4. RESEARCH HYPOTHESES

This paper examines the relationship between social and cognitive presence with collaborative success factors. Duivenvoorde et al. (2009) synthesized several collaboration research studies and proposed the following key dimensions for measuring successful collaboration from a participant perspective: effectiveness, efficiency, productivity, commitment, satisfaction with process and outcome. We posit that these success factors are influenced by cognitive and social presence.

Group effectiveness is the extent to which the resultant collaborative outcome meets the intended goal or outcome. Participants' expectations and the value attributed to collaborative effort are likely to drive their perceptions of effectiveness. It is useful to thus measure intended results as well as expected results (Duivenvoorde et al., 2009). It is hypothesized that individuals who are cognitively involved in the collaborative task by identifying and synthesizing issues and resolving problems will perceive that the group's efforts were successful. Additionally, an individual who indicates high social presence by asking questions and sustaining discussions will be likely perceive the collaborative efforts as successful.

H1a: Cognitive presence positively impacts group effectiveness.
H1b: Social presence positively impacts group effectiveness.

Group efficiency, from a participant's perspective, is the extent to which the resultant net usage of resources meets the expected expense of resources. Resources could be in any form such as time, effort, attention, knowledge, and even physical resources such as money or infrastructure facilities (Duivenvoorde et al., 2009). Individuals indicating high cognitive and social presence are also expected to display high levels of perceived group efficiency.

H2a: Cognitive presence positively impacts group efficiency.
H2b: Social presence positively impacts group efficiency.

Group productivity measures participants' perceptions of the extent to which the expense of resources are commensurate with the quality of results derived from the effort. This balance between time and effort expended and the quality of results is an important success factor, distinct from group efficiency and effectiveness (Duivenvoorde et al., 2009). Similar to group effectiveness and group efficiency, social and cognitive presence are

hypothesized to positively impact the perceived group productivity.

H3a: Cognitive presence positively impacts group productivity.
H3b: Social presence positively impacts group productivity.

Commitment of resources to the group goal is the willingness of the participants to expend resources such as time and effort to achieve group goal (Meyer & Herscovitch, 2001). It also considers the motivation to participate as well as the extent to which participants have a stake in the collaborative goal and their perceived importance of the collaborative effort (Duivenvoorde et al., 2009). Those individuals who expend time and energy to be cognitively involved by identifying key issues, synthesizing ideas, and resolving problems would be expected to display a higher level of commitment than those who do not. Additionally, social aspects of collaborative systems, such as the ability to interact with others and receive feedback from other group members, are expected to impact the commitment toward the group goal.

H4a: Cognitive presence positively impacts commitment.
H4b: Social presence positively impacts commitment.

Participant satisfaction can be measured with respect to the collaborative process as well as the outcome of the process (Duivenvoorde et al., 2009). Emotional satisfaction is implied here, which is a manifestation of a response resulting from a perceived shift in yield with regards to personal goals (Briggs, Reinig, & de Vreede, 2008). A related notion is that of judgmental satisfaction which results from a individual cost-benefit analysis of expending resources with respect to the results and is measured through perceptions of group productivity, effectiveness, and efficiency (Duivenvoorde et al., 2009). An interesting finding reported is that participants reporting higher values of satisfaction with the collaborative outcome have a tendency to report higher values of satisfaction with the process (Reinig, 2003). It is hypothesized that higher levels of cognitive presence and social presence impact both the satisfaction with the collaborative process as well as the satisfaction with the outcome of the collaborative effort.

H5a: Cognitive presence positively impacts satisfaction with the process.

H5b: Social presence positively impacts satisfaction with the process.

H6a: Cognitive presence positively impacts satisfaction with the outcome.

H6b: Social presence positively impacts satisfaction with the outcome.

## 5. METHODOLOGY

In order to test our research model, we conducted an online collaborative activity wherein participants read an article and then engaged in a discussion surrounding specific aspects of the article. Subsequently, participants were administered a survey to assess cognitive and social presence experienced during the collaborative activity as well as collaboration success metrics. Partial least squares (PLS) were then used to assess the measurement model and also the structural model for our research hypotheses.

Participants were drawn from Information Systems courses at two U.S. universities, one in the mid-south and another in the mid-west. Motivation was provided through two different mechanisms: 1) extra credit from the instructor of the class, and/or 2) a drawing to receive one of twenty gift certificates (ranging from $10-$25 in value) for local area restaurants. Chances for the drawings were awarded proportionally based on the amount of participation throughout the collaborative activity which lasted several days. Prospective participants were contacted via email

with details of the study, benefits and risks. Ultimately, sixty-six students initiated the task and thirty-five participants completed the study and the final survey.

For the collaborative activity, participants logged into an artifact-based collaborative system (Meservy et al., 2009) and were assigned to read, discuss and evaluate an article about computer security. This collaborative system was designed to be used to improve distributed, asynchronous collaborative learning by improving the sharing of ideas and comments related to a specific artifact (i.e., article or topic). Major portions of the system were divided into separate web pages which were arranged as "tabs" at the top of the page. In this way, users could easily switch between understanding what they were asked to do (instructions), viewing the article, carrying on an interactive discussion, and viewing how others perceived their contributions (rankings). Figure 3 shows a screen shot showing the discussion view. For more information about the system see (Meservy et al., 2009).

Participants were informed that the goal of the exercise was to develop a deeper understanding about some of the risks of security, costs of preventative actions, and the impact of security breaches. They were also provided with training on how to post and evaluate messages. This topic was selected as it was relevant to the coursework of the student but was also of general interest. The level of task difficulty was intended to foster collaborative learning while being able to be completed in the designated time. Participants were urged to participate in online discussions with other subjects. The discussion was seeded with specific questions intended to encourage collaborative discourse and active learning.

Users were asked to logon to the system once per day for one week to contribute to the discussion. They were given the expectation that the task should take one hour of cumulative effort. Upon completion of the task, the users were directed to complete a survey that sought to assess cognitive

*Figure 3. An annotated snapshot of the main discussion page (Meservy et al., 2009)*

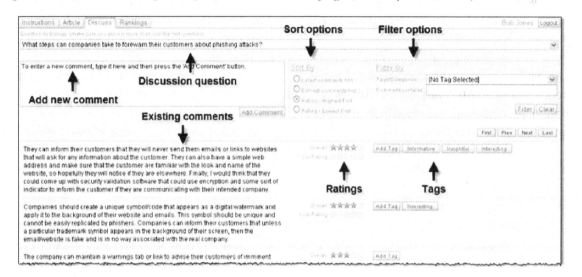

and social presences and also evaluate satisfaction with process and outcome, efficiency, effectiveness, commitment and productivity. The survey utilized questions from two previously validated survey instruments (Duivenvoorde et al., 2009; Garrison, Cleveland-Innes, & Fung, 2004), which were adapted for the distributed, asynchronous context of this study. The adapted survey instrument is provided in the Appendix.

## 6. RESULTS AND DISCUSSION

Partial least squares (PLS) was the data analysis technique used for his study. Given that PLS is better suited for exploratory studies where the theory is under development, and can work for small sample sizes with minimal distributional assumptions (Chin, 1998b), it was considered the analysis technique of choice for this study. SmartPLS (Ringle, Wende, & Will, 2005) was used as the software for conducting PLS analysis.

Throughout the analysis, we followed the recommendations of Straub (1989) and Straub, Boudreau, and Gefen (2004) particularly as they apply to validity.

The questionnaire items were drawn from prior literature in the fields of e-learning and col-

laboration, thus attesting to the content validity of the instrument. Particularly, the instrument items related to the constructs of cognitive presence and social presence have been discussed by Garrison et al. (2004), while those capturing collaboration success have been discussed by Duivenvoorde et al. (2009). The arguments presented therein attest to the representativeness of the measures of these constructs.

Next, construct validity, which relates to the operationalization or measurement between constructs, was considered. Factorial validity, which focuses on establishing the validity of latent constructs, is important in the context of PLS (Gefen & Straub, 2005). Establishing factorial validity implies testing that each indicator variable correlates strongly with a single construct, while correlating weakly or not correlating with other constructs. In PLS, it is assumed that each measurement item reflects only a single latent construct (Gefen, 2003). As such, unidimensionality is assumed to exist a priori. Two other components of factorial validity that capture certain aspects of the goodness of fit of the measurement model are convergent validity and discriminant validity (Gefen & Straub, 2005). Table 1 indicates the outer model loadings, along with the t-values. The t-values were estimated using a nonparametric

*Table 1. Significance test of measurement item loadings*

| Item Code | Item Loading | t-statistic |
|---|---|---|
| Cognitive-1 | 0.888 | 37.529 |
| Cognitive-2 | 0.767 | 18.150 |
| Cognitive-3 | 0.830 | 24.426 |
| Cognitive-4 | 0.880 | 42.825 |
| Cognitive-5 | 0.914 | 58.788 |
| Cognitive-6 | 0.909 | 39.972 |
| Cognitive-7 | 0.830 | 19.420 |
| Cognitive-8 | 0.919 | 48.553 |
| Social-1 | 0.814 | 22.594 |
| Social-2 | 0.857 | 32.443 |
| Social-3 | 0.812 | 18.987 |
| Social-4 | 0.835 | 26.380 |
| Social-6 | 0.853 | 28.154 |
| Effectiveness-1 | 0.928 | 71.321 |
| Effectiveness-2 | 0.903 | 45.536 |
| Effectiveness-3 | 0.885 | 26.926 |
| Effectiveness-4 | 0.907 | 41.366 |
| Effectiveness-5 | 0.862 | 24.875 |
| Efficiency-1 | 0.818 | 26.045 |
| Efficiency-2 | 0.863 | 23.188 |
| Efficiency-3 | 0.934 | 67.085 |
| Efficiency-4 | 0.782 | 16.211 |
| Efficiency-5 | 0.907 | 41.031 |
| Productivity-1 | 0.757 | 12.872 |
| Productivity-2 | 0.784 | 17.159 |
| Productivity-3 | 0.946 | 87.944 |
| Productivity-5 | 0.944 | 108.027 |
| Commitment-1 | 0.803 | 20.301 |
| Commitment-2 | 0.812 | 30.529 |
| Commitment-3 | 0.878 | 36.275 |
| Commitment-4 | 0.735 | 10.724 |
| Commitment-5 | 0.913 | 58.551 |
| Sat-Act-1 | 0.959 | 10.234 |
| Sat-Act-2 | 0.899 | 9.033 |
| Sat-Act-4 | 0.959 | 10.032 |
| Sat-Act-5 | 0.923 | 8.072 |
| Sat-Out-1 | 0.908 | 36.762 |
| Sat-Out-2 | 0.957 | 74.932 |
| Sat-Out-3 | 0.930 | 59.568 |

*Table 2. Square root of AVE scores and correlation of latent variables*

|  | [1] | [2] | [3] | [4] | [5] | [6] | [7] | [8] |
|---|---|---|---|---|---|---|---|---|
| [1] Cognitive | **0.869** | | | | | | | |
| [2] Social | 0.705 | **0.835** | | | | | | |
| [3] Effectiveness | 0.688 | 0.588 | **0.897** | | | | | |
| [4] Efficiency | 0.527 | 0.599 | 0.724 | **0.863** | | | | |
| [5] Productivity | 0.613 | 0.594 | 0.841 | 0.898 | **0.862** | | | |
| [6] Commitment | 0.568 | 0.711 | 0.509 | 0.736 | 0.743 | **0.830** | | |
| [7] Sat-Act | 0.245 | 0.319 | 0.387 | 0.297 | 0.390 | 0.240 | **0.935** | |
| [8] Sat-Out | 0.599 | 0.566 | 0.892 | 0.719 | 0.849 | 0.630 | 0.452 | **0.932** |

bootstrapping procedure using 1000 samples (Chin, 1998a). The loadings for all constructs are significant at α = 0.05 significance level and uniformly high (above 0.7) with a majority above 0.85, attesting to the convergent validity.

Table 2 shows the average variance extracted (AVE) analysis for assessing discriminant validity. To establish discriminant validity, it is recommended that the square root of the AVE of each latent construct should be greater than any correlation between this latent construct and any other latent construct (Chin, 1998b). This indicates that more variance is shared between the latent construct and it's indicators than with another latent construct representing a different set of indicators. Table 2 shows that, in general, discriminant validity exists with the exception of productivity and efficiency.

Table 3 summarizes the results for the structural model constructs. Cronbach's α is used as a measure of internal consistency and values exceeding 0.7 are recommended as a rule of thumb. All constructs fair well on this criterion. Composite reliability is considered a closer approximation of reliability under the assumption that the parameter estimates are accurate. The results show composite reliability (CR) exceeding 0.8 as recommended (Straub et al., 2004). AVE, which can also be considered as a measure of reliability, tends to be more conservative than composite reliability. The results indicate AVE to exceed the recommended 0.5 value, implying 50% or greater variance in each construct is being accounted for (Straub et al., 2004). Together, these statistics attest to the reliability of the instrument.

*Table 3. Summary of results for the inner model constructs*

| Construct | Code | Cronbach's α | Composite Reliability | AVE |
|---|---|---|---|---|
| Cognitive Presence | Cognitive | 0.953 | 0.961 | 0.755 |
| Social Presence | Social | 0.892 | 0.920 | 0.696 |
| Collaboration Effectiveness | Effectiveness | 0.939 | 0.954 | 0.805 |
| Collaboration Efficiency | Efficiency | 0.913 | 0.936 | 0.744 |
| Collaboration Productivity | Productivity | 0.881 | 0.919 | 0.743 |
| Collaboration Commitment | Commitment | 0.888 | 0.917 | 0.690 |
| Satisfaction with Collaboration Process | Sat-Act | 0.956 | 0.966 | 0.875 |
| Satisfaction with Collaboration Outcome | Sat-Out | 0.924 | 0.952 | 0.869 |

Figure 4 illustrates the structural model with the R² value for each of the endogenous constructs. The exogenous constructs, cognitive presence and social presence, are seen to account for 10.2% to 51.4% variation in the endogenous constructs (collaboration success factors), indicating a fairly strong effect overall.

The path coefficients (similar to standardized coefficients in regression analysis) for this inner model are shown along with their respective t-values (p-value < 0.05) in the parentheses. The significant paths are shown with solid lines, while those not deemed statistically significant are shown with dashed lines. Most of the hypotheses

were supported although a few hypotheses did not turn out to be statistically significant. We had expected that those who were cognitively involved in the process would exhibit high levels of commitment. Counter to our expectations, cognitive presence did not positively impact perceived participant commitment. However, social presence did significantly impact commitment (t=6.181) suggesting that the subjects may be motivated to accomplish the activity largely due to social reasons. Similarly, cognitive presence did not significantly impact satisfaction with the activity, but social presence exhibited a significant impact on satisfaction with the activity. Though the effect

*Figure 4. PLS results for the structural model*

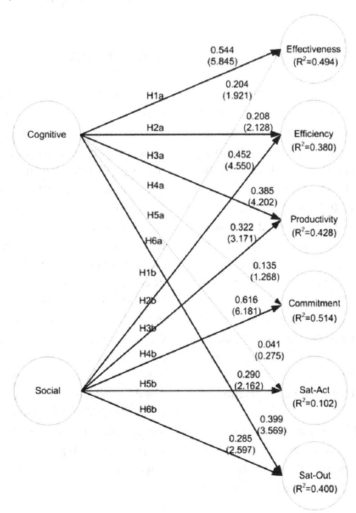

size is minimal, the data suggest that satisfaction with the activity is also impacted by the amount of interactions the participants perceive. Additionally, the structural model shows that social presence does not significantly impact perceived effectiveness. Participants enjoying more high cognitive presence in the collaborative environment perceive having more focus on tangible outcomes, leading to increased perceived effectiveness. However, the results from this study suggest that social presence does not have a significant impact on perceived effectiveness. Detailed investigation is certainly deemed necessary to further our understanding in this direction.

## 7. LIMITATIONS

Like most research there are a number of recognized limitations of this study. For example, while the context of the study (i.e., a distributed, asynchronous learning environment) is becoming more prevalent, it may not be representative of many collaborative environments and the results may not generalize. However, it is our belief that in many collaborative environments these relationships will continue to be significant.

Additionally, in this study, we did not focus on the antecedents of cognitive and social presence. While the presented model is parsimonious, it is likely that there are numerous antecedents that not only impact cognitive and social presence but that also may have a direct impact on the success metrics. There may also be additional mediators of cognitive and social presence on collaboration success. In a similar vein, collaborative success metrics may directly impact each other (e.g., commitment may moderate or mediate satisfaction of the outcome).

It is acknowledged that this study is exploratory in nature and that the small sample size may have attributed to reduced power of statistical inference. It is anticipated that a larger sample size would lead to increased stability of the findings though additional research is needed to validate this assertion.

Further, in our study, constructs were perception based metrics. There are numerous additional approaches that could be utilized for capturing measures including automatically extracting metrics from the collaborative system (e.g., frequency of posting, distribution of posting/reading among subjects, relationship of posting contribution/reading to subject responses). However, these metrics and instruments have not been developed and validated. Finally, the interactions studied in this paper primarily occur through the artifact (i.e., posting ideas, evaluating ideas). In contexts interactions may occur between participants through other channels.

## 8. CONCLUSION

This paper discusses collaboration from the perspective of the distributed, collaborative learning literature and the information systems collaboration literature. The primary contribution of this paper is the introduction and evaluation of a new research model that combines constructs from multiple disciplines. While there are many antecedents of collaboration success, we suggest that cognitive and social presence may mediate the impact of antecedents on collaboration success. At a minimum, these constructs provide yet another set of measurements for collaborative interactions. However, this study suggests that these constructs have additional implications. The previous analysis suggests that these constructs may help to explain variance in success metrics. The data collected from an extensive, distributive, asynchronous activity and survey and subsequent analysis demonstrates that cognitive presence and social presence impact success metrics differently. This is important for a few reasons:

1. These measures may be able to be used as surrogates for other success metrics. Additionally, they may be able to be used earlier in the collaborative process (i.e., the current state of the interaction can be assessed to inform process tailoring decisions).

2. Cognitive and social presence provide an enhanced understanding of why certain collaboration engagements succeed (i.e., certain contexts may impact cognitive and social presence which ultimately lead to success).

3. Understanding the relationship of cognitive and social presence on different success metrics makes designing technology-supported collaborative environments easier. Designing and including features to increase cognitive presence or social presence of group members in collaborative environments is a more concrete and tangible task than focusing on features that increase the more abstract success metrics (e.g., commitment, satisfaction with the process).

The collaboration community is expected to benefit from consideration of cognitive and social presence as mediating factors between collaborative factors and overall collaboration success metrics. This paper lays the foundation for future research work which needs to test contextual factors to see how they impact cognitive and social presence and develop additional collaborative feature sets that further promote cognitive and social presence.

## ACKNOWLEDGMENT

A previous version of this article was presented at the HICSS 44 conference.

## REFERENCES

Bonk, C. J., & Wisher, R. A. (2000). *Applying collaborative and e-learning tools to military distance learning: A research framework*. Arlington, VA: US Army Research Institute for the Behavioral and Social Sciences.

Briggs, R. O., de Vreede, G.-J., & Nunamaker, J. F. Jr. (2003). Collaboration engineering with ThinkLets to pursue sustained sucess with group support systems. *Journal of Management Information Systems, 19*(4), 31–64.

Briggs, R. O., Reinig, B. A., & de Vreede, G.-J. (2008). The yield shift theory of satisfaction and its application to the IS/IT domain. *Journal of the Association for Information Systems, 9*, 267–293.

Chin, W. W. (1998a). Commentary: Issues and opinion on structural equation modeling. *Management Information Systems Quarterly, 22*(1), 7–16.

Chin, W. W. (1998b). The Partial Least Squares approach to structural equation modelling. In Marcoulides, G. A. (Ed.), *Modern methods for business research* (pp. 295–336). Mahwah, NJ: Lawrence Erlbaum.

CyberSmart. (2009). *Web 2.0 tools*. Retrieved from http://cybersmartcurriculum.org/tools/

Denning, P. J., & Yaholkovsky, P. (2008). Getting to "we". *Communications of the ACM, 51*(4), 19–24. doi:10.1145/1330311.1330316

Duivenvoorde, G. P. J., Kolfschoten, G. L., Briggs, R. O., & de Vreede, G.-J. (2009). Towards an instrument to measure successfulness of collaborative effort from a participant perspective. In *Proceedings of the 42nd Hawaii International Conference on Systems Sciences*, Big Island, HI (pp. 1-9).

Fjermestad, J. (1998). An integrated framework for group support systems. *Journal of Organizational Computing and Electronic Commerce, 8*(2), 83–107. doi:10.1207/s15327744joce0802_1

Fjermestad, J., & Hiltz, S. R. (1999). An assessment of group support systems experimental research: Methodologyand results. *Journal of Management Information Systems, 15*(3), 7–149.

Fjermestad, J., & Hiltz, S. R. (2001). Group support systems: A descriptive evaluation of case and field studies. *Journal of Management Information Systems, 17*(3), 113–157.

Garrison, D. R., Anderson, T., & Archer, W. (1999). Critical inquiry in a text-based environment: Computer conferencing in higher education. *The Internet and Higher Education, 2*(2-3), 87–105. doi:10.1016/S1096-7516(00)00016-6

Garrison, D. R., Cleveland-Innes, M., & Fung, T. (2004). Student role adjustment in online communities of inquiry: Model and instrument validation. *Journal of Asynchronous Learning Networks, 8*(2), 61–74.

Gefen, D. (2003). Unidimensional validity: An explanation and example. *Communication of the AIS, 12*(2), 23–47.

Gefen, D., & Straub, D. (2005). A practical guide to factorial validity using PLS-GRAPH: Tutorial and annotated example. *Communication of the AIS, 16*, 91–109.

Gilroy, K. (2001). *Collaborative e-learning: The right approach*. ArsDigita Systems Journal.

Hanover Research Council. (2009). *Current and future classroom and online technologies utilized in higher education*. Retrieved from http://www.hanoverresearch.com

Hiltz, S. R., & Turoff, M. (2005). Education goes digital: The evolution of online learning and the revolution in higher education. *Communications of the ACM, 48*(10), 59–64. doi:10.1145/1089107.1089139

Meservy, T. O., Helquist, J., Deokar, A. V., & Kruse, J. (2009). Enhancing e-learning using artifact-based collaboration. In *Proceedings of the 15th Americas Conference on Information Systems*, San Francisco, CA.

Meyer, J. P., & Herscovitch, L. (2001). Commitment in the workpace toward a general model. *Human Resource Management Review, 11*, 299–326. doi:10.1016/S1053-4822(00)00053-X

Reinig, B. A. (2003). Toward an understanding of satisfaction with the process and outcomes of teamwork. *Journal of Management Information Systems, 19*(4), 65–83.

Ringle, C. M., Wende, S., & Will, A. (2005). *SmartPLS (2.0 beta ed.)*. Hamburg, Germany: University of Hamburg. Retrieved from http://www.smartpls.de

Sidorova, A., Evangelopoulos, N., Valacich, J. S., & Ramakrishnan, T. (2008). Uncovering the intellectual core of the information systems discipline. *Management Information Systems Quarterly, 32*(3), 467–482.

Straub, D. W. (1989). Validating instruments in MIS research. *Management Information Systems Quarterly, 13*(2), 147–169. doi:10.2307/248922

Straub, D. W., Boudreau, M.-C., & Gefen, D. (2004). Validation guidelines for IS positivist research. *Communications of the AIS, 13*(24), 380–427.

Weasenforth, D., Biesenbach-Lucas, S., & Meloni, C. (2002). Realizing constructivist objectives through collaborative technologies: Threaded discussions. *Language Learning & Technology, 6*(3), 58–86.

## APPENDIX

Note: Codes are in parentheses in order to help reader to match survey instrument question with analysis above.

## Survey of Online Learning and Collaboration

This instrument is designed to assess your experiences in online learning. The following questions will assist us in assessing your perceptions with regard to learning in an online environment. Your responses will be held in strict confidence and your identity will not be revealed to anyone other than the researchers in the project. Please complete all pages of this questionnaire. This will take approximately 25-30 minutes.

Compared to previous *face-to-face learning experiences*, how would you rate your online learning experiences with the following?

Rating Scale: Much Better, Better, Same, Worse, Much Worse

## Cognitive Presence (Cognitive)

1.  Identifying key issues?
2.  Stimulating your curiosity?
3.  Identifying relevant new information?
4.  Engaging in exchange of ideas?
5.  Synthesizing ideas?
6.  Resolving problems?
7.  Understanding ideas or concepts?
8.  Applying ideas or concepts?

## Social Presence (Social)

1.  Expressing your emotions?
2.  Being open? (i.e. disclosing your personality)
3.  Asking questions?
4.  Responding to others' comments?
5.  Sustaining discussion?
6.  Feeling part of the class community?
7.  Referring to others by name?

Overall, how would you rate your online learning experience with the following?

The following questions use a 7-point likert scale ranging from 1 - Strongly disagree to 7 - Strongly agree:

## Satisfaction with the Process (SatAct)

1. I feel satisfied with the way in which this learning exercise was conducted.
2. I feel good about this learning exercise's process.
3. I liked the way this learning exercise progressed.
4. I feel satisfied with the activities used in this learning exercise.
5. I feel satisfied about the way we carried out the activities in this learning exercise.

## Satisfaction with the Outcome (SatOut)

1. I liked the outcome of this learning exercise.
2. I feel satisfied with the things we achieved through this learning exercise.
3. When the learning exercise was over, I felt satisfied with the results.
4. Our accomplishments today give me a feeling of satisfaction.
5. I am happy with the results of this learning exercise.

## Commitment (Commitment)

1. I support the goal of this learning exercise as it was presented in the introduction.
2. I had a stake in achieving the goal of this learning exercise as it was presented in the introduction.
3. I was motivated to contribute to this learning exercise.
4. I was willing to put my time and effort into this learning exercise.
5. I found this learning exercise important.

## Efficiency (Efficiency)

1. I found the learning exercise worth the time and effort.
2. The time and effort requested from me was reasonable.
3. I was able to contribute relevant knowledge & experience I had to the learning exercise.
4. The time and effort I spend in the learning exercise was what I expected
5. My input was justified.

## Effectiveness (Effectiveness)

1. The result of the learning exercise had the quality I expected.
2. What we achieved in this learning exercise met my expectations.
3. We achieved what we intended.
4. The result has the quality intended.
5. The result was as I hoped

## Productivity (Productivity)

1. The input asked from me was in balance with the results
2. The result was not a waste of my time and effort
3. What we achieved was worth the time and effort
4. The quality of the results is in balance with the time and effort asked from me
5. The quality of the results justifies my input

*This work was previously published in the International Journal of Social and Organizational Dynamics in IT, Volume 1, Issue 3, edited by Michael B. Knight, pp. 18-33, 2011 by IGI Publishing (an imprint of IGI Global).*

# Chapter 7
# Coding for Unique Ideas and Ambiguity:
## A Method for Measuring the Effect of Convergence on the Artifact of an Ideation Activity

**Victoria Badura**
*Chadron State College, USA*

**Aaron Read**
*University of Nebraska at Omaha, USA*

**Robert O. Briggs**
*University of Nebraska at Omaha, USA*

**Gert-Jan de Vreede**
*University of Nebraska at Omaha, USA & Delft University of Technology, The Netherlands*

## ABSTRACT

*Groups can generate so many ideas during a decision making process involving brainstorming that they become an impediment to group processes. Convergence activities reduce the number of ideas generated by the group and clarify those ideas, allowing the group to move forward with a set of ideas worthy of further attention. Research about convergence and its affect on collaboration is in the early stages. To further this research, measures of convergence are developed in this study as part of an assessment of the effects of convergence on an ideation artifact produced by managers attempting to solve an actual business problem. This paper presents a method for quantifying the reduction and clarification that has occurred through convergence using an assessment of a pre- and post-convergence artifact. This study expands upon understanding of collaboration by presenting the method of characterizing the convergence artifacts.*

DOI: 10.4018/978-1-4666-1948-7.ch007

## INTRODUCTION

Groups consisting of multiple stakeholders with diverse backgrounds, varying degrees of expertise, and with differing, possibly conflicting goals must often work together to make sense of complex problems (Weick, 1993), to make decisions, and to negotiate solutions in domains such as software engineering (Boehm, Grunbacher, & Briggs, 2001; Fruhling & de Vreede, 2006), business process reorganization (den Hengst & de Vreede, 2004; Dennis, Hayes, & Daniels, 1994) and strategic decision making (Vennix, Akkermans, & Rouwette, 1996). Collaboration can be challenging, more so when decisions must be made without a clear understanding of the causes of current conditions and of potential consequences for proposed courses of action. Collaboration experts like professional facilitators, who have specialize collaboration knowledge and skills, can substantially improve group effectiveness and efficiency, but professional facilitators can be expensive, and are not always available to a group (Briggs, de Vreede, & Nunamaker, 2003). Collaboration Engineering (CE) is an approach to designing collaborative work practices for high-value recurring tasks and deploying those work practices to practitioners to execute for themselves without ongoing intervention from professional facilitators (Briggs et al., 2003).

A key goal of collaboration engineering is to distill and codify knowledge and skills into small, easily learnable concepts that non-professionals can readily use. Toward that end, CE researchers identified have six patterns of collaboration that manifest as groups work through a problem-solving process. These patterns characterized the effects of group effort as changes-of-state. The patterns are (Briggs, de Vreede, & Massey, 2008):

- Generate: move from fewer to more concepts
- Reduce: move from more to fewer concepts deemed worthy of more attention

- Clarify: move from less to more shared understanding of concepts
- Organize: move from less to more understanding of relationships among concepts,
- Evaluate: move from less to more understanding of the instrumentality of concepts toward goal attainment
- Build: commitment: move from fewer to more stakeholders willing to commit to a proposal.

Some authors combine the reduce and clarify patterns under the more general heading, *Convergence* (Davis, de Vreede, & Briggs, 2007).

A great deal has been learned about the Generate pattern of collaboration, often called brainstorming or ideation (Diehl & Stroebe, 1987, 1991; Fjermestad & Hiltz, 1999; Fjermestad & Hiltz, 2001; Graham, 1977; Kolfschoten & Santanen, 2007; Lindgren, 1967; Osborn, 1963). Likewise, there are strong researcher streams about building commitment, e.g. team-building (Marks, Zaccaro, & Matthieu, 2000), negotiation (Boehm et al., 2001), and consensus building (Dunlop, 1984; Innes & Booher, 1999; Rosenau, 1962). However, the understanding of the convergence pattern is in its beginning stages.

Convergence patterns of collaboration are useful, as they often follow ideation activities which occur frequently. Often, groups generate more ideas than a group will find useful. In fact, some ideation techniques encourage group members to contribute poor ideas in addition to good ones (Osborn, 1963). A group will find it beneficial, therefore, to have a means of focusing on a reduced set of ideas. In the knowledge economy, attention may be the group's, as well as the organization's, scarcest resource (Davenport & Völpel, 2001). Because they free up a group's attention for the most important issues, convergence activities become especially significant.

In order to measure the effectiveness of technology, we have to measure the value it produces for users. To evaluate technology used for convergence activities, we must be able to measure convergence effects. We therefore perform an exploratory study of technology-supported convergence. Research in this area is critical to better understandings of collaboration because activities that fall under the convergence pattern of collaboration are amongst the most difficult for facilitators to execute (de Vreede & Briggs, 2005), and group members find convergence activities to be a painful and time-consuming (Chen, Hsu, Orwig, Hoopes, & Nunamaker, 1994; Easton, George, Nunamaker, & Pendergast, 1990).

Researchers have begun to delineate concepts to explore the process and results of convergence (Davis, Badura, & de Vreede, 2008; Davis et al., 2007). Not until recently have these concepts been used to characterize convergence (Badura, Read, Briggs, & de Vreede, 2009). The current research presents this method of coding artifacts generated by groups both before and after a group has performed a convergence activity.

Specifically, we present a method of coding for the number of ideas in an artifact in order to characterize the reduction which has occurred in the artifact, as well as a method of coding the ambiguity of these ideas in order to give an indication of the clarification which has occurred as reflected in the artifact. We developed this method in order to quantify the effect of a convergence activity.

It is important that we emphasize that assessing convergence in an artifact is not as accurate as an assessment of convergence which involves the perceptions of the group who generate the ideas in the document. Perceptions of the group participating in a convergence activity are necessary to truly assess to what extent they consider the remaining ideas worthy of further consideration and to truly assess to what extent these ideas are clarified compared to the previous version of the ideas. However, it is useful to have the ability to characterize artifacts resulting from convergence, as a researcher may more readily have access to artifacts as opposed to perceptions of the group members who generated the artifacts.

The organization of the rest of the paper is as follows. The next section contains background information relating to the two constructs we are characterizing in artifacts: ambiguity and idea reduction. In the following section, we present the procedures used in our method of characterizing the convergence. In the next two sections, we validate the coding method and present an example using the coding method with data collected from a large financial services firm and presented in "Exploring the Effects of a Convergence Intervention on Ideation Artifacts: A Multi-Group Field Study" (Badura et al., 2009). We conclude with a discussion of future research and development of the coding scheme.

## BACKGROUND

In this section, we explain why it is important to accurately measure the number of ideas and whether or not these ideas are ambiguous as part of the coding scheme we present. We first explain how these constructs for assessing convergence are in line with those presented by Davis et al. (2007) for an artifact resulting from convergence. To assess convergence, thinkLets that have convergence outcomes are assessed. A thinkLet is a codified packet of facilitation skill that can be applied by practitioners to achieve predictable, repeatable patterns of collaboration (Briggs et al., 2003). Five constructs assess the results of a convergence thinkLet along with five assessing the process of arriving at convergence employed by the thinkLet. As the coding scheme focuses on the results of the thinkLet, we will only discuss the applicable constructs here.

- *Speed*: The length of time taken to perform the convergence activity. This may be captured in the minutes of the meeting in which the convergence activity occurred.
- *Level of Comprehensiveness:* The extent to which all ideas which the group deems

worthy of further attention are included in the set which resulted from convergence.

- *Level of Shared Understanding:* The extent to which a shared context model puts boundaries around what the group is focusing on during a meeting.
- *Rate of Reduction:* The extent of the number of ideas for the group's consideration is reduced. This can be directly assessed as a count of the ideas within the artifact used as a starting point for convergence and the resulting artifact.
- *Rate of Refinement:* The extent to which the artifact resulting from convergence is a refined, polished deliverable.

In our study, we focus on the constructs that can be assessed within a converged artifact itself. This excludes *Speed, Level of Comprehensiveness,* and *Rate of Refinement.* While *Rate of Refinement* and *Level of Comprehensiveness* are measurements of the artifact itself, they cannot be assessed without consulting the group which created the artifact or the individuals who will use the artifact. These were outside the scope of our study.

*Rate of Reduction* can easily be captured as a comparison of the count of ideas in the generated artifact and the converged artifact. The importance of measuring this construct is explained in the following section. *Level of Shared Understanding* is assessed through a measurement of the ambiguity of the statements in the artifact following convergence. As ambiguity decreases, the likelihood of shared understanding of the ideas within the artifact increases. The justification and importance of assessing ambiguity is presented in more detail below.

## Reduction

A reduction in ideas results in a reduction in the number of ideas to process by a group. Theories of cognitive load describe the amount of effort expended as such processing occurs (Barrouillet,

Bernardin, Portrat, Vergauwe, & Camos, 2007; Sweller, van Merrienboer, & Paas, 1998). These theories work in the context of a brain that has a short-term memory with limited processing capabilities and a long-term memory with unlimited memory abilities (Baddeley, 1992). The short-term memory is limited in its processing ability. According to the Time-Based Resource Sharing model of short-term memory (Barrouillet et al., 2007) has a bottleneck allowing only one retrieval from long term memory to occur at a time. Thus as information cues needed to be processed by accessing the long term memory increases, the time to complete the task increases. The smaller number of ideas a group has to process, therefore, equates to less work for a group to perform.

It is important to be able to measure the disaggregated ideas generated by a group, since what a group participant may forward as a single idea may, in fact, contain several ideas. Disaggregated ideas are used as the unit of analysis when considering the relationship between such constructs as quantity and quality of ideas generated by groups (Reinig, Briggs, & Nunamaker, 2007).

## Ambiguity

Reducing ambiguity is key to increasing shared understanding. Ambiguity describes a situation where further information is needed to make meaning more precise (Poesio, 1995). As ambiguity increases, the ability to transfer knowledge decreases (Simonin, 1999), a concept highly related to shared understanding. We define ambiguity or ambiguous as the description of a statement which can be interpreted in more than one way.

In addition to focusing the group on a smaller set of ideas, many convergence thinkLets also help the group to develop a sense of shared understanding which they did not possess beforehand. For example, in the FastFocus thinkLet, the group must come to agreement on the wording of comments proposed by individual group members. Such shared understanding of the meaning of words can be crucial in helping the group to move forward with the decision-making process. Briggs, Reinig, and Nunamaker (2003), for example, cited a case where a group negotiating requirements for a new online bookstore reached an impasse over system rights that should be granted to "affiliates." As it turned out, there were five orthogonal meanings for the word, "affiliate", in that group. Until they reached clarity on those five concepts, they could not move forward with decisions about access rights.

## THE RESEARCH VENUE

We now present the research venue where the artifacts characterized by this coding scheme were generated. These artifacts were collected from the headquarters of a large financial services organization. The company is over a century old and employs more than 2000 individuals.

### Participants

Senior executives and associates from both the home office and the field office were involved in the workshops. Participants represented a wide spectrum of the organization both demographically and based on the departments they represented. Participants ranged in age from 37 to 50 years of age, with an average age of 42.9 years. On average, participants had 23 years of experience in this industry (Badura et al., 2009).

### Task

The company hired an outside paid facilitator to design and conduct a workshop to help participants identify barriers to the organization achieving its strategic objectives. In total, six groups completed the workshop. This study describes the coding process developed to analyze the data from those sessions. The method was used to analyze data from three of those groups. While we also present

a brief analysis of the data here, an analysis of the data from these sessions was reported elsewhere (Badura et al., 2009).

This study was performed by a team of four researchers. One of the researchers acted as a facilitator and enacted a scripted facilitation technique in a technology-supported meeting. This workshop included, among other activities, a brainstorming activity and a convergence activity. The facilitator did not participate in analysis of the data to avoid conflicts of interest. The development of the coding method and analysis was conducted by the other three researchers.

The group went through two workshop activities that are pertinent to this research. In the first workshop activity, the group used an idea generation technique called *FreeBrainstorm* (Briggs & de Vreede, 2001). They generated ideas for 15 minutes in response to the question, "What are the key problems that block us from obtaining our strategic objectives?"

The brainstorming technique allowed all participants to contribute simultaneously and anonymously. The first workshop yielded an artifact containing 124 comments. Subsequent sessions yielded artifacts containing 124 and 77 comments, respectively. Some of the comments contained a single problem. Some contained multiple problems. Some contained no problems. We refer to the artifact from the *FreeBrainstorm* as the *Raw Data Set*.

The second activity performed by the participants was a *FastFocus*. This activity lasted 45 minutes for each session and yielded artifacts containing 29, 31, and 20 problem statements. The artifact from the FastFocus is referred to as the *Reduced Data Set*.

*FastFocus* (Briggs & de Vreede, 2001). During this activity, each participant held a different page from the brainstorming activity. At the beginning of the activity, the facilitator displayed an empty list on a public projection screen where all participants could read it. The participants received the following instructions in accordance with the rules of the FastFocus technique:

*...Each of you is now looking at a different page. You each hold a different part of our brainstorming conversation in your hands. In a moment, I will call on each of you in turn. I will ask you, "What is the most important problem on the page in front of you that blocks us from achieving our strategic objectives?"*

The moderator then began a round robin, calling on each participant in turn. Each participant contributed a single problem statement to the public list. In accordance with the rules of FastFocus, the facilitator screened their contributions for five things:

- *Redundancy:* Participants could only add ideas that were not already on the list.
- *Relevance:* Participants could only add problem statements to the list.
- *Clarity:* Ideas had to be expressed concisely and unambiguously.
- *Levels of abstraction:* Contributions could not be so vague as to be inactionable, nor could they be so specific that they obscured the root causes of the problems.
- *Criticism:* Participants were not allowed to contribute criticisms of the ideas added by other participants. They were told they would have an opportunity to evaluate the ideas later.

When the facilitator was satisfied that a problem statement was non-redundant, relevant, clear, and at a useful level of abstraction, he typed it onto the public list. When every participant had had a chance to contribute one idea to the public list, the facilitator asked participants to switch pages. The facilitator then said, *"What is the most important problem on the page in front of you that has not already been added to the public list?"* Participants added new items to the list as

they discovered them. The facilitator repeated the cycle of contributions and page exchanges until no participant contributed any new problem statements for three successive exchanges of pages.

The groups performed subsequent activities. These activities are outside the scope of this study and are not reported.

## PROCESS OF DISAGGREGATION

In order to determine the effects of a convergence activity on the output of a group's activities, a count of the number of ideas generated by the activity was necessary. An initial attempt to count the number of ideas using an aggregate method met with unacceptable results. Independent coders identified significantly different interpretations of the comments. Inter-rater reliability for one group was as low as .28. Clearly, a different method for determining the number of ideas generated by collaboration activities was needed.

Inter-rater reliability was negatively impacted by the aggregation approach. With disaggregation there is a clear stopping point. Aggregation lacks a clear stopping point. Additionally, in the initial attempt to analyze the data, the researchers were not coding for ambiguity. Since over half of the original comments were deemed to be ambiguous, this may have also interfered with inter-rater reliability.

In the revised scheme, data was coded for each group individually. Three coders were available. It was determined that two coders would analyze each group. The third coder would be available in the event that the primary coders differed in their interpretation.

To that end, the following process was enacted. The process had two phases: a disaggregation phase, where comments were separated into their component parts, and a resolution phase, where disagreements were resolved. Comments were exported from the group support system used for the workshops. The comments were imported into a spreadsheet. Each coder analyzed the comments and inserted disaggregated comments, one per cell, into the spreadsheet below the original comment. In this manner, each coder's interpretations ended up in columns within the spreadsheet that could be easily compared. Coders used brackets and comments to indicate ambiguity.

## Definitions

The purpose of the task was to identify problem statements that met the parameters of the workshop. It was noted, however, that comments generated by participants were frequently formatted as solutions rather than problems. Therefore, researchers developed the following definitions.

*Problem:* A problem is a desired state or outcome that has not yet been attained (e.g., "Our customers do not feel satisfied, although we want them to.").

*Symptom:* A symptom is some unacceptable condition that implies some desired state or outcome that has not yet been attained (e.g., "Customers are returning products.").

Often in order for the disaggregated statement to be useful for further use, missing words needed to be included in the disaggregated statement. To that end, the researchers developed the following.

## Rules

The following section describes the rules developed for the coding scheme. Each rule has a catch phrase associated with it to assist coders in recognizing the appropriate situation while coding. Comments from participants were reduced to the smallest meaningful units possible. The Appendix contains the text of the Rules of Disaggregation used by the coders (Badura et al., 2009).

## Identify Verbs and Nouns

The first step was to identify unique noun-verb-object combinations.

UNIQUE NVO: Each unique noun/verb/object combination that identifies a state or outcome that has not yet been attained was disaggregated into simple problem statements. The following example shows a comment where coders identified identical unique noun-verb-object combinations:

**Original Comment:** There are too many other challenges (people, people processes, technology) that get in the way.

Coder 1 disaggregation:
- *There are too many other challenges that get in the way*
- *There are too many people other challenges that get in the way*
- *There are too many process challenges that get in the way*
- *There are too many technology challenges that get in the way*

Coder 2 disaggregation:
- *There are too many other challenges that get in the way*
- *there are too many people challenges that get in the way*
- *there are too many process challenges that get in the way*
- *There are too many technology challenges that get in the way*

When spelling and typing errors are taken into account these comments disaggregate identically.

ACCEPT SYMPTOMS: Identifying a symptom is an important aspect of framing a problem, so symptoms were accepted as problem statements and disaggregated using the same rules.

MEANINGLESS VERB: Objects were not disaggregated when doing so rendered the verb meaningless, e.g., "We feel torn between our duties to home and work." This was not disaggregated to, "We feel torn between our duties to home" and "we feel torn between our duties to work", because doing so rendered the concept, "feeling torn between", meaningless.

ACCEPT REDUNDANCY: If people say the same thing in multiple ways in the same comment, both wordings were disaggregated into simple problem statements. Redundancy was removed in a later activity. The comment was tagged as redundant for future review.

## Break Phrases

BREAK OUT FIRST CAUSES from CAUSE-AND-EFFECT: When presented with a causal chain, first causes were disaggregated into standalone problem statements. For example, in the comment, "Understaffing leads to overwork, which leads to low morale", we have "understaffing" disaggregated as a separate problem statement.

DISTRIBUTE CAUSES: First causes were distributed across their consequent problem statements to make standalone problem statements. The first cause was included in the problem statement in parentheses so that the ideas could be understood in subsequent analysis steps, (e.g., rushed work) causes low satisfaction. For example, in the comment, "Understaffing leads to overwork, which leads to low morale," the understaffing cause was paired with the overwork effect, and overwork as a cause was paired with low morale, as follows: "(Understaffing) leads to overwork", and "(Overwork leads to) low morale." Thus, this comment was broken out into three problem statements.

MULTIPLE CAUSES: All first causes were combined when distributing across consequent problems, because we don't know whether either of the causes would invoke the effect on its own. For example, in the statement,

"Understaffing and overwork cause low morale", it is not possible to know whether understaffing or overwork each cause low morale, or whether both together cause low morale. Therefore, in this case, both understaffing and overwork would be broken out as first causes (see above) but low morale would be broken out, "(Understaffing and overwork) cause low morale. Thus, this comment was disaggregated into three problem statements, but they differed from the three statements illustrated in the previous rule.

NO THREE DEEP: Distributed causes will not span more than one cause and one effect. There will be no causal chains of three or more clauses in the disaggregated problem statements.

RETAIN DEPENDENT CLAUSES: Dependent clauses were not broken out as separate problem statements unless they were part of a causal chain. (Dependent clauses explain what, how, or when.) (The dependent clause may contain a problem statement when it begins with "to.")

## Determine Ambiguity

BRACKET AMBIGUITY: When coders found the language of the contribution allowed for multiple grammatically sound interpretations that could lead to different disaggregation structures, they made the best interpretation and disaggregated accordingly. The responses to comments that were identified as ambiguous were entered in brackets. The ambiguity was explained by stating at least two possible grammatically sound interpretations allowed by the wording of the original comment. This example shows the two interpretations of an original comment and the coders' indications that the comments were ambiguous.

**Original Comment:** Many classes or meetings that are scheduled around cut offs or month

ends that impact production. The entire Society needs to be aware of these dates!!!!
Coder 1 disaggregation:

- *Many classes are scheduled around cut-offs*
- *Many classes are scheduled around months end*
- *Many meetings are scheduled around cut-offs*
- *Many meetings are scheduled around month ends*
- *[Many classes are scheduled around cut-offs impact production]*
- *[Many classes are scheduled around months end impact production]*
- *[Many meetings are scheduled around cut-offs impact production]*
- *[Many meetings are scheduled around month ends impact production]*

Coder 2 disaggregation:

- *Many classes are scheduled around cut offs that impact production*
- *Many classes are scheduled around month ends that impact production*
- *Many meetings are scheduled around cut offs that impact production*
- *Many meetings are scheduled around month ends that impact production*
- *[The entire society needs to be aware of cutoff dates]*
- *[The entire society needs to be aware of month ends]*

Coding ambiguous statements produced one of four outcomes: First, both coders disaggregated the original comment into two identical responses. Second, the coders each identified grammatically valid interpretations of the comment that were different but did not identify the comment as ambiguous. Third, one coder identified the comment as ambiguous while the other did not. Fourth, both coders identified the ambiguity at the time of coding. The final possibility, one or both

coders identified the comment as too ambiguous to disaggregate.

BRACKET SOLUTIONS DISGUISED AS PROBLEMS: If a problem statement was rhetorically stated as a solution, coders disaggregated it into problem statements, and they used brackets to signify the ambiguity. Brackets were explained.

IGNORE THE POSITIVE: Positive clauses or phrases were not in the set of disaggregated problem statements.

RHETORICAL QUESTIONS: Statements containing rhetorical questions that can be reframed as problem statements were marked as ambiguous and reframed as problem statements. The reframed problem statements were disaggregated according to the rules.

## Ways to Resolve Conflicts and Ambiguities

Once the coders finished disaggregating the comments, the results were compared. This was the resolution phase. Any disagreements were resolved in one of four manners.

NEGOTIATE: All three coders were present for the resolution activities. Possible interpretations were discussed. If one was clearly more plausible, that interpretation was accepted and disaggregated if necessary.

SYNTHESIZE: If a one interpretation was not clearly superior, then the two coders would synthesize a better interpretation together.

ARBITRATE. The third coder was brought in to arbitrate a solution in cases where two plausible interpretations existed and the original coders could not make a determination.

DISALLOW: If coders agreed that it was not possible to determine a valid interpretation, then they would disallow the comment as too ambiguous. They did not disaggregate disallowed comments.

*Table 1. Percentage of agreement and Cohen's Kappa*

| Group | Number of Disagreements | Number of Disaggregated Comments | Number of Comments Agreed Upon | Percentage of Agreement | Cohen's Kappa |
|---|---|---|---|---|---|
| 1 | 11 | 124 | 113 | 91% | 0.71 |
| 3 | 11 | 164 | 153 | 93% | 0.65 |
| 6 | 23 | 280 | 257 | 91% | 0.79 |

## VALIDATION

Three raters independently coded the data from three workshops. Each group was coded by two raters with the third rater adjudicating disagreements.

Of the 70 comments found to be ambiguous by coders in Group 1, 34 were found to be ambiguous by one coder. Of the 34, 11 were found to be ambiguous by only one coder in Group 3. Of the 23 found to be ambiguous in Group 6, 13 were found to be ambiguous by one coder.

To verify the ambiguity of the comments marked ambiguous by one coder, two alternative interpretations were generated for each comment. If upon the second inspection of the comment two valid interpretations could not be generated, the comment was marked unambiguous. The original comment and alternate interpretations were presented to two new coders. The coders were instructed to code each comment that had two valid interpretations as ambiguous.

If any of the comments were not found to be ambiguous, the analysis of the comments reflected

the change. The coders agreed on 89% of the ambiguities. The percentage of agreement for the three groups was 91.1%, 93.2%, and 91.7% for Groups 1, 3 and 6, respectively. Table 1 summarizes the reliability statistics for the three groups.

Percentage of agreement is not wholly sufficient as a measure of inter-rater reliability. It is too likely that the agreement is due more to chance than to agreement amongst the coders. Cohen's Kappa examines inter-rater reliability in light of the percentage of agreement that might be due to pure chance. Cohen's Kappa for Groups 1, 3, and 6 was .71, .65, and .79, respectively. Cohen's Kappa for each group showed substantial agreement on the coding of unique ideas (Landis & Koch, 1977). The Cohen's Kappa for the ambiguity analysis was .527 reflecting moderate agreement. The lower inter-rater reliability for this analysis is likely due to the lack of clear instructions and or the significantly smaller sample size. Ambiguity is a much more subjective concept than unique idea counts. Table 2 shows the interpretations for Cohen's Kappa according to Landis and Koch.

*Table 2. Cohen's Kappa (Landis & Koch, 1977)*

| Kappa Statistic | Strength of the Agreement |
|---|---|
| <0.00 | Poor |
| 0.00 - 0.20 | Slight |
| 0.21 - 0.40 | Fair |
| 0.41 - 0.60 | Moderate |
| 0.61 - 0.80 | Substantial |
| 0.81 – 1.00 | Almost Perfect |

# FIELD TESTING

This coding scheme was used to analyze the data obtained during the aforementioned field study. A detailed explanation of the results of that analysis is reported elsewhere (Badura et al., 2009). The results are summarized here to demonstrate the measurements that can be obtained using the coding scheme. Table 3 contains an analysis of the generated artifact as an example of the way in which the coded data can be used to develop an understanding of how a particular convergence activity affects the artifact of that activity.

The effects of the FastFocus activity upon the generated artifact can be observed through a comparison of the number of disaggregated problem statements and the percentage of ambiguous problem statements in the generated artifact and the artifact which resulted from the FastFocus activity. We report some of the relevant statistics pertaining to the reduced artifact here to demonstrate this effect. The generated or raw artifacts contained, on average, 277 disaggregated problem

*Table 3. Measures calculated based on comments coded using the coding scheme (Badura et al., 2009)*

| Description of Variable | Variable Name | ID | Value | | | |
|---|---|---|---|---|---|---|
| | | | Group A | Group B | Group C | Total |
| Number of Raw Comments Contributed | *Raw Comments* | *RC* | 124 | 124 | 77 | 325 |
| Number of Raw Off Topic Comments (no problem statement disaggregated from the comment) | *Raw Off-Topic* | *RC-Off* | 1 | 7 | 0 | 8 |
| Number of Raw On-Topic Comments | *Raw On-Topic* | *RC- On* | 123 | 117 | 77 | 317 |
| Number of Raw Comments deemed unambiguous | *Raw Unam-biguous* | *RCU* | 70 | 54 | 23 | 147 |
| Number of Raw Comments deemed to be ambiguous | *Raw Ambiguous* | *RCA* | 56 | 63 | 54 | 173 |
| Ratio of Ambiguous Comments to Raw comments (RCA / RC) | *Raw Ambiguity Ratio* | *A/RC* | 0.45 | .50 | .70 | .53 |
| Number of Raw Disaggregated Problem Statements | *Raw Disaggre-gated Problems* | *RCD-Problems* | 280 | 230 | 161 | 671 |
| Number of Unique Raw Disaggregated Problem Statements | *Raw Disaggre-gated Unique* | *RCD-Unique* | 246 | 220 | 154 | 620 |
| Number of Redundant Raw Disaggregated Problem Statements | *Raw Disag-gregated Redundant* | *RCD-Re-dundant* | 29 | 31 | 20 | 80 |
| Number of Raw Problem Statements disaggregated from unam-biguous Raw Comments | *Raw Disag-gregated Prob-lems - From Unambiguous Comments* | *RCD-Unambig* | 165 | 143 | 40 | 348 |
| Number of Raw Problem Statements disaggregated from Raw Ambiguous Comments | *Raw Disaggre-gated Problems - From Ambigu-ous Comments* | *RCD-Ambig* | 115 | 87 | 122 | 324 |
| Average Number of Problem Statements Disaggregated from each Raw Comment | *RC Disaggre-gation Ratio* | (RCD-Unique / RC) | 1.98 | 1.77 | 2 | 1.91 |
| Average Number of Problem Statements Disaggregated from Each Unambiguous Raw Comment | *RC Disaggre-gation Ratio - unambiguous* | (RCD-Unambig / RCU) | 2.35 | 2.65 | 1.74 | 2.37 |

statements, whereas the reduced artifacts contained only 48, on average. On average, 61% of the disaggregated comments in the raw artifacts were ambiguous while only 5% of the disaggregated comments in the reduced artifacts were ambiguous.

On average, coders identified .61 problem statements per unambiguous contribution, and 1.90 unique problem statements per ambiguous contribution.

## DISCUSSION AND CONCLUSION

We present a valid method for coding the number of problem statements and number of ambiguities present in artifacts created by groups through ideation and convergence activities. This coding scheme has been shown to have strong agreement among coders for disaggregation of problem statements. This agreement carried across two sets of independent coders. This ability to measure two key indicators of group convergence activity performance is a significant contribution to the field of collaboration science. Researchers may now evaluate and improve existing convergence activities. Future research should, therefore, build upon this coding scheme by comparing artifacts generated by different convergence activities.

We found during the coding of the ambiguities that roughly 80% of them would likely have been less ambiguous had the group been trained on framing problems as different from solutions. This would include elimination of the word, "need", in specifying a lack of something as well as mentioning nouns without adjectives to describe what about them is problematic. This emphasizes the need to further investigate the effects of brainstorming instructions on the characteristics of results. The coding scheme presented here will be helpful in this research.

The age range of workshop participants (37-50) may not have represented the company studied as a whole. However, we believe that our method of coding ambiguity is applicable to many populations in many organizations. We did not submit ambiguities discovered by both coders to be checked for multiple interpretations as described. In future coding endeavors, a coding of all of the discovered ambiguities for multiple interpretations would give a more accurate reflection of the ambiguity of the artifact. It is, however, likely that, since both coders discovered the ambiguity independently, the statement was indeed ambiguous.

Performing and coding the disaggregation of problem statements and ambiguities took 19-21 person hours to disaggregate—two to three hours for two researchers to perform the disaggregation independently, and roughly five hours for three researchers to code the disaggregation and resolve discrepancies in disaggregation and ambiguity coding. Further effort was needed to find and eliminate redundancies. The labor involved in each effort was highly intensive. Improving the method could be a topic of research in itself. Future research should investigate the convergence measurements *Speed, Level of Comprehensiveness,* and *Rate of Refinement,* as these were not assessed in this study.

The reliability of the coding method will become more apparent as new researchers are able to follow the coding scheme with similar agreement in number of disaggregations and ambiguities as reported here.

This coding scheme could be used for any set of data generated by groups. It is also possible that this scheme would be useful for applications other than collaboration output, since none of the coding rules are inherently tied to collaboration activities.

## REFERENCES

Baddeley, A. (1992). Working memory. *Science, 255*(5044), 556–559. doi:10.1126/science.1736359

Badura, V., Read, A. S., Briggs, R. O., & de Vreede, G. J. (2009). Exploring the effects of a convergence intervention on ideation artifacts: A multi-group field study. In *Proceedings of the Americas Conference on Information Systems*.

Barrouillet, P., Bernardin, S., Portrat, S., Vergauwe, E., & Camos, V. (2007). Time and cognitive load in working memory. *Journal of Experimental Psychology. Learning, Memory, and Cognition*, *33*(3), 570–585. doi:10.1037/0278-7393.33.3.570

Boehm, B., Grunbacher, P., & Briggs, R. O. (2001). Developing groupware for requirements negotiation: Lessons learned. *IEEE Software*, *18*(3), 46–55. doi:10.1109/52.922725

Briggs, R. O., & de Vreede, G. J. (2001). *ThinkLets: A pattern language for collaboration*. Broomfield, CO: GroupSystems Corporation.

Briggs, R. O., de Vreede, G. J., & Massey, A. P. (2008). Introduction to JAIS special issue on collaboration engineering. *Journal of the Association for Information Systems*, *10*, 118–120.

Briggs, R. O., de Vreede, G. J., & Nunamaker, J. F. Jr. (2003). Collaboration engineering with ThinkLets to pursue sustained success with group support systems. *Journal of Management Information Systems*, *19*(4), 31–64.

Chen, H., Hsu, P., Orwig, R., Hoopes, L., & Nunamaker, J. F. (1994). Automatic concept classification of text from electronic meetings. *Communications of the ACM*, *37*(10), 56–73. doi:10.1145/194313.194322

Davenport, T. H., & Völpel, S. C. (2001). The rise of knowledge towards attention management. *Library Hi Tech News Incorporating Online and CD Notes*, *5*(3), 212–222.

Davis, A. J., Badura, V., & de Vreede, G. J. (2008). Understanding methodological differences to study convergence in group support systems sessions. In *Proceedings of the 14th Collaboration Researchers' International Workshop on Groupware*, Omaha, NB.

Davis, A. J., de Vreede, G. J., & Briggs, R. O. (2007). Designing ThinkLets for convergence. In *Proceedings of the 13th Americas Conference on Information Systems*.

de Vreede, G. J., & Briggs, R. O. (2005). Collaboration engineering: Designing repeatable processes for high-value collaboration tasks. In *Proceedings of the 38th Hawaii International Conference on System Sciences* (p. 17). Washington, DC: IEEE Computer Society.

den Hengst, M., & de Vreede, G. J. (2004). Collaborate business process engineering: A decade of lessons from the field. *Journal of Management Information Systems*, *20*, 85–113.

Dennis, A. R., Hayes, G. S., & Daniels, R. M., Jr., (Eds.). (1994). *Proceedings of the Twenty-Seventh Annual Hawaii International Conference on System Sciences*. Washington, DC: IEEE Computer Society.

Diehl, M., & Stroebe, W. (1987). Productivity loss in brainstorming groups: Toward the solution of a riddle. *Journal of Personality and Social Psychology*, *53*(3), 497–509. doi:10.1037/0022-3514.53.3.497

Diehl, M., & Stroebe, W. (1991). Productivity loss in idea-generation groups: Tracking down the blocking effect. *Journal of Personality and Social Psychology*, *61*, 392–403. doi:10.1037/0022-3514.61.3.392

Dunlop, J. T. (1984). *Dispute resolution: Negotiation and consensus building*. Dover, MA: Auburn House.

Easton, G. K., George, J. F., Nunamaker, J. F. Jr, & Pendergast, M. O. (1990). Using two different electronic meeting system tools for the same task: An experimental comparison. *Journal of Management Information Systems*, *7*(1), 85–101.

Fjermestad, J., & Hiltz, S. R. (1999). An assessment of group support systems experimental research: Methodology and results. *Journal of Management Information Systems*, *15*(3), 7–149.

Fjermestad, J., & Hiltz, S. R. (2001). Group support systems: A descriptive evaluation of case and field studies. *Journal of Management Information Systems, 17*(3), 115–159.

Fruhling, A., & de Vreede, G.-J. (2006). Collaborative usability testing to facilitate stakeholder involvement. In Biffl, S., Aurum, A., Boehm, B., Erdogmus, H., & Grünbacher, P. (Eds.), *Value-based software engineering* (pp. 201–223). Berlin, Germany: Springer-Verlag. doi:10.1007/3-540-29263-2_10

Graham, W. K. (1977). Acceptance of ideas generated through individual and group brainstorming. *The Journal of Social Psychology, 101*(2), 231–234. doi:10.1080/00224545.1977.9924013

Innes, J. E., & Booher, D. E. (1999). Consensus building and complex adaptive systems. *Journal of the American Planning Association. American Planning Association, 65*(4), 412–423. doi:10.1080/01944369908976071

Kolfschoten, G. L., & Santanen, E. L. (2007). Reconceptualizing generate thinkLets: The role of the modifier. In *Proceedings of the 40th Annual Hawaii International Conference on System Sciences* (p. 16). Washington, DC: IEEE Computer Society.

Landis, J. R., & Koch, G. G. (1977). The measurement of observer agreement for categorical data. *Biometrics, 33*(1), 159–174. doi:10.2307/2529310

Lindgren, H. C. (1967). Brainstorming and the facilitation of creativity expressed in drawing. *Perceptual and Motor Skills, 24*(2), 350.

Marks, M. A., Zaccaro, S. J., & Matthieu, J. E. (2000). Performance implications of leader briefings and team-interaction for team adaptation to novel environments. *The Journal of Applied Psychology, 85*(6), 971–986. doi:10.1037/0021-9010.85.6.971

Osborn, A. (1963). *Applied imagination: Principles and procedures of creative problem solving* (Rev. ed., *Vol. 3*). New York, NY: Scribner.

Poesio, M. (1995). Semantic ambiguity and perceived ambiguity. In van Deemter, K., & Peters, S. (Eds.), *Semantic ambiguity and underspecification* (pp. 1–47). Stanford, CA: Center for the Study of Language and Information.

Reinig, B. A., Briggs, R. O., & Nunamaker, J. F. Jr. (2007). On the measurement of ideation quality. *Journal of Management Information Systems, 23*(4), 143–161. doi:10.2753/MIS0742-1222230407

Rosenau, J. N. (1962). Consensus-building in the American National Community: Some hypotheses and some supporting data. *The Journal of Politics, 24*(4), 639–661. doi:10.2307/2128039

Simonin, B. L. (1999). Ambiguity and the process of knowledge transfer in strategic alliances. *Strategic Management Journal, 20*(7), 595–623. doi:10.1002/(SICI)1097-0266(199907)20:7<595::AID-SMJ47>3.0.CO;2-5

Sweller, J., van Merrienboer, J., & Paas, F. (1998). Cognitive architecture and instructional design. *Educational Psychology Review, 10*(3), 251–296. doi:10.1023/A:1022193728205

Vennix, J. A. M., Akkermans, H. A., & Rouwette, E. A. J. A. (1996). Group model-building to facilitate organizational change: An exploratory study. *System Dynamics Review, 12*, 39–58. doi:10.1002/(SICI)1099-1727(199621)12:1<39::AID-SDR94>3.0.CO;2-K

Weick, K. E. (1993). The collapse of sensemaking in organizations: The Mann Gulch disaster. *Administrative Science Quarterly, 38*(4), 628–652. doi:10.2307/2393339

## APPENDIX

## Rules of Disaggregation

Source: (Badura et al., 2009)

DEFINITIONS:

PROBLEM: A problem is a desired state or outcome that has not yet been attained (e.g. Our customers do not feel satisfied, although we want them to).

SYMPTOM: A symptom is some unacceptable condition that implies some desired state or outcome that has not yet been attained (e.g. Customers are returning products)

GUIDLINE: Any time you must infer missing words to make a complete noun-verb-object problem statement, add them explicitly to the problem statement in parenthesis.

RULES:

1. Identify Verbs and Nouns
   - UNIQUE NVO: Each unique noun/verb/object combination that identifies a state or outcome that has not yet been attained will be disaggregated into simple problem statements.
   - ACCEPT SYMPTOMS: identifying a symptom is an important aspect of framing a problem, so they are acceptable as problem statements and disaggregated using the same rules.
   - MEANINGLESS VERB: Objects will not be disaggregated when doing so renders the verb meaningless. E.G. "We feel torn between our duties to home and work." We cannot disaggregate the problem to "we feel torn between our duties to home" and "we feel torn between our duties to work," because doing so renders the concept, "feeling torn between" meaningless.
   - ACCEPT REDUNDANCY: If people say the same thing in multiple ways in the same comment, disaggregate both wordings into simple problem statements. Redundancy will be removed in a later activity. Tag it as redundancy for later review.
2. Break Phrases
   - BREAK OUT FIRST CAUSES from CAUSE-AND-EFFECT: When presented with a causal chain, disaggregate first causes into stand-alone problem statements. For example, in the comment, "Under-staffing leads to overwork which leads to low morale," "(we have) understaffing" would be disaggregated as a separate problem statement.
   - DISTRIBUTE CAUSES: Distribute first causes across their consequent problem statements to make stand-alone problem statements. Add the first cause to the problem statement in parentheses so that the ideas can be understood in subsequent analysis steps. e.g. (rushed work) causes low satisfaction. For example, in the comment, "Under-staffing leads to overwork which leads to low morale," The understaffing cause would be paired with the overwork effect, and overwork as a cause would be paired with low morale, as follows: "(Understaffing) leads to overwork, and "(Overwork leads to) low morale." Thus, this comment would be broken out into three problem statements.

- MULTIPLE CAUSES: All first causes must be *combined* when distributing across consequent problems, because don't know whether either of the causes would invoke the effect on its own. For example, in the statement, "Understaffing and overwork cause low morale," it is not possible to know whether understaffing or overwork each cause low morale, or whether both together cause low morale. Therefore, in this case, both Understaffing and Overwork would be broken out as first causes (see above) but low morale would be broken out, "(Understaffing and overwork) cause low morale. Thus, this comment would be disaggregated into three problem statements, but they would differ from the three statements illustrated in the previous rule.
- NO THREE DEEP: Distributed causes will not span more than one cause and one effect - there will be no causal chains of three or more clauses in the disaggregated problem statements.
- RETAIN DEPENDENT CLAUSES - don't break out dependent clauses as separate problem statements unless they are part of a causal chain (Dependent clauses explain what, how or when) (the dependent clause may contain a problem statement when it begins with "to").

3.  Determine ambiguity
    - BRACKET AMBIGUITY: If you find the language of the contribution allows multiple grammatically-sound interpretations that could lead to different disaggregation structures, depending on which interpretation you adopt, make your best interpretation, disaggregate accordingly, but put your responses in brackets. Explain the ambiguity by stating at least two possible grammatically sound interpretations allowed by the wording of the original comment.
    - BRACKET SOLUTIONS DISGUISED AS PROBLEMS: If a problem statement is rhetorically stated as a solution, break it out as a problem statement and bracket it. It is not possibly reliably distinguish solutions from problems during disaggregation. They can be sorted out in a subsequent activity. Explain your brackets.
    - IGNORE THE POSITIVE: Do not include positive clauses or phrases in the set of disaggregated problem statements.
    - RHETORICAL QUESTIONS: If a statement contains a rhetorical question that can be re-framed as a problem statement, mark the comment as ambiguous and re-frame it as a problem statement, and disaggregate it.

4.  Ways to Resolution conflicts and ambiguities.
    - NEGOTIATE. Discuss the possible interpretations. If one is clearly more plausible ACCEPT that interpretation and disaggregate accordingly.
    - SYNTHESIZE a better interpretation together.
    - DISALLOW the comment as too ambiguous if it is not possible to determine which interpretation is more plausible, DO NOT DISAGGREGATE the comment.
    - ARITRATE. If coders discover that they have an irreconcilable disagreement about the meaning of the comment, submit it to a third coder for resolution.

*This work was previously published in the International Journal of Social and Organizational Dynamics in IT, Volume 1, Issue 3, edited by Michael B. Knight, pp. 1-17, 2011 by IGI Publishing (an imprint of IGI Global).*

# Section 2
# Organizational Issues

# Chapter 8
# Towards a Model of Employee Weblog Usage:
## A Process-Oriented Analysis of Antecedents and Consequences

**Philip Raeth**
*EBS Universität für Wirtschaft und Recht, Germany*

**Stefan Smolnik**
*EBS Universität für Wirtschaft und Recht, Germany*

## ABSTRACT

*The recent rise of Web 2.0 ideas, principles, and applications has significantly affected the communication and interaction in social networks. While Web 2.0's Internet usage and benefits have been investigated, certain questions are still unanswered: whether benefits such as enhanced collaboration and knowledge sharing also apply in an organizational context and whether there are more, still uncovered, benefits. Since research on the corporate adoption and use of Web 2.0 technologies is still in its early stages, neither qualitative nor quantitative models that could provide answers have been proposed. As a starting point for further developing this research stream, the authors collected and reviewed the literature on internal corporate blogging. Then the framework by Ives et al. (1980) was chosen to categorize the identified 25 articles for further analysis. The paper describes building a conceptual model and identifying the antecedents and consequences of employee weblog usage within corporations. The findings of the review suggest that employee blogging in corporations is a social and an organizational phenomenon. Individual perceptions and attitudes, peers, and cultures have a crucial influence on weblog usage, while the organization and its culture provide a framework.*

DOI: 10.4018/978-1-4666-1948-7.ch008

# INTRODUCTION

The Web 2.0 movement made its first public appearance at the O'Reilly Media Web 2.0 Conference in 2004. Since then, Web 2.0 has not only been discussed in the mass media, but has also drawn the attention of academia, starting with the ACM's Communications (Vol. 47:12) special issue on the "Blogosphere."

In addition, Web 2.0 tools have also started gaining popularity within the corporate world. A 2008 study by Gartner indicated that that year half of all US companies would use wikis (Morse, 2008). Other companies choose to implement weblogs or social network applications (Cross, Liedtka, & Weiss, 2005). The motive for using such software in the corporate environment is usually to improve communication with customers and business partners, and to encourage collaboration within the company (Bughin & Manyika, 2007).

Although the corporate Web 2.0 research community has made progress recently, the research area is not yet well structured. Most studies have an exploratory character, investigating the understanding of Web 2.0 tools' internal use. Some studies focus on organizational characteristics, others on user characteristics related to weblogs, while still others investigate the content of weblogs. In order to promote further understanding, the factors influencing weblog usage as well as benefits resulting from its use need to be assessed. The antecedents and consequences of system usage have been an issue in research for several decades (Andrew; Burton-Jones & Straub, 2006; Ives et al., 1980; Trice & Treacy, 1988). We therefore align our study with this research stream and explore weblog usage through a literature review examining events prior and subsequent to usage.

A literature review can be applied to a mature topic as well as to one with a much smaller body of literature. In the latter case, the goal of a literature review is initial theorizing (Torraco, 2005; Webster & Watson, 2002). Our aim is therefore to gather literature that discusses the antecedents

and consequences of corporate weblog usage. We ultimately propose a conceptual model summarizing our findings.

The next section describes the background of weblogs in corporate environments and of system usage in general. Subsequently, we briefly present the foundations required to build our conceptual model. This includes the conceptual framework to which we refer, our perspective on literature reviews, and the basics of process theory. Thereafter, we describe the chosen research method and the pursued research process. Next, we present and discuss the results of our study. The conclusion summarizes the results and outlines the implications, limitations, and contribution of this research.

# FOUNDATIONS

## Corporate Weblogs

Weblogs are websites in which an author, or a group of authors, publishes articles sporadically, or at regular intervals. Weblogs on the Internet are often created by individuals or small groups. To date, research on weblogs has focused on the motivations for blogging (Nardi, Schiano, Gumbrecht, & Swartz, 2004), the genres, and types – such as use within public relations and politics (Kelleher, 2008; Trammell, 2007) –, as wells as technical aspects (Du & Wagner, 2006). The number of corporate weblogs is increasing steadily (Du & Wagner, 2006) and their application areas are very diverse. Some corporate weblogs are only for internal use, but companies also apply this technology to market communications and public relation tasks (Cross et al., 2005).

## System Usage

System usage has received wide attention in the information systems (IS) research community. Researchers have focused on a variance-based and process perspective. Variance research has to date

*Figure 1. System usage*

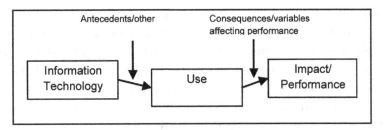

examined different antecedents of IS usage, such as acceptance (Davis, 1989; Straub, Limayem, & Karahanna-Evastiro, 1995; Venkatesh, Brown, & Maruping, 2008; Venkatesh, Morris, Davis, & Davis, 2003) as well as its consequences, such as success (DeLone & McLean, 1992, 2003; Petter, DeLone, & McLean, 2008) and post-adoptive behaviors (Jasperson, Carter, & Zmud, 2005). However, these issues have also been examined from a process-based perspective (Orlikowski, 2000; Soh & Markus, 1995). Figure 1 depicts system usage as illustrated by Trice and Treacy (1988).

Another relevant aspect that Burton-Jones and Gallivan (2007) address in this realm refers to the multilevel nature of system usage. According to Klein and Kozlowski (2000, p. 79), a multilevel perspective "entails more than one level of conceptualization and analysis." Both these authors call for more multilevel IS research, a request

which we try to answer by adopting a user as well as an organizational perspective.

## CONCEPTUAL GROUNDING

## A Model for Computer-Based Research in Management Information Systems

We frame our literature review within the research model by Ives et al. (1980). This model is based on a literature review of preceding frameworks and consists of three IS environments (user, IS development, and IS operations), three IS processes (use, operation, and development), and the information system itself. All the IS-related environments and processes, as well as the information system can be situated in an organizational and external environment, as visualized in Figure 2.

*Figure 2. A framework for computer-based management information systems (Ives et al., 1980)*

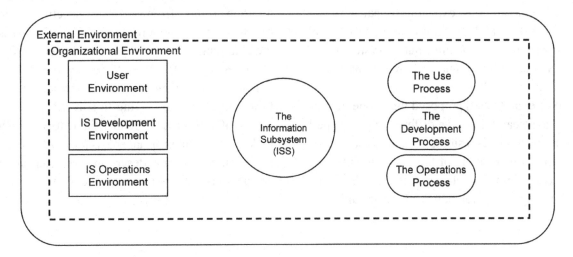

The external environment consists of characteristics or constraints, such as legal, political, or economic factors, that do not originate from an organizational background. Furthermore, the organizational environment is represented by goals, tasks, hierarchies, company size, culture, and related aspects. The user environment is related to the primary users and their tasks, their organization, and various user characteristics. Further, development techniques, design personnel characteristics, and IS development's organization and management are included in the IS development environment. Finally, the IS operations environment contains all the resources necessary for IS operations. These are mainly hardware and software, but also operations personnel, documents, and IS operations' management or organization.

The process variables represent the processes. The use process reflects the interaction between the environmental characteristics and the use of an information system. It expresses the "goodness" of an information system, and can be measured in various ways, such as cost, time, user satisfaction, and implementation success. The operation's process represents the actual functioning of the operation resource. The operation or performance is usually measured by the costs and time expended, or by the staff's satisfaction. Finally, the development process refers to the outcome of the resources invested in the development of the information system. The measures of such an outcome are the time and cost expenditure, participation in, support of, and impact on the organizational environment, etc. The information system is the last element of the framework, represented by a circle in Figure 2.

Ives et al. (1980) proposed this model to categorize research into five different types. Type I research examines a single variable group. Type II studies one or more of the environment characteristics' impact on the process variables. Type III investigates the relationship between information subsystem (ISS) characteristics and process variables. Type IV examines the relationship between ISS characteristics and environmental characteristics or constraints. Finally, type V research analyzes the relationships between one or more of three category variables. In our review, we focus on the user environment, the organizational environment, and the use process (type I and II). On the one hand, this focus is based on the lack of studies investigating the relationship between ISS characteristics and the use process. On the other hand, since Web 2.0 represents emergent technologies, it is mainly driven by organizational and personal characteristics instead of technical aspects (McAfee, 2006).

## A Narrative Perspective in Literature Reviews

A classic, systematic review is difficult when undertaking a literature review of an emerging field. This is due to systematic reviews' additive structure, which is hard to achieve with a small body of literature (Hammersley, 2001). Furthermore, most of the studies examine different aspects by using different sets of research methods, different research questions, and different levels of analysis. This issue can be addressed by adopting a narrative perspective, which is not concerned with aggregating vast amounts of studies investigating the same problem (Denyer & Tranfield, 2006). Instead, it aggregates studies that describe a certain problem from various perspectives, each of which contribute a piece to the puzzle that is the emerging theory (Denyer & Tranfield, 2006; Hammersley, 2001). Accordingly, every article in our literature review contributes a unique piece to the puzzle we are trying to solve. Narratives represent a process embedded in a story, which makes them an appropriate basis for developing a process theory. Before describing how a narrative can be transferred to a process theory, we briefly explain this type of theory.

## Variance and Process Theory

Process theory is best explained by comparing it to its counterpart, variance theory (Mohr, 1982). The difference between variance and process theories lies in their definitions of an occurrence's cause. While variance theory states that a cause is necessary and sufficient when stated in a model, process theory demands sequentially required conditions. Consequently, the presence of a cause does not necessarily lead to the anticipated outcome, as chance and random events are taken into account (Markus & Robey, 1988). Another difference lies in the two meta-theories' assumptions concerning antecedents and consequences. While variance theory assumes that there is an invariant relationship between antecedents and consequences, process theory presumes that the consequences only occur if certain conditions are present. However, the consequences may still not occur. Finally, process theory does not refer to consequences as variables. Instead, they are phenomena representing changes in states (Markus & Robey, 1988). In summary, variance theory explains relationships in terms of dependent and independent variables connected by a causal relationship (more X results in more Y). Process theory concentrates on sequences and its adjunct events that lead to a distinctive outcome (do X, then Y to achieve Z) (Markus & Robey, 1988). Process theory therefore mainly tries to answer the question why variables are related, but not the way they are related to one another (Pentland, 1999).

## Building Process Theory with Narrative

Pentland (1999) introduces different levels of structure in narrative. He postulates that a narrative is structured into four levels of "deepness." Firstly, there is the raw text, which refers to the "particular telling of a story by a specific narrator" (Pentland, 1999, p. 719). Secondly, from this text, a story is created, representing the fabula

from a specific point of view (a fabula describes a different set of events and their relationships, for example, how a person was hired: what happened? Who did what?). Thirdly, a generalized fabula is built from the story, namely a set of events and their relationships. Fourthly, the underlying mechanisms that allow and sanction the fabula can be identified (Pentland, 1999; Van de Ven & Poole, 1995).

Process theory can be created from various sources of narrative (Pentland, 1999). One may also refer to already published sources and treat them as one's own narrative (Martin, Feldmann, Hatch, & Sitkin, 1983), which is also our approach in this paper. This also fits the narrative perspective that we have of literature reviews. Every article has its own narrative and stands on its own at first. By undertaking a cross-case analysis (Eisenhardt, 1989), we try to grasp the mechanism underlying all the narratives under investigation. These narratives may contain all four levels of deepness as previously described.

Hence, we analyzed all the articles within the Ives et al. model by investigating type I as well as type II studies. Within type I studies, we only considered the user and the organizational environment. This helped us understand the antecedents and consequences of the internal weblog usage process.

## METHODOLOGY

### Literature Selection Process

To allow a good overview of the relevant literature, we considered the Web 2.0 literature's emergent status. Consequently, we undertook various steps to ensure that the review had a very broad character. Initially, we defined the literature's scope by first limiting the search to a number of leading IS journals. These were defined by means of the Association of Information Systems (AIS) journal's meta ranking, which is a conglomeration of several journal rankings. Secondly, we included five important and influential IS conference proceedings (ICIS, HICSS, ECIS, AMCIS, CSCW) in the review. In order to include literature from beyond the IS community, we also followed a cross-discipline approach. We consequently examined several research databases (EBSCO, ScienceDirect, and ABI/Inform), which included journals and conference proceedings that fall outside important rankings.

Herring et al. (2005) maintain that weblogs first appeared in 1997; we therefore set the time range from 1997 to 2009. In addition, we used the following 11 keywords – part of the elements describing Web 2.0 (O'Reilly, 2007) –, in a keyword search: weblog, wiki, social network, folksonomy, social software, social computing, tag, collective intelligence, Web 2.0, and Enterprise 2.0. Finally, we conducted a peer review as a quality limitation, which guaranteed that the literature to be reviewed would be of a certain quality. Based on the first set of articles identified through the above-mentioned

criteria, we started a second review round. Each of the articles' references were checked by means of the Web of Science (which allows an article's citation to be tracked) as well as Google Scholar. This allowed us to go back in time by using the references, and to go forward by means of the Web of Science and Google Scholar. This process also enabled us to include articles not contained in the initial set of conferences and journals. This was an important step, as the majority of articles that are relevant for this emerging body of literature are published in rather specialized conference proceedings or journals.

## Framework of Analysis

Our overall analysis framework is based on the five different focal points in Figure 3. We used a bottom–up approach to code the theoretical foundations as well as the unit of analysis. The analysis of the hierarchy of evidence was based on the selected journals or conferences' review

*Figure 3. Analytical framework*

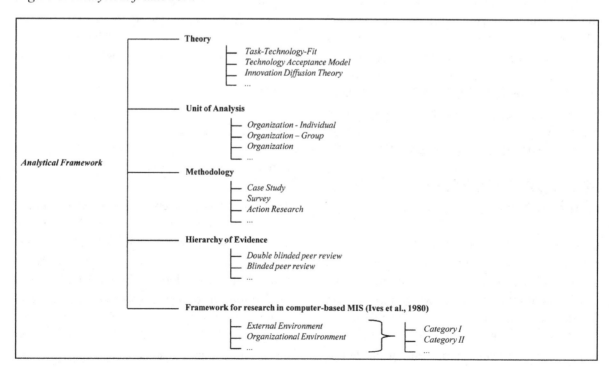

practices. Ives et al.'s (1980) framework for IS research was used as the underlying structure.

## Coding Procedure

We coded the articles identified in our literature review according to the framework. The problem regarding articles that could not be unanimously attributed to a category within Ives et al.'s (1980) framework was solved by discussing the particular discrepancy and obtaining consensus. Furthermore, the remaining articles were coded according to the criteria for internal weblog usage's antecedents and consequences. Disagreement was once again solved through a discussion of the differences.

For the narrative analysis, we coded the stories' basic elements by identifying the actors, their actions, their goals, and the final outcome of their actions – if possible. Further, we differentiated between actual events and hypothesized, generalized, or fictional events. For a more detailed outline of such an analysis, see Ramiller and Pentland (2009). Finally, we also coded for possible constructs by conducting an iterative tabulation of each construct identified in the articles (Eisenhardt, 1989).

## RESULTS

In our review, we found 296 articles dealing with Web 2.0 issues; of these, only 25 articles studied weblogs in corporate intranets (Figure 4).

Our aim was to include type I studies investigating the organizational and user environment, as well as type II studies examining the use process from an organizational and user perspective. Twelve articles fulfilled this requirement (Figure 5).

*Figure 4. Distribution of articles*

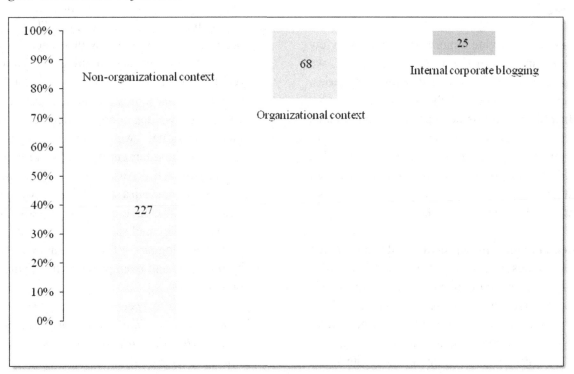

*Figure 5. Distribution of articles (according to the Ives et al. framework)*

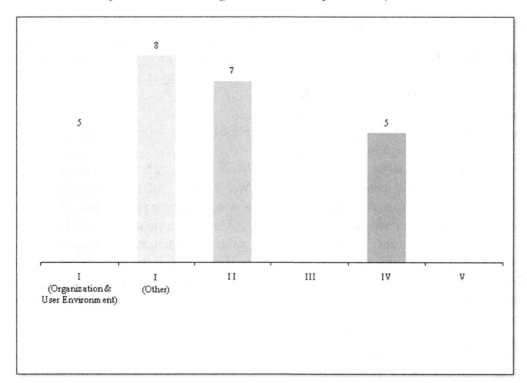

## Antecedents of Internal Weblog Usage

In order to provide a more structured overview of the findings in the antecedents section, we classified them into three different categories. Social factors describe the antecedents of use, which characterize issues related to an individual's social surroundings. Individual factors relate to factors directly linked to the individual. Finally, organizational factors denote criteria associated with a higher or more abstract organizational element than the individual.

**Social Factors:** In respect of social factors, some studies suggest that weblog usage is fostered by the peer group in which the individual is engaged. For example, Jackson et al. (2007) indicate that highly active users engage more in active commenting than in blogging. This suggests that "active involvement with others

on the system" relates to the use of weblogs (Jackson et al., 2007, p. 3). Another study states that individuals are more likely to use a weblog if they know their peers will read and contribute to something they wrote (Ojala, 2004). In addition, Wattal et al. (2009) found a similar indication in their study on employees' weblog adoption. According to them, individuals' weblog usage is higher if most of the other employees working in the same branch also use weblogs. The same point is also made in a study by Efimova and Grudin (2007). In interviews, employees stated that they had started weblogs due to prominent bloggers' influence, examples set by bloggers, and even pressure from other bloggers.

P1: *Users will refer to a peer group when forming their opinions on internal weblog usage, as well as when deciding whether they should start or read a weblog.*

**Individual Factors:** Individual factors appear to be most important when deciding whether to start a weblog. One of the main factors is the perceived weblog benefits. For example, some individuals perceived the time spent blogging as an investment in a future benefit rather than allocating it as a cost factor (Jackson et al., 2007). Others noted that they had visions and ideas of how a weblog could influence their working life and acted upon these (Efimova & Grudin, 2007). Non-users stated that they did not feel that a weblog was a productive tool with which to provide added value within their workplace (Yardi, Golder, & Brozozowski, 2009).

An issue we found to be closely related to the perceived benefit of weblog usage refers to the time and effort it takes to maintain a weblog. People state that they do not have a sufficient time to pursue blogging (Jackson et al., 2007). However, users also argue that, although it takes time, blogging can also play a role in their work-related activities, but only if there is a good rationale for this (Efimova & Grudin, 2007). Users who see a benefit in blogging perceive the time and effort required as rather less restricting.

The perception of blogging and its benefits for work is also influenced by an employee's knowledge of this form of communication. Kosonen et al. (2007) argue that potential users may actually need weblogs in their working environment, but are completely unaware of this. They simply lack knowledge of a weblog's possible uses and benefits. Consequently, marketing and education have a significant impact on the perception of internal weblogs. This issue has also been raised by Stocker and Tochtermann (2008), who found that if weblogs were not promoted, readers were simply unaware of them and tended to overlook them although they could be of interest. Another study mentions that some employees, who did read weblogs, did not realize that they were accessing a weblog. Consequently, the full potential

of such a weblog could not be exploited (Yardi et al., 2009). Finally, Jackson et al. (2007) report that some users complain about not knowing how to get started or doubted that weblogs were relevant to their business. Accordingly, training on these topics might alter their perception of blogging.

Besides marketing and education, experience with Web 2.0 applications also played a role in the use of corporate weblogs. In this respect, however, opinions are mixed. Ip and Wagner (2008) state that employees who are used to weblogs already have enough knowledge to transfer the use of weblogs to corporations. Conversely, Yardi et al.'s (2009) observations tell a somewhat different story. They too noticed that younger employees tend to have more experiences with weblogs, but, rather than frequently using weblogs internally, these employees avoided usage due to the constraints put in place by the corporation. It seems that the perceived benefits they had gained through their experiences outside the corporation decreased their perception of weblogs' benefits behind a firewall. According to another study, the shift from using social media in a private environment to employing it in the workplace does not seem to be as natural as one may think. Without the institutionalization of a Web 2.0 application, its status seems to be rather contentious (Kosonen et al., 2007).

The existence of relevant content and readers is another important observation for the perception of weblogs. Employees complain about the lack of work-related weblog content that is important for their work assignments (Stocker & Tochtermann, 2008). Others criticize weblogs for not finding interesting topics, or for their lack of readership (Jackson et al., 2007). Not surprisingly, readership plays a major role in bloggers' lives. Some are thrilled with the feedback they receive, while others complain about having none (Yardi et al., 2009). The problem with weblogs – as with all content-driven media – is their initial lack of content. A possible solution lies in what Jackson et al. (2007) call a critical mass. At some point, the number of employees commenting on weblog posts will be large enough to serve the needs of a large community.

P2: *Employees assess the value of internal we-blogs through their perceived benefit, which is influenced by the peer group, state of knowledge, experience, and critical mass.*

Control and trust are rather behavioral aspects of weblog usage. Some users are scared of giving away information, as they might lose control of it (Jackson et al., 2007). Some even fear losing their unique position by publishing information that might make their very existence in the organization obsolete (Kosonen et al., 2007). Others complain that the original purpose of blogging – being controversial and personal – is not a valid option in a corporation. They claim that "corporate blogging does not feel natural" (Jackson et al., 2007, p. 8). It is therefore difficult for employees to assess which information has a place in a corporate weblog and which is improper or even risky (Efimova & Grudin, 2007). Consequently, starting a weblog and putting oneself "out there" requires courage (Kosonen et al., 2007). This courage unavoidably leads to a loss of control. Users apparently sense that there are some risks associated with starting a weblog, which could lead to loss of information or even false information, which influences business decisions (Sherer & Alter, 2004).

P3: *Users' decision to use weblogs in their corporation will depend on the control and trust issues raised by the given organizational context.*

**Organizational Factors:** As pointed out earlier, organizational factors are the third group of factors that seem to have a major impact on weblog usage.

The use by and support of the top management have often been mentioned in the IS literature as an important factor of IS use (Thong, Yap, & Ra-

man, 1996). Consequently, it is no surprise that these factors play a major role in the articles that we reviewed. Wattal et al. (2009) suggest that weblog users tend to use weblogs more often if their manager does so. This also holds true if the management provides general top-down support (Yardi, Golder, & Brzozowski, 2008). Managers allow a weblog to be initiated and are therefore also an important barrier to its use if they do not do so. Since managers' attitudes vary from fear to enthusiasm, they assume the role of gatekeepers in their specific area of responsibility. When a weblog has been initiated, managers discuss its areas of application, but also help solve related problems. They could, however, also be completely unaware of the phenomenon and therefore develop a dismissive attitude (Efimova & Grudin, 2007). However, a study by Yardi et al. (2009) suggests that the situation in the company they investigated was slightly different. While blogging was popular within the corporation they analyzed, the dissatisfaction with blogging that employees expressed was mostly related to a lack of management support. Finally, these findings suggest that management support plays a mediating role. This support can either foster or hinder employees' adoption of weblogs.

P4: *Management support, use, and attitude have an influence on weblog usage in corporations in that they can either foster or hinder use.*

Organizational culture is defined as an organization's attitudes, experiences, beliefs, and values (Truban, McLean, & Wetherbe, 2002). It is noticeable that each study of the different elements found to influence internal blogging reveals a slight variance in the common findings. These variances might refer to the studies' different cultural settings. The previously mentioned examples are a case in point. For example, management use of weblogs plays a different role within the various studies. While all the studies acknowledged the importance of management support, the nature of the management's importance and role differs. While some corporations might give their employees the freedom to experiment with weblogs, which seems to be the case in Yardi et al.'s (2009) study, others might be very restrictive (Efimova & Grudin, 2007).

However, even if the management is not restrictive, their employees might still revert to older values and experiences, as indicated in Yardi et al.'s (2009) study. In these authors' study, bloggers point out that, while employees respond strongly to their weblog posts, they do not use the intended channel: comments. Instead, they revert to channels such as email or face-to-face communication. Consequently, organizations deal with weblogs in a totally heterogeneous manner and in keeping with their specific behaviors, values, experiences, and beliefs. Another example is that of a blogger who was reprimanded for putting a certain piece of information on his weblog, although he believed that sharing this information through other communication channels would not have been an issue (Kosonen et al., 2007).

Finally, every corporation will have to deal with weblogs' informal and open character in its own way in order to achieve successful adoption (Kosonen et al., 2007). The corporate culture must, however, somewhat fit the openness that constitutes the crux of blogging (Ip & Wagner, 2008).

P5: *If the organizational culture fits the openness and informality of weblogs, they could be used to a greater extent.*

## Consequences of Internal Weblog Usage

We found that the consequences of blogging comprise three different levels of aggregation. Individual benefit is at the lowest level, community benefit at the middle level, followed by organizational benefit, which is the highest level of aggregation.

**Individual Benefits:** Individual benefits are clustered into four different aspects. Firstly, there are the sheer informational aspects that one might expect from blogging. These are obtaining feedback, receiving information, journaling one's activities (Jackson et al., 2007), and facilitating knowledge transfer (Stocker & Tochtermann, 2008). Secondly, an often-mentioned, much more interesting aspect is the social benefits that individuals gain. For example, people are contacted outside their usual responsibilities and invited to give a talk. Thirdly, their work relationships extend from a rather departmental orientation to a more networked cross-branch connection (Yardi et al., 2009). These networking benefits also provide them with a gain in reputation and, even better, with career possibilities (Jackson et al., 2007). Finally, Jackson et al. (2007) identify other benefits that do not fit into the above-mentioned categories, such as self-expression, working efficiently, or managing upwards. These suggest that weblogs seem to help with achieving strictly individual goals that suddenly become achievable through weblogs' open nature.

P6: *Individuals' benefits from employee blogging stem from informational, social, and unique uses of weblogs.*

**Community Benefits:** Community benefit is a special form of group benefits, as a community represents a group of people connected through their interests and skills. Employees therefore also gain a community benefit. The community-related benefit originates from linking or sharing information within a certain group of people with similar interests. In the studies under investigation, employees often stated they would experience a sense of community membership by maintaining a weblog. Readers expressed this feeling as well (Efimova & Grudin, 2007; Jackson et al., 2007; Trimi & Galanxhi-Janaqi, 2008).

In respect of a community as a peer group of well known colleagues, employees mentioned benefits that facilitate communication. Facilitation refers to a quick, informal, free, wide communication within a context (Jackson et al., 2007). Communities seem to create a set of corporate sub-groups, which accelerates communication between their members and seems to create value for their members that are greater than its parts. This observation is also emphasized by Sippel and Brodt (2008), who propose that blogging communities shape group and organizational identities. That is, they form the emotional and value significance of belonging to an organizational entity, therewith facilitating knowledge transfer for the organization.

P7: *Community benefit is produced when users participate and interact in specific interest or skill groups through which value greater than its parts is realized.*

**Organizational Benefits:** On a corporate level, internal weblogs offer two kinds of knowledge benefits. Firstly, the internal "Blogosphere" provides a glimpse into changes in the corporation. Jackson et al. (2007) mention an example of a pension plan change. As this plan affected quite a large percentage of the employees, it was widely discussed in the weblogs, therefore providing people engaging in the conversation with a wider perspective. Most importantly, however, it made the transition for the company as a whole a lot easier. Stocker and Tochtermann (2008) observed and describe a similar phenomenon. In addition, Kosonen et al. (2007) go one step further by stating that weblogs do not only facilitate changes in corporate strategy, but are also employed to fulfill strategic goals. The communication is, however, not unidirectional. Internal weblogs also allow employees' actual topics to be recognized. To a degree, weblogs help employees gain access to important topics or keep track of what is on people's minds.

P8: *Employee blogging provides organizational benefit by facilitating organizational change and by acknowledging actual employee topics.*

Figure 6 illustrates the described propositions with organizational culture as the moderator.

*Figure 6. A basic model of employee weblog usage*

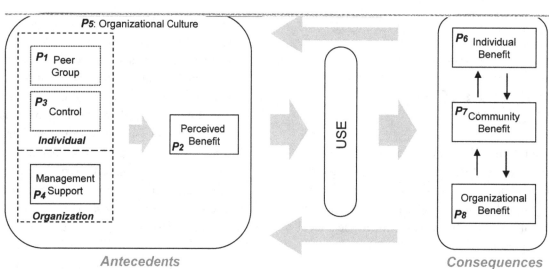

## DISCUSSION

The findings in our review suggest that employee blogging in corporations is a social and an organizational phenomenon. Individual perceptions, peers, and cultures have a crucial influence on weblog usage, while the organization and its culture provide a framework.

This implies a structurationalist perspective as proposed by Giddens (1984) and Walsham and Ham (1991). Structuration suggests that people using technology draw on the properties of the technological artifact. Likewise, they fall back upon on their skills, power, knowledge, assumptions, and expectations. These are shaped by their experiences with other technologies in the social environments in which they sojourn as well as in the institutions in which they live and work. Consequently, the use of technology is structured by the norms, technology, and interpretive schemes in their institution (Orlikowski, 2000). Hence, weblog usage seems to be heavily influenced by the institutional technology, norms, and interpretive schemes in which they are used.

Within the system usage literature, our findings are supported by the body of adoption and acceptance research. For example, the Unified Theory of Acceptance and Technology (UTAUT), which represents an aggregation of acceptance and adoption theories, states that social influence is a major factor with regard to technology acceptance. Additionally, UTAUT's performance expectancy refers to "the degree to which an individual believes that using the system will" help increase his or her job performance (Venkatesh et al., 2003, p. 447). Although perceived benefit covers more than just job performance in our case, this construct as well as other personal benefit dimensions, such as perceived enjoyment (van der Heijden, 2004), may be used in a study. We studied the antecedents and consequences of weblog usage from a multilevel perspective. From a variance perspective, such an endeavor is far more difficult and has been a major issue for researchers other than IS

ones (Burton-Jones & Gallivan, 2007; DeLone & McLean, 1992, 2003; Kline & Kozlowski, 2000; Wixom & Todd, 2005). For example, to take the behavioral (P1), organizational (P5), informational (P2) aspects, as well as the success dimensions into account, researchers could base their model on Wixom and Todd's (2005) integration of user satisfaction and technology acceptance. However, as DeLone and McLean note (2003), attitudes, and their links with behavior, are notoriously difficult to measure. In our model, weblog usage is heavily influenced by attitudes, therefore posing the same problems as stipulated by DeLone and McLean. Consequently, a holistic model – such as the one we propose – has to overcome some barriers to IS theory.

One major finding within our framework is the impact of individual benefits on community benefits and vice versa. These collective benefits are often introduced in existing frameworks (DeLone & McLean, 1992, 2003), but the interaction between the individual and collective success categories is rarely investigated (Andrew Burton-Jones, 2005). Consequently, theories investigating weblog success in enterprises have to incorporate these dimensions in the future.

Finally, our findings also have managerial implications. Managers seeking to understand the benefits to be gained from employee blogging have to be aware that weblogs are an open communication tool. It prospers in organizations that tolerate its free use and provide an open culture.

## CONCLUSION

Our review found that the employee weblog literature is a very small body of work. Most of the studies are of an exploratory character, which meant that we had to engage in a narrative review. By using process theory, we synthesized the literature and proposed a process model for weblog usage.

The research is limited in that the proposed model is merely based on an extensive literature review and on our experiences, therefore perhaps lacking thoroughness, as Tranfield et al. (2003) point out. In addition, the number of articles we studied is small in size and may therefore suffer bias concerning the area of study. Finally, the study of weblogs as well as Web 2.0 in corporations is in its early phase, resulting in a rather scattered image of the phenomenon instead of a complete picture.

Further, while system usage, its antecedents, and its consequences could be criticized for originating from a variance-based perspective of theory, Soh and Markus (1995) demonstrate that the latter can rightly serve as a basis for a process synthesis.

We believe that our model can serve as a starting point for future theorizing. As Gregor (2006, p. 622) points out, process theory can be employed to study "context, content, and settings in which information systems are introduced and isolate some of the more important conditions and events that lead to various outcomes." A variance theoretical approach could be taken to test the degree of relationships between the events. Consequently, our contribution lies in providing an initial model for employee weblog usage that synthesizes the findings to date and smoothes the path for a more thorough understanding of employee weblog usage. Researchers could, for example, engage in either part of our model. That is, for example, testing whether existing models face challenges when explaining elements found in our model. As Majchrzak (2009) suggests regarding wikis, it will also be necessary to investigate whether theories such as structuration, elaboration likelihood, and social capital hold for weblogs in corporations. Our model may serve as an orientation for crafting these studies.

## REFERENCES

Bughin, J., & Manyika, J. (2007). How businesses are using Web 2.0: A McKinsey global survey. *The McKinsey Quarterly*, 32–39.

Burton-Jones, A. (2005). *New perspectives on the system usage construct.* Unpublished doctoral dissertation, Georgia State University, Atlanta, GA.

Burton-Jones, A., & Gallivan, M. J. (2007). Toward a deeper understanding of system usage in organizations: A multilevel perspective. *Management Information Systems Quarterly*, *31*(4), 657–279.

Burton-Jones, A., & Straub, D. (2006). Reconceptualizing system usage: An approach and an empirical test. *Information Systems Research*, *17*(3), 228–246. doi:10.1287/isre.1060.0096

Cross, R., Liedtka, J., & Weiss, L. (2005). A practical guide to social networks. *Harvard Business Review*, *83*(3), 124–132.

Davis, F. D. (1989). Perceived usefulness, perceived ease of use, and user acceptance of information technology. *Management Information Systems Quarterly*, *13*(3), 319–340. doi:10.2307/249008

DeLone, W. H., & McLean, E. R. (1992). Information systems success: The quest for the dependent variable. *Information Systems Research*, *3*(1), 60–95. doi:10.1287/isre.3.1.60

DeLone, W. H., & McLean, E. R. (2003). The DeLone and McLean model of information systems success: A ten-year update. *Journal of Management Information Systems*, *19*(4), 9–30.

Denyer, D., & Tranfield, D. (2006). Using qualitative research synthesis to build an actionable knowledge base. *Management Decision*, *44*(2), 213–227. doi:10.1108/00251740610650201

Du, H. S., & Wagner, C. (2006). Weblog success: Exploring the role of technology. *International Journal of Human-Computer Studies*, *64*(9), 789–798. doi:10.1016/j.ijhcs.2006.04.002

Efimova, L., & Grudin, J. (2007). Crossing boundaries: A case study of employee blogging. In *Proceedings of the 40ᵗʰ Hawaii International Conference on System Sciences*.

Eisenhardt, K. M. (1989). Building theories from case study research. *Academy of Management Review*, *14*(4), 532–550.

Giddens, A. (1984). *The constitution of society*. Berkley, CA: University of California Press.

Greogor, S. (2006). The nature of theory in information systems. *Management Information Systems Quarterly*, *30*(3), 611–642.

Hammersley, M. (2001). On "systematic" reviews of research literatures: A 'narrative' response to Evans & Benfield. *British Educational Research Journal*, *27*(5), 543–664. doi:10.1080/01411920120095726

Herring, S. C., Scheidt, L. A., Bonus, S., & Wright, E. (2005). Weblogs as a bridging genre. *Information Technology & People*, *18*(2), 142–171. doi:10.1108/09593840510601513

Ip, K. F. R., & Wagner, C. (2008). Weblogging: A study of social computing and its impact on organizations. *Decision Support Systems*, *45*(2), 242–250. doi:10.1016/j.dss.2007.02.004

Ives, B., Hamilton, S., & Davis, G. B. (1980). A framework for research in computer-based management information systems. *Management Science*, *26*(9), 911–934. doi:10.1287/mnsc.26.9.910

Jackson, A., Yates, J., & Orlikowski, W. (2007). Corporate blogging: Building community through persistent digital talk. In *Proceedings of the 40th Hawaii International Conference on System Sciences* (p. 80).

Jasperson, S., Carter, P. E., & Zmud, R. W. (2005). A comprehensive conceptualization of post-adoptive behaviours associated with information technology enabled work systems. *Management Information Systems Quarterly*, *29*(3), 525–557.

Kelleher, T. (2008). Organizational contingencies, organizational blogs and public relations practitioner stance toward publics. *Public Relations Review*, *34*(3), 300–303. doi:10.1016/j.pubrev.2008.05.003

Kline, K. J., & Kozlowski, S. W. J. (2000). *Multilevel theory, research and methods in organizations*. San Francisco, CA: Jossey-Bass.

Kosonen, M., Henttonen, K., & Ellonen, K.-H. (2007). Weblogs and internal communication in a corporate environment: A case from the ICT industry. *International Journal of Knowledge and Learning*, *3*(4-5), 437–459. doi:10.1504/IJKL.2007.016704

Majchrzak, A. (2009). Comment: Where is the theory in Wikis? *Management Information Systems Quarterly*, *33*(1), 18–20.

Markus, M. L., & Robey, D. (1988). Information technology and organizational change: Causal structure in theory and research. *Management Science*, *34*(5), 583–598. doi:10.1287/mnsc.34.5.583

Martin, J., Feldmann, M. S., Hatch, M. J., & Sitkin, S. B. (1983). The uniqueness paradox in organizational stories. *Administrative Science Quarterly*, *28*(3), 438–453. doi:10.2307/2392251

McAfee, A. P. (2006). Enterprise 2.0: The dawn of emergent collaboration. *MIT Sloan Management Review*, *47*(3), 21–28.

Mohr, L. B. (1982). *Explaining organizational behaviour*. San Francisco, CA: Jossey-Bass.

Morse, G. (2008). Conversation - Wikipedia founder Jimmy Wales on making the most of company wikis. *Harvard Business Review*, *86*(4), 26.

Nardi, B. A., Schiano, D. J., Gumbrecht, M., & Swartz, L. (2004). Why we blog. *Communications of the ACM, 47*(12), 41–46. doi:10.1145/1035134.1035163

O'Reilly, T. (2007). What Is Web 2.0: Design patterns and business models for the next generation of software. *Communications & Strategies, 65*(1), 17–37.

Ojala, M. (2004). *Weaving weblogs into knowledge sharing and dissemination.* Nord I&D, Knowledge and Change.

Orlikowski, W. J. (2000). Using technology and constituting structures: A practice lens for studying technology in organizations. *Organization Science, 11*(4), 404–428. doi:10.1287/orsc.11.4.404.14600

Pentland, B. T. (1999). Building process theory with narrative: From description to explanation. *Academy of Management Review, 24*(4), 711–724.

Petter, S., DeLone, W., & McLean, E. (2008). Measuring information systems success: Models, dimensions, measures, and interrelationships. *European Journal of Information Systems, 17*(3), 236–263. doi:10.1057/ejis.2008.15

Ramiller, N. C., & Pentland, B. T. (2009). Management implications in information system research: The untold story. *Journal of Management Information Systems, 10*(6), 474–495.

Sherer, S. A., & Alter, S. (2004). Information system risks and risk factors: Are they mostly about Information Systems. *Communications of the AIS, 14*(2), 36–65.

Sippel, B., & Brodt, S. E. (2008). The psychology of blogging communities: Social identities and knowledge transfer across work-groups. In *Proceedings of the 2nd International AAAI Conference on Weblogs and Social Media.*

Soh, C., & Markus, M. L. (1995). How IT creates business value: A process theory synthesis. In *Proceedings of the Sixteenth International Conference on Information Systems.*

Stocker, A., & Tochtermann, K. (2008). Investigating weblogs in small and medium enterprises: An exploratory case study. In *Proceedings of the Workshops on Social Aspects of the Web.*

Straub, D., & Limayem, M., & Karahanna-Evastiro. (1995). Measuring system usage: Implications for IS system testing. *Management Science, 41*(8), 1328–1342. doi:10.1287/mnsc.41.8.1328

Thong, J. Y. L., Yap, C.-S., & Raman, K. S. (1996). Top management support, external expertise and information systems implementation in small businesses. *Information Systems Research, 7*(2), 248–267. doi:10.1287/isre.7.2.248

Torraco, R. J. (2005). Writing integrative literature reviews: Guidelines and examples. *Human Resource Development Review, 4*(3), 356–367. doi:10.1177/1534484305278283

Trammell, K. D. S. (2007). Candidate campaign blogs: Directly reaching out to the youth vote. *The American Behavioral Scientist, 50*(9), 1255–1264. doi:10.1177/0002764207300052

Tranfield, D., Denyer, D., & Smart, P. (2003). Towards a methodology for developing evidence-informed management knowledge by means of systematic review. *British Journal of Management, 14*(3), 207–223. doi:10.1111/1467-8551.00375

Trice, A. W., & Treacy, M. E. (1988). Utilization as a dependent variable in MIS research. *Database, 19*(3-4), 33–42.

Trimi, S., & Galanxhi-Janaqi, H. (2008). Organisation and employee congruence: A framework for assessing the success of organisational blogs. *International Journal of Information Technology and Management, 7*(2), 120–133. doi:10.1504/IJITM.2008.016600

Truban, E., McLean, E., & Wetherbe, J. (2002). *Information technology for management* (3rd ed.). New York, NY: John Wiley & Sons.

Van de Ven, A. H., & Poole, M. S. (1995). Explaining development and change in organizations. *Academy of Management Review, 20*(3), 510–540.

van der Heijden, H. (2004). User acceptance of hedonic information systems. *Management Information Systems Quarterly, 28*(4), 695–705.

Venkatesh, V., Brown, S. A., Maruping, L., & Bala, A., Hillol. (2008). Predicting different conceptualizations of system use: The competing roles of behavioral intention, facilitating conditions, and behavioral expectation. *Management Information Systems Quarterly, 32*(3), 483–502.

Venkatesh, V., Morris, M. G., Davis, G. B., & Davis, F. D. (2003). User acceptance of information technology: Toward a unified view. *Management Information Systems Quarterly, 27*(3), 425–473.

Walsham, G., & Ham, C. K. (1991). Structuration theory and information systems research. *Journal of Applied System Analysis, 17*, 77–85.

Wattal, S., Racherla, P., & Mandviwalla, M. (2009). Employee adoption of corporate blogs: A qualitative analysis. In *Proceedings of the Hawaii International Conference on System Sciences*.

Webster, J., & Watson, R. T. (2002). Analyzing the past to prepare for the future: Writing a literature review. *Management Information Systems Quarterly, 26*(2), xiii–xxiii.

Wixom, B. H., & Todd, P. A. (2005). A theoretical integration of user satisfaction and technology acceptance. *Information Systems Research, 16*(1), 85–103. doi:10.1287/isre.1050.0042

Yardi, S., Golder, S. A., & Brozozowski, M. J. (2009). Blogging at work and the corporate attention economy. In *Proceedings of the 27th International Conference on Human Factors in Computing Systems*.

Yardi, S., Golder, S. A., & Brzozowski, M. (2008). *The pulse of the corporate blogosphere*. Paper presented at the Computer Supported Collaborative Work Conference.

*This work was previously published in the International Journal of Social and Organizational Dynamics in IT, Volume 1, Issue 3, edited by Michael B. Knight, pp. 34-49, 2011 by IGI Publishing (an imprint of IGI Global).*

# Chapter 9

# Examining the Varying Influence of Social and Technological Aspects on Adoption and Usage of Knowledge Management Systems

**Andrea J. Hester**
*Southern Illinois University Edwardsville, USA*

## ABSTRACT

*Knowledge management strives for effective capture and application of organizational knowledge, a resource imperative in sustaining organizations. To better achieve knowledge management initiatives, examination of factors influencing adoption and usage of knowledge management systems (KMS) are of great interest. Implementation of technological solutions considered organizational innovation is subject to potential problems of resistance, implying analysis of social factors equally important to technological factors. With Innovation Diffusion Theory as a foundation, this research examines factors influencing adoption and usage of KMS. The model is extended to include Reciprocity Expectation, an important factor affecting knowledge management processes. Results indicate that some factors are important in determining adoption while others are important for continued usage. This research emphasizes careful consideration and re-evaluation of both social and technological factors throughout all stages of technology implementation; more specifically, Reciprocity Expectation may be an important factor affecting length of adoption, but insignificant in determining continued usage.*

## INTRODUCTION

The latest trend in technology involves systems and applications encompassing higher levels of social interaction and collaboration. With globalization of organizations also gaining in popularity, the

DOI: 10.4018/978-1-4666-1948-7.ch009

ability to work more effectively and efficiently with the aid of technology provides considerable benefit including quick and easy access to information at any time and any place. Even before information technology became prevalent in the work environment, organizations were faced with an on-going challenge to balance management of a variety of resources including both physical resources and human resources. Today's organizations are faced with the additional obstacle of managing technological resources.

As organizations strive to maximize resource acquisition and utilization, one of the most valuable resources is intellectual capital, comprised of organizational knowledge residing in either individuals or in collective actions of a group. The importance of intellectual capital has motivated the field of knowledge management, which has in turn facilitated development of a wide variety of knowledge management systems (KMS). While the content of a KMS is the knowledge itself, an overall KMS also includes processes, goals, strategies and culture (King, 2007). KMS provide a technological solution to support processes of knowledge capture and knowledge application. Nonetheless, the human component and subsequent social aspects are also important to successful knowledge management.

Despite development of systems allowing for increased capabilities to support organizational knowledge processes, adoption of KMS remains enigmatic (Wagner & Bolloju, 2005). Even when KMS are in place, studies show that the majority of knowledge relevant to an organization is not represented in systems (Frappaolo & Capshaw, 1999). With capture of organizational knowledge continuing to be a problem for current KMS, new solutions need to be analyzed (Wagner, 2006). While the stream of research on adoption of IS is extensive, newer technologies facilitating collaborative processes are in need of further examination. Furthermore, collaboration is imperative to successful KMS utilization, warranting specialized technologies of great interest. The aim of this research is to examine both social and technological factors affecting adoption and usage of KMS. We seek to investigate the importance of social factors compared to technological factors and the possible difference among these factors impacting length of adoption compared to extensiveness of usage. The model proposed by this research is based on Innovation Diffusion

Theory (IDT) (Moore & Benbasat, 1991), and is comprised of independent variables measuring social factors (Voluntariness, Visibility, Image) and technological factors (Ease of Use, Trialability, Relative Advantage, Result Demonstrability), with dependent variables of Adoption and Usage. In order to focus on processes more specific to knowledge management, the model is extended to include another socially influenced independent variable, Reciprocity Expectation. As KMS users need to both contribute and acquire knowledge from other users, perceptions of Reciprocity Expectation may provide further insight into the specific case of KMS adoption and usage.

## Conceptual Framework

When viewed as intellectual capital, knowledge is a crucial element of today's organizations. A recent study found that four factors influenced short-term alignment: shared domain knowledge, IT implementation success, communication between IT and business executives, and connections between IT and business planning (Reich & Benbasat, 2000). Of these factors, only one was found to influence long-term alignment: shared domain knowledge. A direct, positive relationship exists between communication and knowledge sharing (Joshi, Sarker, & Sarker, 2007). Creating an environment allowing members of the organization to engage in various forms of communicating, socializing and collaboration may foster increased knowledge sharing. Subsequently, an improved knowledge sharing environment may be characterized by increased perceptions of Reciprocity Expectation. The resulting collaboration can provide benefits in the form of deeper resource pools, a variety of domain knowledge, and multiple viewpoints (Mohtashami, Marlowe, Kirova, & Deek, 2006).

Knowledge management is a key initiative in organizations seeking to harness knowledge as a resource for sustained competitive advantage (Kankanhalli, Tan, & Wei, 2005). An important element required for achieving effective knowledge management comes in the form of a KMS, a technological solution to support the knowledge processes of creation, storage/retrieval, sharing/transfer and application. While the content of a KMS is the knowledge itself, an overall KMS also includes processes, goals, strategies and culture (King, 2007). Thus, although KMS can provide great benefits, the technological aspects should not be over emphasized while neglecting the social aspects (Butler, 2003).

While legacy systems can still be used effectively, today's organizations often seek new technologies to resolve issues in knowledge management. The specific case of technological innovation involves advances in computing capability consisting not only of a technological component, but also potentially new business processes and organizational structure (Lyytinen & Rose, 2003). Advances in technology have fostered new approaches to knowledge management in the form of web-based collaborative technologies supporting environments of social computing. Wiki technology is an example of an emerging trend providing an effective knowledge management system with benefits of improved communication and collaboration, work processes, and knowledge sharing. Regardless of technological platform, the introduction of a new system can produce wavering results depending on the overall approach of the implementation.

Two of the most commonly used models in prior research (Compeau, Meister, & Higgins, 2007; Straub & Burton-Jones, 2007) of technology adoption and implementation are Davis' Technology Acceptance Model (TAM) (Davis, 1989) and Moore and Benbasat's model of Innovation Diffusion Theory (IDT) (Moore & Benbasat, 1991). Studies incorporating TAM are quite numerous with many proving TAM's predictive validity in IS use contexts (Lee, Kozar, & Larsen, 2003; Venkatesh, Davis, & Morris, 2007). However, there is debate within the IS field as to whether the use of TAM has been exhausted, and that broadening and deepening the research through development of

more context-specific models with greater richness is needed. Although TAM does include an element of user behavior, the model ignores social factors and the model is often criticized for focusing on the intention to use as opposed to actual usage. TAM, as well as other models based on intention, is more effective for situations prior to adoption, serving as a tool to help predict whether a technology may or may not be adopted by users (Davis, Bagozzi, & Warshaw, 1989; Straub, Limayem, & Karahanna, 1995; Venkatesh, Brown, Maruping, & Bala, 2008).

Competing models of TAM are often approached with the view that introducing a new technology constitutes an organizational innovation. Early research on innovation was developed by Rogers (1962). Diffusion of Innovation Theory (Rogers, 1962) focused on organizational innovation in general as opposed to technological innovation. More recent work involves the development of Innovation Diffusion Theory (IDT) (Moore & Benbasat, 1991). IDT has been shown to be an effective model in numerous settings (Compeau et al., 2007). An important difference between Rogers' theory and the model developed by Moore and Benbasat is the level of analysis. Rogers' attributes of innovation adoption are defined such that the focus in on the innovation itself. Moore and Benbasat transformed the original definitions to describe the behavior of using the innovation, and labeled the behaviors "Perceived Characteristics of Innovating (PCI)".

IDT places some focus on technological aspects, and incorporates user behaviors and social factors associated with a technology. However, the way the dependent variable is defined and operationalized varies among studies. Some published works continue to focus on behavioral intention (Agarwal & Prasad, 1997; Karahanna, Straub Jr., & Chervany, 1999) while others focus on actual usage (Agarwal & Prasad, 1997; Compeau & Higgins, 1995; Igbaria, Pavri, & Huff, 1989; Limayem & Hirt, 2003; Venkatesh et al., 2008). Measuring actual usage in subjective (duration, frequency, intensity) or objective (system logs) terms may provide more explanatory power than measurements based on intention to use a technology (Limayem & Hirt, 2003; Limayem, Hirt, & Cheung, 2007; Plouffe, Hulland, & Vandenbosch, 2001; Venkatesh et al., 2008). Studies of IDT focusing on adoption tend to simply target either adopters or non-adopters for evaluation (Lu, Quan, & Cao, 2009) or model adoption as a dichotomous variable (Cooper & Zmud, 1990), thus ignoring a variable level of adoption. Improved measures of the dependent variables may enhance the model.

Although several studies involving technology innovation acceptance have provided empirical evidence supporting the influence of various factors, examples of ineffective implementation still exist (Alavi & Leidner, 2001; Bansler & Havn, 2003; Butler, 2003; Wagner & Bolloju, 2005). More specifically, adoption of KMS remains enigmatic due to problems associated with acquiring and sharing knowledge (Wagner & Bolloju, 2005). One problem with successful KMS utilization can be described as the *knowledge acquisition bottleneck*. Although knowledge may be acquired, the knowledge cannot be shared or applied until it is stored in a system that supports channeling the knowledge to other organizational members. Another potential problem is related to the inter-organizational balance of power. Resistance to technology implementation may occur if users perceive that utilization of the system may result in a loss of power (Armistead & Meakins, 2007; Markus, 1983). This research proposes a new model expanding IDT to include a construct motivated by the increasing level of social interaction involved in knowledge processes. Reciprocity Expectation reflects user's perceptions of how the social environment affects technology usage by examining the degree to which contributing knowledge will result in the reciprocal action of receiving knowledge. Therefore, as behavior of users engaging in knowledge processes involves additional social complexity, extending the IDT

model may provide a more thorough understanding of KMS adoption and usage.

## Research Model

Technology implementation is a multi-stage process beginning with the organization's decision to adopt and evolving from initial implementation to widespread acceptance and diffusion of the technology. This project involves analysis of only a portion of the extensive process. It is assumed that the technology has been implemented by the organization and users are at some level of adoption and usage. The adoption stage may vary from early adoption to later stages of adoption. Furthermore, as the scenarios of the respondents vary, the specific factors of Voluntariness and Trialability are assumed to vary. Use of the technology may be either voluntary or mandatory and the technology may or may not allow for trialability. Results will indicate the user's perceptions of these factors as opposed to any organizational or technological mandate.

The research model is depicted in Figure 1. This study encompasses a wide range of respondents employed in a variety of organizations and engaged in technology usage at various stages of adoption. As pre-adoption stages are not the focus of the study, measuring behavioral intentions to adopt or use the technology are inappropriate. Therefore, the dependent variable is measured according to both adoption level and subjective measures of usage level. Adoption is measured as length of individual adoption indicating the approximate stage in which the respondent is engaged. Although subjective or self-reported usage measures are often criticized as potentially inaccurate measures of actual usage, this issue can be improved by incorporating multiple dimensions of usage (Igbaria et al., 1989), allowing for a richer assessment of the extent of usage. Therefore, usage is operationalized by measuring the construct along four dimensions: frequency, total number

*Figure 1. Research model*

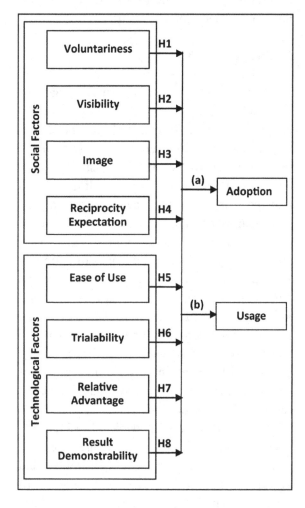

of tasks, total number of systems utilized, and level of expertise.

The factors influencing adoption and usage are categorized as either social factors or technological factors. Social factors reflect characteristics of the individual or situations of social influence from others. Technological factors are more direct indicators of characteristics of the technology or outcomes of the technology.

## Social Factors

Voluntariness is defined as the degree to which use of the KMS is perceived as being voluntary

(Moore & Benbasat, 1991). Adoption is not always a choice for the user as organizations mandate use of a technology in some instances. If use of the system is not mandated by the organization, Voluntariness may be viewed as a form of social influence through compliance processes (Bandyopadhyay & Fraccastoro, 2007; Karahanna et al., 1999). Perceptions of Voluntariness also vary over time. A study focusing on World Wide Web usage indicated that Voluntariness was a factor in the early stages of usage, however insignificant regarding intentions of future usage (Agarwal & Prasad, 1997). This contradicted findings by Karahanna et al. that potential adopters perceived initial use as voluntary, but continued use as more mandatory (Karahanna et al., 1999). The longitudinal study focusing on pre-adoption and post-adoption beliefs found that although the organizational level decision to initially adopt a technology was not an important factor, continued use may be influenced by social norms, with users being pressured not to abandon the technology, thus perceptions were different depending on the adoption stage.

H1: The perceived voluntariness of the KMS will be positively related to both (a) adoption and (b) usage.

Visibility is defined as the degree to which using the KMS is visible within the organization (Moore & Benbasat, 1991). Visibility refers to the ability to see other's use of the technology. Observation of other's use can influence a greater sense of usability (Compeau & Higgins, 1995). Visibility may also be viewed as a normative pressure from peers being most influential in the early stages of adoption when users may tend to comply with others' views (Venkatesh & Morris, 2000). In situations where use of the technology is not mandatory, Visibility may serve as a mechanism to motivate users to adopt in order to achieve a sense of belonging.

H2: The perceived visibility of the KMS will be positively related to both (a) adoption and (b) usage.

Image is defined as the degree to which the use of the KMS enhances one's image or status within the organization (Moore & Benbasat, 1991). While Image is most often associated with organizational identity, a user's image also plays an important role. Perceptions of Image incorporate into the model an aspect of social influence. Drawing on Image, subjective norms and social factors, social influence is an important construct in the UTAUT model (Venkatesh, Morris, Davis, & Davis, 2003). Users may be more willing to share or contribute knowledge when they feel that it will strengthen their image. Image can be of particular importance as users gain experience, meanwhile placing lesser emphasis on factors such as usefulness, ease-of-use and result demonstrability (Karahanna et al., 1999).

H3: A user's perceived image will be positively related to both (a) adoption and (b) usage.

Defined as the degree to which use of the KMS for knowledge contribution will lead to future requests for knowledge being met, Reciprocity Expectation is an important construct from Social Capital Theory. Consideration of Social Capital Theory research may help to explain how group characteristics, norms, and trust may influence knowledge sharing and collaboration. With knowledge sharing, users may experience reciprocal benefits, whereby contributing knowledge may lead to receiving knowledge from others when requested (Kankanhalli et al., 2005). Reciprocity Expectation has also been found to positively influence attitude toward knowledge sharing (Bock, Zmud, Kim, & Lee, 2005), knowledge contribution to electronic knowledge repositories (Kankanhalli et al., 2005) and electronic networks of practice (Wasko & Faraj, 2005).

H4: A user's perceived reciprocity expectation will be positively related to both (a) adoption and (b) usage.

## Technological Factors

As a component of both TAM and IDT, Ease of Use is extensively researched and continues to prove to be a relevant factor. Ease of Use is defined as the degree to which the KMS is easy to learn and use (Moore & Benbasat, 1991). In a meta-analysis of TAM research, replications of the model reported Ease of Use as having a significant impact on word processors, graphics, spreadsheets, e-mail, voice mail, text editors and GDSS (Lee et al., 2003). Substantial empirical evidence of the importance of Ease of Use as a component of IDT also exists (Compeau et al., 2007). Perceived lack of Ease of Use can present a considerable obstacle to technology adoption and usage. If using a technology requires a tremendous effort on the part of the user, usage will be seriously affected, and in fact, adoption may not occur at all.

H5: The perceived ease of use of the KMS will be positively related to both (a) adoption and (b) usage.

Trialability is defined as the degree to which it is possible to try using the KMS (Moore & Benbasat, 1991). A certain degree of Trialability also exists in the presence of others' use of a technology as users are able to experiment with the technology vicariously (Compeau et al., 2007). Trialability may be more important for early adopters as the ability to try the technology will decrease levels of uncertainty. However, as users gain experience, the importance of Trialability will most likely decline.

H6: The perceived trialability of the KMS will be positively related to both (a) adoption and (b) usage.

Relative Advantage is defined as the degree to which using the KMS is perceived as being better than using its predecessor (Moore & Benbasat, 1991). Rogers conceptualization of Relative Advantage is very similar to the perceived usefulness construct from TAM (Moore & Benbasat, 1991), however the idea differs in that it refers to a predecessor. Relative Advantage can often take on a variety of dimensions depending on the environment and technology studied. For instance, in a study involving adoption of new computing architectures, Relative Advantage was considered a combination of better software quality, lower costs, better acceptance, and more backward compatibility (Bajaj, 2000). Compared to proprietary operating systems, the open source software Linux was perceived as having increased Relative Advantage in terms of cost and reliability (Dedrick & West, 2004).

H7: The perceived relative advantage of the KMS will be positively related to both (a) adoption and (b) usage.

Result Demonstrability is defined as the degree to which the results of using the KMS are observable to others (Moore & Benbasat, 1991). In a study comparing pre- and post-adoption beliefs pertaining to the Windows operating system, Result Demonstrability and Image were the only important factors prior to adoption (Karahanna et al., 1999). Agarwal and Prasad (1997) also found Result Demonstrability to be an important factor in World Wide Web adoption; however, contrary to Karahanna et al.'s findings, the effect was significant for intentions of future use as opposed to initial use.

H8: The perceived result demonstrability of the KMS will be positively related to both (a) adoption and (b) usage.

## RESEARCH METHODOLOGY

The theoretical population for the study comprises of any and all employees of business organizations. The study population involves individuals engaging in usage of knowledge management systems in an organizational setting. A wide range of respondents were desired representing various types and sizes of organizations as well as various types of knowledge management systems. E-mails and postings to various on-line groups, such as LinkedIn groups and Yahoo! Groups, were used to invite potential respondents to participate in the survey. Within the websites utilized, a keyword search was performed to find groups that may consist of members using KMS. The majority of groups targeted exhibited an interest in knowledge management or collaborative technologies. Just a few examples of the groups invited to take the survey include Information, Access and Search Professionals (IASP), KM Practitioners Group, KM_Best_Practices, and TikiWiki CMS/Groupware. In each case, a brief description of the research was given and a link was provided to access the survey. Participants were required to be engaged in organizational usage of KMS as opposed to personal usage. The definition of KMS was given as follows: *"A KMS refers to a generally IT-based system for managing knowledge in organization, supporting creation, capture, storage and dissemination of information. It can comprise a part of a Knowledge Management initiative. The idea of a KMS is to enable employees to have ready access to the organization's documented base of facts, sources of information, and solutions."*

The usable sample size was 129, consisting of 86 females and 43 males. Further details regarding the respondents as well as a profile of the organizations are given in Table 1.

*Table 1. Descriptive statistics*

| Age | Frequency (%) |
|---|---|
| 20-29 | 10 (8) |
| 30-39 | 48 (37) |
| 40-49 | 34 (26) |
| 50-59 | 33 (26) |
| 60 or Over | 4 (3) |
| **Education Level** | **Frequency (%)** |
| Some College | 9 (7) |
| Associate's Degree | 4 (3) |
| Bachelor's Degree | 41 (32) |
| Master's Degree | 62 (48) |
| Doctorate | 13 (10) |
| **Job Profile** | **Frequency (%)** |
| Administrative& Clerical | 9 (7) |
| Technical | 28 (22) |
| Middle Management | 48 (37) |
| Top Management | 10 (8) |
| Executive | 14 (11) |
| Other | 20 (16) |
| **Organization Type** | **Frequency (%)** |
| Professional Services | 10 (8) |
| Education | 19 (15) |
| Finance/Accounting | 14 (11) |
| Government | 10 (8) |
| Healthcare | 6 (5) |
| Information Technology | 14 (11) |
| Manufacturing | 10 (8) |
| Other | 19 (15) |
| **Organization Size** | **Frequency (%)** |
| 1-50 | 32 (25) |
| 51-200 | 17 (13) |
| 201-500 | 11 (9) |
| 501-1000 | 10 (8) |
| 1001-2000 | 8 (6) |
| Over 2000 | 51 (40) |

## Analysis

The partial least squares (PLS) method was used to examine the hypotheses, as it is recommended for complex models focusing on prediction, and allows for minimal demands on measurement scales, sample size, and residual distribution (Chin, Marcolin, & Newsted, 2003). A two-stage analysis was performed using confirmatory factor analysis to assess the measurement model followed by examination of the structural relationships. Path modeling and analysis was performed on the standardized data using SmartPLS (Ringle, Wende, & Will, 2005). The survey measures were derived from previously published studies and are given in Appendix A, along with the corresponding means and standard deviations. All items were measured using a seven-point Likert scale, from "strongly disagree" to "strongly agree".

The measurement model was assessed for multicollinearity, reliability and validity. One of the original constructs of the IDT model, Compatibility, was removed due to multicollinearity. After removal of two additional indicators, EOU2 and RELADV3, adequate scores for indicator reliability were achieved. The resulting Cronbach's alpha scores ranging from .46 to .79 (See Table 2). Values for Cronbach's alpha are considered fair (.45 - .54), good (.55 - .62), very good (.63 - .70), or excellent (.71 and higher) (Comrey, 1973).

Validity of the measurement model was assessed by examining content validity, convergent validity and discriminant validity. Content validity was ensured by utilizing measurement items validated by existing research and pilot-testing the survey. Convergent validity was assessed by examining composite reliability and the average variance extracted (AVE). For composite reliability, a threshold of .50 is considered to indicate the majority of the variance accounted for by the construct, although values greater than .70 (Chin et al., 2003) are more desirable. Results for composite reliability values ranged from .72 to .85 (See Table 2). Values of .50 and greater are considered acceptable for AVE (Fornell & Larcker, 1981). AVE values ranged from .47 to .72 (See Table 2). Although the AVE for Trialability was below .50, the variable was retained as complete

*Table 2. Reliability and validity measures*

|  | Cronbach's alpha | Composite Reliability | AVE |
|---|---|---|---|
| Voluntariness | .59 | .83 | .71 |
| Visibility | .74 | .85 | .66 |
| Image | .79 | .85 | .66 |
| Reciprocity Expectation | .58 | .76 | .52 |
| Ease of Use | .58 | .83 | .70 |
| Trialability | .46 | .72 | .47 |
| Relative Advantage | .61 | .83 | .72 |
| Result Demonstrability | .55 | .82 | .69 |

removal of the variable did not improve the subsequent performance of the model.

Convergent validity is further defined as the degree to which the operationalization is similar to other operationalizations to which it theoretically should be similar, whereas discriminant validity is defined as the degree to which the operationalization is not similar to other operationalizations that it theoretically should not be similar to (Fornell & Larcker, 1981). This can be assessed by examining the correlation matrix, given in Table 3.

The bold and italic numbers in the diagonal of the table indicate the square root of the average variance extracted for each construct. This number should be greater than the values for the correlations between the given construct and each of the other constructs to indicate discriminant validity (Fornell & Larcker, 1981). One potential problem is indicated by the correlation between Relative Advantage and Reciprocity Expectation, as the correlation value is only slightly lower than the diagonal value for Relative Advantage. No action was taken as neither removal of additional indicators nor variables had a significant impact on the results.

Assessment of the structural model involves examining the path coefficients and the $R^2$ values. Path coefficients reflect the strengths of the relationships between the independent and dependent variables. Significance of the paths is determined by using a bootstrap resampling method (500 samples) (Chin, 1998). The $R^2$ value indicates the predictive power of a model for the dependent variables. Results are shown separately for Adoption (Figure 2) and Usage (Figure 3) (EOU: Ease of Use; IMG: Image; RAD: Relative Advantage; RCX: Reciprocity Expectation; RDM: Result Demonstrability; TRL: Trialability; VIS: Visibility; VOL: Voluntariness). This model accounts for 16 percent of the variance in Adoption and 32 percent of the variance in Usage. All outer loadings were significant (p < .01 level). Eight paths were found significant as indicated in the following figures.

## RESULTS AND DISCUSSION

Results indicate that some factors are important in determining Adoption while others in determining Usage. Significance of hypotheses is based on the t-test with the corresponding t-values and p-values given in Table 4. Voluntariness, Visibility, Reciprocity Expectation and Result Demonstrability were found to be important factors having a positive effect on adoption level. Visibility, Trialability, and Relative Advantage were found to be important factors having a positive effect on usage level. Thus, 3 out of 4 social factors were significant compared to 1 out of 4 technological factors for adoption. On the other hand, for usage, 1 out of 4 social factors compared to 2 out of 4 technological factors were significant. This may

*Table 3. Convergent and discriminant validity measures*

|  | EOU | IMG | RAD | RCX | TRL | VIS | RDM | VOL |
|---|---|---|---|---|---|---|---|---|
| **EOU** | *0.838* | | | | | | | |
| **IMG** | 0.074 | *0.811* | | | | | | |
| **RAD** | 0.264 | 0.456 | *0.722* | | | | | |
| **RCX** | 0.406 | 0.426 | 0.716 | *0.847* | | | | |
| **RDM** | 0.354 | 0.259 | 0.366 | 0.476 | *0.830* | | | |
| **TRL** | 0.375 | 0.432 | 0.495 | 0.541 | 0.376 | *0.688* | | |
| **VIS** | 0.354 | 0.310 | 0.226 | 0.260 | 0.369 | 0.314 | *0.809* | |
| **VOL** | 0.080 | -0.005 | 0.094 | 0.096 | 0.135 | 0.183 | -0.087 | *0.840* |

indicate that social factors are more important in the early stages of adoption, whereas technological factors are more important for continued usage. Thus, users may feel more pressure or social influence to adopt a technology, but after adoption they may rely on the technological aspects to encourage sustained use.

The significant impact of Voluntariness on Adoption is consistent with the findings of Agarwal and Prasad (1997) that the construct is important in early stages, however insignificant for continued use. Thus, when use of a system is Voluntary during initial adoption by the organization, the system is more likely to be adopted. The positive influence of Result Demonstrability on

*Figure 2. Structural model results for adoption*

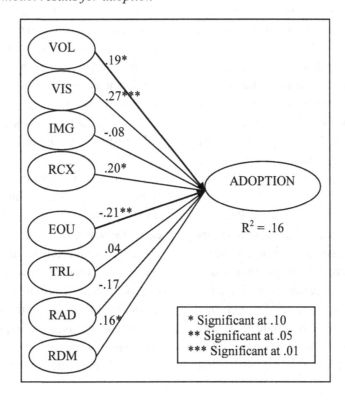

*Figure 3. Structural model results for usage*

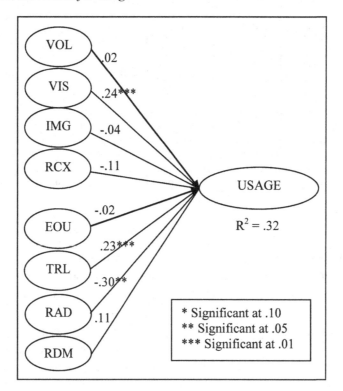

Adoption as opposed to Usage supports findings of Karahanna et al. (1999). The ability to observe the results of using the KMS is more important when users make the initial decision to adopt the system as opposed to continue using the system. It is also important to the initial adoption phase for the user to have perceptions of Reciprocity Expectation, indicating the viewpoint that by adopting the system and sharing knowledge, those actions will be reciprocated by other users in the organization.

The significant positive influence of Relative Advantage on Usage supports previous indications that the construct is consistently found to be an important factor. Relative Advantage is defined as "the degree to which using the KMS is perceived as being better than using its predecessor", which may explain why the construct is important for Usage as opposed to Adoption. When users have yet to adopt a system, they are less able to compare that

system to the one they are accustomed to using. However, as users attain more continued use, they are able to see the advantages of using the new system compared to the system used previously. A similar interpretation may explain the significance of Trialability on Usage. The more users are able to try using the system, the more experience they gain, resulting in higher levels of usage.

Visibility is the only factor having a positive impact on both Adoption and Usage. This supports previous research indicating Visibility as important in early stages of adoption (Karahanna et al., 1999; Riemenschneider, Hardgrave, & Davis, 2002; Venkatesh & Morris, 2000), while the significant impact on Usage may be indicative of higher levels of normative pressure influencing users to continue to use the system. Although all of the constructs were hypothesized to have a positive influence on both adoption and usage, the results are consistent with previous findings

*Table 4. Significance of hypotheses*

| | ✓ | Path Coeff. | t-Value | p-Value |
|---|---|---|---|---|
| H1a | ✓ | .192* | 1.802 | .07 |
| H1b | | .019 | 0.209 | .83 |
| H2a | ✓ | .270*** | 2.880 | .00 |
| H2b | ✓ | .244*** | 2.712 | .01 |
| H3a | | -.080 | .558 | .56 |
| H3b | | -.037 | .681 | .68 |
| H4a | ✓ | .200* | 1.62 | .10 |
| H4b | | -.114 | .93 | .35 |
| H5a | | -.211** | 1.927 | .05 |
| H5b | | -.022 | 0.261 | .79 |
| H6a | | .044 | 0.694 | .69 |
| H6b | ✓ | .227*** | 2.508 | .01 |
| H7a | | -.173 | 1.123 | .26 |
| H7b | ✓ | .305** | 2.220 | .03 |
| H8a | ✓ | .159* | 1.807 | .07 |
| H8b | | .113 | 0.272 | .27 |

* Significant at .10, ** Significant at .05,
*** Significant at .01

suggesting that certain factors are important in the early stages of adoption while other factors are important for continued use.

Although the negative relationship between Ease of Use and Adoption initially appears to be counter-intuitive, a plausible explanation may exist. Several studies have in fact indicated either a negative effect or lack of effect of Ease of Use on Usage. In a study involving a hospital computer system, Ease of Use had no effect on use intensity with the moderating effect of Relative Advantage considered the source of the unexpected result (Compeau et al., 2007). Student intentions to use a University website were not affected by Ease of Use due to the moderating influence of perceived enjoyment (Sun & Zhang, 2006). Ease of Use had no direct effect on website navigability but instead directly influenced self-efficacy (Pavlou & Fygenson, 2006). Finally, a study of adoption of Internet TV reported no effect of Ease of Use which was attributed simply to the fact that the technology successfully exhibited user-friendly design (Hsieh, Rai, & Keil, 2008).

One of the more commonly cited explanations for unexpected results with Ease of Use is the confounding factor of experience (Compeau et al., 2007). Experience level for the sample may be ascertained by level of expertise. Survey participants were asked to indicate their level of expertise with the current technology utilized most as their knowledge management system with an overwhelming 82% of respondents indicating an expertise level of 5 or greater (measured on a scale from 1, low, to 7, high). Future research requires further investigation of this phenomenon.

## CONCLUSION

With organized and usable knowledge being a key ingredient to organizational success, ensuring productive creation and sharing of knowledge can be deemed advantageous for organizations. Successful implementation of KMS may provide considerable support for achievement of knowledge management initiatives. This research identifies social and technological factors facilitating increased adoption and usage of KMS. Results of the study support prior research indicating that some of the factors analyzed are important in determining Adoption, while others are important in determining Usage. More importantly, inclusion of consideration of Reciprocity Expectation is in fact important to length of adoption of KMS.

Absence of a significant impact of some of the factors may be explained by flaws with the original IDT model, such as the multicollinearity issue with Compatibility. Another potential issue may be the confounding impact of level of experience or perhaps the relatively high education level of the sample. Substantial prior research suggests the importance of consideration of experience level, which is also supported by these findings. Further limitations are presented by the nature of the study. Respondents represented a rather wide variety of organizations and systems. This may explain the relatively low $R^2$ scores presented by the results. Further testing of the model is necessary for more generalizable results. Focus on specific stages of adoption or specific technologies may be needed.

In addition to addressing the limitations of this study, future research may involve further exploration into other social factors such as social identity and social network ties, or inhibitors of knowledge processes such as perceptions of loss of knowledge power. Organizational culture may also be of particular interest to the case of knowledge management systems. More careful examination of the specific case of collaborative technologies such as Wiki technology could provide valuable insight into the plausibility of alternatives to traditional knowledge management systems.

Results of this study may prove insightful to both researchers and practitioners. Researchers may find that extensions to basic adoption models are needed. Additional direct factors as

well as moderating factors are of interest. Also, the varying importance of factors throughout an entire implementation indicates that flexibility in the model may also be required. Practitioners involved in KMS implementation may benefit by allowing initial adoption by users on a voluntary basis, along with targeting of users who may serve as early adopters making their use of the KMS visible. Demonstrable results of new technologies may also facilitate increased adoption. Efforts made to foster a knowledge sharing community engaging in reciprocal actions may also have a positive effect on adoption of KMS. As the stages move beyond initial adoption, increased usage of the KMS may be facilitated by ensuring that the use remains visible and provides the means for trialability as well as recognizable advantages over previous technologies.

# REFERENCES

Agarwal, R., & Prasad, J. (1997). The Role of Innovation Characteristics and Perceived Voluntariness in the Acceptance of Information Technologies. *Decision Sciences*, *28*(3), 557–582. doi:10.1111/j.1540-5915.1997.tb01322.x

Alavi, M., & Leidner, D. E. (2001). Review: Knowledge Management and Knowledge Management Systems: Conceptual Foundations and Research Issues. *Management Information Systems Quarterly*, *25*(1), 107–136. doi:10.2307/3250961

Armistead, C., & Meakins, M. (2007). Managing Knowledge in Times of Organisational Change and Restructuring. *Knowledge and Process Management*, *14*(1), 15–25. doi:10.1002/kpm.268

Bajaj, A. (2000). A Study of Senior Information Systems Managers' Decision Models in Adopting New Computing Architectures. *Journal of the Association for Information Systems*, *1*, 4.

Bandyopadhyay, K., & Fraccastoro, K. A. (2007). The Effect of Culture on User Acceptance of Information Technology. *Communications of the Association for Information Systems, 19*, 522–543.

Bansler, J., & Havn, E. (2003). Building Community Knowledge Systems: An Empirical Study of IT-Support for Sharing Best Practices Among Managers. *Knowledge and Process Management, 10*(3), 156–163. doi:10.1002/kpm.178

Bock, G.-W., Zmud, R. W., Kim, Y.-G., & Lee, J.-N. (2005). Behavioral Intention Formation in Knowledge Sharing: Examining the Roles of Extrinsic Motivators, Social-Psychological Forces and Organizational Climate. *Management Information Systems Quarterly, 29*(1), 87–111.

Butler, T. (2003). From Data to Knowledge and Back Again: Understanding the Limitations of KMS. *Knowledge and Process Management, 10*(3), 144–155. doi:10.1002/kpm.180

Chin, W. W. (1998). The Partial Least Squares Approach for Structural Equation Modeling. In *Modern Methods for Business Research* (pp. 295–336). Mahwah, NJ: Lawrence Erlbaum Associates.

Chin, W. W., Marcolin, B. L., & Newsted, P. R. (2003). A Partial Least Squares Latent Variable Modeling Approach for Measuring Interaction Effects: Results from a Monte Carlo Simulation, Study and an Electronic-Mail Emotion/Adoption Study. *Information Systems Research, 14*(2), 189–217. doi:10.1287/isre.14.2.189.16018

Compeau, D. R., & Higgins, C. A. (1995). Application of Social Cognitive Theory to Training for Computer Skills. *Information Systems Research, 6*(2), 118–143. doi:10.1287/isre.6.2.118

Compeau, D. R., Meister, D. B., & Higgins, C. A. (2007). From Prediction to Explanation: Reconceptualizing and Extending the Perceived Characteristics of Innovating. *Journal of the Association for Information Systems, 8*(8), 409–439.

Comrey, A. L. (1973). *A First Course in Factor Analysis*. New York: Academic Press.

Cooper, R. B., & Zmud, R. W. (1990). Information Technology Implementation Research: A Technological Infusion Approach. *Management Science, 36*(2), 123–139. doi:10.1287/mnsc.36.2.123

Davis, F. (1989). Perceived Usefulness, Perceived Ease of Use, and User Acceptance of Information Technology. *Management Information Systems Quarterly, 13*(3), 319–339. doi:10.2307/249008

Davis, F., Bagozzi, R. P., & Warshaw, P. R. (1989). User Acceptance of Computer Technology: A Comparison of Two Theoretical Models. *Management Science, 35*(8), 982–1003. doi:10.1287/mnsc.35.8.982

Dedrick, J., & West, J. (2004, January 5-8). An Exploratory Study into Open Source Platform Adoption. Paper presented at the 37th Hawaii International Conference on System Sciences, Waikoloa, HI.

Fornell, C., & Larcker, D. (1981). Evaluating Structural Equation Models with Unobservable Variables and Measurement Error. *JMR, Journal of Marketing Research, 18*(1), 399–350. doi:10.2307/3151312

Frappaolo, C., & Capshaw, S. (1999). Knowledge Management Software: Capturing the Essence of Know-How and Innovation. *Information Management Journal, 33*(3), 44–48.

Hsieh, J. J. P.-A., Rai, A., & Keil, M. (2008). Understanding Digital Inequality: Comparing Continued Use Behavioral Models of the Socio-Economically Advantaged and Disadvantaged. *Management Information Systems Quarterly, 32*(1), 97–126.

Igbaria, M., Pavri, F., & Huff, S. (1989). Microcomputer Applications: An Empirical Look at Usage. *Information & Management, 16*, 187–196. doi:10.1016/0378-7206(89)90036-0

Joshi, K. D., Sarker, S., & Sarker, S. (2007). Knowledge transfer within information systems development teams: Examining the role of knowledge source attributes. *Decision Support Systems*, *43*, 322–335. doi:10.1016/j.dss.2006.10.003

Kankanhalli, A., Tan, B. C. Y., & Wei, K.-K. (2005). Contributing Knowledge to Electronic Knowledge Repositories: An Empirical Investigation. *Management Information Systems Quarterly*, *29*(1), 113–143.

Karahanna, E., Straub, D. W. Jr, & Chervany, N. L. (1999). Information Technology Adoption Across Time: A Cross-Sectional Comparison of Pre-Adoption and Post-Adoption Beliefs. *Management Information Systems Quarterly*, *23*(2), 183–213. doi:10.2307/249751

King, W. (2007). Keynote paper: Knowledge Management: A Systems Perspective. *International Journal of Business Systems and Research*, *1*(1).

Lee, Y., Kozar, K. A., & Larsen, K. R. T. (2003). The Technology Acceptance Model: Past, Present, and Future. *Communications of the Association for Information Systems*, *12*, 752–780.

Limayem, M., & Hirt, S. G. (2003). Force of Habit and Information Systems Usage: Theory and Initial Validation. *Journal of the Association for Information Systems*, *4*, 65–97.

Limayem, M., Hirt, S. G., & Cheung, C. M. K. (2007). How Habit Limits the Predictive Power of Intention: The Case of Information Systems Continuance. *Management Information Systems Quarterly*, *31*(4), 705–737.

Lu, Y., Quan, J., & Cao, X. (2009). The Perceived Attributes of Wi-Fi Technology and the Diffusion Gap among University Faculty Members: A Case Study. *Communications of the Association for Information Systems*, *24*, 69–88.

Lyytinen, K., & Rose, G. M. (2003). The Disruptive Nature of Information Technology Innovations: The Case of Internet Computing in Systems Development Organizations. *Management Information Systems Quarterly*, *27*(4), 557–595.

Markus, M. L. (1983). Power, Politics, and MIS Implementation. *Communications of the ACM*, *26*(6), 430–444. doi:10.1145/358141.358148

Mohtashami, M., Marlowe, T., Kirova, V., & Deek, F. P. (2006). Risk Management for Collaborative Software Development. *Information Systems Management*, 20–30. doi:10.1201/1078.105805 30/46352.23.4.20060901/95109.3

Moore, G. C., & Benbasat, I. (1991). Development of an Instrument to Measure the Perceptions of Adopting an Information Technology Innovation. *Information Systems Research*, *2*(3), 192–222. doi:10.1287/isre.2.3.192

Pavlou, P. A., & Fygenson, M. (2006). Understanding and Predicting Electronic Commerce Adoption: An Extension of the Theory of Planned Behavior. *Management Information Systems Quarterly*, *30*(1), 115–143.

Plouffe, C. R., Hulland, J. S., & Vandenbosch, M. (2001). Research Report: Richness Versus Parsimony in Modeling Technology Adoption Decisions - Understanding Merchant Adoption of a Smart Card-Based Payment System. *Information Systems Research*, *12*(2), 208–222. doi:10.1287/isre.12.2.208.9697

Reich, B. H., & Benbasat, I. (2000). Factors That Influence the Social Dimension of Alignment Between Business and Information Technology Objectives. *Management Information Systems Quarterly*, *24*(1), 81–113. doi:10.2307/3250980

Riemenschneider, C. K., Hardgrave, B. C., & Davis, F. (2002). Explaining Software Developer Acceptance of Methodologies: A Comparison of Five Theoretical Models. *IEEE Transactions on Software Engineering, 28*(12), 1135–1145. doi:10.1109/TSE.2002.1158287

Ringle, C. M., Wende, S., & Will, A. (2005). *SmartPLS (Version 2.0 beta)*. Hamburg, Germany: University of Hamburg.

Rogers, E. M. (1962). *Diffusion of Innovations* (4th ed.). New York: The Free Press.

Straub, D. W., & Burton-Jones, A. (2007). Veni, Vidi, Vici: Breaking the TAM Logjam. *Journal of the Association for Information Systems, 8*(4), 223–229.

Straub, D. W., Limayem, M., & Karahanna, E. (1995). Measuring System Usage: Implications for IS Theory Testing. *Management Science, 41*(8), 1328–1342. doi:10.1287/mnsc.41.8.1328

Sun, H., & Zhang, P. (2006). Causal Relationships between Perceived Enjoyment and Perceived Ease of Use: An Alternative Approach. *Journal of the Association for Information Systems, 7*(9), 618–645.

Venkatesh, V., Brown, S. A., Maruping, L. M., & Bala, H. (2008). Predicting Different Conceptualizations of System Use: The Competing Roles of Behavioral Intention, Facilitating Conditions, and Behavioral Expectation. *Management Information Systems Quarterly, 32*(3), 483–501.

Venkatesh, V., Davis, F., & Morris, M. G. (2007). Dead or Alive? The Development, Trajectory and Future of Technology Adoption Research. *Journal of the Association for Information Systems, 8*(4), 267–286.

Venkatesh, V., & Morris, M. G. (2000). Why Don't Men Ever Stop to Ask for Directions? Gender, Social Influence, and Their Role in Technology Acceptance and Usage Behavior. *Management Information Systems Quarterly, 24*(1), 115–139. doi:10.2307/3250981

Venkatesh, V., Morris, M. G., Davis, G. B., & Davis, F. (2003). User Acceptance of Information Technology: Toward a Unified View. *Management Information Systems Quarterly, 27*(3), 425–478.

Wagner, C. (2006). Breaking the Knowledge Acquisition Bottleneck Through Conversational Management. *Information Resources Management Journal, 19*(1), 70–83.

Wagner, C., & Bolloju, N. (2005). Supporting Knowledge Management in Organizations with Conversational Technologies: Discussion forums, Weblogs and Wikis. *Journal of Database Management, 16*(2).

Wasko, M. M., & Faraj, S. (2005). Why Should I Share? Examining Social Capital and Knowledge Contribution in Electronic Networks of Practice. *Management Information Systems Quarterly, 29*(1), 35–57.

# APPENDIX A

*Table A1. Survey items*

| | Survey Item | Mean | Std. Dev. |
|---|---|---|---|
| VOL1 | My use of the KMS is voluntary (as opposed to required) by my superiors or job description. | 4.92 | 2.21 |
| VOL2 | My boss does not require me to use the KMS. | 4.02 | 1.86 |
| VOL3 | Although it might be helpful, using the KMS is certainly not mandatory in my job. | 3.84 | 1.87 |
| RAD1 | Using the KMS enables me to accomplish tasks more quickly. | 5.65 | 1.20 |
| RAD2 | Using the KMS improves the quality of work I do. | 5.60 | 1.20 |
| RAD3 | Using the KMS makes it more difficult to do my job. | 5.98 | 1.32 |
| IMG1 | People in my organization who use the KMS have more prestige than those who do not. | 3.63 | 1.62 |
| IMG2 | Using the KMS does not improve my image within the organization. | 4.40 | 1.66 |
| IMG3 | People in my organization who use the KMS have a high profile. | 4.15 | 1.55 |
| EOU1 | I believe that it is difficult to get the KMS to do what I want it to do. | 4.94 | 1.41 |
| EOU2 | Overall, I believe that the KMS is easy to use. | 5.64 | 1.23 |
| EOU3 | Learning to operate the KMS is easy for me. | 6.05 | .87 |
| RDM1 | I believe I could communicate to others the outcomes of using the KMS. | 5.77 | 1.08 |
| RDM2 | The results of using the KMS are apparent to me. | 5.81 | 1.09 |
| RDM3 | I would have difficulty explaining the advantages of using the KMS. | 5.34 | 1.66 |
| VIS1 | In my organization, one sees the KMS on many computers. | 5.38 | 1.57 |
| VIS2 | The KMS is not very visible in my organization. | 4.94 | 1.75 |
| VIS3 | It is easy for me to observe others using the KMS in my firm. | 5.11 | 1.57 |
| TRL1 | I know where I can go to satisfactorily try out various uses of the KMS. | 5.30 | 1.46 |
| TRL2 | Before deciding whether to use the KMS, I was able to properly try it out. | 4.80 | 1.68 |
| TRL3 | I was not permitted to use the KMS on a trial basis long enough to see what it could do. | 5.29 | 1.70 |
| RCX* | When I share my knowledge through the KMS, I believe that my queries for knowledge will be answered in future. | 4.87 | 1.39 |
| RCX2* | When I share my knowledge through the KMS, I expect somebody to respond when I'm in need in the future. | 5.14 | 1.55 |
| RCX3* | When I contribute knowledge to the KMS, I do not expect to get back knowledge when I need it. | 4.44 | 1.72 |

Notes: (1) All items adapted from Moore and Benbasat (1991) except for those indicated by * (Kankanhalli, et al. 2005).

(2) All items measured on a seven-point Likert scale (Strongly Disagree, Disagree, Somewhat Disagree, Neutral, Somewhat Agree, Agree, Strongly Agree).

*This work was previously published in the International Journal of Social and Organizational Dynamics in IT, Volume 1, Issue 1, edited by Michael B. Knight, pp. 49-65, 2011 by IGI Publishing (an imprint of IGI Global).*

# Chapter 10
# A Model for Operationalising Influencing Factors in IT Strategy Deployment

**Tiko Iyamu**
*Tshwane University of Technology, South Africa*

## ABSTRACT

*The reliance on information technology (IT) keeps increasing and rapidly as technology advances. Information technology has become so significant that it is critical to the success or failure of many organisations. Hence the organisations emphasises on strategy for IT, to enable and support their processes and activities, periodically. The IT strategy is influenced by many factors at both development and implementation levels. These factors enable and at the same time constraint during the development and implementation of the IT strategy in the organisation. The research examines the types of factors which exist during the development and implementation of IT strategy. This includes the roles of the factors and how they manifest to influence IT strategy. In achieving this object of the research, a case study method was employed and Structuration Theory was applied to examine the factors which emerge and how they impact the development and implementation of IT strategy in the organisation.*

## 1. INTRODUCTION

Over the years, the need for IT has become increasingly important in the organisations it supports (Scarbrough, 1998; Lederer & Sethi, 1988). Hence it is important to align the IT strategy to the business strategy (Weiss & Anderson, 2002). According to Sohal and Ng (1998), IT strategy has a great impact on the business strategy and

some organisations rely completely on their IT strategy to succeed. It has also become a significant resource in enabling business goals and objectives. The roles and expectations of IT and the changing business needs have made it necessary to have a strategy for IT development, execution and use (Walsham & Waema, 1994; Wolff & Sydor, 1999). For example, the growth of web technology has expanded and changed the scope of the applications of IT. Two decades ago the focus of applications was more on internal

DOI: 10.4018/978-1-4666-1948-7.ch010

use. It was largely automation of processes to improve organisational operations. But, during the last decade, not only are people within an organisation increasingly 'connected' but so too are people outside the organisation connected with the organisation through the application of IT.

Understanding the development and implementation of IT strategy within the organisation implies making sense of it in their human and technological contexts. According to Iyamu and Roode (2010), there are various agents, some involved in the development of IT strategy while others are not. The study focused on the structures that existed, as created by humans and within which they operated, which influence the technology and organisation, groups of individuals and their organisational activities and tasks, their philosophical viewpoints on work as well as the organisation and IT strategy.

Regardless of the degree to which an employee may commit him or herself to the objectives of the organisation, personal interests are likely to be different from those of the employer. Employees seek to satisfy not only the organisational interests, but also their own wants and needs which are driven by self-interest (Markus, 1983). Mintzberg (2000) points out that people apply strategy in several different ways. Also, it is the management of the powerful resources (such as technology and people) and the environment they create that allow a difference to be made. According to Iyamu and Adelakun (2008), People's willingness to accept or reject the IT strategy will therefore be highly influential in the outcome of the IT strategy.

The research examined how the interplay between structures and humans derail IT strategy in the organisation. The focus was on technical and non-technical factors in the development and implementation of IT strategy in the organisation. Based on the data analysis and findings, a model for operationalising the influencing factors in IT strategy deployment was developed. The study adopted qualitative interpretive case study for the research approach including, for the data collection.

## 2. RESEARCH METHODOLOGY

Qualitative, interpretive case study approaches were adopted in the study. This was due to the nature of the study, which sought to understand the impact of the interplay between the existing structures and humans in the development and implementation of IT strategy. Rowlands (2005) argued that the interpretive research method acknowledges the intimate relationship between the researcher, what is being explored, and the factors which shapes process. The study was unpinned by the Structuration Theory (ST), a theory by Anthony Giddens (1984). The analysis was carried out using the duality of structure from ST.

It was believed that the case study approach was the appropriate research strategy. This was primarily because of the advantages and opportunities it presented to create novel and profound insights and to examine the rich contextual influences (Myers, 1997; Yin, 2009). Other approaches could have been adopted. However, this would not have revealed in detail the unique experiences of individuals in the organisations and the factors influencing their IT strategy. According to Noor (2008), the case study approach is best used in probing particular area of interest.

The organisation used for the case study is an insurance company in South Africa, founded over hundred years ago. It has twelve thousand employees, of which four hundred and twenty are in the computing environment. The data collection was from primary and secondary sources, interviews and documentation, respectively.

The primary data collection sources were structured and semi-structured interviews which were tape recorded. Roode's (1993) description of a process-based research framework for information systems research was used to generate the most appropriate questions for this research. A total of 23 interviewees were carried out in the organisation: 14 white and 9 non-white; 11 senior and 12 junior; 12 female and 11 male employees were interviewed. A set of balanced respondent demographics was formulated and adhered to, as it was a key factor in achieving a true reflection of the situations. The demographics included different races, genders and various levels in the IT organisational hierarchy - senior employees: IT Executives, IT Managers, Business Managers, IT Architects and Project Managers; and junior employees: Programmers, Analyst and Network Administrators.

The secondary sources included documents about organisational hierarchy, Business and IT strategic alignment and IT strategy materials. The materials were used to develop the background information on the technical and non-technical contexts of the organisation and its hierarchy, which helped to construct the history of the computing environment. This help to understand the organisational hierarchy as presented in the Agent and Structure subsections of the analysis section.

The study applied Structuration Theory (ST) in the analysis. ST was selected primarily because, it holds: that human actions are enabled and constrained by structures, and emphasizes that these structures are the result of previous actions (Orlikowski, 1992); consists of rules and resources, and they do not exist independently of human action, nor are they material entities. According to Pozzebon and Pinsonneault (2001), the theory of Structuration recognizes and accommodates both subjective and objective dimensions of social reality, and assumes a duality of structure and action.

The key elements of Structuration Theory are Agency, Structure, which Giddens (1984) argues that they are a duality that cannot be conceived separate from one another) and Duality of Structure. These elements were used in the analysis of the case study.

Agency refers to humans' ability to act. According to Giddens (1984), human agency has the 'capacity to make a difference'. Further, the loss of the capacity to make a difference is powerlessness. Hence, agency is intimately connected to power. In this study, the agency was used to identify actors, activities in the development and implementation of IT strategy.

Structures are described by Giddens (1984) as rules and resources; they only have virtual existence, as 'traces in the mind', and argue that they exist only through the actions of human beings (Jones, 1999). Only through the activities of human actors can structure exist (Orlikowski, 1992). Structures both enable and constrain the daily actions and thought processes of people, but do not wholly determine them (Rose & Hackney, 2002). Individual choices are not independent of the structures within which they take place. This was applied to examine the rules and regulation that existed, and the enactment of the structures enabling or constraining in the development and implementation of IT strategy.

The duality of structure was used to understand the contextual dynamics within which organisational dilemmas interplayed; how structures embodied the organisation's norms, which were influenced by actions; whether these actions by agents led to changes in how rules and resources influence interactions and to the reinforcement of the norms upon which these interactions were based, during the development and implementation of IT strategy in the organisation. Iyamu and Roode (2010) argue that Structuration theory mutually reinforces the nature of agents and structure interaction, conceptualising structure as flexible and recognising that rules and resource control mechanisms are continued process.

For analytical purposes, Giddens (1984) distinguishes different structurational dimensions, namely, signification, domination and legitimation. Associated with each structural dimension are mediating components, which are interpretative schemes, facilities, and norms, whereby concepts embedded in the structure are given specific by social agents through their actions, which are at the same time, enabled and constrained by the structural properties. The notion of embodied structure was complemented with that of emergent structure, and the notion of user appropriation with that of enactment.

Thus, as human actors communicate, they draw on interpretative schemes to help make sense of interactions; at the same time those interactions produce and reproduce structures of signification. Similarly the facility to allocate resources is enacted in the wielding of power, and produces and reproduces social structures of domination. Finally, moral codes (norms) help determine what can be sanctioned in human interaction, which iteratively produces and reproduces structures of legitimation.

The dimensions of the duality of structure were applied in a vertical and horizontal manner in the analysis of the case study.

# 3. ANALYSIS

The analysis focuses on the actions within the structures, and how the agents acted and were acted upon during the development and implementation of IT strategy in the organisation. The analysis begin by exploring the agency, thereafter examined the types of structures that existed during the development and implementation of IT in the organisation.

## 3.1. Agency

The agents were intimately connected with rules and resources. In the organisation, the agents involved in the development were different from those who were responsible for the implementation of IT strategy. The employees involved in the development and implementation of IT strategy had different backgrounds and skills, including managerial and technical skills. Also, the employees were made up of different races and age generations.

The Executive Committee (Exco) of the organisation mandated the IT Director to be responsible and accountable for all IT related activities in the organisation. The IT Director used the mandate to include the IT Executive in the responsibility of IT strategy.

The computing environment of the organisation was hierarchically structured with several teams. Within the hierarchy, roles and responsibilities were respectively accorded and mandated, on the basis of the rules and regulations of the organisation. The IT Executive team delegated responsibilities and authority to their various managers and authorities were wielded primarily by the exploitation of rules and resources in the development and implementation of IT strategy.

## 3.2. Structure

The resources such as technologies and employees in the computing environment were managed by the IT Director through the rules of the organisation. In the order of hierarchy, the responsibilities were further delegated to the IT Executive team and other IT managers for the development and implementation of IT strategy in the organisation.

The different activities including responsibilities were conducted within rules. The individuals in the computing environment used the resources within their reach to carry out their responsibilities in the development and implementation of IT strategy. The rules were as important as the resources as they depended on each other during the development and implementation of IT strategy. As a result of the dependencies, the manner in which the rules were interpreted and used by the different employees was critical. This led to the use of the dimensions of the duality of structure in the case study, as discussed in the next section.

## 3.3. Dimensions of the Duality of Structure

Structure and human interaction in the computing environment was divided into three dimensions for the primary purpose of analysis. The recursive character of these dimensions is illustrated by linking modalities, as described in the methodology section.

### 3.3.1. Duality of Structure: Signification and Communication

Executive Committee (Exco), the highest decision making body of the organisation, held IT strategy with high significance and as such, assigned it to the IT Director. The relevance of IT strategy to the organisation required it to have a wide range of input and audience within the computing environment of the organisation.

The IT Director and IT Executive team communicated the objectives of the IT strategy to the next level of management, the IT managers. Subsequently, the various IT managers did the same by providing the necessary information to the rest of the employees.

The development of IT strategy was divided into different components. Members of the IT Executive team were responsible and accountable for these components, which included Business Applications, Infrastructure and Architectural components. The main purpose of the components was to assign roles and responsibilities as guided by the rules of the organisation. Another reason was to ensure balanced resources for the different IT Executive team members.

Employees within the computing environment were made aware of the developed IT strategy. Different media such as the company intranet and team meetings were used as communication platforms. According to some of the employees, the most popular and value-adding communication platform was the departmental workshop.

Some of the employees were not satisfied with the level of awareness that was created by the IT Executive team. These employees thought (perspective and perception) that the IT Executive could do more to create awareness about IT strategy in the organisation. On the other hand, some employees felt that there was enough access to information about IT strategy.

The main aim for creating the awareness was for the employees to understand the importance of IT strategy so that they could contribute to the implementation in their various ways. Some employees were also concerned with the flow of information. Those who were concerned say that they would prefer a two-way information flow between the junior and senior employees in the computing environment. Most of the junior employees interviewed emphasized that such flow of information could enhance their understanding of IT strategy.

Some of the senior managers acknowledged that there was a problem with communication in the computing environment. This was attributed by some to the spoken language used in the organisation. In addition to these oral communication problems, there was also a problem of understanding some of the documentation relating to IT strategy. Some of the Afrikaans speaking employees find it difficult to read and understand documents that were written in English, and *vice versa*. According to one of the managers, *"One of the problems in my opinion was that it's an Afrikaans company and our strategy was written in English . . . which creates problems. When I go to speak to my manager to explain or help explain the document, my manager is not able to explain it to me in my own language; he's explaining it to me in his second language, which creates problems"*.

### 3.3.2. Duality of Structure: Legitimation and Sanction

The IT Director was responsible and accountable for IT strategy in the organisation. As such, she strived to ensure that IT strategy was accepted in the organisation, starting with the Exco. The IT Director presents IT strategy to Exco for approval.

Upon the approval, the IT Management team tries to get the buy-in of the IT managers reporting directly to them, and encouraged the various IT managers to get the buy-in of their respective employees.

There was incentive to the staff. The incentive was based on performance as assessed by the individual IT managers. This was aimed to motivate them in carrying out their tasks and responsibilities. Even though incentive was offered, some employees were reluctant and others, for various reasons, did not accept the IT strategy. For example, some employees felt that the information shared or communicated to them was either incomplete or was incorrect; as a result, they did not trust the IT Management team.

There was a strained relationship between the IT Management team and the rest of the employees, and both parties realized the extent of the problem. Even though the rules of the organisation mandate the IT Management to allocate tasks, it became difficult to do so as the employees were unwilling or only reluctantly accepted their individual tasks.

The strained relationship between the IT Management team and the rest of the employees led to lack of trust and confidence. This affected the capacity and capability to share, as well as carry out task in the development and implementation of IT strategy. The constant suspiciousness questioned the integrity of the IT managers in the allocation of tasks during implementation.

Many of the employees who did not sanctioned the IT strategy alleged that they could not read or didn't understand the document as it was written in a language they were not fluent in.

### 3.3.3. Duality of Structure: Domination and Power

The authority to develop and implement IT strategy in the organisation was mandated from the Executive Committee of the organisation to the IT Director and the IT Management team. The IT managers including the rest of the employees were by virtue of their employment supposed to support the IT Director's initiative unreservedly.

To communicate the developed IT strategy, IT Management organized a workshop. Attendance at the workshop was a success in that almost every employee in the computing environment attended.

All IT managers, as instructed by the IT Director, allocated tasks to their employees. This enabled the IT managers to use their authority to coerce employees to implement the IT strategy by allocation of tasks and resources.

Some employees who have been in the organisation for a long time were more knowledgeable and had more information about the organisation and the organisation's businesses and activities than some of their colleagues, particularly those with a fewer number of years of service in the organisation. Their stocks of knowledge created a feeling of superiority toward their colleagues during the implementation of IT strategy in the organisation.

The majority of the employees felt that the rules of the organisation gave them little or no room to negotiate their differences. Their reaction to this differed.

Understanding of the developed IT strategy was critical for successful implementation. There were concerns that if information was not properly shared or communicated in terms of a two-way flow, IT strategy may not be well understood, leading to incorrect implementation. Some of the employees pointed out that incorrect implementation could hamper the business processes and activities that IT strategy was supposed to enable and support.

The implementation of IT strategy in the organisation first of all required the acceptance of the developed IT strategy by employees. The level of acceptance formed the basis for the actions of individuals, teams and groups, and, therefore, their participation, which was essential for successful implementation. However, with a low level of acceptance, and issues of mistrust permeating the ranks of employees, implementation inevitably was bound to be severely hampered. IT Management therefore used its authority to enforce acceptance. Using the performance appraisal approach, IT managers, as instructed by the IT Director, allocated tasks and resources to employees involved in the implementation of IT strategy. Employees accepted instructions or commands with little or no negotiation. It was clear, however, that employees at the lower levels in general did not have a good understanding of the IT strategy they were supposed to be implementing.

## 4. FINDINGS

The empirical data were analyzed using Structuration Theory, and the interpretation (findings) of the analysis is now presented. Of the factors which impact the structures in the development and implementation of IT strategy, six were most critical:

### 4.1. Control of Resources

Control of resources was prevalent in the computing environment. This was based on how significant the resources were in the development and implementation of IT strategy.

The structures within the computing environment determined and defined the tasks during the development and implementation of IT strategy, and actors enacted these structures in their daily practice. The mandate allowed the IT Director and IT Management to make particular operational rules for the various units, and also gave them autonomous control over resources under their auspices. In some instances, the resources were used according to individual interests. IT managers also used their mandate to determine employees' access to facilities in their interactions with colleagues, with authorities, and with technology during implementation of IT strategy. This meant that the participation of individual employees in the implementation of IT strategy was influenced by factors outside their control. At the same time, employees used their individual knowledge such as technical know-how and information within their reach to gain advantage over others.

IT managers were granted the authority over resources, and the authority to allocate tasks to employees under their control. Coupled with the fact that the prevailing culture in the organisa-

tion did not allowed for the questioning of any decisions by managers, this meant that managers dominated employees during the implementation of IT strategy. This practice was not sanctioned by many of the employees.

The prerogatives of IT managers as mandated by the structures of the organisation meant that they were vulnerable to favouritism and nepotism towards employees, during allocation, as well as in the assessment of the tasks. As a result of the mandate, the IT managers continued to interfere on the employees activities in carrying out their tasks and responsibilities. This created conflict of interests at the expense of the organisation.

### 4.2. Human Interference

The organisational hierarchy in the computing environment allowed the management team to coerce employees to adhere to instructions. Thus, older employees had to work with a younger generation of employees, which created tension because of differences in approach and understanding. This "generation gap" co-operation was therefore based on a foundation of unwillingness to work together and led to the younger employees not getting enough information from their older colleagues who were more knowledgeable about the organisation and its needs.

Based on the limited information made available to them, some employees could not easily understand how to carry out their individual tasks during the implementation of IT strategy. This was a serious problem for some of the employees within this group and it affected the larger computing environment in terms of collaboration and interdependency of the processes and activities of the implementation of IT strategy.

There was also a growing concern of ownership and control of the available resources between the older and younger generations. Some of the older generation felt insecure and as a result, acted individually in order to achieve and satisfy their own goals and objectives. For example, some of the older employees knew that certain senior managers had more respect for them because of their age, and that whatever they said would carry more weight than the words of the younger employees. They exploited this, and were driven by personal interests in their actions. Also, the older employees were more knowledgeable, and, they used this to maintain job security and to dominate younger employees.

These result to different interest groups being formed. Certain actions were clear manifestations of personal interest. As a result, there was sharp division, which led to serious lack of cooperation between the different groups in the computing environment. This affected the implementation of IT strategy, a great deed. This was blamed on the organisational rule which give employees little or no choice, as it coerces them to adhere to management instruction.

## 4.3. Organisational Rules

The prevailing culture of dominance within the computing environment meant that the actions and decisions of IT managers could not be questioned by lower level employees. Consequently, some of the IT managers had a nonchalant attitude towards their subordinates. Preferences were accorded to employees as they wished. The IT managers and their preferred employees became dominant.

Language was one of the issues through which the rules of the organisation became a constraint. This derailed processes and activities in the implementation of IT strategy in the organisation. English and Afrikaans were legitimised as official languages for communication in the computing environment, but unfortunately, some employees were not fluent in Afrikaans and found it difficult to understand and interpret IT strategy related documents. It also made it difficult for them to participate in meetings where the development and implementation of IT strategy were discussed in Afrikaans.

Some of the IT Management team members and the IT managers applied their personal discretion in the way information was shared and how Afrikaans was used as a medium of communication. This obviously affected the actions of some of the employees during the implementation of IT strategy. There was cultural Diversity in the organisation, hence multi-lingual was allowed as medium of communication. However, some employees felt that they were being dominated and that Afrikaans was used to exclude them from being part of the implementation of IT strategy. The challenge arises as a result of conservatism among certain employees who did take cognisance of their colleagues' language of preference. Other employees felt that IT managers deliberately accorded preferential treatment to certain employees when they used Afrikaans in meetings. This, the employees felt, was irrational and as such, they found it difficult to sanction the development and this clearly affected the implementation of IT strategy.

## 4.4. Cultural Diversities and Conservatism

As evident in the data about the organisation, the organisation was founded over hundred years ago. There was rich cultural diversity in the computing environment of the organisation. Instead of celebrating this diversity, pervasive elements of conservatism counteracted the advantages that could have been gained from the diversity.

The diversity in the computing environment contributed to how tasks for the implementation of IT strategy were allocated in the organisation. The diversity related to age generation gaps, cultural differences and the use of spoken and written languages among the employees. As a result, getting the employees to be interested in the IT strategy was very difficult, with implementation suffering as a result

There was also a cultural conservatism among the employees in the computing environment.

This was particularly prevalent among the older generation of employees. The conservatism, which was about "doing things like we always did", created little or no support for transformation in the organisation. This became a dominant factor because those who indulged in the practices of the old culture were more knowledgeable about the organisation and they were not interested in change. As such, they reluctantly enrolled in the implementation of the IT strategy.

The response to these changes was to be unco-operative. Some employees were not contributing their knowledge which had been gained from experience. On the other hand, the new intakes into the environment also had difficulty in performing their individual tasks in the new cultural setting. These were attributed to historical effects. At the time of this study, the new and old cultures had not found a point of compromise. The non-acceptance of the new culture created considerable barriers, which derailed processes and activities during the implementation of IT strategy in the organisation.

## 4.5. Historical Effects

The historical shift in the politics of South Africa forced the organisation to amend some of its traditions. Traditionally, non-white people were not employed in the computing environment of the organisation. In the new dispensation, the organisation embarked on transformation in order to align with the government policy of 'Affirmative Action', which was in process during the study. This was to balance the number of employees in the computing environment along racial lines. The transition from the old to the new political dispensation has been a challenge and has affected the development and implementation of IT strategy in the organisation with 'new intakes' having to learn about the organisation while at the same time being allocated tasks.

Between the new and older employees, an antagonism developed. The affirmative action candidates claimed that because of the discrimi-

nation, information about IT strategy was not appropriately circulated or shared with them. They felt they were being discriminated against and that their white colleagues had more power as a result of the resources within their reach. In response to this domination, the affirmative action candidates acted in their individual interests and half-heartedly supported the implementation of IT strategy. This led to unco-operative actions and manifestations of defensive behaviour by the affirmative action employees

The reluctance to co-operate, or the complete lack of co-operation from both the affirmative action candidates and other employees, including managers, who had jurisdiction over the resources available to them, was used by these same managers as a source of power to exclude unco-operative employees from the implementation of IT strategy.

## 4.6. Irregularities Caused by Personal Interests

Employees' actions unfortunately, employees were influenced by different personal interests, which had detrimental effects, especially for the implementation of IT strategy. IT managers' personal interests manifested themselves through irregularities such as favouritism and nepotism, while the rules of the organisation protected them in the execution of these acts.

Personal values, beliefs and attitudes sanctioned the actions of actors and produced and reproduced structures of legitimation. Naturally, these norms were seldom articulated, but nevertheless were used by actors to sanction their actions that then reproduced the structures of legitimation. Similarly, personal interests mediated early decisions about IT strategy in the organisation that eventually wielded their greatest influence during the implementation stage.

The relationships between IT Management and employees revolved around rules, regulations and resources during development and implementation of the IT strategy. Between IT managers and

*Figure 1. Impact of non-technical factors on IT strategy*

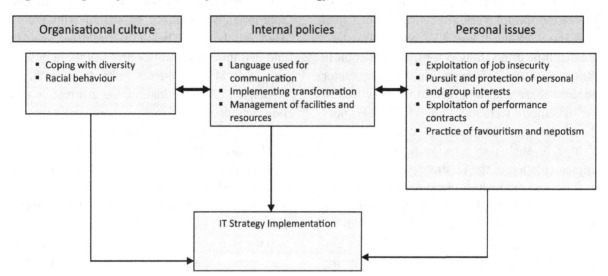

employees, IT strategy was interpreted, tasks were negotiated and allocated, and information was shared and communicated. However, this all happened with varying degrees of outcome. Employees did not believe that the organisation could fairly judge their performances and qualification for salary increases and promotion. Consequently, employees resorted to manoeuvring because they believed that managers had no objective way of differentiating effective people from those who were less effective, and were in fact practicing nepotism and favouritism. As we have seen above, this was indeed the case. From the analysis and findings, a model for operationalising the influencing factors in IT strategy deployment was developed, as presented in the next section.

## 5. A MODEL FOR OPERATIONALISING THE FACTORS INFLUENCING THE IT STRATEGY

In presenting the above findings, we necessarily have to move to a higher level. Figure 1 shows that the various non-technical factors that influence and impact the development and implementation of IT strategy have been accommodated in three main components, namely, organisational culture issues, internal policies and personal issues. This represents a generalization of the results of the case study, and puts forward the proposition that these three main components would also accommodate non-technical factors that would be found in other organisations.

The various non-technical factors are, as has been shown, not independent, but deeply interdependent. The three main components proposed in Figure 1 are similarly not independent. Certain factors of a personal nature need a particular organisational culture in which to thrive, or would feed on particular internal policies. Similarly, certain internal policies would only be possible within a particular organisational culture. In the case study, the latter was illustrated forcefully: the organisation's policy of acknowledging both Afrikaans and English as official languages had serious consequences – not so much as a result of the policy itself, but as a result of the organisational culture in which this policy was promulgated. The culture coped poorly with diversity, and the additional diversity created through the policy transformed into another divide, linking with existing divides and reinforcing them and itself.

The advantage of a general model such as shown in Figure 1 is that it enables a greater understanding of how non-technical factors manifest in the implementation of IT strategy. While non-technical factors could never be eradicated, using a model such as Figure 1 could assist in removing some of the feeding grounds of non-technical factors, or counteracting them with appropriate measures.

## CONCLUSION

The study investigates the impact of non-technical factors on IT strategy and probes the interaction between these issues in the development and implementation of IT strategy. It vividly exposed the fact that culture, policy and personal issues enable IT strategy as much as it constrains it, whether consciously, unconsciously or by practical unconsciousness.

Some of the findings, such as cultural diversity, of the study are known facts in many organisations. But it was thought to be known by few. As a result, it was easy to turn a blind eye to the practice. Other matters were considered to be too sensitive to address. The findings of the study will instill confidence in IT managers to boldly confront the signs such as language manipulation.

Structuration Theory was identified as suitable theory to underpin the research. As such it provided an ontological and epistemological basis for the research: both an understanding of the essence of what was investigated in the study, and how to obtain knowledge about the phenomena studied.

The empirical findings of this study contribute to the understanding of the impact and influence of people and process both in the development and implementation of IT strategy in the organisation. In addition, the study contributes to a better understanding of human implications, the roles of actors, structures and the individuals and groups of individuals involved in the implementation of IT strategy. Also, the study revealed insights such as use of dominance of race and age groups, and language to align with position of influence, which professionals including IT managers would not have detected or observed.

## REFERENCES

Giddens, A. (1984). *The constitution of society: Outline of the theory of structuration.* Cambridge, UK: John Polity.

Iyamu, T., & Adelakun, O. (2008). The impact of non-technical factors on information technology strategy and e-business. In *Proceedings of the 12th Pacific Asia Conference on Information Systems* (pp. 1214-1222).

Iyamu, T., & Roode, D. (2010). The use of structuration and actor network theory for analysis: A case study of a financial institution in South Africa. *International Journal of Actor-Network Theory and Technological Innovation, 2*(1), 1–26. doi:10.4018/jantti.2010071601

Jones, M. (1999). Structuration theory. In Currie, W. L., & Galliers, R. D. (Eds.), *Rethinking management information systems* (pp. 103–134). Oxford, UK: Oxford University Press.

Lederer, L., & Sethi, V. (1988). The implementation of strategic information systems planning methodologies. *Management Information Systems Quarterly, 12*(3), 445–461. doi:10.2307/249212

Markus, L. (1983). Power, politics, and MIS implementation. *Communications of the ACM, 26*(6), 430–444. doi:10.1145/358141.358148

Mintzberg, H. (2000). *The rise and fall of strategic planning.* Upper Saddle River, NJ: Prentice Hall.

Myers, M. D. (1997). Qualitative research in information systems. *Management Information Systems Quarterly, 21*(2), 241–242. doi:10.2307/249422

Noor, K. (2008). Case study: A strategic research methodology. *American Journal of Applied Sciences*, *5*(11), 1602–1604. doi:10.3844/ajassp.2008.1602.1604

Orlikowski, W. (1992). The duality of technology: Rethinking the concept of technology in organizations. *Organization Science*, *3*(3), 398–427. doi:10.1287/orsc.3.3.398

Pozzebon, M., & Pinsonneault, A. (2001, June 27-29). Structuration theory in the IS field: An assessment of research strategies. In *Proceedings of the 9th European Conference on Information Systems*, Bled, Slovenia (pp. 205 -217).

Roode, J. D. (1993). Implications for teaching of a process-based research framework for information systems. In *Proceedings of the 8th Annual Conference of the International Academy for Information Management*, Orlando, FL.

Rose, J., & Hackney, R. (2002). Towards a structurational theory of information systems: a substantive case analysis. In *Proceedings of the 36th Hawaii International Conference on System Sciences* (Vol. 8, p. 258).

Rowlands, B. (2005). Grounded in practice: Using interpretive research to build theory. *Electronic Journal of Business Research Methodology*, *3*(1), 81–92.

Scarbrough, H. (1998). Linking strategy and IT-based innovation: The importance of the "management of expertise". In Galliers, R. D., & Baets, W. R. J. (Eds.), *Information technology and organisational transformation: Innovation for the 21st century organization*. Chichester, UK: John Wiley & Sons.

Sohal, A., & Ng, L. (1998). The role and impact of information technology in Australian business. *Journal of Information Technology*, *13*(3), 201–217. doi:10.1080/026839698344846

Walsham, G., & Waema, T. (1994). Information systems strategy and implementation: A case study of a building society. *ACM Transactions on Information Systems*, *12*(2), 159–173. doi:10.1145/196734.196744

Weiss, J., & Anderson, D. (2002). CIOs and IT professionals as change agents, risk and stakeholder managers: A field study. In *Proceedings of the 36th Hawaii International Conference on System Sciences*.

Wolff, S., & Sydor, K. (1999). Information systems strategy development and implementation: A nursing home perspective. *Journal of Healthcare Information Management*, *13*(1), 2–12.

Yin, K. (2009). *Case study research, design and methods* (2nd ed.). Newbury Park, CA: Sage.

*This work was previously published in the International Journal of Social and Organizational Dynamics in IT, Volume 1, Issue 4, edited by Michael B. Knight, pp. 48-59, 2011 by IGI Publishing (an imprint of IGI Global).*

# Chapter 11
# Playing Virtual Power Games:
## Micro-Political Processes in Inter-Organizational Networks

**Monique Janneck**
*Luebeck University of Applied Sciences, Germany*

**Henning Staar**
*University of Hamburg, Germany*

## ABSTRACT

*Although virtual organizations and networks have been studied, there is still need for research regarding their inner dynamics and the mechanisms of leadership and governance. This paper investigates micro-political processes i.e. informal actions of individual actors to gain power and exert influence, which is a well-researched concept in traditional organizations with respect to inter-organizational networks. This study investigates structures and strategies of power within virtual networks. Results show that micro-political tactics known from research in traditional organizations are used in inter-organizational settings. Additional micro-political tactics, specific to virtual networks, are identified. The latter are related to the use of information and communication technology (ICT). A second quantitative study surveyed 359 members of inter-organizational networks on their use of micro-political tactics. Results confirm that micro-political strategies are widely used in virtual networks. The degree of virtuality was associated with the use of certain tactics. Possible implications for the structure and governance of virtual networks and the design of the technology that is used to support virtual cooperation are discussed.*

## INTRODUCTION

Due to globalization and technological developments, *virtual organizations and networks* have emerged in the last decade as new organizational structures and continue to gain importance on the

market. This is especially true for networks of freelancers and small and medium-sized enterprises.

Although virtual networks have been studied for quite some time (Davidow & Malone, 1992; Goldman, Nagel, & Preiss, 1995; Kock, 2000; Travica, 2005), there is still need for research regarding their inner dynamics and the mecha-

DOI: 10.4018/978-1-4666-1948-7.ch011

nisms of leadership and governance: The vast majority of research has focused predominantly on the level of single network *organizations* when dealing with aspects of network governance and leadership. The individual-related perspective focusing on the interacting *people*, however, has played a minor role in the existing literature on governance in collaborative settings (Huxham & Beech, 2008).

In this paper we investigate whether the concept of *micro-politics* is useful to explain behavior in virtual networks. The term 'micro-politics' refers to informal actions of individual stakeholders to gain power and exert influence within an organizational setting. Originating in organizational science and psychology, micro-political behavior within organizations has been extensively researched in the last decades (Ferris, Hochwarter, Douglas, Blass, Kolodinsky, & Treadway, 2002; Vigoda-Gadot, 2003).

The aim of our paper is to transfer the concept of micro-politics from the *intra*-organizational setting to the *inter*-organizational level. So far, micro-political behavior of individual network members has hardly been examined (Huxham & Beech, 2008). Nevertheless, focusing on informal influence processes is particularly interesting due to the fact that inter-organizational networks are typically characterized by a lack of formal hierarchies and roles and have no *formal* structure of leadership (Janneck & Finck, 2006; Rittenbruch, Kahler, & Cremers, 1998; Travica, 2005). Thus, it is sensible to assume that *informal* actions of individual stakeholders play a crucial role in shaping and governing the network.

To investigate whether micro-political behavior is a feasible perspective on virtual networks, we initially conducted a qualitative interview study with representatives of various networks, questioning them about their perception and use of actions to gain power and influence. Secondly, we conducted a quantitative study to test the generalizability of the qualitative results.

In essence, the contribution of our work is to *extend* the concept of *micro-politics* to *inter-organizational*—or virtual—*networks* and to provide first *empirical* insights into structures and tactics of power within such networks.

The paper is structured as follows: First, we discuss and define virtual networks as we understand them in our study. Afterwards, we introduce the concept of micro-politics *within* organizations and transfer it to *inter-organizational* relations. The next section presents the methodology and results of the qualitative interview study (study 1). The quantitative study, based on an online survey (study 2), is presented in the subsequent section, and followed by a comprehensive discussion of both studies. We conclude the article by discussing implications for the design of virtual networks and the supporting ICT from a researcher's as well as a practitioner's viewpoint and describing prospects for future work.

## VIRTUAL NETWORKS

Virtual organizations can take various forms (Travica, 2005). However, most definitions agree that virtual organizations are forms of "inter-organizational, cross-border ICT-enabled collaboration between legally independent entities, usually with a specific economic goal" (Pitt, Kamara, Sergot, & Artikis, 2005, p. 373).

Beyond those basic properties, virtual organizations can vary considerably regarding the stability of membership and participation and also regarding the duration and goals of the cooperation.

In our research, we take a view of virtual organizations as *networks* of independent enterprises or entrepreneurs. Members (or member organizations, respectively) engage in this form of cooperation because they expect economic advantages, e.g. by sharing resources, forming buying syndicates, organizing vocational training together, attracting new customers and expanding their range of services or products or developing new products and services together. This is especially important for small and medium-sized enterprises (SMEs) that might be in danger of losing their competitiveness in a globalized market.

However, network members often still act as individual competitors on the market. Thus, collaboration in virtual business networks has also been termed 'coopetition' (Brandenburger & Nalebuff, 1997): A permanent and delicate balancing act between cooperation and competition.

The virtual networks we studied are mostly *polycentric networks*, i.e. highly distributed (Gumm, 2006) and loosely coupled associations with high degrees of autonomy of their members. This implies that there is typically no formal leader with special authority or someone superior to the other members. The networks we investigated are constituted predominantly by small and medium-sized enterprises (SMEs) or freelancers.

In such networks typical elements of virtual organizations become especially apparent, such as a lack of formal hierarchies and roles and a heavy reliance upon information and communication technology (Rittenbruch et al., 1998; Travica, 2005).

Furthermore, facing the 'coopetition' explained above, a certain amount of trust among members is crucial to deal with the insecurity and informality of the situation (Rittenbruch et al., 1998): Thus, *personal relations* between network members (or representatives of member enterprises, respectively) play a vital role. For example, members might possess a high degree of influence due to their personal experience or charisma and thus emerge as informal network leaders. Therefore, micro-political behavior, which contributes to the establishment of structures, processes, and roles, seems to be an especially promising concept to investigate virtual networks.

Based on this characterization, we will use the terms 'virtual networks' and 'inter-organizational networks' interchangeably in this paper.

## THE CONCEPT OF MICRO-POLITICS

Organizations consist of individual actors who interact constantly. In organizational science, micro-political processes are understood as strategies of individuals to negotiate their interests in interaction with others and gain and exert influence. Micro-political behavior is a central concept of organizational theory as well as an everyday occurrence in organizations: Organizational actions are neither fully formalized nor based on rational decisions only. Thus, micro-political processes become relevant when people have a certain scope of action to achieve their goals, realize ideas, or push certain interests. Typical situations in which micro-political processes become relevant include career advancement opportunities or "bottom-up leadership", i.e. employees seeking to influence their supervisors (Yukl & Falbe, 1990; Falbe & Yukl, 1992).

Even though these processes are typically informal in nature and not organizationally sanctioned, they nevertheless influence power structures within organizations (Elron & Vigoda-Gadot, 2006; Vigoda & Cohen, 2002).

## INTRA-ORGANIZATIONAL MICRO-POLITICAL PROCESSES

In the last decades there has been a rapid growth in theoretical publications and empirical studies in organizational science and psychology that focused on influence and politics in intra-organizational settings (Falbe & Yukl, 1992; Ferris & Kacmar, 1992; Gandz & Murray, 1980; Pfeffer, 1992; Vigoda-Gadot & Drory, 2006).

One approach to micro-political processes that has been extensively discussed focuses on the organizational members' political behavior. On this note, micro-politics is regarded as part of a general set of social behaviors contributing to the basic functioning of organizations (Pfeffer, 1992).

*Table 1. Influence tactics in traditional organizations*

| Tactics | Explanation |
|---|---|
| Rational Persuasion | Using logical arguments and facts; giving information to persuade the other that a desired result will occur. |
| Ingratiation | Using praise and flattery or helpful behavior to get the other person in a good mood or to think favorably of oneself; making the other person feel important. |
| Coalitions | Using the assistance of others or securing other persons' support to achieve the desired goal. |
| Personal Appeals | Appealing to the other's feelings of loyalty and friendship towards oneself. |
| Inspirational Appeals | Arousing enthusiasm by appealing to universal or common values, ideals, and aspirations. |
| Assertiveness | Seeking compliance by using demands, threats, frequent checking, or persistent reminders. |
| Upward Appeals | Causing pressure to conform by invoking the influence of higher levels in the organization (making a formal appeal to superiors or obtaining their informal support). |
| Blocking | Ignoring other people or spreading (wrong) information to thwart others. |
| Sanctions | Threatening to prevent benefits or job security. |
| Legitimating | Indicating that a request is consistent with organizational policies, rules, practices or traditions. |
| Exchange | Offering an exchange of positive benefits, indicating willingness to reciprocate at a later time or promise a share of the benefits if the other person helps accomplish a task. |
| Consultation | Asking for participation in decision-making when the other person's assistance and support are desired; showing willingness to modify a proposal to deal with the other's concerns and suggestions. |
| Self-Promotion | Presenting oneself as competent, smart, successful, and proficient; showy behavior. |

Accordingly, micro-political processes have been investigated by means of observing typical informal behavioral patterns of employees on different hierarchical levels (Yukl & Falbe, 1990), the use of power bases (French & Raven, 1959), or skills that might be helpful in "getting one's way" (Ferris et al., 2007). However, micro-political processes have been studied most frequently regarding employees' *influence tactics*. Such influence tactics used at work can be aimed at different goals and self-focused as well as organization-focused (Kipnis, Schmidt, & Wilkinson, 1980). Work in this field has led to a variety of typologies of influence tactics, as well as their possible antecedents and consequences (Kipnis et al., 1980; Vigoda-Gadot, 2003; Yukl & Falbe, 1990).

In Table 1 we summarize a representative set of tactics that were identified in seminal studies (Ansari, 1990; Kipnis et al., 1980; Yukl & Falbe, 1990) and have been extensively re-examined since then (Blickle, 2003; Ferris et al., 2002).

## Inter-Organizational Micro-Political Processes

In our view, micro-politics is a useful concept to study and understand inter-organizational relations, especially *polycentric* networks without formal structures and rules of governance, giving way to informal processes and tactics of influence and negotiation and also raising actors' consciousness regarding the importance of 'political' behavior (Gandz & Murray, 1980). As formal structures of leadership are missing, individual activities to form coalitions and build an influential position in order to benefit from the cooperation should be especially effective in inter-organizational networks.

Furthermore, communication and coordination of work activities in network collaboration is often enabled and facilitated through an extensive use of information and communication technology (ICT). Accordingly, former research on political processes in virtually organized collaborations

(Elron & Vigoda-Gadot, 2006) suggests that technology-based interactions may be especially susceptible to informal influence processes. Moreover, ICT used by inter-organizational networks might not only contribute to but even constitute micro-political processes, as technology serves both: making existing processes and structures more explicit as well as bringing forth new roles and rules (Janneck, 2009). Network actors who are well experienced in the use of ICT might use their knowledge to gain power.

Therefore, in our studies we investigated the following main research questions:

1.  What micro-political processes can be identified within inter-organizational networks? Are they different from typical tactics found in the intra-organizational context?
2.  How successful is micro-political behavior in an inter-organizational setting? How does it affect the virtual network?
3.  How are micro-political processes enacted through technology in virtual networks?

## STUDY 1

## Method

The study was conducted in spring 2009 as part of a larger research project concerned with governance and innovation in inter-organizational networks (http://www.kreanets.com). By means of a systematic Internet research we recruited members of inter-organizational networks for a qualitative interview study. The networks needed to fulfill the following criteria to be included in the study: a) horizontal relationships between members/member organizations, b) polycentric governance, and c) a minimum of three member organizations (ranging from sole proprietorships to SMEs).

Overall, we conducted 15 semi-structured in-depth interviews (Miles & Huberman, 1994)

with members of virtual networks from different sectors and industries (IT, media design, shipping industry, real estate business, consulting business, labeling industry, medicine, farming). The enterprise size ranged from single-person enterprises to SMEs with up to thirty members. The network size ranged from three to twelve members/member organizations. Our interview partners were between age 28 and 61, six were female, nine male.

Economic goals such as joint customer projects or sales orders were named as the network's primary objective by 13 of the 15 network representatives. Slightly different, the medical network's aim was to facilitate communication and exchange across different medical sectors and, therewith, to improve patients' medical treatment. The network of farmers acted as an agricultural cooperative. All networks were aimed at long-term existence and arranged their collaboration mainly through the use of information and communication technologies. The technologies applied ranged from exchange via e-mail and telephone to sophisticated communication and groupware platforms. Table 2 summarizes the sample characteristics.

To obtain comprehensive and valid data on interpersonal influence processes, we focused on individuals whose network positions allowed lively interactions and exchange with the other network partners, or—in other words—who were likely to be both the source and aim of influence attempts. Therefore we concentrated on freelancers and representatives of small and middle-sized enterprises, acting as the organizations' *boundary spanners* (White & Dozier, 1992) within the network.

The interview partners were asked about their experiences with influence and politics, leadership, and power within their networks, i.e. what tactics and behaviors they had either been using *themselves* or *other* network members had been using to push their interests within the network, and how *successful* these tactics had proven. To elicit these experiences, we asked the interviewees

*Table 2. Sample characteristics*

| Sample characteristics | |
|---|---|
| Business sectors | IT, media design, shipping industry, real estate business, consulting business, labeling industry, medicine, farming |
| Enterprise size | 1-30 employees |
| Network size | 3-12 member organizations |
| Primary objective of network | Economic goals (n=13)<br>Improve medical treatment (n=1)<br>Agricultural cooperative (n=1) |
| Interviewees' gender | 6 female, 9 male |
| Interviewees' age | 28-61 yrs (M=41.0) |

to describe so-called 'critical incidents' or key situations in which influence attempts had occurred, following the common procedure of prior research on micro-politics (Dosier, Case, & Key, 1988; Kipnis et al., 1980; Yukl & Falbe, 1990). Concerning the effectiveness of micro-political behavior, no fixed criteria for success were determined beforehand; instead the interviewees were asked for their subjective judgment whether the tactics applied had worked out for them or other network members. This open criterion of success as simply 'getting one's way' has been commonly used in other studies on micro-politics as well (Kipnis et al., 1980).

Furthermore, the interviewees were asked about the emergence of the network, the issue of competition and trust, processes of innovation, and the use of ICT. Data on formal aspects such as network size, duration, geographical distribution etc. was also collected.

The interviews (30-90 minutes duration) were audiotaped and transcribed literally according to a fixed set of transcription rules that had been defined beforehand. A qualitative content analysis was conducted using a combined a-priori/post-hoc approach: In a first step, the interview data was structured according to a category system deduced from the literature on micro-political processes within organizations (a-priori analysis). In a second step, the category system was refined by adding further categories of tactics identified

through the described behaviors and actions of network agents in the data (post-hoc analysis). A total of 31 distinguishable concrete micro-political actions in 15 different categories were identified.

The stability *(intra coder reliability)* (Krippendorf, 1980) of the newly developed category system was tested by repeated coding three weeks after the first analysis. Cohen's Kappa was calculated as reliability index. Intra-coder reliability was excellent (k=.91). Likewise, the *inter-coder reliability* (tested by having the material coded by three independent raters) proved to be very good (k=.77).

## Results

In the next sections, we present the results of the deductive (a-priori) and inductive (post-hoc) analyses.

**A-priori analysis: Use of intra-organizational micro-political tactics:** The a-priori analysis showed that the micro-political tactics known from research within organizations (Ferris et al., 2002; Vigoda-Gadot, 2003) (Table 1) are also relevant in inter-organizational contexts. Table 3 shows the number of different tactical actions described by the interviewees that could be assigned to the respective tactical categories.

*Table 3. Intra-organizational tactics used in virtual networks*

| Category | $N_{TACT}$ | Paraphrased Text Samples |
|---|---|---|
| Rational Persuasion | 2 | Gathering additional information in view of a forthcoming discussion |
| Ingratiation | 3 | Being charming to gain resources |
| Coalitions | 2 | Spending more time beyond network meeting with some partners |
| Personal Appeals | 1 | Appealing to someone's friendship to get support for one's own plans |
| Inspirational Appeals | 2 | Evoking the common network idea |
| Assertiveness | 3 | Stopping discussions at meetings on one's own authority |
| Blocking | 2 | Circulating rumors, ignoring network partners |
| Sanctions | 1 | Counting single agents from the network community |
| Legitimating | 2 | Referring to network contracts |
| Exchange | 2 | Reminding others of a prior favor |
| Consultation | 1 | Obtaining an opinion from network partners for a planned project |
| Self-Promotion | 3 | Emphasizing one's own good reputation |

All categories of micro-political tactics known from the intra-organizational setting (except for *Upward Appeals* to supervisors, which obviously does not apply to virtual networks without formal hierarchies) were named by at least one interview partner to be one of their own tactics. The category mentioned most often in the interviews is *Rational Persuasion*, both as a tactic the interview partners used themselves and as well as one which is used by others. 'Competitive' tactics such as *Blocking* are attributed more to other network members than to oneself. This issue will be discussed further on.

**Post-hoc analysis: Micro-political tactics specific to virtual networks:** Beyond the micro-political tactics known from the intra-organizational context three additional tactics specific to virtual networks could be identified: *Mediating, Being Visible*, and *Claiming Vacancies.*

*"Being Switzerland": Mediating:* In four cases interviewees reported gaining influence by taking a neutral, mediating position ("being Switzerland", as one interviewee put it). Contrary to intra-organizational settings there will seldomly be a dyadic relation of influence between actors, but an individual's position within the network as a whole will be crucial regarding his or her influence and power. Being seen as a mediator seems to strengthen this overall network position. The following quote exemplifies the tactic:

$N_{TACT}$: No. of different *tactical actions* that were assigned to this category across the whole sample.

*"I always tried to keep myself out of the playing around, the feuds and coalitions. But when you're active and still keep a kind of neutral position, that neutrality gives you a central position, and somehow you are the contact person for the others, something like a mediator. And when the others wouldn't find a common ground, my word was important."*

The interviewees described this more reluctant, mediating role not as putting one's own interests back or avoiding conflict as such, but as tactical measure in the sense of "when two people fight, the third decides". By 'being Switzerland' actors maneuver themselves in a better strategic position.

*"Add your two cents!": Being Visible:* Six of the reported tactics referred to frequent presence and good visibility within the network as a means to gain influence. Contrary to teams coordinating their work in traditional organizations, members of virtual networks are typically distributed not only organizationally, but also in time and space (Gumm, 2006). Therefore, distributed teams often suffer from a lack of awareness (Dourish & Bellotti, 1992) concerning each other's activities: Different members' ways of working and also their respective contributions are often not transparent to others. In such a setting, frequent visibility might serve as 'evidence' of members' efforts and achievements—quite irrespective of the quality of their contribution.

Naturally, information, coordination, and co-operation processes in virtual networks are largely based on electronic communication. Therefore, being visible is often tied to frequent use of the network's different communication channels and tools. Members who are visible become a central 'communication knot'. How visibility serves as a tactic to gain influence is exemplified by the following interview quote:

*"I would definitely say that sometimes quantity is much more effective than quality. I always kept the others informed. E-mails, phone calls, postings in the forum. Of course, everybody benefitted from my activities. And at the same time due to that persistent presence, permanent showing that you're there, you get the status of an active and effective network partner: "Wow, he's active!" You get to be a core player of the network if you're so omnipresent. There is no getting around you when you have that presence."*

Unlike the established category of *Self-Promotion*, which focuses on emphasizing one's importance, competencies, and success, the tactic of being visible is not aimed primarily at showing off one's capability, but rather activity as such to gain influence.

*"Filling the vacuum": Claiming Vacancies.* Another tactic specific to virtual networks that was reported in five cases aims at strategically searching and taking up (new) tasks and roles within the network. Especially in the network's initial phase, tasks and roles are often not specifically tied to certain individuals. Furthermore, taking responsibility is mostly voluntary in poly-centric networks, therefore leaving room for individuals to assume tasks and roles that suit their respective interests, competencies, and needs. Examples for taking up roles as a means to gain influence include serving as a host/moderator of meetings (with the possibility to set the agenda) or administrating the network platform. The following quotes point out this tactic:

*"You know, there is always a vacuum, some tasks or positions are not clearly assigned to someone—especially at the very beginning. And so it is up to you to take advantage of it. (...) As the moderator of the meeting, of course, you are in the position to co-determine the agenda. Your matters come first, when everyone is listening."*

*"And some of the partners always arrived pretty late after the meetings had started already. And, OK, I knew they would argue against my proposal. So the vote was set at the very beginning. Bad luck for them."*

Again, it becomes clear that information and communication technology used within the network serves as a vehicle for micro-political processes:

*"One of our partners was very good in technical things. So it was him from the very beginning who created our Internet appearance and answered the customers' e-mails and, well, of course he did that to his own benefit I would say."*

Further examples show that the power of being an administrator is also due to the possibility to act as a 'gatekeeper' and filter or use incoming information first before distributing them to the other network members. Similarly, administrators make use of the possibility to influence the network's outside presentation (e.g. by controlling web sites) in a way that is favorable for them (e.g. to attract certain groups of customers).

**Acceptance and success of micro-political tactics in virtual networks:** To sum up, micro-political behaviors known from intra-organizational research as well as actions specific to inter-organizational networks could be identified in our study. Table 4 summarizes all tactics that were reported by our interviewees.

Success is a fundamental criterion of micro-political behavior (Vigoda-Gadot, 2003), raising the question of the *effectiveness* of the micro-political tactics that were identified in this study. Therefore, the interviewees were also asked about the acceptance and success of the micro-political tactics they used and experienced. No fixed criteria for success or failure were determined beforehand; instead the interviewees voiced their own judgment if and how the tactics worked out for them or other network members.

Results show that *Rational Persuasion* is not only the tactic named most, but also the one that is seen as the most promising and successful to promote and push one's own interests within the network. This tactic was also judged as collaborative (Simmers, 1998), since it is seen as preserving not only one's own position within the network but the network as a whole as well.

$N_{FREQ:}$ No. of interviewees mentioning this tactic.
$N_{SELF:}$ No. of interviewees reporting this as *own* tactic.

*Table 4. Micro-political tactics used in virtual networks*

| Category | $N_{FREQ}$ | $N_{SELF}$ |
|---|---|---|
| Rational Persuasion | 14 | 14 |
| Ingratiation | 6 | 3 |
| Coalitions | 8 | 3 |
| Personal Appeals | 2 | 1 |
| Inspirational Appeals | 9 | 5 |
| Assertiveness | 4 | 2 |
| Blocking/ Manipulating | 3 | 1 |
| Sanctions | 2 | 1 |
| Legitimating | 3 | 1 |
| Exchange | 6 | 3 |
| Consultation | 4 | 3 |
| Self-Promotion | 6 | 3 |
| Mediating | 4 | 2 |
| Being Visible | 6 | 2 |
| Claiming Vacancies | 5 | 3 |

Other collaborative tactics named by the interviewees were especially *Inspiring Appeals* and *Being Visible*. Contrary, *Blocking and Manipulating* was seen as a highly competitive tactic. It was also judged as being only temporarily successful, but detrimental in the long run—for the individual position as well as for relations within the network as a whole.

*Self-Promotion* and *Assertiveness* were evaluated inconsistently: Some interview partners (from more 'traditional' areas such as farming and shipping) judged these tactics as clearly competitive and not effective, while others (from newer fields such as media design) praised them as highly effective and important.

One interviewee describes the effectiveness of assertive behavior as follows:

*"We were all in the same boat, but I tried to get them to row in the same direction. That means that sometimes you simply have to bang your fist on the table and call everyone to order—quite gruffy if necessary, because men are pretty simple and a firm stand was understood much better than the whole diplomatic seesaw."*

The disparity between the judgments of interviewees from more traditional industries compared to those from non-traditional business sectors was reflected in the general use of tactics, too: Tactics such as *Self-Promotion* were mentioned more frequently by interviewees from younger economic fields. As one interviewee put it:

*"Nowadays you have to be a real show-off in business life. Pretending and showing what you've got has become pretty essential".*

Generally it became clear that 'open' tactics are the most accepted and also the most effective micro-political behaviors in networks. 'Hidden fouls' behind the backs of others (e.g. *Blocking and Manipulating*) or tactical 'wheeling and dealing'

(*Coalitions*) were seen as jeopardizing trust and equal cooperation in virtual networks.

## STUDY 2

## Method and Sample

In a next step, we aimed at developing a standardized questionnaire to quantitatively measure the use of micro-political tactics in inter-organizational networks. Based on a foregoing literature and instrument research, think tank roundtable discussions, and the results of the qualitative interview study described above relevant constructs of tactical actions were identified. Building on that pool of network-related influence behavior, a pool of items was formulated. Along the lines of existent instruments from intra-organizational research (Ferris et al., 2002; Ansari, 1990; Kipnis et al., 1980; Blickle, 2003), the items focused on a self-assessment of 'how to get one's way' on a 6-point Likert scale ranging from never (1) to very often (6). Thereby, we largely refrained from a direct adoption of scales or items as the intra-organizational inventories in their original form did not meet the network context in word and content and, thus, had to be reworded.

On this note, as the general basis of the questionnaire's item inventory tactic categories from different sources were incorporated: Tactics already known from research in intra-organizational settings, the empirically identified tactics (*Mediating*, *Being Visible*, and *Claiming Vacancies*) as well as tactical actions reflecting network-specific phenomena like *Inspiring Trust*, i.e. the facilitating role of trust and reciprocity on cooperative behavior in virtual collaborations (Wehmeyer & Riemer, 2007).

With the objective of shortening the questionnaire and keeping only the most suitable items and scales, several psychometric criteria were defined for the scale and item selection, such as:

*Table 5. Internal consistencies (Cronbach's Alpha) of subscales*

| Subscale | Cronbach's α |
|---|---|
| Rational Persuasion | .75 |
| Inspirational Appeals | .90 |
| Assertiveness | .77 |
| Exchange | .83 |
| Self-Promotion | .81 |
| Mediating | .71 |
| Being Visible | .73 |
| Claiming Vacancies | .76 |
| Inspiring Trust | .85 |

- Clear pattern of factor loadings (factors should be clearly marked by high loadings for items reflecting the same underlying construct and low loadings for others)
- Acceptable internal consistencies of subscales (alpha coefficients of $\alpha > .70$)
- Items help to increase their subscale's reliability
- Exclusion of items with extreme mean values
- Sufficiently high dispersion about the mean (standard deviation and variance of the sample)
- Low proportion of missing values to exclude items that respondents seemingly had trouble understanding.

Therefore, not all of the 15 tactical categories originally reported in the qualitative study where finally included in the questionnaire. Several subscales had shortcomings especially regarding a lack of occurrence or an insufficient selectivity. As a consequence, six tactical categories were excluded from further examination at a very early stage of questionnaire development.

Thus, the final version of the questionnaire to be used contained 30 items, consisting of 9 subscales measuring different micro-political tactics (see Appendix A).

The subscales revealed acceptable to good internal consistencies (Table 5). As new scales and items were devised in the course of the development process, an EFA (principal components analysis, Promax rotation) was conducted on the 30-item pool to evaluate the dimensionality of the subscales. On the basis of factor loadings >0.5, nine resulting factors confirmed the theoretically derived subscale structure with a total of 72.8% of explained variance. Additionally, a conducted minimum average partial test (Velicer, 1976) supported the nine-factor solution. This can be interpreted as a sign of construct validity.

An online survey was conducted in summer 2009 with members of inter-organizational networks. Criterion for participation was actual or former engagement in one or more inter-organizational collaborations with economic goals as the primary objective. In addition to the Micropolitics questionnaire described above, participants were asked about the characteristics of their inter-organizational networks and especially about media usage among network partners. Respondents were contacted via social networking websites and business networks such as XING (http://www.xing.com) and asked to participate in the survey.

359 people completed the survey. 35% of participants were female, 65% male. Average age was 39.5 years (SD=9.8).

*Figure 1. Frequency of computer-mediated communication among network partners*

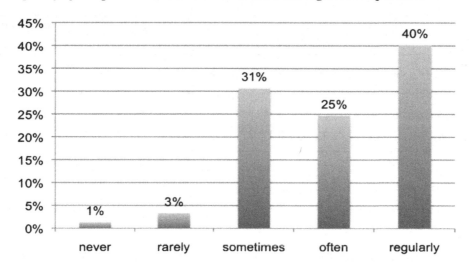

## Results

**Characteristics of virtual networks:** The size of the networks varied considerably. However, 72% of networks had 10 members or less. The vast majority (83% of respondents) said that their network included potential competitors on the market, giving the issue of power and influence particular relevance.

Almost half of the networks (48%) were founded 2007 or later. Only 8% of networks had been established before 2000. Two thirds (64%) of network members said that cooperation was open-ended, while in 23% cooperation was project-bound (13%: not specified).

The networks' goals included exchange of knowledge and experiences, efficiency, and reduction of costs.

**Use of electronic communication media:** Naturally, computer-mediated communication plays an important role for the network members. Two thirds of respondents used electronic communication media often or regularly (Figure 1).

The respondents mainly used basic communication media to communicate with their fellow network members (89%, Figure 2). A sizable part of networks also use groupware systems that are either provided by one of the network partners (39%) or even exclusively established for the network (29%). Other communication tools that are used quite frequently include VoIP (40%), video/internet conferencing (25%) and shared file systems (32%).

**Use of micro-political tactics.** The frequency of using different micro-political tactics varies substantially. Table 6 shows the mean values and standard deviations for the subscales.

The most frequently used tactics include *Inspiring Trust*, *Rational Persuasion*, and *Being Visible*. Also, *Inspirational Appeals*, *Mediating*, and *Claiming Vacancies* are tactics more commonly used. The tactics less reported are *Exchange*, *Assertiveness*, and *Self-Promotion*, each with 45% or more of respondents stating that they "rarely" or "never" use this tactic. Figures 3a and 3b show the frequency distributions for the subscales.

Therefore, results from the quantitative study mainly confirm the results from our qualitative

*Figure 2. Types of electronic communication media used in inter-organizational networks (in percent)*

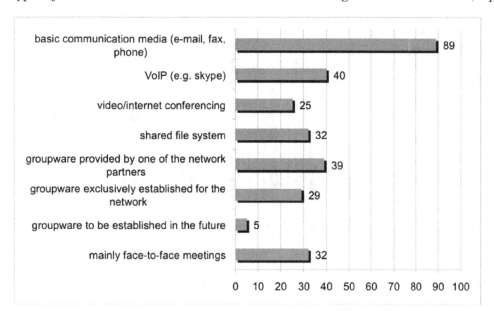

*Table 6. Use of micro-political tactics, mean value and standard deviation for subscales (scaling: 1 = never, 2 = rarely, 3 = sometimes, 4 = fairly often, 5 = often, 6 = very often)*

| Scale | M | SD |
|---|---|---|
| Inspiring Trust | 4.9 | 0.937 |
| Rational Persuasion | 4.61 | 0.92 |
| Being Visible | 4.45 | 1.179 |
| Inspirational Appeals | 3.71 | 1.37 |
| Mediating | 3.58 | 1.09 |
| Claiming vacancies | 3.29 | 1.182 |
| Exchange | 2.74 | 1.315 |
| Assertiveness | 2.73 | 1.01 |
| Self-Promotion | 2.46 | 1.224 |

study: Open, non-manipulative tactics play a major role in inter-organizational networks.

Regarding *demographic variables*, only marginal differences were found. Men apply the tactic of '*Being Visible*' more frequently than women (p=.05). Furthermore, younger men (>35 years) use *assertive* tactics more frequently than older men (p=.05).

There are some hints in the data that the *maturity* of the networks (in terms of duration)

plays a role regarding the occurrence of micro-political processes. Unfortunately, since the bulk of networks existed for two years or less, sample sizes were too small to calculate detailed inter-group comparisons. Therefore, networks that had existed for 1-2 years or 3-5 years, respectively, were compared exemplarily. Members of the older networks used *Rational Persuasion* (p=.05), *Assertiveness* (p=.05), and *Being Visible* (p=.06)

*Figure 3a. Frequency distribution for subscales; b. Frequency distribution for subscales*

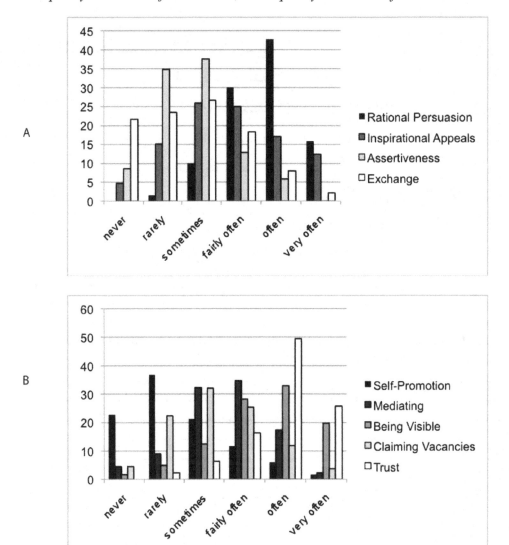

more often than members of younger networks (Mann-Whitney-U test).

Quite interestingly, no differences in micro-political behavior could be found regarding net-work *size*. However, due to the uneven distribution of member counts, again detailed comparisons could not be calculated.

**Relations between micro-political behavior and use of electronic communication media:** To investigate the relations between micro-political behavior and the use of ICT

we included several items measuring the participants' assessment and use of ICT within their network (Table 7). The items addressed *virtual presence* (access to information resources, visibility of activities, roles and responsibilities), the *meaning and importance of ICT* for the network, and *changes of interaction patterns* within the network through ICT.

Group comparisons (unpaired t-tests) showed that participants with frequent vs. infrequent use of certain micro-political tactics differ significantly in their use and assessment of ICT. This is especially true for the newly identified tactics of *Being Visible* and *Claiming Vacancies*, but also for *Self-Promotion* and, to a lesser degree, *Inspirational Appeals*, *Exchange*, *Mediating*, and *Assertiveness*: Participants who used these tactics more frequently also made more use of electronic communication, placed more weight on the general meaning of ICT and ICT skills for networking and were also aware of the meaning of ICT for presence and visibility within the network (Table 7).

## DISCUSSION

The aim of the studies presented in this paper was to investigate micro-political processes in virtual networks. Micro-politics is a well-researched concept in organizational science and psychology describing informal tactics to gain influence and power in traditional organizations.

By transferring this approach from the *intra-organizational* to the *inter-organizational* level, we aimed to shed light on the occurrence, characteristics, acceptance, and success of micro-political behavior in virtual networks.

Results indicate—despite some limitations discussed below—that the concept of micro-political behavior in organizations is indeed feasible and useful to explain the dynamics of virtual networks, which comprise actors from different enterprises. In the absence of clear hierarchies, structures, and roles, which is a key characteristic of the virtual networks we explored, micro-political behavior even seems to fall on especially fertile ground.

*Table 7. Comparison of participants with high vs. low usage of micro-political tactics in terms of their assessment of the use and meaning of ICT for their network (unpaired t-test, \*: p<0.05, \*\*: p<0.01, \*\*\*: p<0.001, +: p<0.10)*

| Item | Being Visible | Claim. Vac. | Self Prom. | Insp. Appeals | Exch. | Med. | Asser-tivenes |
|---|---|---|---|---|---|---|---|
| All network members have equal access to electronic information resources. | n.s. | n.s. | .001** | .01** | n.s. | n.s. | .014* |
| I took over new responsibilities and roles in my network through the use of ICT. | .01** | .000** | .000** | .08+ | .03* | n.s. | n.s. |
| Individual commitment for the network becomes visible through the use of ICT. | .000** | .001** | .002** | .06+ | n.s. | .02* | n.s. |
| I predominantly use electronic media for communication with network partners. | .002** | .07+ | .018* | n.s. | n.s. | n.s. | n.s. |
| Skills in the use of ICT are important for working together in our network. | .005** | n.s. | .007** | n.s. | n.s. | n.s. | n.s. |
| The use of ICT is important for our network. | .000** | n.s. | n.s. | n.s. | n.s. | n.s. | n.s. |
| Communication in our network has become more efficient through the use of ICT. | .000** | n.s. | n.s. | n.s. | .007** | n.s. | n.s. |
| Communication in the network has become more lively through the use of ICT. | n.s. | n.s. | .05* | n.s. | n.s. | n.s. | n.s. |

This leads us to the question whether micro-political behavior in inter-organizational networks is at all different from tactics found within traditional organizations. Our results show that members of virtual networks use many of the micro-political tactics known from traditional organizations. However, there are some differences.

For one thing, we identified tactics *specific* to virtual networks and organizations, namely *Mediating, Being Visible, Claiming Vacancies, and Inspiring Trust*. Future studies might discover additional ones.

We argue that these results are indeed new, since in the extensive body of research on intra-organizational micro-political tactics, these specific tactics have not been identified so far (Ansari, 1990; Blickle, 2003; Ferris et al., 2002; Kipnis et al, 1980; Yukl & Fable, 1990).

In our view, the newly identified tactics are rooted in the *non-hierarchical* character of virtual networks (e.g. forming and seizing (new) tasks and roles), but also in the reliance on *technology-supported interaction*. The interviewees gave clear examples of how they use ICT for micro-political actions, such as exploiting the possibilities of electronic communication for visibility within the network or using new roles associated with ICT (e.g. administrator or web master) to influence the network's outward appearance or communication flow. The quantitative analysis confirmed that network members differed in their use of micro-political tactics depending on their assessment and frequency of use of ICT: Members who showed higher technology-savvy and awareness also reported more frequent use of micro-political tactics. This holds true especially for those micro-political tactics that were newly identified as network-specific in our study.

However, it is an interesting research perspective to explore whether and how micro-political processes are enacted through technology in traditional organizations as well (for example in intra-organizational virtual teams).

Furthermore, networks are typically characterized by especially strong interdependencies between individual actors. Therefore individuals have more opportunities to 'control' others and push their own interests by micro-political behavior than in traditional organizations.

Nevertheless, unlike one might assume, micro-political behavior in virtual networks is not excessive or detrimental. It seems to be restrained by a self-regulating mechanism: As soon as competitive tactics threaten the integrity or stability of the network, micro-political behavior 'backfires' on the actor. Thus, actors have a strong motivation to abandon the behavior and protect the network as well as their own position.

A prerequisite for this self-regulatory mechanism seems to be a somewhat stable network structure and set of rules, legitimizing or sanctioning certain behaviors. As transparency, reciprocity, and trust are essential for successful cooperation in virtual networks, especially transparent and co-operative micro-political tactics (Simmers, 1998) seem to be viable and successful in the long run.

Quite generally, micro-politics is a controversial topic (Block, 1988). The negative connotations often associated with 'power' or 'politics' seem to contradict the positive notions of trust and cooperation on an equal footing associated with virtual networks. However, cooperation always involves interaction of humans—and humans do not act strictly 'rational' or as representatives of organizations, but also according to their very personal interests and needs.

Combining a qualitative and quantitative approach allowed us to make a profound first inquiry and generate a broad picture of the participants' subjective views and experiences in different types of networks and industry sectors, but also test these results on a broader basis, thus improving generalizability. The quantitative study confirmed the network-specific tactics that were identified in the interview study. Furthermore, it confirmed the observation that micro-political behavior in virtual networks is associated with the use of

ICT: Apparently, network members who apply micro-political behavior are especially aware of the potential of utilizing electronic communication media to establish a better strategic position within the network.

Moreover, we were able to develop a standardized questionnaire that can be used in future studies to measure micro-political behavior in virtual networks.

However, a clear limitation of both studies is that we did not collect independent measures of the effectiveness of micro-political behavior. Likewise, we were not able to judge the networks' overall success.

Furthermore, we have to bear in mind that *social desirability* plays a vital role in investigations of power and influence. Therefore, when interpreting the results, we have to be careful, especially when it comes to the question of *who* is using certain (more or less desirable) tactics: Quite interestingly, in the interview study competitive or egoistical tactics were mostly attributed to *other* network members. In the quantitative study, only the participants' self-assessment of their own use of micro-political tactics was measured. Again, participants stated that they mainly used cooperative tactics.

In future studies, it is necessary to triangulate the members' subjective views with other measures. E.g., micro-political behavior could be investigated through observations of network interactions and communication patterns. An analysis of *electronic* artifacts and communication records seems especially promising in this regard.

Measures of *effectiveness* could include the networks' stability (e.g. duration of individual membership, fluctuation, growth etc.), conflicts within the network, as well as economic indicators.

Furthermore, it would be desirable to include *whole* networks (or at least a larger number of their members) in future studies. This would also serve as a means to test the *convergence* of senders' and receptors' perception of micro-political processes, and thus help to validate results—or

gain further insights into the mechanisms of 'virtual micro-politics'.

It is important to note that our results describe micro-political processes in inter-organizational networks with a *polycentric* structure, which consist of independent members or member organizations and lack formal hierarchies and roles (cf. section 'Virtual networks'). More formalized types of virtual organizations might experience other forms of micro-political behavior.

## IMPLICATIONS AND FUTURE WORK

In this concluding section, we briefly discuss possible implications for the structure and governance of virtual networks as well as the design of the technology that is used to support virtual cooperation and identify issues for further research in the area.

### Implications for Research and Practice

**Structure and Governance of Virtual Networks:** Based on the results of our studies it is feasible to assume that micro-political behavior influences interaction, communication, and decision-making processes in virtual networks in a decisive way. Therefore, the way the 'virtual micro-politics' are played will probably affect the outcome, stability, and success of virtual networks. It is an open research question of the future to shed light on these mechanisms.

Our results suggest that different networks develop distinctive 'organizational' cultures, in which different levels and strategies of micro-political behavior are accepted and endorsed. Therefore, we hypothesize that individual micro-political tactics and preferences play a role in the process of becoming (and staying) a member of a certain network. If virtual networks manage to convey their 'micro-political culture' they might be more successful regarding these (self) selection processes, resulting in greater stability and less conflicts within the network. Again, these effects need to be clarified in future research.

**Design and Use of Technology:** The results of our studies also show that technology is an important carrier of micro-political behavior. Therefore, as designers of groupware and other information and communication technology, we should take a closer look on how design decisions facilitate or constrict micro-political behaviors.

For example, showing presence by means of electronic communication media is closely related to the design of *awareness features* in shared workspaces (Dourish & Bellotti, 1992; Janneck, 2009). Albeit the extensive body of research in the area, it still needs to be investigated e.g. how people *purposely* use awareness features for influence and power.

**Practical Implications:** As stated above, there are numerous implications for the structure and governance of virtual networks that are of equal interest for researchers as well as practitioners. Examples include selecting new members, handling conflicts, devising network rules, assigning roles, or even choosing technology.

However, at this early stage of research on micro-political processes in virtual networks, detailed recommendations are hard to make.

As a general statement—learning from research on intra-organizational micro-political processes— organizations are well advised not to ignore or try to restrain informal rules and behavior. Micro-politics is part of the organizational reality that can also have beneficial effects as it unleashes employees' creativity and motivation. Likewise, members of virtual networks should accept micro-political behavior as 'part of the game'.

Given the negative associations of power, this might not be an easy task: "*The taboo about power is still perhaps more profoundly rooted in conscience of modern man than the taboo about sex*" (Crozier, 1973, p. 214).

Similarly, prior research has shown that members of virtual networks often try to avoid the issue of *competition*, which is undoubtedly another reality of inter-organizational cooperation (Janneck & Finck, 2006).

Overcoming these taboos is a challenge for the organizational development of virtual networks, which might be addressed in consulting processes.

## Future Work

In our own research, we plan to take a closer look at the *associations* between *technology* and *virtual micro-politics*. Research questions to ask include how different types of media encourage or prove efficient regarding different micro-political tactics. In doing so, we will especially investigate electronic artifacts and communication patterns in virtual networks.

Furthermore, we plan to investigate micro-political behavior at *different stages* of cooperation in virtual networks: For example, specific tactics might exist in the initial phases of cooperation (e.g. pretending to possess certain resources) that might become obsolete or even detrimental later on. Also, the processes of entering and leaving virtual networks will be analyzed with respect to micro-political behavior.

There are some hints in the qualitative as well as the quantitative data that actors make use of different tactics depending on their *age*, *gender*, and also their *professional background* or the *industry sector* they come from. Also, network maturity seems to play a role. We will continue to investigate these variables in future studies.

To account for the methodological aspects discussed before, we also plan to conduct complete surveys of all (or at least a great number of) members belonging to a virtual network.

## ACKNOWLEDGMENT

We would like to thank the anonymous reviewers for their thorough assessment of our work and their valuable suggestions that helped tremendously to improve this paper. An earlier version of this paper was published in the proceedings of HICSS 2010 (Janneck & Staar, 2010).

This work has been funded by the German Federal Ministry of Research and Education (BMBF) and the European Social Fund (ESF) as part of the funding program "Working—Learning—Developing Skills. Potential for Innovation in a Modern Working Environment" under grant no. 01FM07047.

## REFERENCES

Ansari, M. A. (1990). *Managing people at work. Leadership styles and influence strategies.* London, UK: Sage.

Blickle, G. (2003). Convergence of agents' and targets' reports on intra-organizational influence attempts. *European Journal of Psychological Assessment, 19,* 40–53. doi:10.1027//1015-5759.19.1.40

Block, P. (1988). *The empowered manager: Positive political skills at work.* San Francisco, CA: Jossey- Bass.

Brandenburger, A. M., & Nalebuff, B. J. (1997). *Coopetition.* Eschborn, Germany: Riek.

Crozier, M. (1973). The problem of power. *Social Research, 40*(2), 211–228.

Davidow, W. H., & Malone, M. S. (1992). *The virtual corporation.* New York, NY: Harper-Collins.

Dosier, L., Case, T., & Key, B. (1988). How managers influence subordinates: An empirical study of downward influence tactics. *Leadership & Organization Development Studies Journal, 9*(5), 22–31. doi:10.1108/eb053645

Dourish, P., & Bellotti, V. (1992). Awareness and coordination in shared workspaces. In *Proceedings of the ACM Conference on Computer-Supported Cooperative Work* (pp. 177- 114). New York, NY: ACM Press.

Elron, E., & Vigoda-Gadot, E. (2006). Influence and political processes in cyberspace: The case of global virtual teams. *International Journal of Cross Cultural Management, 6*(3), 295–317. doi:10.1177/1470595806070636

Falbe, C. M., & Yukl, G. (1992). Consequences for managers of using single influence tactics and combinations of tactics. *Academy of Management Journal, 35,* 638–652. doi:10.2307/256490

Ferris, G., Hochwarter, W., Douglas, C., Blass, F., Kolodinsky, R., & Treadway, D. (2002). Social influence processes in organizations and human resources systems. In Ferris, G., & Marmocchio, J. J. (Eds.), *Research in personnel and human resources management* (*Vol. 21,* pp. 65–127). Amsterdam, The Netherlands: Elsevier.

Ferris, G. R., & Kacmar, K. M. (1992). Perceptions of organizational politics. *Journal of Management, 18,* 93–116. doi:10.1177/014920639201800107

Ferris, G. R., Treadway, D. C., Perrewé, P. L., Brouer, R. L., Douglas, C., & Lux, S. (2007). Political skill in organizations. *Journal of Management, 33*(3), 290–320. doi:10.1177/0149206307300813

French, J. R., & Raven, B. (1959). The bases of social power. In Cartwright, D. (Ed.), *Studies in social power.* Ann Arbor, MI: University of Michigan Press.

Gandz, J., & Murray, V. V. (1980). The experience of work place politics. *Academy of Management Journal, 23*(2), 237–251. doi:10.2307/255429

Goldman, S. L., Nagel, R. N., & Preiss, K. (1995). *Agile competitors and virtual organizations: Strategies for enriching the customer.* New York, NY: Van Nostrand Reinhold.

Gumm, D. C. (2006). Distribution dimensions in software development projects: A taxonomy. *IEEE Software*, 23(5), 45–51. doi:10.1109/MS.2006.122

Huxham, C., & Beech, N. (2008). Inter-organizational power. In Cropper, S., Ebers, M., Huxham, C., & Ring, P. S. (Eds.), *The handbook of inter-organizational relations* (pp. 555–579). Oxford, UK: Oxford University Press. doi:10.1093/oxfordhb/9780199282944.003.0021

Janneck, M. (2009). Designing for social awareness of cooperative activities. In *Proceedings of the 5th International Conference on Web Information Systems* (pp. 463-470).

Janneck, M., & Finck, M. (2006). Making the community a hospitable place—identity, strong bounds, and self-organisation in web-based communities. *International Journal of Web Based Communities*, 2(4), 458–473. doi:10.1504/IJWBC.2006.011770

Janneck, M., & Staar, H. (2010, January). Virtual micro-politics: Informal tactics of influence and power in inter-organizational networks. In *Proceedings of the 43th Annual Hawaii International Conference on System Sciences* (p. 10). Washington, DC: IEEE Computer Society.

Kipnis, D., Schmidt, S. M., & Wilkinson, I. (1980). Intra-organizational influence tactics: Explorations in getting one's way. *The Journal of Applied Psychology*, 65, 440–452. doi:10.1037/0021-9010.65.4.440

Kock, N. (2000). Benefits for virtual organizations from distributed groups. *Communications of the ACM*, 43(11), 107–112. doi:10.1145/353360.353372

Krippendorf, K. (1980). *Content analysis. An introduction to its methodology*. Thousand Oaks, CA: Sage.

Miles, M. B., & Huberman, A. (1994). *Qualitative data analysis: An expanded sourcebook*. Thousand Oaks, CA: Sage.

Pfeffer, J. (1992). *Management with power*. Boston, MA: Harvard Business School Press.

Pitt, J., Kamara, L., Sergot, M., & Artikis, A. (2005). Formalization of a voting protocol for virtual organizations. In *Proceedings of the Fourth International Joint Conference on Autonomous Agents and Multiagent Systems* (pp. 373-380). New York, NY: ACM Press.

Rittenbruch, M., Kahler, H., & Cremers, A. B. (1998). Supporting cooperation in a virtual organization. In *Proceedings of the International Conference on Information Systems* (pp. 30-38).

Simmers, C. A. (1998). Executive/ board politics in strategic decision making. *Journal of Business and Economic Studies*, 4(1), 37–56.

Travica, B. (2005). Virtual organization and electronic commerce. *SIGMIS Database*, 36(3), 45–68. doi:10.1145/1080390.1080395

Velicer, W. F. (1976). Determining the number of components from the matrix of partial correlations. *Psychometrika*, 41(3), 321–327. doi:10.1007/BF02293557

Vigoda-Gadot, E. (2003). *Developments in organizational politics*. Cheltenham, UK: Edward Elgar.

Vigoda-Gadot, E., & Cohen, A. (2002). Influence tactics and perceptions of organizational politics. A longitudinal study. *Journal of Business Research*, 5, 311–324. doi:10.1016/S0148-2963(00)00134-X

Vigoda-Gadot, E., & Drory, A. (2006). *Handbook of organizational politics*. Cheltenham, UK: Edward Elgar.

Wehmeyer, K., & Riemer, K. (2007). Trust-building potential of coordination roles in virtual organizations. *The Electronic Journal for Virtual Organizations and Networks*, *8*, 102–123.

White, J., & Dozier, D. M. (1992). Public relations and management decision making. In Grunig, J. E. (Ed.), *Excellence in public relations and communication management* (pp. 51–84). Mahwah, NJ: Lawrence Erlbaum.

Yukl, G., & Falbe, C. M. (1990). Influence tactics and objectives in upward, downward and lateral influence attempts. *The Journal of Applied Psychology*, *75*(2), 132–140. doi:10.1037/0021-9010.75.2.132

# APPENDIX A

*Table A1. Subscales and items of the Micro-Politics Questionnaire (translation of the original German questionnaire)*

| Subscale | Items |
|---|---|
| | *To achieve my goals within the network...* |
| **Rational Persuasion** | ...I tried to convince others with my knowledge in that matter.<br>...I used rational arguments to convince my network partners.<br>...I described in detail the reasons for my concerns.<br>...I spread information to the network partners to clarify my concerns. |
| **Assertiveness** | ...I clearly expressed my displeasure towards my network partners.<br>...I had to engage in open confrontation with my network partners.<br>...I put pressure on my network partners. |
| **Inspiring Trust** | ...I tried to appear open-minded about my network partners' concerns from the very beginning.<br>...I purposefully tried to show that I am a good and worthy network partner (showing mutual exchange, trustworthiness, etc.).<br>...I purposefully presented myself as a network partner who is willing to share information and resources.<br>...right from the start I tried to show my reliability towards the other network members. |
| **Inspirational Appeals** | ...I tried to highlight that we are all in the same boat.<br>...I called upon our common vision, the basic idea of a network.<br>...I emphasized the need to pull together for being successful. |
| **Mediating** | ...I achieved my goals better when I behaved neutrally towards my partners.<br>...I tried to stay neutral and mediated between partners during negotiations and discussions.<br>...I kept a non-committed position in discussions and controversies instead of taking sides with a party straight away.<br>...I tried to be the mediating tie in cases of disagreement. |
| **Self-Promotion** | ...I emphasized my efforts regarding the network collaboration.<br>...I emphasized my value for the network.<br>...I referred to positive outcomes due to my work and/or the central position of my company within the network. |
| **Being Visible** | ...I always tried to show presence via electronic media.<br>...I purposefully used electronic media to call attention to my concerns.<br>...I always tried to be available and present on all communication channels. |
| **Exchange** | ...I affirmed that I would show my gratitude for a partner's favor.<br>...I offered to do my network partner a favor in return.<br>...I promised to reciprocate for my network partner's support. |
| **Claiming Vacancies** | ...I looked for opportunities to play an additional part in the network beyond my primary role.<br>...I adopted some additional tasks as they turned out to be advantageous.<br>...I took over new tasks and/or roles within the network to extend my scope of action. |

*This work was previously published in the International Journal of Social and Organizational Dynamics in IT, Volume 1, Issue 2, edited by Michael B. Knight, pp. 46-66, 2011 by IGI Publishing (an imprint of IGI Global).*

# Section 3
# Virtual and Software Issues

# Chapter 12
# 3D Virtual Worlds:
## Assessing the Experience and Informing Design

**Sean P. Goggins**
*Drexel University, USA*

**Matthew Schmidt**
*University of Missouri, USA*

**Jesus Guajardo**
*University of Texas Health Science Center, USA*

**Joi L. Moore**
*University of Missouri, USA*

## ABSTRACT

*Teams meet in 3D virtual worlds more frequently than ever before, yet the tools for evaluating 3D collaboration environments are underdeveloped. To close the 3D collaboration tool evaluation gap, the authors integrate lessons from the gaming industry and distributed work research. They develop two complementary approaches. First, the individual user's perspective using eye-tracking (ET) is addressed, and second, the collaborative experience of the group using a technique called All-Views-Qualitative-Analysis (AVQA) is evaluated. The latter integrates the points-of-view of all subjects in a small group collaborating on a creative work task in a 3 dimensional virtual world. The authors show how these techniques enable evaluation of 3D environment design from the perspective of human computer interaction theory and theories related to distributed work. The paper discusses why designers should seek ways to leverage the advantages of 3D collaboration technologies and avoid recreating mirrors of physical space in these environments.*

DOI: 10.4018/978-1-4666-1948-7.ch012

# INTRODUCTION

Over one billion hours of collaborative play have been logged in the game Halo (Grossman, 2007). Put into easily understood commercial terms, that's about 526,315 person years of work effort; or the entire population of Ljubljana, Slovenia playing Halo instead of going to work, school or anywhere else during the day for an entire year. This milestone underscores the increasing acceptance of virtual worlds as legitimate, compelling places for humans to interact with one another, making it likely that 3D interaction technologies will be adopted beyond the realm of play. In fact, there is evidence that 3D virtual worlds are becoming a prominent framework for human-computer interaction (HCI) to support distributed, collaborative work (Kaptelinin & Czerwinski, 2007).

Much of what is known about HCI in 3D emerges from the study of video games. Qualitative studies of how gamers experience virtual worlds show that new games are adopted faster if they follow familiar interaction styles (Clarke & Duimering, 2006), and that game play sometimes leads to a new category of virtual community (Nardi & Harris, 2006). These studies provide preliminary guidance for HCI designers searching for new metaphors that might support deeper engagement in collaborative work among geographically dispersed groups (Carroll, 2003; Dyck, Pinelle, Brown, & Gutwin, 2003; Rapeepisarn, Wong, Fung, & Depickere, 2006). Designing software for distributed group work is recognized as a wicked problem with many challenging dimensions (Fitzpatrick, 1998). Grudin (1994) identified eight of the most significant challenges of designing software for collaborative work. Each of Grudin's eight challenges takes a slightly different form as technology changes. In this paper, we specifically address one of Grudin's eight challenges for the 3D generation of collaboration technologies: Evaluation.

Before explaining how evaluation of 3D environments might be different than evaluation of other types of collaborative work systems, we need to understand how users experience 3D collaboration differently. Dyck et al.'s (2003) analyses of gaming as an interaction metaphor reveals the core dimensions of effortless community, learning by watching, deep customizability and fluid system-human interaction. These dimensions of 3D games present an opportunity for 3D collaboration software designers to transfer ideas from gaming (Rapeepisarn et al., 2006). Wrapped up with this opportunity are challenges to long accepted heuristics for interface design, including simplicity, consistency & ease of use for all users. Dyck et al (2003) describe how these accepted HCI design heuristics do not transfer to 3D interaction design. HCI convention is further undermined by evidence that gamers enjoy learning a game quickly but then wish for it to become more difficult as they advance through different stages.

Gaming style interactions like those encountered in 3D environments are more compelling than conventional windowing systems (Paiva et al., 2002; Larson, 2007) and could form the basis for more engaging and productive HCI. The evaluation heuristics that we communicate to designers of these types of systems must, then, necessarily reflect both the fundamental differences and potential advantages of 3D collaboration. First, we must make a critical distinction between 3D virtual worlds and games: In the 3D environments tuned for work, collaboration is measured by creative output and group efficacy, not by a body count or other discrete score. One of the premises underlying the work presented here is that while the HCI community might learn from the example of game developers, building worlds to support creative collaboration is distinct from the challenge of creating a really great first person shooter (FPS) game. While the gaming community knows what works (Crawford, 1982; Rollings & Adams, 2003), the development and evaluation of collaborative 3D environments are in a more formative state.

There are a few aspects of 3D games that are salient to 3D interaction more generally and not tightly coupled to gaming interaction. First, interaction in 3D environments is more immersive, includes interactions with avatars and other social-emotional representations of people, and follows a set of interaction metaphors that have no corollary in traditional user interfaces. Each 3D environment embeds some combination of its own navigational scheme and existing conventions for movement, like the WASD buttons on a QWERTY keyboard (used for walking around and setting direction of a user within the world). Second, emotion is a more prevalent dimension in 3D interaction, the frequently lampooned legacy of Microsoft's Bob in HCI notwithstanding (Linnett, Fries Duvall, & Powelson, 1997). Avatars add emotional dimension to interaction in 3D spaces that is not present in conventional user interfaces designed to support collaborative work. Our evaluation design, then, must make sense of how users adapt to new types of interactions associated with the first aspect, and new types of collaboration associated with the second aspect of 3D environments.

In order to learn more about navigation and user experience in 3D environments, we set out to define an evaluation protocol for capturing and analyzing both the paths of individual user adaptation to 3D tools, and the patterns of group adoption of these kinds of tools. We choose eye-tracking (ET) technology to capture the nuances of how users make sense of avatar controls and interaction strategies in 3D environments because ET captures information at the 1/16th of a second level of detail, and makes it clear what users are attending to while navigating this new world. While insightful at the individual level of interaction analysis, ET is insufficient for building a comprehensive understanding of group interactions in 3D virtual worlds. This leads us to develop a complementary method for assessing 3D virtual world interactions through the integration of remote screen recording and formal usability lab

observation of subjects, which we describe as the all-views-qualitative-analysis (AVQA) method.

Next we examine the foundations of eye tracking as an HCI evaluation method. We then describe how eye-tracking data is captured and analyzed. This is followed by a description of how this type of data capture might be applied to the evaluation of user experience in a 3D environment.

## EYE TRACKING TECHNOLOGY

Duchowski (2002) reviews the development and application of eye-tracking technology over the past 40 years, outlining historical phases in the fields of cognitive psychology, industrial engineering, neuroscience and computer science (HCI). The central value of eye-tracking is based on what Just and Carpenter (1980) and others call the eye-mind hypothesis, which states that the location of a person's gaze directly corresponds to the most immediate thought in a person's mind. Early eye-tracking research is centered in cognitive psychology and neuroscience. Duchowski (2002) describes the present era in eye-tracking as *interactive*, with the most recent preceding era characterized as *diagnostic*. The key differentiation between these two eras is how eye-tracking technology is applied. In the diagnostic era, eye tracking is focused on understanding what a user is viewing. In the interactive era, eye-tracking technology becomes an aspect of user input. In both eras, eye-tracking application in the fields of industrial engineering and HCI increases (Duchowski, 2002). In the context of interactions in windowed, 2D spaces, the sequential framing of these eras is supported in the literature. However, the use of eye-tracking to refine 3D interactions either diagnostically or interactively remains practically unexamined and potentially quite fruitful.

## Capturing Eye-Tracking Data

There are two primary eye-tracking technology architectures, fovea-based and non-fovea-based. The fovea is a part of the eye that can be tracked to indicate where a person is looking. Fovea-based eye-tracking uses special equipment in a laboratory setting to monitor where a user is looking. Fovea tracking can be conducted with or without a head mounted device. Head mounted fovea-trackers are less expensive and more precise, but require the user to attach a cyborg-like device to their head. The drawback of both types of fovea tracking systems is that they require a laboratory environment, limiting insight into how user gaze is influenced by their natural environment.

Non-fovea-based eye-tracking systems take a variety of approaches, and most have been designed with the intention of overcoming either the cost or lab-based limitations of fovea-based eye-tracking systems. Mousetracks (Arroyo, Selker, & Willy, 2006) captures mouse movement over an interface, with the expectation that user gaze follows the cursor. In a sense, this extends the eye-mind hypothesis into an eye-mind-mouse hypothesis. Another non-fovea-based eye-tracker is Tarasewich and Fillion's (2004) enhanced restricted focus viewer, which achieves results similar to those of a full eye-tracking apparatus by blurring most of a user interface, rendering only a small section of the screen visible. This visible section is controllable by a user through a mouse or comparable pointing device. Li, Babcock, and Parkhurst (2006) developed a head-mounted eye-tracking apparatus from commodity hardware, in effect tackling the cost challenge of fovea-based eye tracking by open-sourcing the capture of gaze information. This accomplishment may signal the imminent commoditization of fovea-based eye-tracking technologies. It may also signal a decline in the exploration of non-fovea-based eye tracking, which is less authentic and less precise.

Eye-tracking to examine windowed applications advances understanding of how systems are learned and used, especially when traditional HCI evaluation methods do not reveal important shortcomings. For example, standard HCI evaluation methods do not account for user efficiency with a system when time is of the essence (emergency response applications, for example) or adequately explain user confusion or scenario failure (Karn, Ellis, & Juliano, 1999). Users new to 3D environments often encounter difficulty (Moore, Gathman, Ducheneaut, & Nickell, 2007). We suggest that knowledge of how users adapt and learn to use 3D environments will be enhanced by the use of eye tracking as an evaluation tool.

## Eye-Tracking Data Analysis

There are two primary views on how to analyze eye-tracking data, and how this information may be most useful for understanding user interactions with a computer system. The first view is that fixations and saccades reveal the most compelling explanation of how a user is experiencing a system (Karn et al., 1999; Karn, 2006). A fixation is a place where the user stares for a specified period of time. A saccade occurs when a user's gaze is moving from place to place in an interface. As might be expected, the distinction between fixation and saccade becomes more controversial with slower eye movements. The question "when does a fixation become a saccade?" continues to be a subject of debate in the eye-tracking research community (Salvucci & Goldberg, 2000). In a study of stroke patients, Müri et al. (2009) devised a taxonomy of fixation and saccade that included an intermediate concept they call foveation, which they define as rapid eye movements in a small visual field. These are distinguished from saccades in their research by the understanding that during sweeping saccades little visual input is processed by the brain, but during foveation, the brain processes significant visual input.

The second view of how to interpret and apply eye-tracking information is reviewing areas of interest (AOI) in the data. The AOI approach focuses on the density of total time spent in a particular area. The distinction between a fixation and a saccade is less critical than knowing where a user spends most of their time. Almost all analysis of eye tracking data falls into one of these two camps.

A number of studies argue that analyzing areas of interest provides as much insight for many tasks as analysis that distinguishes between fixations and saccades (Goldberg, Stimson, Lewenstein, Scott, & Wichansky, 2002; Santella & DeCarlo, 2004; Guan, Lee, Cuddihy, & Ramey, 2006). Other studies (West et al., 2006) find critical information present in the distinction between fixations and saccades, in some cases valuing the simpler, coarser but related concept of scanpaths, which are the heavily traveled visual roads between two points. As eye-tracking technology is applied to an increasing variety of Human Computer Interaction questions, ranging from web information usage (Cutrell & Zhiwei, 2007) to visual search (Byrne, 2001), we expect eye tracking data analysis methods to be distinguished by the types of questions they help us to answer.

## EYE TRACKING AND 3D WORLDS

Eye tracking is an evaluation method that will help 3D environment designers understand what parts of the rich interface a user is attending to during use. One of the key distinctions between a 3D environment and a windowed system is the presence of avatars and characters, which display emotional cues that are interpreted and acted upon by subjects. If these worlds are to be extended beyond applications focused on play, knowledge of the specific avatar characteristics attended to by subjects will aid designers. Further, consideration of how collaboration, idea sharing and innovation are best facilitated demands designer and researcher attention to what system users pay attention to during system use. Avatars and

fine-grained controls are aspects of 3D interaction that eye-tracking technologies directly address.

Blascovich et al. (2001) suggest that anthropomorphized avatars – those who subjects earnestly believe represent another human being – have a higher degree of social presence than agent-avatars and as a result are more likely to induce authentic social influence effects in a collaborative virtual environment. There is an interaction between the nature or importance of this belief about the avatar's social presence, and the realism of the avatar's representation. In general, the social presence of the avatar is positively influenced if it is identifiably a "human-avatar" (the user or subject knows the avatar is controlled by another human). As a result, the behavioral realism of the on screen representation can be low and still result in an authentic social interaction. By contrast, if the avatar is perceived as being agent driven instead of representative of a human, the behavioral realism of the representation must be higher in order for social influence effects to occur.

Blascovich's theory suggests two important ideas to 3D environment designers. First, it suggests that low quality avatars may be sufficient if the subjects know that the avatars are representations of real people. Second, realistic avatars may not require the locus of control for the avatar to be "human". Therefore, improvements in the efficacy of virtual environments for fostering social interaction may be possible through either an increase in the identifiably human nature of the avatars, which can be established through human like dialogue or through an increase in the realism of the avatars representation of the human form. Better graphics are not necessarily the answer to better 3D collaboration tools. Perhaps more significantly, if the attention of 3D environment designers is turned toward collaboration and knowledge creation, fine-grained study of what subjects focus on in these contexts may reveal starkly different design characteristics for collaboration and knowledge creation than for gaming.

Our study experiments with, refines and extrapolates methods for examining the relative importance of social presence and avatar realism in 3D environment interaction. Human attention to others, and the choice of whom to and how to interact in the world is powerfully affected by emotions, and emotional expectations of users (Wadlinger & Isaacowitz, 2006). Facial features that people attend to when discerning the emotional state of others are well established in the literature. The importance of facially expressed emotion compels the development of a method for applying eye-tracking technology to the evaluation of 3D collaboration environments. Our protocol integrates the importance of emotion into the eye-tracking experiment. We ask subjects to distinguish emotional states in human faces and avatars while eye-tracking data is captured. Next, we integrate ideas from previous work like Mousetracks and the enhanced restricted focus viewer to discern what users are attending to in a virtual environment with traditional usability lab protocols.

Knowing what individual users are attending to while participating in a 3D environment helps designers evaluate user controls. Increasing social and task oriented interactions in a 3D environment requires the study of multiple users in the environment at once. To ensure we evaluate both individual user interactions and collaborative work processes as they occur in a 3D environment, we developed a method we refer to as all-view-qualitative-analysis (AVQA). This method is distinguished by its integration of multiple user views, recorded from sessions of group work in 3D collaborative environments.

The remainder of this paper is organized as follows. First, two experiments where we capture eye-tracking information from subjects are described. Second, we describe the results from those experiments. Third, we discuss the results and provide a generalized method and toolset for consistently analyzing 3D environments using heat maps. Fourth, we describe the AVQA method, and insights gathered from our pilot studies. Lastly, we articulate a research agenda for the continued development of technologies for understanding human-avatar interaction in 3D environments.

## EXPERIMENT

### Eye-Tracking Apparatus

For the eye-tracking component of our method, subjects were seated in a desk chair in front of a computer screen with eye-tracking software configured. The eye tracking equipment used was an ASL R6 with VHT (video head tracking). Eye movements were recorded using this equipment, which was located in a human-computer interaction usability lab at a large university. The ASL R6 was selected over other eye-tracking technologies because it does not require a head mounted display.

### Stimulus Material

The facial expressions and animated avatars used in the eye-tracking part of our study were selected because they each present distinct, emotional states. For this study, images used as stimulus material included pictures of real human faces and dynamic avatars that were obtained from http://www.dotolearn.com. To operationalize our protocol, a PowerPoint presentation was created displaying: a.) six faces of a man showing different emotional status (Figure 1), b.) six faces of a woman showing different emotional status, c.) an animated avatar exhibiting different emotions (Figure 2).

### Protocol Design

Subjects in this study are not provided with any incentives, time constraints or other external motivation for performance. Working with eye-tracking lab equipment in virtual environments like those we are studying was viewed as compelling by subjects, and recruitment was based on this

*Figure 1. Emotionally expressive faces*

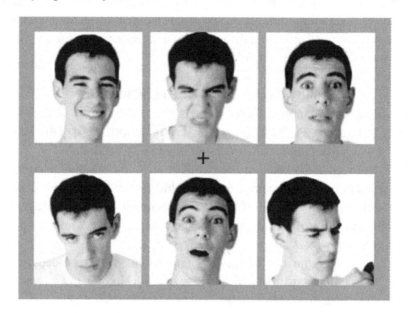

*Figure 2. Animated, 3 dimensional avatar representing fear*

intrinsic interest. All subjects were provided with a description of the study context, and their role in it as outlined in the protocol. A researcher provided instructions and walked the subjects through an initial example of the first of two protocol components. The first protocol component included a set of static images that were numbered 1 to 6. Each of the pages had six individual faces with different emotions on each face. There were two sets of face-image pages, one with a male face, and the other with a female face. The male version is shown in figure one.

The second part of the protocol involved interacting with an animated avatar, and the subsequent identification of the appropriate emotion being displayed by the animated avatar (the avatar we used to display fear is shown in Figure 2). The limitations of the printed page prevent our inclusion of the animated version here.

There are two phases to our study. In the first phase, we are focused on refining our use of eye tracking for the study of 3D environments. In the second phase, our focus is the development of our AVQA methodology. We present our phase one results in several stages, below. Followed by phase 2 results.

## PHASE ONE RESULTS

Seven individuals participated in studies of our eye tracking protocol. The subjects included three females (one Caucasian, one African American and one Asian) and four males (three Caucasian and one Hispanic) ranging in age from 27 to 48. The first five yielded substantial preliminary data using a think-aloud protocol common to usability studies (Carroll, 2003). The findings from these data enable us to refine our methods for capturing further data using eye-tracking equipment. Having refined our protocols and analysis mechanisms, we perform extended eye tracking data analysis on the final two subjects' experiences with our virtual environment, yielding compelling results and a repeatable method. It is noteworthy that two of the seven subjects had difficulty correctly identifying the emotions present in the static images, although all subjects correctly identified emotions represented by the animated avatar.

Results were gleaned from the analysis of eye tracking data captured while subjects went through the protocol. Data representing the X and Y coordinates of the subjects' gaze on a screen were obtained from the subjects using the ASL R6 eye tracking apparatus. A simple representation of the data in graph format (scatter plot) is shown in figure three and figure four. These scatter plots show a single data point for each instance of gaze location captured by the equipment. High X, Y coordinates, for example, are representative of the subject looking in the upper right-hand corner of

the screen, low X, Y coordinates are representative of the subject looking in the lower left-hand corner of the screen. Graphs were created from the two sessions for each subject. Figure 3 and Figure 4 are examples from one session using the static image protocol for two different subjects. One can quickly detect that each subject is scanning a series of equidistant objects, ultimately settling on one or two. This is notable because it represents an identifiable pattern of gaze behavior and demonstrates that the equipment accurately captures evidence of the subjects' gaze patterns. The distinguishing nature of the gaze pattern when the subject is scanning static images is emphasized when compared to data from the animated avatar sessions, which show a clearly different scanning pattern in the case of subject B, and a nominally different scanning pattern in the case of subject A.

Achieving our goal of integrating eye-tracking information with virtual environments required the addition of an image overlay to the representations of data from subjects A and B. This overlay brings the context of the subjects' gaze into focus. Noting the X, Y coordinates of the image on the screen, calibrated for each subject, and then aligning the image with those coordinates results in the overlays below. This is accomplished by placing a scatter plot graphic over a photographic image used in the study. The two graphics were calibrated to be the same size, and coordinates 0, 0 and 300,300 in perfect alignment, resulting in pixel-perfect accuracy, as shown in the overlays in Figure 5 and Figure 6.

Reviewing the images side by side for each of the subjects analyzed in this manner reveals both similarity and difference in the gaze patterns among subjects. The overlays reveal which aspects of the photos were attended to, but they do not provide the fine-grained cues needed to distinguish intensity of gaze in particular locations. To accomplish that, we analyzed the data using an open source heat mapping tool, initially intended for website usability, called "Clickheat" (http://www.labsmedia.com/clickheat/index.html). When we

*Figure 3. Subject A, avatar data*

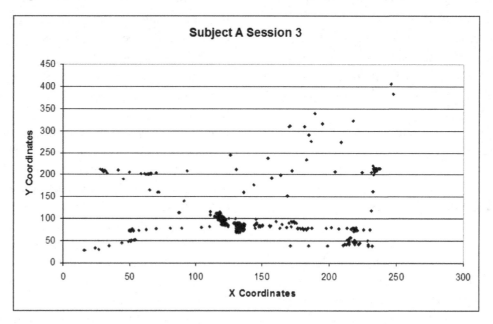

*Figure 4. Subject B, avatar data*

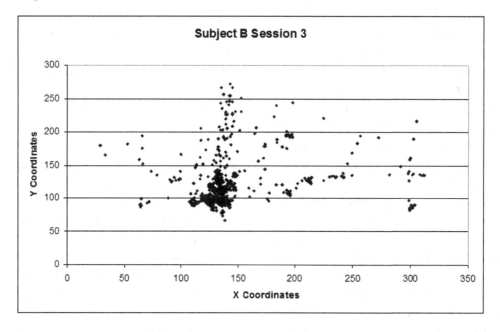

added the eye tracking data as heat map overlays to our static images using 640x480 resolution, the heat maps were nearly perfectly aligned with the static images, with a skewing of the data in toward the center from the edges, which we were able to correct for in Figure 7 and Figure 8.

*Figure 5. Participant A, static image 2 scatter plot overlay*

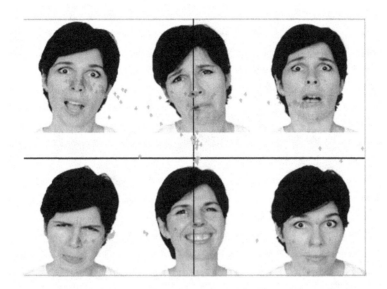

*Figure 6. Participant B, static image 1 scatter plot overlay*

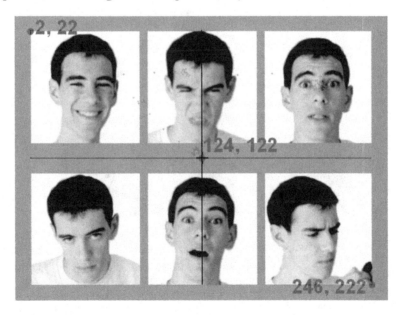

## Eye-Tracking Over Moving Pictures (Avatars)

For the animated avatars, we conducted similar heat map analysis, and produced an animated data analysis that allowed researchers to follow the gaze in context. Figure 9 shows a static image of that analysis tool.

Note the use of the heat map discussed in the static section, combined with animated black cross-hairs played for each 1/16th second of gaze from the user in Figure nine. By dynamically illustrating AOI and fixation-saccade data in this interface, we establish a repeatable protocol for capturing, analyzing and understanding gaze behavior in 3D collaborative environments. We

*Figure 7. Participant A, static heat map 1*

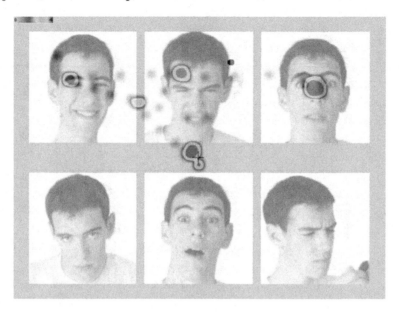

*Figure 8. Participant B, static heat map 1*

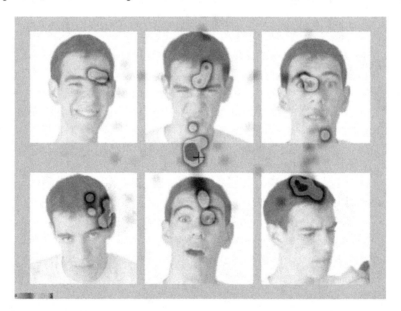

later apply the exact same protocol, using the avatars illustrated earlier, to perform ET data analysis in a dynamic environment. The result is a repeatable process for understanding where users look when interacting with avatars in 3D collaborative environments.

## METHOD FOR HEAT MAP ANALYSIS

Heat maps provide a powerful and intuitive way to graphically visualize gaze data. Typically, these visualizations are represented using the color red for drawing attention to areas that are intensely observed and the color blue for less-intensely

*Figure 9. Animated cursor following eye-tracking data points over time*

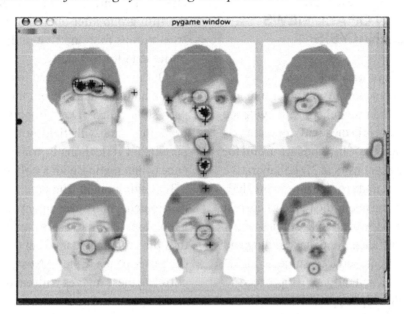

observed areas. The longer a user gazes at a given area, the warmer the color in that area becomes. Areas that are not observed are represented using white (and sometimes black or even no color at all). To draw an analogy, just as peaks are represented in red and valleys in blue on topographical maps, so also is the intensity of gaze represented in heat maps.

Plotting eye-tracking data on a graph enables the researcher to observe all eye tracking data points simultaneously, but does not provide a context for interpreting these data. Nonetheless, because these scatter plots are derived mathematically and the results can be replicated, the researcher can have confidence that these scatter plots provide a true representation of the underlying data. A simple way to provide context to these scatter plots is to overlay them onto the images that were used in the study; however, such images do not provide as clear of an analysis as the heat maps. Our challenge, then, is to devise a method of analysis using heat maps that we can prove to be as aligned with a ground truth about focus areas as the scatterplots.

Principal to meeting this challenge is our ability to pixel-perfectly align our heat maps to our mathematically proven scatter plots. First, we use linear transformations to convert the raw data provided by the eye tracking apparatus into X and Y coordinate data that correspond to a resolution of 640x480 pixels. Next, we feed the data into our heat map creation software. Third, we analyze the initial output, which shows a 35 pixel skew. Fourth, we correct for this skew using linear transformations that resize the output. Fifth, we have produced heat maps as semi-transparent overlays on the experiment images. Comparison of these heat maps with scatter plots show perfect correlation across all of our subjects. Finally, the production of heat maps, with integrated tracking data over dynamic avatars provide a combination of AOI analysis and saccade fixation analysis required for more focused examination of interaction in 3D virtual environments.

## EYE-TRACKING ANALYSIS AND THE DAWN OF ALL VIEWS QUALITATIVE ANALYSIS

The adaptation of eye-tracking technologies for the analysis of interaction in 3D environments provides analysts and researchers with evidence of what individual users in these environments attend to. As we hoped, these methods are useful for identifying where user errors in 3D collaborative environments occur, and provide important clues that inform theorizing about the range of correct design responses. However, our studies show that this data is insufficient for understanding and explaining interactions between subjects in 3D environments. To close that gap, we proceed to develop a multi-threaded approach to analyzing user interaction in 3D environments. In this method a small group of users come together to complete a simple, collaborative task while we capture the interaction from each individual's point of view. Next, we analyze the resulting data and use it to inform our discussion of 3D environment design.

### Studies of Novices in Virtual Worlds

To explore how novices might adapt 3D environments for a collaborative work task, we study groups using an online environment based on Croquet (Consortium, 2007), while they perform a work task that involves the synthesis of multiple, related artifacts into a single, final version. We record the sessions from the point of view of three different subjects, observing one of the subjects in the usability lab at our university. Our method includes the installation of dynamic screen recording software on the local computers of two remote subjects. In each study, a third subject joins the group from our usability lab, which is equipped with a two monitor system, audio recording, facial expression recording, key stroke tracking and other features available in the usability evaluation software package, Morae[1]. We observe a total of five groups performing identical tasks in the same 3D collaboration. We stopped at the fifth group after obtaining few new insights from groups four and five, indicating saturation of our data for this study.

Our method is designed to capture user navigation and interaction from the point of view of each subject in a 3D environment. We then integrate this data with field notes, interviews and participant reflections to triangulate the experience of interacting with a collaborative group in a 3D environment. The data we glean from our distributed, multi-participant recordings enable us to observe where users navigate to and where they direct their avatars from the point of view of each user of the system. Next, we integrate and correlate these images with each other. In AVQA, we also look at the same session in a 3D environment from each participant's point of view. This is conceptually similar to observing a sporting event from multiple camera angles at the same time. All of the sessions last between 1.5 and 2 hours. Our analysis includes annotation of four panels of recorded video from the 3D environment, using Anvil[2]. Our annotations are combined with field notes, participant reflections and interview transcripts and analyzed using line by line coding in the grounded theory tradition.

## PHASE TWO RESULTS

When initially introduced to the 3D environment, users interact with each other playfully, learning to jump, move around, and drag documents in and out of the environment. Our additional findings emerge from two general observations of common engagement behavior across groups. First, the chat tool, which is integrated in the 3D environment, is the primary means of communication between subjects. This is observed in the lab, and in analysis of screen recordings by distributed 3D environment collaborators in our study. Second, three out of the five group members who participated in the laboratory role during our study broke out a laptop in order to open an additional communication channel. This behavior suggests that the high degree of social presence afforded by the 3D environment supports interaction and a desire to interact which the 3D environment itself was unable to provide. The tools brought up on the second computer by users in the lab included the course management system shared by students in the class, as well as Google Documents that the groups used to share information. This use of a second computer is not something we staged; it is something we did not anticipate or guard against, but which results in a rare chance to observe authentic user behavior in a laboratory setting.

Our observations of interactions between users, undertaken both 'live' and from the side by side comparison of simultaneous session recordings, reveal four primary patterns:

1.   Group formation appears similar to that experienced in the real-world.
2.   Novices bring social cues with them from the physical world.
3.   3D environment collaborators are usually engaged in multiple simultaneous activities.
4.   Environment use declines following group formation.

## Group Formation

Like groups placed together in a physical setting, the absence of clear boundaries and well understood organizational structure lead to initial group formation phases described by Tuckman (1965) as 'storming, forming, norming', although in the 3D virtual environment these phases are a playful type of interaction, even during the "storming" phase. Of course, theories of group development and collaboration have come a long way since Tuckman. Finholt and Sproull (1990) describe how groups emerge through email distribution lists, characterizing unique forms of influence and identity formation that take place in electronic groups.

Keisler and Cummings (2002) provide a thorough review of what we know about distributed work through 40 years of research. In it, they note that people are more likely to be social, comply with and interact with people are who physically near them. These phenomena appear to generalize to shared social settings, in the tradition of ecological views of group work. Our observation of the groups in our 3D environment suggests that this environment is experienced as a shared social setting in the same sense that Keisler and Cummings described. Groups form and interact in our 3D environment as though they are in physical space. They do not experience the same degree of extended negotiation around technology or the new experience as described in studies of distributed groups brought together with asynchronous tools (Finholt & Sproull, 1990; Goggins, Laffey, & Tsai, 2007).

The group formation sequences occur quickly in the virtual environment and task combination that comprise our study, especially by comparison with similar activities among physically collocated groups. This is consistent with past findings of game designers and researchers. First, our groups experiment with the environment for between 11 and 15 minutes. The groups are led into more structured activities by the first member to take initiative toward the assigned task. Other members follow. Analysis of the group experiences through annotation of each user's perspective, side by side with other user's perspectives, shows that most users focus on the artifacts (text documents, word processing documents, web pages, pictures and presentations) on the walls in the virtual world, and then, only later, focus on their final work products. Text chat is the dominant coordination technology during this period.

The open space of the environment is a factor in creating an increased sense of social presence. Khan (all subject names are pseudonyms), a member of group one, says he feels more comfortable and open with his group in the 3D environment because he is able to interact with them visually, and 'see' what other members were doing. Being in a space with group members increases the social interaction compared with text chat. Gestures, such as approaching other members and gathering together around an object that represents the group's purpose are both factors reported by our subjects to heighten their experience of being in a group online. Subjects uniformly describe these features of the 3D environment as helping group formation, but providing limited support for the completion of work.

## Social Cues

Our subjects pay attention to virtual equivalents of social cues and norms that are common in the physical world. While these experiences increase the sense of social presence our subjects describe, it impedes discovery, the reading of shared artifacts and ultimately the efficient completion of work in the 3D environment. For example, subjects do not move their avatars in front of or close to another avatar when reviewing shared material. Khan reported "*I did not want to get in Steven's way. So, I dragged the document to my desktop to read it, and then copied my changes into the online version once Steven was done*". Reflecting on the same events, Steven reports that he is waiting for Khan to contribute, and somewhat frustrated by the lack of engagement in the virtual world at first. Khan experiences the collaboration in the virtual world as 'invading [Steven's] personal space'. The result is that obedience to physical world metaphors limits the potential advantages of the 3D collaborative environment.

Social customs carried over from the physical world lead to a muting or reversal of the advantages of social presence experienced in 3D environments. We respect personal space around our fellows in the physical world as a matter of culture, tradition and personal comfort. Carrying these traditions into the virtual world does not serve a function, and suggests that the physical metaphor of this 3D environment provokes customs from the physical world that serve no

purpose in the environment. This translation of physical traditions to the 3D environment in our study is "natural" according to our informants. In the fourth group, after observing this behavior consistently, we ask our subjects why they thought they respected personal space in the 3D environment in the same way they respect personal space in the physical world. Responses varied from, "*I did not think about the difference, I just tried to get to know my team mates*" to "*That's a really good question; I think it's because I saw myself and I saw my group members and I didn't want to ... get in the way or be rude*".

Whether an outcome of reflection or an operationalized behavior translated to virtual space, this consistent experience by members of our groups suggests something important about 3D environments. The use of avatars and representations of space modeled after the physical world may place an artificial ceiling on the quality of collaboration in 3D environments. Virtual interaction is guided by physical traditions in this case. Although the 3D environment we study enables members to gather around an object, their compliance with social cues from the physical world prevent this. Our 3D environment, modeled after physical space, has advantages for creating a sense of social presence, but disadvantages for completion of work.

## Multiple Simultaneous Activities

In our lab, Khan used the monitor on the Morae equipped station, as well as his own laptop for participation in the group. Lucy, another subject in the lab during a different group session, restricted her work to a single monitor, but nonetheless frequently referred to her notes, and "slipped out" of the 3D environment to check assignments and status in an online discussion board. The world itself, engaged in from the lab computers, served as an instrument or mode of communication. Information seeking, note taking and assimilation of shared knowledge occurred either by jumping out of the 3D environment completely, or by turning away from the environment to another computer, as in the case of Khan's laptop. Simply put, the collaborative world provided by the software makers is not the totality of the knowledge creation and innovation for groups in these environments. Distinct from a gaming context, the subjects we observed are not immersed in the 3D environment they use to collaborate. Creative activity, unlike gaming, appears to support the 'in and out' nature of these engagements.

## Decline in Environment Use Over Time

Three dimensional virtual worlds prove useful to our subjects as a social, "group formation" place at the beginning of a creative collaboration, but become less central to the joint endeavor as creative work progresses. Our observation across sessions is that the distributed teams build an identity and a shared understanding of the problem within the virtual world, but move fluidly in and out of it as creative work (in this case the construction of a course design document) increases. In the case of Khan's group, while members are willing subjects in our study of the 3D environment, and actually design their collaborative work product to incorporate it as a central mechanism for learning (describing at one point their team 'jumping together in collaborative ecstasy'), they never do return to it for collaboration after the initial creative session. Instead, they rely on easier to coordinate, asynchronous means for collaboration, such as discussion boards, shared editors (wiki spaces, etc.) and archived chat. For ongoing work, 3D environments appear to simply be too much work for too little return.

## THE EMERGENCE OF A METHOD

In this study we set out to devise a method for evaluating technology mediated collaborative work in 3D environments. This addresses one of the eight challenges of designing for collaborative work (Grudin, 1994) for the 3D era. Working

iteratively through laboratory and laboratory-field integrated studies; we capture and describe the experiences of engagement among team members through 3D environments. Our subjects perform creative tasks in a virtual environment; we develop a protocol that can be used to continue the study of 3D environments for distributed work, and to inform the design of future 3D environments.

The protocol we define here includes the use of Camtasia studio for screen recording on Windows (and now MAC) based PCs[3]. Users login to the system after starting the screen recording software, and we make a clock available as the first shared object in the workspace. Through these simple devices, we are able to synchronize and analyze sessions to understand how groups behave, how they interact and ultimately to determine the nature of 3D environment enhanced collaboration. Detailed, minute-by-minute annotation of each session is then compared across sessions, and specific types of interactions are noted and analyzed at varying depths, depending upon the research question. The four primary types of virtual engagement between avatars observed in our pilot study included:

1.  Playful engagement, like jumping around.
2.  Shared engagement around an artifact.
3.  Disengagement or isolation (walking around and exploring the space independently).
4.  Chat engagement.

There are a very limited number of 'face to face' engagements between avatars in the collaborative space we studied. This could be a side effect of the task, or possibly a more general discovery. Another important limitation to note is that users in our study are clearly engaged in other activities that are not captured by our screen recording software. For example, when our lab users break out their laptops and being working on shared documents outside the 3D environment, we have an indication of the collaboration, but not the social (or non-social engagement). This limitation in our analysis is nonetheless helpful for researchers and designers seeking to inform future 3D environment designs for information systems, collaboration or other forms of distributed work.

## IMPLICATIONS FOR DESIGN

Designing 3D collaboration environments creates a new set of challenges. First, the individual user experience comes with different demands and expectations than a 2D windowed environment. We address this through our eye-tracking protocol. Second, collaboration in 3D spaces occurs near the intersection of gaming, face to face interaction and previous studies of technology mediated groups. Together, these two methods show designers how the individual participants interact with the tools, and also how the individual participants interact through the tools. Previous, independent instantiations of these analyses methods are separately useful for usability evaluation. Together, these methods provide a complete evaluation toolkit that enables designers to co-evolve the tools, and interactions within tools as they design next generation socio-technical systems.

This study suggests that the design of collaborative 3D environments must move in a different direction than game design. Having 3 dimensions does not necessitate the use of metaphors from the physical world. For example, text chat is the dominant coordination tool, subjects do not engage with each other in a face to face manner and, unlike the case of gaming, subjects are not fully immersed in these 3D environments. Multi-tasking dominates. Inspired by the success of gaming, 3D technology is being incorporated into collaboration tools in a way that recreates the sense of physical space that exists in the real world. While this metaphor is both apt and optimal for games whose focus is often shooting at another person or scoring points in a virtual football game, it falls short when trying to support thought work.

The possibility of designing human computer interactions that incorporate three dimensions of space to support distributed work is powerful, but infinitely more complex than designing a space that supports warfare or virtual games. The gaming industry is ahead of the collaborative work, distributed work and computer mediated communication research communities because their design problem is simple, though their technology problem is significant. The evaluation tools developed through this study will help designers meet the design challenges of applying 3D technology to distributed work problems.

Three dimensional interaction technologies are a new and exciting way for HCI designers to engage distributed workers. The research presented here demonstrates that 3D environments modeled after the physical world increase the sense of social presence among users. As a next step, designers must begin to think about how three dimensions can be used to support information exchange, creativity, awareness, and creative work among distributed groups.

## CONCLUSION

There are theoretical and methodological implications of this work. From the perspective of theory, the way our subjects used 3D technologies for distributed work suggest that existing theory about the irreplaceable nature of physical presence should be challenged. The use of 3D environments by themselves does not replace physical presence. However, the natural occurrence of multiple device multi-tasking by our subjects suggests that given enough channels, people naturally move to recreate as much of the physical world as they can in virtual environments. Three dimensional environments with avatars permit the recreation of gesture. They also permit the organization of high dimensional information spaces. Given an integrated set of technologies it is possible that we might not replace the capacity of physical co presence, but possibly, for the performance of task work, exceed it.

Methodologically, this paper presents a year of work developing two distinct but interconnected methods for HCI evaluation of 3D environments. Our integrated approach has four main benefits to the HCI community. First, the application of existing eye-tracking technology to 3D environments provides a fine-grained toolset for identification of basic navigational issues experienced by novices. Second, knowledge of subject attention to the emotions presented in avatar facial expressions is enabled through eye-tracking. Third, our AVQA method offers designers the opportunity to know how members of a 3D environment see each other, and separately attend to the objects and activities in these types of environments. Fourth, the integration of these two methods to examine a series of different 3D virtual environments – ideally by a number of different research teams – will advance the use of 3D collaborative spaces for work and learning at a very rapid pace.

Three-dimensional technology is presently very successful at engaging people in play. We hope that by outlining these methods, and suggesting their integrated use, we will inspire serious discussion about how to design and evaluate 3D environments for collaboration and learning across geographical, linguistic and cultural boundaries. We seek to advance the role that design based research, Human Computer Interaction and the design profession in general are able to play in the creation of better worlds within our world.

## ACKNOWLEDGMENT

We would like to thank several anonymous reviewers for their feedback on this article, and an earlier version of it, which we presented at the Hawaii International Conference on System Science, 2010. We would also like to thank Cynthia Jobe for her editorial review and feedback.

## REFERENCES

Arroyo, E., Selker, T., & Willy, W. (2006). Usability Tool for Analysis of Web Designs Using Mouse Tracks. In *Proceedings of CHI 2006*.

Blascovich, J., Loomis, J., Beall, A. C., Swinth, K. R., Hoyt, C. L., & Bailenson, J. N. (2001). Immersive Virtual Environment Technology as a Methodological Tool for Social Psychology. *Psychological Inquiry*.

Byrne, M. D. (2001). ACT-R/PM and Menu Selection: Applying a Cognitive Architecture to HCI. *International Journal of Human-Computer Studies*, *55*, 41–84. doi:10.1006/ijhc.2001.0469

Carroll, J. M. (2003). *HCI Models, Theories, and Frameworks: Toward a Multidisciplinary Science*. San Francisco, CA: Morgan Kaufmann.

Clarke, D., & Duimering, R. (2006). How Computer Gamers Experience the Game Situation: A Behavioral Study. *ACM Computers in Entertainment*, *4*(3), 1–23.

Consortium, C. (2007). *Croquet: Invent the Future*. Retrieved September 14, 2007, from http://www.opencroquet.org/index.php/Main_Page

Crawford, C. (1982). *The Art of Computer Game Design: Reflections of a Master Game Designer*. New York: McGraw-Hill.

Cutrell, E., & Zhiwei, G. *(2007). What Are You Looking For? An Eye-Tracking Study of Information Usage in Web Search*. In *Proceedings of CHI 2007*, San Jose, CA.

Duchowski, A. (2002). A Breadth-First Survey of Eye-Tracking Applications. *Behavior Research Methods, Instruments, & Computers*, *34*(4), 455–470.

Dyck, J., Pinelle, D., Brown, B., & Gutwin, C. (2003). Learning From Games: HCI Design Innovations in Entertainment Software. In *Proceedings of the Graphics Interface*, Halifax, Nova Scotia, Canada.

Finholt, T., & Sproull, L. S. (1990). Electronic Groups at Work. *Organization Science*, *1*(1), 42–70. doi:10.1287/orsc.1.1.41

Fitzpatrick, G. (1998). *The Locales Framework: Understanding and Designing for Cooperative Work*. Brisbane, Australia: University of Queensland.

Goggins, S., Laffey, J., & Tsai, I.-C. (2007). Cooperation and Groupness: Community Formation in Small online Collaborative Groups. In *Proceedings of the ACM Group Conference 2007*, Sanibel Island, FL.

Goldberg, J. H., Stimson, M. J., Lewenstein, M., Scott, N., & Wichansky, A. M. (2002). Eye Tracking in Web Search Tasks: Design Implications. In *Proceedings of the ETRA 2002*, New Orleans, LA.

Grossman, L. (2007). *The Man in the Mask*. Technoculture.

Grudin, J. (1994). Eight Challenges for Developers. *Communications of the ACM*, *37*, 92–116. doi:10.1145/175222.175230

Guan, Z., Lee, S., Cuddihy, E., & Ramey, J. (2006). The Validity of the Stimulated Retrospective Think-Aloud Method as Measured by Eye Tracking. In *Proceedings of chi 2006*, Montreal, Canada.

Just, M. A., & Carpenter, P. A. (1980). A Theory of Reading: From Eye Fixations to Comprehension. *Psychological Review*, *87*, 329–354. doi:10.1037/0033-295X.87.4.329

Kaptelinin, V., & Czerwinski. (Eds.). (2007). *Beyond the Desktop Metaphor: Designing Integrated Digital Work Environments*. Boston: MIT Press.

Karn, K. S. (2006). Eye Tracking for Usability testing, You've Got to Know Your Strengths and Weaknesses. In *Proceedings of CHI 2006*.

Karn, K. S., Ellis, S., & Juliano, C. (1999). The Hunt for Usability: Tracking Eye Movements. In *Proceedings of CHI 1999*.

Keisler, S., & Cummings, J. N. (2002). What do We Know About Proximity and Distance in Work Groups? A Legacy of Research. In Hinds, P., & Kiesler, S. (Eds.), *Distributed Work* (pp. 57–111). Cambridge, MA: MIT Press.

Larson, J. (2007). Out of the Video Arcade, into the Office: Where Computer Games Can Lead Productivity Software. *Interaction*, 18–22. doi:10.1145/1189976.1189992

Li, D., Babcock, J., & Parkhurst, D. J. (2006). open-Eyes: A Low-Cost Head-Mounted Eye-Tracking Solution. In *Proceedings of the ETRA 2006*.

Linnett, B. J., Fries Duvall, K. E., & Powelson, L. H. (1997). *Software Platform Having a Real World Interface with Animated Characters*. Hoboken, NJ: Microsoft Corporation.

Moore, R. J., Gathman, E. C. H., Ducheneaut, N., & Nickell, E. (2007). Coordinating Joint Activity in Avatar-Mediated Interaction. In *Proceedings of the CHI 2007*, San Jose, CA.

Muri, R. M., Cazzoli, D., Nyffeler, T., & Pflugshaupt, T. (2009). Visual exploration pattern in hemineglect. *Psychological Research*, *73*(2), 147–157. doi:10.1007/s00426-008-0204-0

Nardi, B., & Harris, J. (2006). Strangers and Friends: Collaborative Play in World of Warcraft. In *Proceedings of CSCW '06*, Banff, Alberta, Canada.

Paiva, A., Andersson, G., Hook, K., Mourao, D., Costa, M., & Martinho, C. (2002). SenToy in FantasyA: Designing an Affective Sympathetic Interface to a Computer Game. *Personal and Ubiquitous Computing*, *6*, 378–389. doi:10.1007/s007790200043

Rapeepisarn, K., Wong, K. W., Fung, C. C., & Depickere, A. (2006). Similarities and Differences Between "Learn Through Play" and "Edutainment". In *Proceedings of the 3rd Australasian conference on Interactive entertainment IE '06*.

Rollings, A., & Adams, E. (2003). *Andrew Rollings and Ernest Adams on Game Design*. New Riders.

Salvucci, D. D., & Goldberg, J. H. (2000). Identifying Fixations and Saccades in Eye-Tracking Protocols. In *Proceedings of the ETRA 2000*.

Santella, A., & DeCarlo, D. (2004). Robust Clustering of Eye Movement Recordings for Quantification of Visual Interest. In *Proceedings of the ETRA 2004*.

Tarasewich, P., & Fillion, S. (2004). Discount Eye Tracking: The Enhanced Restricted Focus Viewer. In *Proceedings of the Tenth Americas Conference on Information Systems*, New York.

Tuckman, B. W. (1965). Developmental Sequence in Small Groups. *Psychological Bulletin, 63*, 384–399. doi:10.1037/h0022100

Wadlinger, H. A., & Isaacowitz, D. M. (2006). Positive Mood Broadens Visual Attention to Positive Stimuli. *Motivation and Emotion, 30*, 89–101. doi:10.1007/s11031-006-9021-1

## ENDNOTES

1    http://www.techsmith.com/morae/
2    http://www.anvil-software.de/
3    http://www.camtasiastudio.com

*This work was previously published in the International Journal of Social and Organizational Dynamics in IT, Volume 1, Issue 1, edited by Michael B. Knight, pp. 30-48, 2011 by IGI Publishing (an imprint of IGI Global).*

# Chapter 13
# Toward an Understanding of Software Piracy in Developed and Emerging Economies

**Bruce A. Reinig**
*San Diego State University, USA*

**Robert K. Plice**
*San Diego State University, USA*

## ABSTRACT

*The software industry loses billions of dollars annually to software piracy and has raised awareness of the high software piracy rates worldwide, particularly in emerging economies. In this paper, the authors build a general model of software piracy that includes three economic and social factors suggested by the literature, including per capita GNI, the relative size of a country's IT market, and government corruption. The paper demonstrates that the relationship between national software piracy and per capita GNI is nonlinear, with additional gains in per capita GNI, producing marginally smaller reductions in software piracy. No structural variation is found in the model with respect to whether an economy is developed or emerging, using the OECD membership as a proxy. However, a structural break did exist with respect to the relative size of a country's IT market. The analysis suggests that the classification of an economy as developed or emerging does not necessarily advance the understanding of the causal mechanisms that give rise to software piracy. Findings suggest that more insight can be gained by focusing on strategies that take into account the relative size of a country's IT market.*

## INTRODUCTION

*"While emerging economies account for 45 percent of the global PC hardware market, they account for less than 20 percent of the PC software market. If the emerging economies' PC software share were* the same as it is for PC hardware, the software market would grow by $40 billion a year." (Business Software Alliance, 2009)

The above quotation is from a joint report of the Business Software Alliance (BSA) and International Data Corporation (IDC), reflecting their belief that software companies suffer losses

DOI: 10.4018/978-1-4666-1948-7.ch013

of their intellectual property rights (IPR) disproportionately in emerging economies. The BSA is the largest IT industry group and is comprised of 29 major software companies, such as Adobe, Microsoft, HP, and SAP. The BSA-IDC annual software piracy report highlights decreasing, but still remarkably high, piracy rates in certain developing economies such as China (80%), Indonesia (85%), and Venezuela (86%) (BSA, 2009). The BSA suggests that software piracy is inhibiting development in emerging economies and estimates that 600,000 new jobs would be created and $24 billion in tax revenue would be generated if the piracy rate could be lowered by 10 percent over the next four years (BSA, 2008). The BSA and its members have worked with governments to encourage the enforcement of IPR with notable progress in key economies such as Russia and China. With billions of dollars at stake, few issues are of greater importance to the software industry than the protection of their IPR through a reduction of software piracy.

Whereas the software industry suggests that software piracy inhibits a country's economic development in terms of per capita gross national income (GNI), a number of researchers argue that the direction of this relationship is actually reversed; that is, increases in per capita GNI reduce software piracy (e.g., Banerjee, Khalid, & Sturn, 2005; Gopal & Sanders, 1988; Shin et al., 2004). The rationale for this perspective is straightforward: A key motivator of piracy is a desire to save money and the relative cost of software is much higher for people with low disposable income than for people with a high disposable income. We adopt this perspective in the current study, and examine the national software piracy rate as a function of per capita GNI. We also explore the effects of a strong national IT industry and government corruption, as suggested in the literature, on software piracy in both developed and emerging economies.

This paper complements existing research into software piracy in a number of ways. One stream

of prior research has examined behavioral mechanisms that lead to software piracy, and has suggested policies that can moderate such behavior. The papers making up this literature contain both complementary and contradictory aspects. Thong and Yap (1998) studied the role of deontological theories (which assume that a set of universal rules define what is right) and teleological theories (which address the rightness or wrongness of an action on the basis of its consequences) in forming intentions to pirate software. They found that both considerations play a role in the decision to pirate. Peace, Galletta, and Thong (2003) used survey research to test a model of intention to pirate, and found that individual attitudes, subjective norms, and perceived behavioral control are significant precursors. Moores and Chang (2006) used survey research student subjects to test a model of ethical decision making, and found that the deontological aspects of recognizing software piracy as an infringement of intellectual property rights did not play a strong role in deciding on the morality of piracy. Gopal and Sanders (1997) considered how preventive and deterrent controls (broadly aimed at enhancing deontological and teleological considerations) affect the profitability of software firms. They found that preventive controls can operate to increase profits, while deterrent controls actually decrease profits.

A second stream of literature, within which this paper fits, focuses on the economic precursors of software piracy (Bagchi, Kirs, & Cerveny, 2006; Banerjee, Khalid, & Sturn, 2005; Gopal & Sanders, 1998; Gopal & Sanders, 2000). Cheng, Sims, and Teegen (1997) determined that economic considerations play a strong role in motivating piracy, noting that "software too expensive" was the number one reason given for committing piracy. Sundararajan (2004) analyzed an analytical model to reveal how price interacts with deterrence in influencing piracy, and found that price discrimination can substitute for technological deterrence in managing piracy. This paper builds upon these findings, by examining the relationships between piracy, economic development, and income levels.

The first objective of this paper is to build a general model of software piracy by examining key explanatory factors from the literature. We then examine the relationship between these factors and country classifications as developed versus emerging economies. Regression analysis is used to validate the model and test for structural variation that would support the chief implication of the software industry's analysis, namely, that an economy's level of economic development is significant as an explanator of its piracy rate (i.e., that it is necessary to model piracy differently in emerging and developed economies). We also examine differences in IT intensive versus IT non-intensive, and high corruption versus low corruption economies.

## THEORY

We take national software piracy rate as the dependent variable and include independent variables that are suggested by the literature. Software piracy is defined by the BSA as the unauthorized copying or distribution of copyrighted software. Software copyrights can be infringed upon in a number of ways. Counterfeit software may be introduced in the distribution channel after being illegally produced by organized crime syndicates in hidden factories (BSA, 2009). Such counterfeit software is often sold on internet auction sites and street markets, for example. Software can also be pirated through illegal file sharing over the internet or between acquaintances, and when corporate IT departments install more copies than their licenses permit (BSA, 2009).

We are interested not in the absolute amount of software that is pirated in a country, but the relative amount as measured by the ratio of pirated software to total software deployed. Thus, our dependent variable is national software piracy

rate and ranges from zero (all of the piracy in use is authorized) to unity (all of the software in use is unauthorized).

## Overall Model

As shown in Figure 1, we focus on three factors that have been identified as explanators of software piracy at the country level, namely, per capita GNI, the relative size of the IT industry, and the level of government corruption (Bagchi, Kirs, & Cerveny, 2006; Banerjee, Khalid, & Sturn, 2005; Gopal & Sanders, 1998; Gopal & Sanders, 2000). Because wealthier people have less economic incentive to pirate software compared to poorer people, we expect that software piracy will be a negative function of per capita GNI. Per capita GNI has no theoretical upper bound, so we expect this relationship to be nonlinear. That is, additional increases in GNI cannot reduce piracy below zero, and thus the relationship between the two variables is likely to be asymptotic and approaching zero at high levels of per capita GNI. Such a relationship would be characterized by a

*Figure 1. Theoretical model of the effects of income levels, IT share of the economy, and government corruption on software piracy*

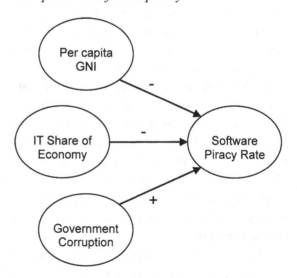

negative and increasing slope. This expectation is consistent with the findings of Gopal and Saunders (2000), who tested for a negative linear relationship between software piracy and per capita GNI. They reported a steeper slope for economies with a per capita GNI of less than $6,000 as compared to economies with a per capita GNI greater than $6,000. We model the relationship through all levels of per capita GNI by including a non-linear component. Thus, our first hypothesis:

H1: National software piracy rate is a negative, curvilinear function of per capita GNI. The impact of additional increases in per capita GNI diminishes as per capita GNI becomes large (i.e., the slope is negative and asymptotically approaching zero).

Countries vary with respect to their incentives to reduce software piracy. Gopal and Sanders (1998) argued that a government's incentive to protect IPR is a function of the size of the domestic software industry, regardless of income levels. It is not surprising, for example, that the country with the largest software industry, the United States, also has the world's lowest national software piracy rate, at 20 percent (BSA, 2008). The software industry also notes that an inverse relationship exists between the size of a country's IT market and its software piracy rate (BSA, 2005a). Thus, our second hypothesis:

H2: National software piracy rate is a negative linear function of the relative size of a country's IT market.

The rationale for the second hypothesis is that a country with an economy more dependent on IT *relative* to other industries (e.g., agriculture, manufacturing, tourism) will tend to decrease software piracy because it is in its own interest to do so. To a certain extent, this is likely to be a reinforcing relationship. That is, a country that develops an IT industry will be incentivized to

support that industry by protecting IPR and IT companies may be more interested in setting up operations in countries with a reputation for protecting IPR.

Government or public sector corruption has been identified as a non-economic factor that is positively related to software piracy (Bagchi, Kirs, & Cerveny, 2006). Countries with a high level of corruption are less likely to implement laws designed to protect IPR and are otherwise less likely to actively seek to catch and prosecute copyright offenders (Bagchi, Kirs, & Cerveny, 2006). Traphagan and Griffith (1998) note that effective enforcement of legal protections must be in place to reduce piracy and that high incomes, in and of themselves, are not sufficient to predict low piracy rates. Thus, our third hypothesis:

H3: National software piracy rate is a positive linear function of the level of corruption.

The three hypotheses are summarized in Figure 1.

## Structural Variation

As noted above, a key objective of this paper is to explore whether the hypothesized relationships in the model must be parameterized differently depending on the level of development within an economy, the size of an economy's IT sector, or the extent of corruption within society. Such structural differences, if found to be present, could yield insight into formulating anti-piracy strategies. On the other hand, if the model is structurally identical for emerging and developed economies, it would suggest that the categorization of economic development as developed vs. emerging is less useful than other possible factors for understanding piracy.

It can be difficult to distinguish between emerging and developed economies. Although some countries are clearly developed, such as the United States, Japan, and Germany, and other are clearly emerging, such as India, Brazil, and South Africa, the demarcation is often difficult on what is clearly a multi-dimensional continuum. For this reason, economists and sociologists sometimes make use of membership in the Organization for Economic Co-operation and Development (OECD) to establish a designation of a developed economy. The OECD is a forum of 30 market democracies that work to help governments "… foster prosperity and fight poverty through economic growth, financial stability, trade and investment, technology, innovation, entrepreneurship and development co-operation" (OECD, 2008). The 30 OECD members produce nearly 60 percent of the world's goods and services and are committed to a market economy and a pluralist democracy (OECD, 2008). OECD membership is used as a holistic designation of developed economy status for the purpose of our study.

Although OECD membership is useful for designating a country as developed, the complement of OECD membership (i.e., non-membership) is not particularly useful for establishing a country as an emerging economy. For example, Hong Kong, Singapore, and Israel are not members of OECD but would generally be recognized as developed economies rather than emerging ones. In recognition of this limitation, we also examine median splits on the independent variables in the model, including per capita GNI, which would place Hong Kong, Singapore, and Israel in the upper half of all countries with respect to income.

## ANALYSIS AND RESULTS

We gathered data on each of the variables represented in Figure 1, then tested for structural variation based on OECD membership. Software piracy rate data was obtained from the "Second Annual BSA and IDC Global Software Piracy Study" (BSA, 2005b). Piracy rate is defined as the proportion given by dividing the unsold software units that are in use by the total amount of

software units in use (both sold and unsold). Per capita GNI data was measured using purchasing power parity and was obtained from the World-bank database (World Bank, 2007). Relative size of IT market was measured using the IDC Worldwide IT Spending Reports as published in the Expanding the Frontiers of our Digital Future report (BSA, 2005a). This measure consists of IT spending by consumers, business, governments, and educational institutions on IT relative to GDP, but not taking into account exports or imports and excluding telecommunications services (BSA, 2005a). Finally, government corruption was measured using the Transparency International Corruption Perceptions Index 2004 (2004). The corruption perceptions index (CPI) is a composite score developed from multiple surveys (referred to as a "poll of polls") that ranges from 10 (low corruption) to 0 (high corruption). The CPI reflects the perceptions of business people and country analysts as to the level of corruption that exists among public officials and politicians in each country.

The most recent year in which all of these measures were freely available was 2004. The software piracy rate, CPI, and per capita GNI are published annually and publicly available, but the last year in which the IT market data was freely available was 2004 [appearing in 5]. Thus, we use 2004 data for all measures. The four sources of data intersected on 62 countries, 28 of which are members of OECD (Appendix A).

OECD membership proved to be a meaningful grouping for comparing the unweighted mean values of the variables included in this study (Table 1). All four variables (i.e., software piracy rate, GNI per capita, IT sector as a percent of GDP, and corruption perception index) reveal statistically significant differences ($p < .001$) in the mean values when examined by OECD membership. OECD members enjoy a mean national software piracy rate of 38.14 percent compared to 65.74 percent for non-members, a mean per capita GNI that is more than 200 percent greater than nonmembers,

*Table 1. Summary statistics and comparisons of variances and means between selected OECD and Non OECD countries*

| Variable | OECD (n=28) | | Non OECD (n=34) | | F-test for equality of $\sigma^2$ | t test for equality of $\mu$ |
|---|---|---|---|---|---|---|
| | M | S | M | S | | |
| Software Piracy Rate (percent) | 38.14 | 13.09 | 65.74 | 15.75 | $F_{(33,27)}$=1.45 | $t_{(60)}$=-7.40*** |
| GNI per capita ($1,000s) | 25.92 | 8.43 | 10.93 | 6.94 | $F_{(27,33)}$=1.48 | $t_{(60)}$=7.68*** |
| IT Sector as a percent of GDP (percent) | 2.35 | .78 | 1.54 | .68 | $F_{(27,33)}$=1.33 | $t_{(60)}$=4.42*** |
| Corruption Perception Index (CPI) | 6.93 | 2.17 | 4.26 | 1.77 | $F_{(27,33)}$=1.51 | $t_{(60)}$=5.34*** |

Notes: 1. ***p<.001, 2. CPI is coded as 10=low corruption, 1=high corruption.

and significantly less government corruption as measured by the corruption perceptions index. The IT sector also plays a significantly larger role in the economy for members (2.35 percent of GDP) compared to nonmembers (1.54 percent of GDP). The F-test for equality of variances was non-significant for each of the aforementioned comparisons. Given the stark differences in the mean values of these variables it is understandable why practitioners find the classification of developed vs. emerging as a useful explanator of software piracy. However, we are interested in knowing whether the relationships among these variables are indeed different between the two groups.

## Multiple Regression Results for the Overall Model

We use multiple regression to test the hypotheses across all data and then make use of the Chow (1960) test to determine whether the regression model performs differently for OECD and non-OECD countries. The software piracy rate, rounded to the nearest percent, is the dependent variable for all models. H1 is tested using a natural log transformation of per capita GNI to model the non-linear aspect of the relationship ($H1: \beta_{\ln GNI} < 0$). The logarithmic transformation has the advantage here of producing a curve that has a positive but decreasing slope, which is the nature of the relationship hypothesized in our study. The logarithmic transformation tests the hypothesis that although additional increases in per capita GNI decrease software piracy, they also produce diminishing returns as per capita GNI becomes large. H2 was tested by including the IT sector as a percent of GDP ($H2: \beta_{IT} < 0$). H3 was tested by including the CPI index as a variable in the model ($H3: \beta_{CPI} < 0$).

The regression results are presented in Table 2. The overall model is statistically significant

*Table 2. Regression results using all data (n=62)*

| Parameter Estimates: | B | s.e. | Model fit |
|---|---|---|---|
| Intercept | 112.55*** | 4.52 | $F_{(3,58)}$=91.30*** $R^2$=.825 adjusted $R^2$=.816 |
| Natural Log Transformation of GNI per capita (thousands of dollars) | -13.83*** | 2.83 | |
| IT Sector as a percent of GDP (percent) | -6.22** | 2.17 | |
| Corruption Perception Index (CPI) | -1.97* | .97 | |

Note: *p<.05, **p<.01, ***p<.001

and accounts for 82.5 percent of the variance in the software piracy rate among the 62 countries (adjusted $R^2$=.816). H1 was supported at a p<.001 level of significance, H2 was supported at a p<.01 level of significance, and H3 was supported at a p<.05 level of significance. Thus, there was support for the overall model and varying levels of support for the individual hypotheses.

Multicollinearity diagnostics were examined to determine if the regression coefficients were influenced by high correlations among the predictor variables. For example, one would expect corruption and GNI per capita to be correlated because high levels of corruption are typically associated with low levels of per capita GNI. The variance inflation factors (VIFs) were examined for each parameter estimate and all were below the recommended threshold of 10 (Hair et al., 2004) with CPI having the largest value (4.35). Thus, it was concluded that multicollinearity did not interfere with a meaningful interpretation of the parameter estimates.

## Testing for Structural Variation

Although the model gives insight into understanding the factors that influence software piracy, a primary objective of this paper is to determine whether the parameter fit is equivalent in developed and emerging economies. We begin by conducting a Chow (1960) test to determine whether a structural difference exists for the regression model using OECD countries compared to the same model with non-OECD countries. The null hypothesis assumes that the vector of parameter estimates is equal for both groups. In the present case, we have four parameter estimates, including the intercept (i.e., $\beta_0, \beta_{\ln GNI}, \beta_{IT}, \beta_{CPI}$). The alternative hypothesis is that one or more of the five parameter estimates is unequal. There was not a statistically significant structural variation based on OECD membership ($F_{(4,54)}$=1.54, p=.204), indicating that the observations for OECD

and non-OECD countries can be pooled and analyzed as a single model.

We then tested the model for other possible structural variation by conducting a median split on each of the three independent variables. A structural difference based on per capita GNI, for example, would suggest that the influence of the variables on software piracy differs between wealthy (above the median) and poor (below the median) countries. However, there was not a significant structural break on a median split of per capita GNI. We conducted the equivalent test with a median split on CPI and again found no structural break (Table 3). We proceeded to test for a structural break with respect to IT sector as a percent of GDP. The test was less straightforward because there were three observations that shared the median value of 1.70. These three observations include Columbia, China, and OECD member Poland. The three observations were eliminated from the analysis, and the test yielded a significant structural difference at $F_{(4,51)}$=3.50 (p=.013). If the three median observations are placed in the low IT share group, the test yields a significant result of $F_{(4,54)}$=2.68 (p=.041); if the three median observations are placed in the high IT share, the test yields a significant result of $F_{(4,54)}$=3.18 (p=.020). The results of the four structural variation tests, including the median split on IT sector as a percent of GDP with the three median observations removed, are presented in Table 3.

The presence of a structural difference based on the relative size of IT market indicates that the observations should not be pooled, because one or more of the parameter estimates in the two separate models are unequal. An analysis was conducted to determine where the inequality exists. First, a separate regression model was fitted for each of the two groups (i.e., high IT share countries and low IT share countries). Second, a pooled model was fitted using all of the observations and including five additional independent variables for testing the significance of the slope differentials between the two groups. These vari-

*Table 3. Results of structural break tests for OECD membership and median splits on independent variables*

| Grouping | Chow (1960) test |
|---|---|
| OECD Membership | $F_{(4,54)}=1.54$ |
| Median split on GNI per capita | $F_{(4,54)}=0.74$ |
| Median split on IT Sector as a percent of GDP | $F_{(4,51)}=3.50^*$ |
| Median split on Corruption Perception Index | $F_{(4,54)}=2.05$ |

Note: $^*p<.05$

ables are set equal to the value of the corresponding observations in the high IT share countries and zero in the low IT share countries. The five variables then have parameter estimates that equal the difference between the two separate regression models, providing a test to determine if the difference is statistically significant. Two variables were found to have significantly different slope estimates between the two models: IT sector as a percent of GDP, which was significant in the high IT share countries and non-significant in the low IT share countries; and corruption, which was non-significant in the high IT share countries and was significant in the low IT share countries (Table 4).

## DISCUSSION

Our results provide insight into the factors that influence software piracy rate and a potentially useful perspective for shaping country specific approaches to combating software piracy and protecting IPR. The overall model was supportive of each of the hypothesized relationships in Figure 1. Software piracy is reduced by increases in per capita GNI and the relative size of a country's IT industry. Software piracy is also reduced in countries where governments are less corrupt. These results suggest that software piracy is a complex issue and is influenced by a mix of economic and social factors.

*Table 4. Regression models for median split grouping on IT as a percent of GDP*

| | High IT Countries (n=30) | | Low IT Countries (n=29) | | |
|---|---|---|---|---|---|
| Model Fit: | $F_{(3,26)}=26.90$ ***, R²=.756 adjusted R²=.728 | | $F_{(3,25)}=21.29$***, R²=.719 adjusted R²=.685 | | |
| Parameter Estimates: | B | s.e. | B | s.e. | Differential slope estimates |
| Intercept | 115.80*** | 11.12 | 101.55*** | 7.13 | 14.26 |
| Natural Log Transformation of GNI per capita (thousands of dollars) | -17.60*** | 4.88 | -12.13** | 3.58 | -5.47 |
| IT Sector as a percent of GDP (percent) | -9.93** | 3.04 | 8.97 | 6.42 | -18.90** |
| Corruption Perception Index (CPI) | .50 | 1.24 | -4.45** | 1.44 | 4.95* |

Notes: 1. Sig. levels for F tests and two-tailed t tests are indicated with $^*p<.05$, $^{**}p<.01$ and $^{***}p<.001$

2. High IT Countries: Australia, Austria, Belgium, Brazil, Canada, Croatia, Czech Republic, Denmark, Estonia, Finland, France, Germany, Hong Kong, Hungary, Israel, Japan, Latvia, Malaysia, Netherlands, New Zealand, Norway, Singapore, Slovakia, Slovenia, South Africa, South Korea, Sweden, Switzerland, United Kingdom, United States

3. Low IT Countries: Argentina, Bulgaria, Chile, Costa Rica, Dominican Republic, Egypt, Greece, India, Indonesia, Ireland, Italy, Kuwait, Lithuania, Mexico, Panama, Peru, Philippines, Portugal, Romania, Russia, Saudi Arabia, Spain, Thailand, Turkey, UAE, Ukraine, Uruguay, Venezuela, Vietnam

The results provide a more nuanced perspective on the oft cited relationship between per capita GNI and software piracy. Gopal and Sanders (2000) provided empirical support of their assertion that income levels reduced software piracy rates and, further, that the impact of an additional thousand dollars of income was more pronounced for low income countries than it was for high income countries. Specifically, Gopal and Sanders (2000) conducted separate analyses for countries with a per capita GDP of less than $6,000 and one for countries with a per capita GDP of greater than $6,000. Their results show that the slope for the poorer countries was six times greater than that of the wealthier countries. However, the y-intercepts for these two analyses differ substantially (88.7 for poorer countries and 67.1 for wealthier countries) leading to some odd conclusions if the models were to be used to predict software piracy (such as a country with $5,000 in per capita GDP having an estimated piracy rate of 59.2 percent and a country with $7,000 in per capita GDP having an estimated piracy rate of 60.8 percent). We contend that there is nothing particularly special about $6000 of income and demonstrate that the relationship can be modeled with a single y-intercept if its non-linear nature is taken into account. The marginal benefit of additional per capita GNI becomes small as per capita GNI increases. For example, an increase in per capita GNI from $4,000 to $5,000 is associated with a reduction of 3.09 percent in software piracy whereas an increase in per capita GNI from $24,000 to $25,000 is associated with a reduction of .56 percent in software piracy. Our model further validates and then builds on the work of Gopal and Sanders (2000) in terms of the relationship between income and software piracy.

There are two unanticipated findings with respect to structural variation in the model. First, there is no structural difference when comparing OECD members to non-OECD members. OECD membership clearly differentiated between the mean value of each of the four variables considered (Table 1), but the estimated parameter estimates in the hypothesized relationships do not differ from one group to the next. This was also true when separating the countries by income level. This may suggest that the distinction between developed and emerging economies is not particularly useful for understanding the complex relationships that give rise to software piracy. Much is made of this differentiation by the software industry, but in terms of software piracy it may be more useful to see where a country resides on a variety of economic and social dimensions rather than its classification as developed or emerging. Such one-dimensional designations can be ambiguous and fail to consider the underlying causal mechanisms that give rise to software piracy. It is true that developed nations tend to enjoy higher incomes and less government corruption than emerging nations, for example, but this is not true in all cases and there exists substantial variance on these measures within both groups of economies.

The second unanticipated finding is the structural difference that exists for a median split on the relative IT share of the economy. That this occurred in the absence of a structural difference based on per capita GNI provides additional support for the assertion by Gopal and Sanders (1998) that the relative size of a domestic software industry influences software piracy independent of income. We note, however, that we examined the relative size of the IT industry (BSA, 2005b) whereas Gopal and Sanders (1998) focused exclusively on the software industry. It is also notable that the break revealed significant differences on two parameters (Table 3). Within high IT countries, IT share is a significant predictor of software piracy rates: A one-percent increase in the relative size of the IT market would result in 9.93 percent of all software converting from unauthorized to authorized. By contrast, relative IT share is not statistically significant in low IT countries. Corruption, on the other hand, has a nearly opposite effect. Corruption is non-significant in high IT countries while a one-point increase in CPI would result in a reduction in piracy of 4.45 percent of total software in low IT countries.

These results suggest that different approaches to reducing piracy may be called for in high IT economies versus low IT economies. In both groups, piracy rates decline when there are increases in per capita GNI, but the software industry might do well to focus on countering government corruption in low IT countries and seeking to expand the IT market in high IT economies. At the very least, IT share appears to be a more meaningful distinction to draw between economies than does the concept of general economic development when the goal is to understand how software piracy is influenced by economic and social factors.

## Limitations

There are a number of limitations in this study that should be considered when interpreting and generalizing the results. First, there is measurement error associated with each of the variables. For example, per capita GNI fails to take into account income inequality. The mean income for a given country may not be a typical income in that country. Government corruption is difficult to measure and, as such, we need to rely on a perceptual measure rather than an observed measure. The CPI is a sound measure of perceived corruption but it is nonetheless subject to measurement error inherent in any link between perceptions and reality. Second, the data analyzed is cross-sectional and limited to one year. Additional research can examine these relationships over multiple years to see if they continue to hold. Third, we assume that the BSA statistics on software piracy are computed independently of the World Bank statistics on per capita GNI. However, Png (2010) challenges this assumption which could call into question the inclusion of both variables in the regression model. Finally, although we gathered data from as many countries as possible, our model may not accurately reflect the relationships that exist between these variables in countries not included in the model.

## CONCLUSION

We report on a study that examined the influence of three factors on the software piracy as suggested by the literature. We developed a regression model that supported a hypothesized nonlinear relationship between per capita GNI and linear relationships with relative IT market and corruption with software piracy. The model performed equally well in developed versus emerging economies as designated by OECD membership. The results suggest that the demarcation of developed versus emerging was not particularly meaningful in terms how the independent variables in this study influence software piracy. Future research may examine additional independent variables to see if structural breaks exist among them. We hope that our model will contribute insight into the development of successful strategies for reducing software piracy.

## ACKNOWLEDGMENT

An earlier version of this manuscript was published in the *Proceedings of the Forty-Third Annual Hawaii International Conference on System Sciences*.

## REFERENCES

Bagchi, K., Kirs, P., & Cerveny, R. (2006). Global Software Piracy: Can Economic Factors Alone Explain the Trend? *Communications of the ACM, 49*(6), 70–75. doi:10.1145/1132469.1132470

Banerjee, D., Khalid, A. M., & Sturm, J. E. (2005). Socio-economic development and software piracy. An empirical assessment. *Applied Economics, 37,* 2091–2097. doi:10.1080/00036840500293276

Business Software Alliance. (2005a). *Expanding the Frontiers of Our Digital Future: Reducing Software Piracy to Accelerate Global IT Benefits.* Washington, DC: BSA.

Business Software Alliance. (2005b). *Second Annual BSA and IDC Global Software Piracy Study.* Washington, DC: BSA.

Business Software Alliance. (2008). *The Economic Benefits of Lowering PC Software Piracy.* Retrieved June 1, 2009, from http://www.bsa.org/upload/idc-findings_summary.pdf

Business Software Alliance. (2009). *Sixth Annual BSA-IDC Global Software 08 Piracy Study.* Retrieved June 1, 2009, from http://global.bsa.org/globalpiracy2008/studies/globalpiracy2008.pdf

Cheng, H. K., Sims, R. R., & Teegen, H. (1997). To purchase or to pirate software: An empirical study. *Journal of Management Information Systems, 13*(4), 49–60.

Chow, G. (1960). Tests of Equality Between Sets of Coefficients in Two Linear Regressions. *Econometrica, 28,* 591–605. doi:10.2307/1910133

Gopal, R. D., & Sanders, G. L. (1997). Preventive and deterrent controls for software piracy. *Journal of Management Information Systems, 13*(4), 29–48.

Gopal, R. D., & Sanders, G. L. (1998). International Software Piracy: Analysis of Key Issues and Impacts. *Information Systems Research, 9*(4), 380–397. doi:10.1287/isre.9.4.380

Gopal, R. D., & Sanders, G. L. (2000). Global Software Piracy: You Can't Get Blood Out of a Turnip. *Communications of the ACM, 43*(9), 83–89. doi:10.1145/348941.349002

Hair, J. F. Jr, Anderson, R. E., Tatham, R. L., & Black, W. C. (2004). *Multivariate Data Analysis* (4th ed.). Upper Saddle River, NJ: Prentice Hall.

Moores, T. T., & Chang, J. C. J. (2006). Ethical decision making in software piracy: Initial development and test of a four-component model. *Management Information Systems Quarterly, 30*(1), 167–180.

Organization for Economic Co-operation and Development. (2008). *The OECD. OECD Media Relations.* Retrieved June 1, 2009, from http://www.oecd.org

Peace, A. G., Galletta, D. F., & Thong, J. Y. L. (2003). Software piracy in the workplace: A model and empirical test. *Journal of Management Information Systems, 20*(1), 153–177.

Png, I. P. L. (2010). On the Reliability of Software Piracy Statistics. In *Proceedings of the 43rd Hawaii International Conference on Systems Sciences,* Los Alamitos, CA. Washington, DC: IEEE Computer Society Press.

Shin, S. K., Gopal, R. D., Sanders, G. L., & Whinston, A. B. (2004). Global Software Piracy Revisited. *Communications of the ACM, 47*(1), 103–107. doi:10.1145/962081.962088

Sundararajan, A. (2004). Managing digital piracy: Pricing and protection. *Information Systems Research, 15*(3), 287–308. doi:10.1287/isre.1040.0030

Thong, J. Y. L., & Yap, C. (1998). Testing an ethnical decision-making theory: The case of softlifting. *Journal of Management Information Systems, 15*(1), 213–237.

Transparency International. (2004). *Transparency International Corruption Perceptions Index 2004.* Retrieved September 17, 2007, from http://www.transparency.org/policy_research/surveys_indices/cpi/2004

Traphagan, M., & Griffith, A. (1998). Software Piracy and Global Competitiveness: Report on Global Software Piracy. *International Review of Low Computers, 12*(3), 431–451. doi:10.1080/13600869855298

World Bank. (2007). *Key Development Data and Statistics.* Retrieved July 17, 2007, from www.worldbank.org/data/countrydata/countrydata.html

## APPENDIX

Countries or regions included in the study.

OECD Members:

Australia, Austria, Belgium, Canada, Czech Republic, Denmark, Finland, France, Germany, Greece, Hungary, Ireland, Italy, Japan, Mexico, Netherlands, New Zealand, Norway, Poland, Portugal, Slovakia, South Korea, Spain, Sweden, Switzerland, Turkey, United Kingdom, United States.

Non OECD Members:

Argentina, Brazil, Bulgaria, Chile, China, Colombia, Costa Rica, Croatia, Dominican Republic, Egypt, Estonia, Hong Kong, India, Indonesia, Israel, Kuwait, Latvia, Lithuania, Malaysia, Panama, Peru, Philippines, Romania, Russia, Saudi Arabia, Singapore, Slovenia, South Africa, Thailand, UAE, Ukraine, Uruguay, Venezuela, Vietnam

Note: Two OECD members (Iceland and Luxembourg) were not included in the study.

*This work was previously published in the International Journal of Social and Organizational Dynamics in IT, Volume 1, Issue 1, edited by Michael B. Knight, pp. 1-12, 2011 by IGI Publishing (an imprint of IGI Global).*

## Chapter 14

# Getting Lost in the Labyrinth:
## Information and Technology in the Marketplace

**John Conway**
*Art Institute of Pittsburgh, USA*

## ABSTRACT

*The importance of the labyrinth as a trope in the Western tradition can hardly be overstated. Far from being a metaphor that describes just anything, it is a sign whose meaning appears in specific contexts. This article argues how the labyrinth's triple function as visual, verbal and spatial sign—as well as its paradoxical function as unicursal and multicursal structure—makes it flexible enough to represent the paradoxical and complex nature of the modern workplace, the city, the mall and the individual subject's position within an ever burgeoning network of relationships brought about by consumerism, capitalism, and commodification. Understanding the labyrinth trope helps people to understand the subject's relationship to power and the very technology that we have created and in which we are trapped.*

## INTRODUCTION

According to Attali (1999) in his book, *The Labyrinth in Culture and Society*, human beings are in the "process of becoming virtual nomads: working and shopping at home, navigating without a guide through networks of information and power, with fantasies of belonging to that future elite of deluxe nomads who migrate from pleasure to pleasure" (p. xxv). We live within vast and complicated networks and grids that overlap, confuse, and

make dizzying connections very quickly. Our road and highway systems are just more labyrinths that we traverse daily to our places of work which themselves resemble mazes with their twisting corridors, confusing hallways, and dead end cubicles. The cityscape, the suburb, the school, the mall—all of these are contemporary labyrinths in which we live, navigate, and get lost. The virtual spaces we explore in the Worldwide Web (its name connoting a series of confusing bifurcations) is an endless series of hallways, rooms, and networking connections, calling forth the infinitely large library in Borges' story, "The Library of Babel,"

DOI: 10.4018/978-1-4666-1948-7.ch014

where all possible letter configurations (even the meaningless ones) were contained in one total and complete library-universe. It has become easy to become lost within the vast virtual libraries whose information we have created and collected. The labyrinth is the symbol of our creations and our imprisonment within them. According to Attali (1999), "Understanding labyrinths will soon become essential to a mastery of the modern condition" (p. xxv).

But why is this? Why has the labyrinth become such a pervasive modern symbol? What does it mean to describe our lives, our technology, and our information systems in this way and to use this particular trope instead of countless others? Why not a forest or a constellation? Why the labyrinth? To answer this question fully one must understand the history and genealogy of the labyrinth as well as the variety of texts in which it is featured. To understand what the labyrinth means is to understand our relationship to those things that we create. This discussion will incorporate a variety of texts including Attali's (1999) study but also including Aarseth's (1997), *Cybertext: Perspectives on Ergodic Literature*; Berman's (1982), *All That is Solid Melts Into Air*; Veel's (2003) "The Irreducibility of Space: Labyrinths, Cities, Cyberspace," Mitchell's (1992) "Orientalism and the Exhibitionary Order" and Benjamin's (2004) labyrinthine work about 19th century life called *The Arcades Project* as well as other works that discuss the history of the labyrinth concept. The idea is to understand what the metaphor means in terms of how it is used now in relation to how the concept has been deployed in the past. In doing this we will learn that the labyrinth is a flexible trope who's multiple and paradoxical meanings do a great deal in helping us understand our complex relationships with each other and the machines and technology we use. The labyrinth is a dual visual and verbal symbol (triple if you count spatial) and ambiguous trope. About the labyrinth Foucault (1986) commented in his book, *Death and the Labyrinth*, that it was one of the "two great mythic

spaces so often explored by Western imagination" (p. 80). He describes labyrinthine space as "rigid and forbidden, surrounding the quest, the return, and the treasure" (p. 80). The second great mythic space is of the metamorphosis: "communicating, polymorphous, continuous, irreversible" (p. 80). We will learn that the labyrinth actually in practice encompasses both of these spaces. It is a place to get lost as well as a place of wondrous transformation. It is both rigid and flexible, allowing creative freedom as well as imprisonment. What better way to explain our lives as moderns?

Before we discuss a history of the labyrinth and what it means to us as nomads in the information jungle, let's consider two contemporary media texts that prominently feature the labyrinth as a site where we do business and work [located here: http://www.youtube.com/watch?v=Now74xATro4&NR=1 and here: http://www.youtube.com/watch?v=-N-Htse4sPI]. The first is a commercial, "SHRM Commercial Version 1" (YouTube, 2001) for the Society of Human Resource Management and the second is a commercial, "Barclays: fake," for the British banking interest, Barclays. Both of these brief texts say a great deal about how we as subjects navigate labyrinthine networks of information.

The SHRM commercial (YouTube, 2001) begins by stating that "your most important business assets walk out the door every night," ("SHRM commercial version 1") and it shows a stream of employees walking outside and away from a large office building set amongst a confusing cluster of other tightly packed buildings in a large metropolitan area. SHRM states it is their job to "make sure they come back every morning" (YouTube, 2001). A man is shown guiding the employees back into the building via an escalator. Interestingly, the very building that the workers are entering morphs into a multicursal hedge maze that features the same man as guide. The man finds a way out of the labyrinth but then the image morphs again to show him superimposed on top of a labyrinthine grid that signifies a graph.

The SHRM commercial concludes that their organization helps a business meet the challenges of a changing world (YouTube, 2001). On the surface the argument of the commercial is that SHRM can help a business succeed by helping to navigate the tricky labyrinths associated with strategy and economics. But why is a labyrinth used to signify a business environment? Why a hedge maze? Why might we as an audience easily associate a city and an office building with a labyrinth and what does this say about how we frame our professional lives? What does it mean to conflate business, information, and the labyrinth via this human resources commercial?

The "Barclays: fake" (YouTube, 2009) commercial is more subtle if not just plain disturbing with its implications. The commercial is the short story of a man realizing that what he considers to be "real" is actually a vast, complicated, simulated stage, a labyrinthine stage set only meant to *look* real. The commercial begins when a business professional in suit and tie leaves a crowded, lively bar only to enter a simulacrum featuring fake, mannequin-people on what was once a busy, lively street. Pigeons fly about as if the street scene has been abandoned by human life. The man wanders through the streets, beginning to panic as he realizes that nothing is "real." He attempts to pick up a newspaper, but realizes the pile of newspapers is only a hollow stage prop. He attempts to exit via a subway entrance but realizes the stairway is painted onto the floor. He runs in between more of the lifeless drone-like statues and through the streets, tries to enter a building, only to have his foot fall through the cardboard steps. He realizes he is caught within a kind of stage set when whole pieces of the backdrop begin to fall over, revealing an empty and isolated beach on top of which the wooden frames of the set have been built. Strangely, the man doesn't exit the fake set, but chooses to enter back into the labyrinth. Once he finds the Barclays building (which is a substantial structure, something "real" inside the otherwise fake set), a "real" man greets him, and then the

entire scene reverts back to its "normal" and lively state (YouTube, 2009). Has the man found "reality" or only another layer to the labyrinth? What is "reality" within this labyrinth?

Both of these scenes are important because of the way they feature employees as subjects navigating a business world featured as a labyrinth. In each commercial the company in question is featured as the way to "exit" the labyrinth, when disturbingly, it is apparent the labyrinth hasn't been exited at all. The exit from the hedge maze in the SHRM commercial only deposits the employee within a labyrinth of information that must be interpreted by the SHRM agent. The man inside the simulated Barclays environment doesn't even choose to exit the labyrinth at all, but the implication is that we always already reside within a fake, contrived structure, even if it does appear "real." In both the labyrinth is an important metaphor in how we view reality and how we see ourselves as modern subjects. We will learn that the labyrinth signifies how man creates and then becomes trapped within what he has wrought, whether it be the office spaces he or she occupies or the entire economic system which he has constructed. The labyrinth is the only metaphor available which helps to explain how we create and become controlled by what we have made. In this way we can never exit the labyrinth; we can only trick ourselves into thinking that we might exit it, or we must learn how to navigate it ourselves. This is what Attali (1999) means when he says "We must relearn labyrinthine thinking and restudy strategies necessary for our evolution towards a reinvention of the secrets of this ancient wisdom" (p. xxv). This kind of thinking helps us to detail in depth the intersection of the concept of the labyrinth, the rhizomatic Internet, as well as how commodification complicates how we navigate the information maze.

Before we can understand better the connection between the labyrinth, our technology, and our culture, let's take a look at a brief genealogy of the labyrinth concept. What makes the labyrinth trope unique is its triple function as a visual, verbal and spatial sign. The history of the labyrinth concept is a story of this kind of development, tension, and synthesis between these different signs. Kern (2000) in his book, *Through the Labyrinth*, proposes the original concept of the labyrinth was actually a group dance whose intricate pattern was inscribed as a unicursal labyrinth. He argues that the earliest visual representations of the Bronze Age petroglyphs are images that depict the path of the dance (pp. 25-26). His evidence of this is literary. He explains that Homer, Plutarch, and Virgil describe the labyrinth in terms of dance movement that seem "to be reflections of this original expression: attempts at recording the ephemeral movements of the dance" (p. 27). So in short, the earliest material form recorded are Bronze Age petroglyphs (inscribed above tombs and mines) which are theorized to be visual forms of ritualistic dance movements. Kern (2000) categorizes the concept of the labyrinth into three groups: 1) the labyrinth as literary motif (usually a maze), 2) the labyrinth as dance movement, and 3) the labyrinth as image (p. 27). The labyrinth as image predates its textual manifestation by at least 1,000 years. Kern (2000) suggests that the transition from the labyrinth's meaning as a dance to that of a place is that it designated the stage or foundation upon which the dance was performed (p. 27). In this regard the first instance of the meaning of the labyrinth is that of a performance stage, not a palace or maze. This is important in understanding how, for example, we understand the labyrinth constructed around us as being simulated (via the Barclays commercial) but also the way we construct our reality using language (also seen as labyrinthine).

To understand the concept of the labyrinth it's important to understand that there are two contradictory meanings: the unicursal and the multicursal. The unicursal labyrinth is a kind of spiral that leads to the center. There are no possible choices; the path leads the walker to the center and then out again. The multicursal labyrinth is more readily recognizable as a maze with multiple branchings and paths that force the walker to become lost. The unicursal labyrinth is seen as an exercise in patience and endurance whereas the multicursal labyrinth is an exercise in choice and "finding oneself." The most difficult aspect of understanding the labyrinth as a trope is to see that both forms and their paradoxical natures have developed together over at least the past 5,000 years. Additionally, there is a difference between the visual form which is inscribed as a pattern onto surfaces versus the verbal (or textual) sign as it appears in writing.

The earliest textual evidence of the labyrinth comes from three sources: 1) a small Mycenaean clay tablet dated at Knossos around 1400 BC; 2) a Samian architect who compares himself in the sixth century to the famous labyrinth builder called Daedalus; and 3) an account by Herodotus of an Egyptian labyrinth in the fifth century BC. Although in all three instances the labyrinth is the name of a structure, Kern (2000) points out that the meaning is not that of what we consider to be a "maze." In fact, the visual image of labyrinth as maze doesn't occur until the 15th century (but the concept of labyrinth as maze does occur much earlier) as is seen by a series of drawings by a Venetian doctor, Giovanni Fontana, who proposes the labyrinth as multicursal maze. Kern references a book that Fontana wrote (now lost) called *Little Book of Labyrinths* where he proposes a series of maze-like drawings. Fontana is credited by Kern as having drawn the first mazes, but these are not textual instances of the maze, only the first time the image is a multicursal series of choices that the modern reader would associate with mazes (pp. 138-139). Kern (2000) concludes by saying that the term was widely accepted as a maze in the late Hellenistic era simultaneously with the labyrinth as unicursal figure (p. 139). It is from these two meanings that the concept disseminates.

The labyrinth as visual and verbal sign is closely related to the development of sedentary civilization, itself a function of tool building and technology. Kern (2000) posits that the labyrinth was inherited by the Minoans via the Neolithic era at its earliest since its cosmological and astral aspects coincide with a people who were farmers and who were concerned about death and the afterlife (petroglyphs inscribed on tombs support this). Paleolithic hunters and gatherers had no use for the symbol, so the labyrinth has grown beginning with the earliest semblances of human civilization. The nomadic wanderings of past peoples are converted into the winding path of the labyrinth for a people who have stopped moving. This knowledge must be reprised to help us understand the mobility demanded by modernity and our technology. With the coming of the Industrial Revolution Attali (1999) argues that its function as ornament and game ended and it once regained meaning to help conceptualize modern cities, market economies, as well as "networks of power and influence, diagrams of business and governmental organizations, university curricula, or personal careers" (p. xxiii). Straight lines don't do the kind of work that the labyrinth does to explain modern life and its complicated relationships and networks: "We instead find a succession of convolutions, traps, dead ends, wrong paths, and jealously guarded sanctums. Wealth and power are henceforth to be found within the terminus of the labyrinth" (p. xxiii). For Attali understanding the labyrinth is no parlor game, it is crucial to understanding our cultural selves and identities. We are becoming virtual nomads who wander from virtual place to virtual place.

To understand better the labyrinth and how it relates to how we perceive our culture and technology it's important to look at Doob's (1990) excellent study called *The Idea of the Labyrinth* which explores the meaning of the trope during the Middle Ages. As was stated earlier, the labyrinth is a flexible trope, deriving two contradictory meanings from its unicursal and multicursal forms as well as its visual, verbal and spatial nature. The trope incorporates "order and disorder, clarity and confusion, unity and multiplicity, artistry

and chaos....Our perception of labyrinths is thus intrinsically unstable: change your perspective and the labyrinth seems to change" (p. 1).

Doob's (2000) etymology is incredibly useful in understanding the concept. She begins with the common medieval, Latinate spelling "laborintus" which is opposed to the Greek derived "labyrinthus." From the latter we get the meaning "house of difficult exit," but Doob prefers the former word as etymological study. "Laborintus" is derived from "labor" and "intus." "Labor" denotes as a verb to fall, perish, err or go wrong within. As noun it means "hardship, or fatigue, or exertion, or application to work" (p. 97). "Intus" means "lies within" and so what happens within the labyrinth is more important than getting in or getting out, highlighting process or even transformation. According to Doob (2000), this meaning is preferred because it is "far more ambiguous, suggestive, and indeterminate" (p. 97) than the typical "House of Daedalus" meaning of labyrinthus: "Etymologically speaking, then, the labyrinth is a process involving internal difficulty (or error, or artistry, or fatiguing effort); and what happens inside is more important than whether it is hard to get in or get out" (p. 97).

Since the English medieval people thought of labyrinths as mazes, Doob (2000) discusses the etymology of the word "maze" through its Old and Middle English meanings. It is derived from *amased* and *masedli* in the thirteenth century which means "out of one's mind, irrational, foolish," but Doob points out at this time there is no labyrinthine connection (p. 98). The noun *mase* appears in 1300 meaning "a source of confusion or deception; vision, fantasy, delusion, deceit" (p. 98). Doob (2000) cites the first instance when the word takes on labyrinthine connotations in 1325 with the phrase "They went ashore as mazed men; they didn't know where they were" (p. 98). There is no explicit connection, but it does reflect a "labyrinthine experience" (p. 98). Doob (2000) cites instances in the late 1300's that suggest by the end of the century the word *mase* is clearly linked to the labyrinth. Doob concludes that the word begins in Old English as a state of mind but transitions to signify the labyrinth because the confusion and bewilderment of both words makes for a logical connection: "If a mazed man is confused and deluded and a labyrinth confuses and deceives, then a labyrinth is a maze. *Maze* comes to signify *labyrinth* by a kind of metonymy, the effect giving its name to the cause" (p. 98).

Based on this etymology alone, it becomes easier to see the connections made between the concept and our lives as working professionals in the 21st century. The labyrinth is a place in which difficult, fatiguing work is done. It is a place without egress in which we labor and create. "House of Daedalus" seems to be an appropriate pseudonym, given the inventor's creative spirit and drive as well as how he became lost in the very creation he produced. The fact that Doob emphasizes process shows the recursive nature of the labyrinth, especially how it is viewed today. Nobody seeks egress out of the labyrinth (this might explain the Barclays commercial and the man who doesn't wish to exit). There is only the labyrinth and process, never a center, never a revelation, only fatiguing effort. The ambiguity of the labyrinth suggests both a prison-like effect as well as creative freedom and hard work. Doob's discussion of "maze" is also relevant. It is a source of confusion, of vision, fantasy, and delusion. What better way to describe the culture and the places we work?

Modernity and its products have also contributed to our labyrinthine experiences. An interesting instance of how new materials and technology can help us create our own labyrinths is given by McCullough (2004) in his book called *The Unending Mystery: A Journey Through Labyrinths and Mazes*. According to McCullough, the hedge maze arrived in America in the 19th century via a religious group called The Harmonists who settled in Pennsylvania and Indiana and wrought complicated hedge mazes around their communities. According to McCullough, the hedge maze

morphed into the "glass house" or mirror maze. The reason for this transformation is only because of new materials that were ideal for traveling carnivals since they were easy to setup and dismantle. What made these portable, easy-to-carry mirrors ideal for a carnival is that by the optical trick of reflecting mirrors, they were able to make a small space seem six times larger than it actually was, perfect for setting up in a limited space. According to McCullough, "the typical glass house consisted of, first, a corridor, which often doubled back on itself, lined with distorting mirrors having curved glass that made the walkers look taller or fatter or smaller than they were" (pp. 157-158). Some of the corridors were decorated with "house-of-horrors" touches like cobwebs, spooky lighting, and prop skeletons and monsters.

It wouldn't take much to see how this particular case might signify our own lives and relationships with our information systems, especially our virtual lives where we work and play. The Internet-as-labyrinth is a kind of mirror house where virtual space opens up indefinitely within a small space (our computers) and in which we imagine ourselves wandering. The distorted effect of the mirrors themselves are perfect metaphors for how advertising makes us see ourselves as being too fat, or too ugly, or not beautiful enough. It's important, though, to see that the Internet isn't the only labyrinth, but that our virtual lives reach out to us in whatever form marketing and advertising can utilize including the mall, the television, or the billboard sign. The walls of the labyrinth are adorned with such messages everywhere we go.

So far we have laid the foundation for understanding the complexity of the labyrinth trope, but we need to do more work to understand how the labyrinth is deployed in the context of our modern lives and our relationship to our technology and information systems. To begin to make these connections, time will be spent discussing modernity and the labyrinth, leaning on Berman's (1982) *All That Is Solid Melts Into Air*. This book is important because it discusses our experience as moderns using the same kind of duality that the labyrinth so easily conveys; in fact, Berman states that to be modern is to live a paradoxical and contradictory life (p. 13). It is these paradoxes and contradictions that he spends a great deal of time explaining. His book does a great deal to help us understand the confusion inherent to our every day experience in which the individual subject is overpowered by vastly labyrinthine, bureaucratic organizations that control and have the power to destroy our communities, lives, and values. Yet in the face of these powers we fight to change and make the world our own (p. 13). The duality of the labyrinth speaks to us here. We are both controlled by our passage through the very thing that we have wrought. As Berman (1982) so eloquently states, "To be modern is to find ourselves in an environment that promises us adventure, power, joy, growth, transformation of ourselves and the world—and, at the same time, that threatens to destroy everything we have, everything we know, everything we are" (p. 15). How is this so?

Modern life, we are reminded by Berman (1982), is a maelstrom fed from many sources including 1) discoveries in the physical sciences, 2) the industrialization of production (transforming scientific knowledge into technology), 3) the increase in the tempo of life because of technology, 4) the creation of vast bureaucratic power in the form of corporations and nation states, 5) urban growth, and 6) mass communications (p. 18). "Modernization" is the concept which describes the technological phenomena that bring these forces into being and keep them going, making the individual simultaneously both a powerful subject and automated object. One of the great successes of Berman's (1982) book is the way that he describes the dizzying, terrifying, transforming atmosphere that we all take for granted. The following passage is worth quoting in its entirety:

*This is a landscape of steam engines, automatic factories, railroads, vast new industrial zones; of teeming cities that have grown overnight, of-*

*ten with dreadful human consequences; of daily newspapers, telegraphs, telephones and other mass media, communicating on an ever wider scale; of increasingly strong national states and multinational aggregations of capital...of mass social movements....of an ever-expanding world market embracing all, capable of the most spectacular growth, capable of appalling waste and devastation, capable of everything except solidity and stability (pp. 18-19).*

The subject wanders within this vast, networked landscape, and Berman (1982) uses labyrinthine language to describe the modern artist Pollock's drip paintings as "forests in which spectators might lose (and, of course, find) themselves" (p. 24). But what does Berman say about modern man and his relationship to technology?

Berman (1982) explains two poles, two positions that attempt to explain our relationship to technology. The first position would be akin to the celebration of modern technology espoused by the Italian Futurists where technology is the catalyst for change, even for the transformation of humans into something amoral, even non-emotional in favor of the "powerful bodily electric" (p. 25). Berman (1982) rightfully states that the problem here is "there is precious little for modern man to do except to plug in" (p. 27). The opposite pole is one that decries Modernism and all things technological in an "iron cage" metaphor written about by Max Weber. According to Berman (1982), "[N]ot only is modern society a cage, but all the people in it are shaped by its bars; we are beings without spirit, without heart, without sexual or personal identity" (p. 27). In this view "Modernity is constituted by its machines, of which modern men and women are merely mechanical reproductions" (p. 29).

Having said that, one of the more positive impulses of modernity and modern thinking is the opening of oneself to the richness and variety of things brought forth and made possible by modernization (p. 32). It was this kind of grand vision and openness that was lost in the 70's, according to Berman (1982), and which made discussions of modernism bleak and sterile (p. 33). It might be possible that the invention of the labyrinthine Internet and its rhizomatic power and freedom have rekindled some of the liberating modern impulses that were lost. Berman attributes this duality to our economic system of capitalism that destroys the possibilities it creates. It is a paradox, and it offers endless and creative possibility and production alongside the stagnation and destruction of the same. The bourgeoisie cannot follow the path toward true freedom and production offered by modernization because those avenues are shut down by the hoarding of profit associated with the bottom-line (pp. 95-96). What better metaphor for this kind of dualism than the labyrinth that conceals as it reveals, offers both revelation and loss of self in the same trope? Berman (1982) lays out Marx's paradoxical vision of capitalism and the "culture of modernism:"

*The theme of insatiable desires and drives, permanent revolution, infinite development, perpetual creation and renewal in every sphere of life; and its radical antithesis, the theme of nihilism, insatiable destruction, the shattering and swallowing up of life, the heart of darkness, the horror (p. 102).*

Underneath the chaos, creative power, and tumult of modernity and the individual subject's position within the labyrinth is the mythical narrative that supports and penetrates the modern meaning; it's incredibly interesting to read the labyrinth myth's themes on top of this account since they appear to be so relevant. The Cretan labyrinth on Knossos is the result of Queen Pasiphae's bestial lust and desire for the white bull given to Minos by Poseidon (but not sacrificed). Her insatiable lust creates the Minotaur but only with the help of Daedalus who constructs a hollow bull into which she places herself to consummate this desire. Minos imprisons Daedalus into the very labyrinth that he creates, not only to hide the result

of the bestial union (the Minotaur) but probably as a result of his complicity. Daedalus is a wonderful metaphor for creativity and its misuses. Even the hero Theseus who defeats the Minotaur with the help of Minos' daughter, Ariadne, demonstrates his dual nature by leaving the distraught Ariadne alone on an island after the celebration of the defeat of the Minotaur is over. Within this tale is the greed and power of Minos and his ruthless handling of Daedalus. There is also the creative spirit and ambivalence of Daedalus himself who during the same visit creates the technology to help Pasiphae sate her unnatural desire, builds the labyrinth for Minos to imprison the fruit of that desire, and then creates the technology and the means to escape that imprisonment himself. Creative power, greed, lust, and ingenuity could all be seen as qualities of modern men and women.

Up to this point we have seen why the labyrinth is a powerful trope for men, women, and their technologies in a complicated society and how the history of the concept relates to this. Although Berman offers some insightful avenues into the problematics associated with modernity, technology, and the labyrinth, how might we begin to more closely link the labyrinth as a trope with technology? One passageway into this discussion is an article written by Veel (2003) called "The Irreducibility of Space: Labyrinths, Cities, Cyberspace." Veel (2003) highlights the debate surrounding whether scholars should occupy themselves with the new media. On one side are those who believe that literary scholars should use their abilities to understand the technology and what it means. On the other side are those concerned that the neutral quality of the Internet blurs our sense of history and continuity (p. 151). The distrust of information technology as a subject of study in the humanities, according to Veel (2003), relates to the technology becoming more prominent during a time when post-structuralism has framed the world in terms of fragmentation and decentered meaning of which the Internet was seen as proof. The result of this was that a "humanistic" approach was not adapted to this technology (p. 151). Veel (2003) argues that scholars need to explore the possibilities that the technology can provide, not what they fear it will become (p. 151). Central to Veel's (2003) study is how the labyrinth is complicit in how we understand cyberspace as well as the city, arguing that "orientation and navigation in cyberspace is indeed governed by a highly physical and even geographical experience of space" in which the labyrinth plays an important role (p. 152). Although the purpose of Veel's study is not to connect the labyrinth to a larger cultural and historical context like we are doing here, her article clarifies the meaning and use of the labyrinth in the field of information technology.

Veel (2003) links how we perceive cyberspace to a cognitive semantic term known as "schemata" which connects abstract concepts to physical space; for example, the "source-path-goal schema" conceptualizes progress toward a goal as a physical journey through physical space" (p. 153). Although this by itself doesn't necessarily answer why the labyrinth is used in the face of other "schemata"—like conceptualizing cyberspace as a constellation with its various nodes and links—it does help to see how "real" space is connected to "virtual" space. The labyrinth is an obvious contender in this regard. Veel (2003) points out that the labyrinth trope is central to a variety of metaphors used in relation to cyberspace: "network," "web," "information highway," and "shopping mall" (p. 153).

Veel's article seeks to show how the dual and ambiguous nature of the labyrinth trope informs our notions of cyberspace when it is described in labyrinthine terms. Veel (2003) discusses the labyrinthine city as an example of how a subject can be both viewer and walker since the city "is the most immediate antecedent to cyberspace that has exposed the human subject to a radicalized change of the meaning of space (p. 157). For example, "technologies such as the bicycle, telegraph, telephone, electric light, power networks,

and railway were all part of changing the prevailing paradigms for understanding cities, space, and time which were rooted in the preindustrial past" (p. 157). Veel's (2003) most interesting point is that the move from the unicursal to the multicursal labyrinth is in part made possible by the technologies that helped create the modern city and which helped us conceptualize space differently. What makes our experience labyrinthine is how our physical bodies occupy urban space: "The interaction between the urban order and the physical body is what is central to the labyrinthine experience" (p. 161). All of this, she argues, is important in understanding how we view cyberspace as being labyrinthine.

Since we are already linking our bodies to the labyrinth via our modern experience of the city, we are easily able to frame our virtual experiences within the Internet as labyrinthine. Concerning cyberspace, Veel (2003) states:

*"What we experience as a space in which we can navigate consists in fact of numerical data. As an example, a digital image is made up of discrete elements, or pixels, each assigned a specific numerical value that determines its position and shade. The space created is thus essentially a mathematical space in which body and sensory perceptions have no place insofar as it is not a human space in the traditional sense" (p. 163).*

However, even though mathematics and statistics "conjure" it up, it's perceived as space being that it is brought into a human environment (p. 163). When navigating cyberspace it is not possible to "create an all-encompassing view of the entire structure" (p. 164) because of the amount of information in the network as well as the subjective and divergent experiences offered by the same structure (p. 164).

According to Veel (2003), we experience the Internet as a labyrinth in which we are both the viewer and walker. That is to say the labyrinthine experience of the Internet depends upon our shifting position as subjects able to see and map the maze from above while simultaneously walking and getting lost within it (p. 165). In this way the labyrinthine city still serves as an excellent precursor. Veel's (2003) study is a persuasive exploration of how the spatial characteristics in cyberspace are a result of the medium's mimicry of three-dimensional space via the conceptual constellation of labyrinth, city, and cyberspace (p. 170).

In so doing Veel (2003) concludes that a contradiction occurs when "cyberspace is infused with redemptive and liberating qualities and conceived of as 'other' space that is cut off from geographical space" (p. 170). That is to say the interesting contradiction is a result of seeing the rhizomatic, liberating Internet as such when we are also mired within a labyrinthine experience. This might not be such a contradiction, though, since the labyrinth does operate in both capacities. It is a place of revelatory transformation as well as a prison-like place to get lost. This again demonstrates the labyrinth's flexibility as a trope. Veel (2003) concludes her study with the warning: "Since we encounter and handle cyberspace every day, its familiarity makes achieving the necessary distance to deal with it as an object of study in an academic framework problematic" (p. 170). This does seem to contradict Veel's earlier statement that we can be both viewer and walkers of the labyrinth. Her last comment definitely leans more toward the subject as walker lost within the structure versus the viewer looking from above.

Another aspect of modernity that is developed with the labyrinth trope—in addition to the technological transformations of modernization—is the way power acts upon the subject in society. Here we return to Attali's (1999) book, *Labyrinth in Culture and Society*, since he spends some time discussing our experience of becoming lost within the bureaucratic and governmental landscape and how power is a function of this. According to Attali (1999), the labyrinth glorifies power (p. 52). Architectural and structural labyrinths (of

any kind) created by man are only possible with the marshalling of massive resources and capital centralized under authority (this harkens back to the labyrinth built by Daedalus at the behest of King Minos). This is the case with ancient labyrinths, with aristocratic hedge mazes, with the labyrinthine city, and with the rhizomatic, networking Internet. Attali (1999) argues that the labyrinth is a "weapon of power" in the way it is used to imprison and to obstruct the citizenry's access to power. The Cretans used it as a prison and European sovereigns built them where they lived and traversed them during their coronations (pp. 53-54). Attali (1999) states, "When bourgeois society developed the pretense of power that was no longer apart and isolated from the people, the labyrinth as authoritarian symbol became unnecessary" (pp. 54). The sovereign cultivated the idea that access to power was direct and straight and open to all, "and even that they might take his place." The myth was perpetuated that anyone could become anything with hard work. This is the "founding myth of capitalist society in general, and American society in particular" (pp. 54).

Attali (1999) warns that today power hides within the labyrinth. It is becoming more and more impossible to determine where power resides within an ever complicated and bureaucratic network. Is there a center or not? Is there a Bastille to be stormed? Haven't we all expressed frustration with labyrinthine call centers where it is impossible to get an answer? "We have passed from the labyrinth of one central power to that of multiple and changing centers, with powers circulating ceaselessly between them" (p. 55). Future power will seek to restrict circulation and control the access within the labyrinth (p. 55).

Control and access of information as well as our dependency on complicated energy grids is the new form of power, a sphere we must navigate like subjects within a labyrinth. With electrical and transportation grids that overlap one another, the straight line is replaced with the bifurcated path which endlessly divides and then divides again.

Attali (1999) tells us that the simple act of dialing a number is a process of bifurcation: "The straight line no longer rules today, with portable telephones acting as a kind of thread of Ariadne for new urban nomads, and answering machines and voice mail serving to render them 'reachable' or 'unreachable' for others in search of them" (p. 63). Furthermore, Attali (1999) theorizes that future communication will become even more labyrinthine in nature:

*"Television, transportation, and the countless shopping and business networks are like mazes already. Freeways themselves will cease to obey the straight line, which causes more traffic jams as well as accidents due to drowsiness; mazes that multiply road choices between one point and another actually improve circulation. Already, today's freeways are becoming mazes superimposed on one another, with express lanes, interchanges, and one-way access roads. The most effective subway transport systems have multiple redundant maps" (p. 63).*

Ultimately, the Internet has become the uber labyrinth and Attali's (1999) succinct account of the history of the Internet is also an exercise in the labyrinthine. The nature of the labyrinth was built into the internet from the beginning with the creation of hypertext in 1965 which allowed for passages to be created in a subterranean and rhizomatic way that ran counter to a straight, "orderly," hierarchical organization of information. Ted Nelson, the inventor of hypertext, envisioned "linking up all existing texts in a vast structure, like the absolute library [from the short story called "The Library of Babel"] envisioned by Jorge Luis Borges" (p. 64). In 1969 Cerf and Kahn, two American engineers, designed communication protocols enabling computers to connect with one another in a labyrinthine network. The system became public in 1980: "In 1991, the Gopher system allowed the creation of 'tunnels,' linking places in a labyrinth with no direct connection

between them. At the same time, the Worldwide Web appeared, with its explicit debt to a spider's labyrinth" (p. 64). According to Attali, this new form of connection used "overlapping, interlinked alleys and driveways" which passed through into unexpected encounters or resulted in dead ends. Attali calls "information superhighway" misleading because it connotes a straight, express path, when in fact the rhizomatic nature of the Internet is anything but with its winding, circuitous, subterranean nature that resembles a medieval town with "electronic street-mazes." However, if one takes the highway in the vein of Kerouac, Hunter S. Thompson, and DeLillo, it's easy to see how the "information superhighway" can connote both the easy transfer of information enabled by the Internet as well as the labyrinth of the road with all its exits and entrances, off-ramps, curves, and dead ends. The super highway is just one part of the labyrinthine road system. Control of these labyrinths is the new battleground. The debates and concerns of Julian Assange and Wikileaks is an example of this. Whoever controls this information wields a certain kind of power.

Up this point we have discussed how we have become subjects lost within vast, bureaucratic networks of power, roaming the landscape with mobile cell phones in labyrinthine structures like the city, the super highway, and the Internet. The next important point to make is the effect that framing our information technology as a labyrinth has on us and what this means, especially when we read and interpret using those technologies. Aarseth (1997) explores the intersection between information technology and the labyrinth metaphor in his book, *Cybertext: Perspectives on Ergodic Literature,* which explores cybertexts and the act of reading. As Aarseth (1997) explains, "the concept of cybertext focuses on the mechanical organization of the text, by positing the intricacies of the medium as an integral part of the literary exchange" (p. 1). The process is centered around the user of the text. Aarseth (1997) calls "ergodic" any kind of reading that requires "nontrivial effort" in its process, like reading of a cybertext. A cybertext is differentiated from other texts in that "when you read from a cybertext, you are constantly reminded of inaccessible strategies and paths not taken, voices not heard" (p. 3). Too often this difference is mistaken for literary ambiguity instead of being a real difference in the act of reading. With a cybertext there is real possibility to miss certain meanings of the text, depending on one's choices. An objection to the uniqueness of cybertexts is that they still have to be read as a linear text (a reader can only choose one path at a time), so there's no use in making the differentiation. Aarseth (1997) objects on the grounds of the kind of metaphors that are used to understand the reading process (p. 3). This is how the labyrinth enters into the conversation.

According to Aarseth, one of the reasons that verbal ambiguity of linear texts is read into the non-linear text is the metaphor of the labyrinth that is the rhetorical model used to explain the reading process. Aarseth (1997) explains that the idea of the narrative text being thought of as a "labyrinth, a game, or an imaginary world, in which the reader can explore at will, get lost, discover secret paths, play around, follow the rules…" leads to a "systematic misrepresentation of the relationship between narrative text and reader" which results in a "spatiodynamic fallacy" (p. 3). The narrative text is perceived as the world itself and not as representation of that world. The linear text emphasizes the interpretive and the cybertext emphasizes the interactivity of the text (Aarseth does address the overlapping of the two as well). The problem with taking the labyrinth metaphor of the linear text and using it to understand the cybertext is that the cybertext IS a labyrinth in a way that the linear text is not. Whereas the linear narrative text presents itself as a labyrinth, the cybertext "*is* a game-world or world-game; it *is* possible to explore, get lost, and discover secret paths in these texts, not metaphorically, but through the topological structures of the textual machinery" (p. 4). These distinctions are

important for Aarseth since reading cybertext as a linear text misses some of the important dynamics of cybertextuality.

To state this more succinctly: Aarseth believes the labyrinth metaphor to be useful for both narrative and cybertexts, but he believes that projecting the labyrinth metaphor onto a "real" labyrinth (like the Internet or cybertext) is problematic. Even more interesting is that Aarseth (1999) suggests that understanding how cybertexts are indeed labyrinths exposes some of the deficiencies in how we view narrative texts as labyrinths (p. 5). To understand this Aarseth discusses the history of the labyrinth concept via Doob's book, *The Idea of the Labyrinth*. Doob's important point is that the multicursal and unicursal forms existed simultaneously in the same category even though we perceive these two to be opposites. That is to say that there was no need to distinguish between the difficult progress leading to a goal of the unicursal labyrinth with the complex design, and the inextricability or impenetrability of the multicursal labyrinth. Aarseth (1997) suggests that the rich duality of the labyrinth as both unicursal and multicursal form existing in the same category lost some of its complexity when the labyrinth as multicursal maze took predominance in how we view narrative texts. As a result, the labyrinth metaphor as multicursal maze doesn't quite do justice to understanding narrative texts. In fact, Aarseth suggests that the unicursal model is best applied to narrative texts while the multicursal model is best for cybertexts since the linear nature of narrative doesn't allow for choice or for the reader to "get lost" in the same way that a cybertext "player" can get lost (p. 7). To put it another way, since the meaning of the unicursal labyrinth is not used as frequently, the multicursal form is wrongly associated with narrative texts when the more accurate use would be for cybertexts.

Aarseth includes an interesting discussion of what constitutes ergodic literature, and since this figures prominently in this discussion about labyrinths and information technology, some time should be spent understanding what exactly this kind of labyrinthine literature entails. Aarseth (1997) begins with stating how ergodic literature, being a spatial activity itself, developed alongside linear writing. He cites as an example Egyptian inscriptions which were read three-dimensionally from wall to wall or room to room inside temples (p. 9). He also cites the *I Ching* as an example of ancient cybertext that is able to generate multiple textual meanings in a non-linear way. Other examples include those that engage the "reader" in choosing different pathways or endings. They are labyrinthine because the participant chooses a path from within instead of standing above the whole in a grand act of interpretation.

With the advent of digital computing, computer language emerged as a textual genre: "Short, simple programs are often linear, but longer programs generally consist of collections of interdependent fragments, with repeating loops, cross-references, and discontinuous 'jumps' back and forth between sections" (p. 11). Aarseth (1997) also cites the textual computer game Adventure that requires the active participation of the player in a story which can only exist with that player's decisions. "Hyperfictions" which rely on the hypertext link also represent "literary labyrinths" that can be explored by the reader (p. 13). Aarseth's last example is the "multi-user dungeon" which was a textual game where multiple users could access the computer via modem and then create a kind of community. These are obvious pre-cursors to the popular MMORPG's.

Time has been spent discussing how technology can produce ergodic texts that create a labyrinthine experience for the reader. Some time was also spent in discussing what it means to attach the labyrinth trope to our experience of modernity and technology. In doing this we have learned that a labyrinthine experience connotes a certain kind of encounter between the subject and his or her environment. Some time was spent relating this experience to our lives within the labyrinth of the city as well as our virtual lives on the Internet.

In so doing we have seen that the labyrinth is a flexible trope given its tradition as both a verbal, visual and spatial sign. One more turn that we must take to make this discussion complete is to understand how consumerism and commodification is complicit in our lives as buyers and sellers on the Internet and where we live and do work. Given the similarity of the Internet with the labyrinthine "House of Mirrors" with its distorting glass and how advertising and marketing acts upon us by its distorting force, it may not be surprising that the concepts of the labyrinth, consumerism, and commodification have been explored. What can be said about our experience within these kinds of labyrinthine structures as it pertains to how we do business and how we live our lives within these places both virtual and "real?" To understand this further, Walter Benjamin's concept of the *flaneur* will be useful.

Benjamin's (2004) 1,000 paged book, *The Arcades Project*, begun in 1927 but first published in 1982, is itself a labyrinthine text that studies the Paris arcades which Benjamin considered to be the most important architectural form of the nineteenth century and which he linked to literary, philosophical, political, economic, and technological concerns of the time (p. ix). Benjamin (2004) sought to do this by collecting the "detritus of history, the half-concealed, variegated traces of daily life" (p. ix). The idea was to understand the modern foundation by exploring cultural artifacts from the nineteenth century. Benjamin's (2004) project was interested in examining how "high capitalism" affected our most intimate areas of life and work. He called this the "commodification of things" (p. xii). It is within this "phantasmagoria" that the *flaneur* wanders.

One general comment that could be made is that our cultural reaction to capitalism and its technology is labyrinthine in structure. The Paris arcades might best be described as a kind of proto-mall of the nineteenth century. In the following discussion we want to keep one eye on how the labyrinthine Paris arcades serve as foundational experience for the business we do as virtual flaneurs on the Internet. The following quote could almost be directly linked to the Internet although it's a description of the arcades themselves: "In the dusty, cluttered corridors of the arcades, where street and interior are one, historical time is broken up into kaleidoscopic distractions and momentary come-ons, myriad displays of ephemera, thresholds for the passage of 'the ghosts of material things" (p. xii). With its virtual corridors where the public and private merge (think of our social networking pages and our blogs) the Internet has become a site where our experiences are fragmented into all of those myriad images and virtual malls where we are so easily distracted and where material objects truly do become ghost-like. What does Benjamin say about arcades and our experience as subjects in the process of commodification? How is the labyrinth related?

Benjamin (2004) describes the arcades as a forerunner to the department store (itself a labyrinthine structure) that emerged because of a textile boom and the use of iron in the decade after 1822. The arcades were glass roofed and marble-lined corridors extending in a labyrinthine network through entire blocks of buildings. What was once exterior street became interior passage-way, "so that the passage is a city, a world in miniature" (p. 3). Like so much modern growth, the structure and form that new technology and innovation takes is labyrinthine. It is within these structures that the "universe of commodities" is propagated (p. 8), a phantasmagoria of the market which a person abandons him or herself to as a distraction (p. 14). The arcades exist as part of the city and not as a separate structure like a mall. In this way they are a kind of labyrinth within a labyrinth.

And who are the people who wander these corridors? According to Benjamin (2004), the flaneur is an alienated man. He is the private individual who exists in between the public and private worlds of work and home (p. 10). He is a threshold figure, in between the public and

private as well as the transition from pre-modern life into modern life. The flanuer is created as a type because of Paris and its arcades, a place that he wanders like a "werewolf restlessly roaming a social wilderness" (p. 418). But the flaneuer is also a casualty of the economic system in which he thrives, a place of "unfeeling isolation" and paradoxical crowding. The flaneur wanders in the crowd to become anonymous, a man of "fifty professions" (p. 428). The labyrinth is his home: "The city is the realization of that ancient dream of humanity, the labyrinth. It is this reality to which the flaneur, without knowing it, devotes himself" (p. 429). As Veel (2003) suggests in her article, the flaneur goes astray in the crowd in an act of desire and repulsion, much like one would submit themselves to a baroque maze garden (p. 160). The flaneur "turns the boredom of bourgeois life into an adventure by getting lost in the labyrinth of the streets" (p. 159). The ambiguity of modernity is represented well with the ambiguity and duality of the labyrinth trope which allows for a double perspective of being above and within at the same time. As Veel (2003) states, "For Benjamin the modern city is a place in which oppositions such as modern and archaic, sacred and profane, public and private, exterior and interior come together and demand another logic and legibility from the person who wants to navigate this space" (p. 162). The nature of the labyrinth's dual function is noticeable here as well as the nature of the subject as both viewer and walker (something that Doob does a good job of exploring). The city enables this duality in the subject and the labyrinth's dual nature as metaphor helps us understand this dizzying effect. Veel (2003) relates how Michael de Certeau in his book *Practice of Everyday Life* discusses how the city can be viewed as a map meant to be read, interpreted, and understood versus being a walker inside the city and at its mercy (p. 160). The flaneur, being a figure in between, traverses the city as one who wishes to get lost but also who seeks to orient themselves in the shifting world of commodification and phantasmagoria.

The last turn to take before returning to the Barclays and SHRM commercials is to understand how the labyrinth becomes a site for commercial contrivance and even control. The labyrinth is really an excellent trope for the creation and commercial exchange of image and identity. In "Orientalism and the Exhibitionary Order" Mitchell (1992) argues that the world is created as an endless exhibition (ex. World exhibits, museums) in which the purpose is to effect order and certainty. The artificiality creates an "external reality" in which essentialism, otherness, and absence are prevalent in the fabulation of the Orient by Westerners. That is, the exhibition and its construction creates the illusion of the "external reality" of the Orient that it portrays and then reinforces it. Representation not only creates meaning and order but it is also integral to the construction of otherness in the colonial project (p. 290). This kind of colonial construction is necessary for "the order of representation itself." As example, Mitchell (2003) discusses the reconstruction of the streets of Medieval Cairo as seen by four members of the Egyptian delegation to the Stockholdm Orientalist conference in Paris in 1889 (p. 291). Mitchell (2003) argues that Europeans have a unique concern to render the world as viewable: "Middle Eastern visitors found Europeans a curious people with an uncontainable eagerness to stand and stare" (p. 292). Many Middle Eastern accounts make note of this European penchant for curiosity as well as "a corresponding *objectness*" (p. 292). According to Egyptian accounts, the French constructed sets around visiting dignitaries for the French public: "The Khedive stayed in the imitation palace during his visit and became a part of the exhibition, receiving visitors with medieval hospitality" (p. 293). As we will see, the shape of this construction is labyrinthine, a place with no entrances or exits.

In exhibits like Mitchell is discussing, indeed within the very fabric of our commodity system which extends out into the virtual space of the In-

ternet, disorientation is experienced at the blurring line of the artificial and the real, the representation and the reality: "Exhibitions were coming to resemble the commercial machinery of the rest of the city. This machinery, in turn, was rapidly changing in places such as London and Paris, to imitate the architecture and technique of the exhibition" (p. 299). As exhibitions become more complicit with the commercial machinery of the city, this same machinery changes the architectural structure of the city to enable more exhibition effects. For example, small, individually owned shops give way to "the larger apparatus of shopping arcades and department stores....Just as exhibitions had become commercialized, the machinery of commerce was becoming a further means of engineering the real indistinguishable from that of the exhibition" (p. 299). The labyrinthine arcades tranforms the city itself. Mitchell (2003) comments that this is unique to the West and cites the first fictional account of Europe published in Arabic in 1882 which recounts a labyrinth that the Egyptian characters accidentally find themselves in when they enter a wholesale supplier, finding themselves lost in the long corridors, some of which end in mirrors and reflect images back of themselves (p. 300). Mitchell states compellingly "The West, it appears, is a place organized as a system of commodities, values, meanings, and representations, forming signs that reflect one another in a labyrinth without exits" (p. 300).

The exhibition does not cut us off from reality but persuades us that there is such a thing as objective reality which the exhibit is supposed to represent. There is no door to reality, no exit from the exhibition. The labyrinth is an obvious trope to help us understand the world arranged as an exhibit and it calls forth the "reality as stage" as portrayed in the Barclays commercial: "It is not the artificiality of the world-as-exhibition that should concern us, but the contrasting effect of a lost reality to which such supposed artificiality gives rise" (p. 300). Why doesn't the man leave the staged props of the city scene in the Barclays commercial? Because there is no "real" platform to move to, no place devoid of contrivance and plot. The labyrinth signifies the artificiality and maze-like confusion of the world wrought as consumer maze as well as the immersive "real" experience of the Orient. The exhibition persuades us the world is divided into the representation and the original; "But 'reality,' it turns out, means that which can be represented, that which presents itself as an exhibit before an observer" (p. 309). The only thing "outside" the exhibition is "a further extension of that labyrinth that we call an exhibition. What matters about this labyrinth is not that we never reach the real, never find the promised exit, but that such a notion of the real, such a system of truth, continues to convince us" (p. 313). The labyrinth as a fabricated structure, easily mistaken for "reality" with its extensive and organic nature, is the perfect trope for this dizzying effect of representations.

This discussion has sought to explain why we view our technology and working lives in the market place as labyrinths. It also has been an attempt to reflect on what it means to frame the places that we work and do business in as labyrinths. The labyrinth is a complicated trope that fits the paradoxical complexity of how we experience our modern lives. The SHRM commercial not only helps us to see the city as labyrinth but also how the labyrinth can be used to signify business and governmental organization and control. If the working environment weren't a labyrinth, one would not need a guide. One might even posit that organizations and companies like SHRM and Barclays have much invested in selling the business world as one vast labyrinth that must be navigated by professional experts (knowing full well that no escape is ever possible, only an infinite series of labyrinths). The very bureaucracies that propose exit are the ones that resemble labyrinths themselves. The labyrinth is a stage, a fabrication, something that is separated from reality but also which signifies it. The labyrinth signifies the fabricated reality that we live and work

in and what it is like to become lost within the thing we create. Capitalism expands human powers through science, technology, and rationality. In doing so as Berman (1982) tells us, it releases "demonic powers that erupt irrationality, beyond human control, with horrifying results" (p. 101). All things built must be rebuilt constantly again and again to be remade in more profitable forms. The organic disorder of the reshaping takes on the structural and functional effect of the labyrinth. It is a site of power that bureaucratic forces use to confuse and bewilder, a place that we must wander and navigate.

In case we become too distraught by all of this, Attali (1999) gives some cause for hope. Although it is considered a bad thing to be a "loser" in industrial society, we must learn to accept this disorientation and vertigo, even crave it. If we take more pleasure in being lost, we may have more opportunity to think about and reconsider the direction we are taking. In being lost we overcome fear. In straying we discover what we might not have found. As Attali rightfully tells us, "On the Internet, it is by getting lost that we find out things that we did not realize we needed to know" (p. 80). It is in the labyrinth that we best understand who we are.

## REFERENCES

Aarseth, E. J. (1997). *Cybertext: Perspectives on ergodic literature*. Baltimore, MD: Johns Hopkins University Press.

Attali, J. (1999). *Labyrinth in culture and society: Pathways to wisdom*. Berkeley, CA: North Atlantic Books.

Benjamin, W. (2004). *The arcades project*. Cambridge, MA: Harvard University Press.

Berman, M. (1982). *All that is solid melts into air: The experience of modernity*. New York, NY: Penguin.

Borges, J. (1998). The library of babel. In Hurley, A. (Ed.), *Collected fictions* (pp. 112–118). New York, NY: Penguin Books.

Doob, P. R. (1990). *The idea of the labyrinth: From classical antiquity through the middle ages*. Ithaca, NY: Cornell University Press.

Foucault, M. (1986). *Death and the labyrinth*. New York, NY: Doubleday and Co.

Kern, H. (2000). *Through the labyrinth: Designs and meanings over 5,000 years*. New York, NY: Prestel.

McCullough, D. W. (2004). *The unending mystery: A journey through labyrinths and mazes*. New York, NY: Pantheon Books.

Mitchell, T. (1992). Orientalism and the exhibitionary order. In Dirks, N. B. (Ed.), *Colonialism and culture* (pp. 289–317). Ann Arbor, MI: University of Michigan Press.

Veel, K. (2003). The irreducibility of space: labyrinths, cities, cyberspace. *Diacritics*, *33*(3-4), 151–172. doi:10.1353/dia.2006.0014

YouTube. (2001). SHRM commercial version 1. Retrieved from.http://www.youtube.com/watch?v=Now74xATro4&NR=1

YouTube. (2009). *Barclays: fake*. Retrieved from http://www.youtube.com/watch?v=-N-Htse4sPI

*This work was previously published in the International Journal of Social and Organizational Dynamics in IT, Volume 1, Issue 3, edited by Michael B. Knight, pp. 50-65, 2011 by IGI Publishing (an imprint of IGI Global).*

# Chapter 15
# Using an Ethical Framework to Examine Linkages Between "Going Green" in Research Practices and Information and Communication Technologies

**Maliha Zaman**
*Drexel University, USA*

**Claire A. Simmers**
*Saint Joseph's University, USA*

**Murugan Anandarajan**
*Drexel University, USA*

## ABSTRACT

*The link between "Going Green" in research practices and Information and Communication Technologies (ICTs) is studied using general ethics and social psychology literature. This paper investigates and concludes that a researcher's ethical judgment is the strongest factor influencing their intention to follow green research practices (GRP). Their ethical judgment is molded indirectly by the researcher's attitude towards environmental awareness. Their intention towards GRP is influenced by existing research practices and experience in using a technology touted as a greening enabler, Web 2.0. The strength of the relationship suggests there is no pivotal turning point in the research practices to become green. This paper concludes that GRP represent a smaller, albeit important, paradigm shift affecting the conduct and dissemination of research with positive spillover effects for the environment.*

DOI: 10.4018/978-1-4666-1948-7.ch015

## INTRODUCTION

Researchers are probably unthought-of offenders in increasing the world's carbon footprint. In this article, we examine the transition from research practices anchored mainly in travel and paper (what we call traditional research practices) to work facilitated by Information Communication Technologies (what we call green research practices). We argue that research work using Information Communication Technologies (ICT's) is a part of a paradigm shift in researchers' attitudes and behaviors towards "Going Green." We view "Going Green" in research practices, not as change representing a pivotal turning point in scientific development as described by Kuhn in his influential work, *The Structure of Scientific Revolutions* (1970). Instead, we propose that green research practices represent a smaller, albeit important, shift affecting the conduct and dissemination of research with positive spillover effects for our environment. While Kuhn's (1970) focus was on the process of scientific discovery in a general context, subsequent scholarly work extended his theory to many disciplines and types of changes (Driver-Linn, 2003; Jones, 2008; McDonagh, 1976; Polsby, 1998; Price, 2006). We also propose using Kuhn's (1970) work as a superstructure in our attempt to understand the adoption of green research practices. Our interest in this topic is in response to a general study of research practices in the digital age which called for scholarly communication and the development of a research infrastructure, that was coherent, and *sustainable* (emphasis added) (Houghton, Steele, & Henty, 2003 p. ix). To date, however, we found no studies answering this call. Our study begins to address this gap by examining, within an ethical framework, the intentions of researchers to use greening practices enabled by ICTs. We first offer a summary of Kuhn's theory and its application to our work. Then we detail our research objectives, followed next by our proposed model and

hypotheses. We conclude with our methodology, results, and discussion.

Kuhn (1970) wanted to understand better, how scientific knowledge grew. He suggested that the development of scientific knowledge was characterized by periods of calm acceptance of the current scientific knowledge, punctuated by revolutions of change. The growth of scientific knowledge was not based on seamless transitions, but rather he saw distinct stages when rival theories stood together with ensuing periods of argument, sometimes, heated, and the eventual adoption of one theory (Polsby, 1998). Central to Kuhn (1970) is the importance of social-psychological elements in change; mechanisms of persuasion and judgment within a community of scientists blend with logical proofs as the conversion process from an old to a new paradigm enfolds (McDonagh, 1976). One of the critical contributions of Kuhn (1970) is the expansion of science from traditional cognitive components to include affective and normative components. All scientific discoveries reveal a process of psychological transformation with the increasing awareness of an anomaly, the gradual and simultaneous emergence of both observational and conceptual recognition of alternatives and the replacement of the existing theory, all accompanied by resistance. Key to emerging as the "winning" alternative is the ability to communicate and persuade.

It is not always possible to know which innovation will "win" (Rogers, 2003) until an innovation becomes part of the organizational life. We suggest that the linkage of going green in research practices with information and communication technologies is an innovation in the early stages before what Kuhn calls the phenomenon of "conversion" (Polsby, 1998). Consistent with Kuhn (1970) we develop a research model that includes both affective and normative components and seek to understand how the traditional ways of conducting research maybe transitioning to the digital ways of conducting research.

## RESEARCH OBJECTIVES

"Going Green" or "Doing Green" is a very popular phenomenon for organizations and individuals; sustainability is at the heart of the movement to go green. The World Commission on Environment and Development (United Nations, 1987, p. 8) described sustainable development as: "Humanity has the ability to make development sustainable –to ensure that it meets the needs of the present without compromising the ability of future generations to meet their own needs." There are numerous activities under the greening movement umbrella, for example, conserving forests, decreasing pollution, lowering the carbon footprint, producing eco-friendly goods, and creating green process (Boerner, 2008). Researchers investigated many aspects of the green movement already, the majority of these investigations focused on the green behaviors of consumers (Chan, Wong, & Leung, 2008; Manaktola & Jauhari, 2007; Phau & Ong, 2007) or organizations (Florida & Davison, 2001; Harris & Crane, 2002; Peng & Lin, 2008). Most of these studies broadly study consumer or organizational practices within general ethics literature (Shaw & Shiu, 2003) or the ethics of examining specific consumer practices such as bringing your own bags to the store (Chan et al., 2008), and grocery shopping (Memery, Megicks, & Williams, 2005). The findings suggest that ethical beliefs (Chan et al., 2008) and environmental beliefs (D'Souza, Taghian, & Khosla, 2007) anchor greening decisions among consumers. Greening research on the organizational level uses firm level frameworks such as organizational learning (Zhu, Sarkis, Cordeiro, & Hung, 2008), institutional theory (Peng & Lin, 2008) and organizational culture (Harris & Crane, 2002). Most found positive linkages with green management adoption.

At an individual level, studies have neither focused on the willingness of researchers to follow green behaviors in their research nor empirically investigated the enabling role of ICTs, particularly Web 2.0 in their decisions to work green. Researchers as a work group is an important occupational group, rising from an estimated 5.8 million worldwide in 2002 to 7.1 million in 2007 (UNESCO, 2009). Thus given the rising popularity of the greening movement and the increasing number of researchers, we feel it is important to examine researchers' green research intentions. Additionally, since Information and Communication Technologies are so pervasive in the workplace, we are interested in the role that ICTs play in greening decisions among researchers.

Information and Communication Technologies, defined by Preston (2004, p. 35) as "the cluster or interrelated systems of technological innovations in the fields of microelectronics, computing, electronic communications including broadcasting and the Internet…" is part of everyday professional and personal life (Mansell, Avegerou, & Silverstone, 2009). A subset of ICTs is Web 2.0 technologies, described by O'Reilly (2005), as person-to-person online communication tools for connecting, communicating, and collaborating, thus creating communities of like-minded individuals. Web 2.0 represents changing trends in the use of the World Wide Web technology and web design that aim to enhance creativity, communications, secure information sharing, collaboration and functionality of the web. Web 2.0 concepts led to the development and evolution of interactive web culture communities and hosted services such as social–networking sites, video sharing sites, wikis, and blogs (Campesato & Nilson, 2010). Even though the term Web 2.0 is identified as a consumer phenomenon, the technology behind it being adopted in organizations as well (Daft, 2009). Organizations are using Web 2.0 technologies to streamline their processes in areas of collaboration (Coleman & Levine, 2008), business communication (Flynn, 2006) and knowledge management (Lytras, Damiani, & Ordóñez de Pablos, 2008). All of which could contribute towards the greening movement even though it may not have been their initial objective for implementing Web 2.0; in such ways as reducing the amount of paper generated in printing, and reducing the need for travel. Although there is also some work which suggests that researchers should use Web 2.0 technology to enhance productivity (McKinnon, 2009; Zhang, Cheung, & Townsend, 2008). To date, there is little empirical work on the Web 2.0 technology linkage with green researcher practices.

Consistent with prior work examining greening decisions at the individual level (Chan et al., 2008; D'Souza et al., 2007), we use an ethical theoretical framework to present and test a model delineating the major factors likely to affect researchers' intentions to use green research practices (called "green research practices" or "GRP" intention). GRP is defined in this paper as any measure (e.g. reading articles online vs. printing them on paper first) taken by researchers to contribute towards the "greening" movement. We propose that researchers can contribute to the "greening" movement by modifying their practices to use more Web 2.0 technologies in their work. We seek to further our understanding of how researchers' current research practices, their experiences with Web 2.0 technology, their "green" attitudes and behaviors and their basic moral philosophies influence their ethical judgment concerning GRPs and their intention to engage in these practices (WGRPs intention). In the following sections, we review the literature on current research practices using ICTs, we then present our research framework and model, concluding with the hypotheses we seek to test.

## Research Practices and Information Communication Technologies

Earlier studies on researchers and the use of new Information and Communication Technologies in scholarly work found that although usage was low, external demand for sharing as well as the necessary infrastructure increased electronic communication practices (Walsh & Bayma, 1997). The institutional and social environment within the organization also affected the adoption of ICTs in research work. Lack of institutional support through incentive systems meant less likelihood of the usage of ICTs in research practices, even if the technology was available (Budd & Connaway, 1997). At a social level, the influence of less technologically experienced mentors and senior faculty constrained the adoption of ICTs, even by more technological savvy junior faculty and doctoral students (Covi, 2000).

More recently, the rapid advances in ICTs sparked a growing trend for collaborative research and an internationalization of collaborative activity (Houghton & Schmidt, 2005; Vincent-Lancrin, 2006). According to a comprehensive Australian study on research practices (Houghton & Schmidt, 2005), project team communication was primarily via frequent e-mails and phone calls. Face-to-face interactions, even with substantial travel, were important to a quarter of the respondents. An average of seventy-five percent of survey respondents searched and browsed online. However, only 10% reported reading and studying online; the clear preference was for using printed documents. E-mail was the principal means for circulation of papers within both project teams and the wider networks of research and scholarship. Few indicated that they put material on institutional or personal websites. An important conclusion of the study was

New digital object access management systems will be required, and there will be increasing demand for collaborative research support applications and research support systems that enable researchers to bring together the increasingly disparate digital objects used in research in such a way as to facilitate enhanced integrated analysis (Houghton & Schmidt, 2005, p. 127)

In the 1990's studies, the predominant research practice was paper-based. By the early 2000's, we see most researchers using localized ICTs such as email and computer storage primarily resident on local computers. These localized ICTs became known as Web 1.0. The popular term Web 2.0

*Figure 1. Key elements of web 2.0*

Source: (Anandarajan et al., 2008)

became increasingly common during the early 2000's . The key aspects of Web 2.0 technology (Figure 1) are "the interconnectivity and interactivity of web-delivered content" all being generated by the users themselves (Anandarajan, Arinze, Govindarajulu, & Zaman, 2009; De Kool & Van Wamelen, 2008; Lai & Turban, 2008; Zhang et al., 2008).

Web 2.0 is proposed here as a critical enabling technology (Deering, Van Hall, Jonk, & Cook, 2008) making Green Research Practices possible. Web 2.0 consists not only of applications driven

by software but by network databases driven by explicit or of implicit user contribution (O' Reilly, 2008). Table 1 summarizes the changes in research process that are now possible based on the evolution of capabilities (Coleman & Levine, 2008; Nickull, Governor, & Hinchcliffe, 2009) from Web 1.0 to Web 2.0.

*Table 1. Differences in research practices based on information and communication technologies*

| Research tasks | Pre Web1.0 | Web 1.0 | Web 2.0 |
|---|---|---|---|
| Document storage | All hard copies | Some Soft copies | Online – remotely Mostly soft copies |
| Document transfer | Snail mail, physical delivery | Email, snail mail | Centrally located virtually– accessible by all with permission |
| Travel | Physically to location | Physically to location | Web conferencing, some physical travels |
| Collaboration | Restricted to college, department | Conferences, ease of interaction due to e-mail | Research 2.0 web applications e.g. MyNetResearch.com |
| Research topic | Restricted to one field Geographically restricted | Restricted to one field Wider research scope | Inter and Intra fields of research. Global perspective |

## PROPOSED MODEL AND HYPOTHESES

This study uses the basic ethical decision making model proposed by Hunt and Vitell (1986) which attempts to explain the "decision-making process of marketers involved in ethical situations" (Rallapalli & Vitell, 1998, p. 158). The model used here is a modified version of the original model and does not include the constructs personal experience (e.g. moral development) or those related to cultural, industry or organization environment. Our model proposes the construct Environmental Awareness influences Ethical Judgment indirectly through deontological evaluation like Teleological evaluation. Furthermore, true to the original mode both Ethical Judgment and Teleological evaluation will influence researcher's Intention to use GRP. The Intention to USE GRP is also proposed to be influenced by researcher's Web 2.0 experience and their existing research practices (Figure 2).

## General Theory of Marketing Ethics

An individual, when faced with making an ethical judgment, considers a set of action-based alternatives. These alternatives stem from a person's deontological (duty-based) and teleological (goal-based) evaluations. Deontological evaluation is conducted by applying deontological norms elicited by the ethical dilemma to each alternative. Deontological norms are predetermined guidelines based on independent, moral rights and duties focusing on what are right rather than the result). For example, the act of printing out long documents when the material is possible to read on the computer should be avoided not because it is detrimental to someone else but because the act in itself is wrong. In short, evaluation is based on the inherent righteousness of an action (Murphy & Lacxnial, 1981). Teleological evaluations on the other hand stress the end result or consequence of an individual's action. For example, an individual may consider the consequence on the forest and environment before printing the next document. According to the model, these two evaluations influence a person's ethical judgment and sub-

*Figure 2. Proposed model*

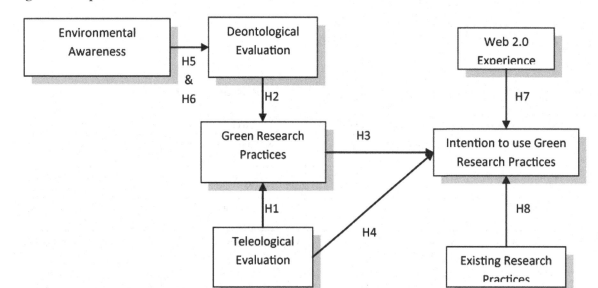

sequently, their intention to carry out an action. The action investigated in this study is the use of GRP by researchers.

Based on discussion above, we propose that a researcher, before reaching a decision on their intention to use GRP, will first evaluate the alternatives based on deontological and teleological considerations and come to an ethical judgment. This judgment will have a direct influence on the final intention of the researcher. Hence:

Hypothesis 1: Teleological evaluations influence the ethical judgment of researchers on green research practices

Hypothesis 2: Deontological evaluations influence the ethical judgment of researchers on green research practices

Hypothesis 3: The ethical judgments of researcher's on green research practices influence intentions to use green research practices

The model also postulates that in some instances, a person may bypass their ethical judgment to achieve or avoid specific consequences (Chan et al., 2008). Hence:

Hypothesis 4: Teleological evaluations directly influence a researcher's intentions to use green research practices

## Environmental Awareness

Deontological norms present "rules of behavior" (Hunt & Vitell, 1986, p. 9). According to Hunt and Vitell (1986), deontological norms can range from "general beliefs" (e.g. cheating) to "issue-specific beliefs" (e.g. environmental effect on global warming). For this study, deontological norms represent issue-specific beliefs on a broad range of environmental issues. A researcher's environmental awareness represents their attitude and 'rules of behavior' towards environmental issues which in turn may influence whether they believe it is a duty to be green and how they will behave. Hence:

Hypothesis 5: Attitudes towards general environmental issues significantly influence a researcher's deontological evaluation of green research practices

Hypothesis 6: Behavior towards general environmental issues influences a researcher's deontological evaluation of green research practices

## Web 2.0 Experience

We use the theory of Planned Behavior (TPB) (Ajzen, 1991; Ajzen & Fishbein, 1980) to explain the connection of Web 2.0 experience to intentions to use Green Research Practices. A person's perceived behavioral control influences their behavioral intention. Perceived behavioral control refers to people's perceptions of their abilities to perform a given activity (Ajzen, 1991; Ajzen & Fishbein, 1980). Social psychology literature suggests that experience on performing the activity forms this perception (Ajzen, 1991; Ajzen & Fishbein, 1980; Chan et al., 2008; Conner & Armitage, 1998). Hence, experience is an important determinant of intention (Taylor & Todd, 1995). Knowledge needed to influence intention towards an activity is made "more accessible" (Taylor & Todd, 1995, p. 563) by the experience a person has with that activity (Aarts, Verplanken, & van Knippenberg, 1998; Karahanna & Straub, 1999; Taylor & Todd, 1995). However, a recent study by Bamberg, Rolle, and Weber (2003) found that experience at times might not be a strong predictor of behavioral intention. Based on these contradictory findings, this study investigates whether a researcher's experience with Web 2.0 will influence their intention to use green research practices. Following prevailing knowledge, we predict that, a researcher with Web 2.0 experience is likely to have positive behavioral intentions towards green research practices. Hence:

Hypothesis 7: A Researcher's Web 2.0 experience will positively influence their intention to use green research practices.

## Existing Research Practices (Habit)

Habit is a "learned sequences of act that become automatic responses to specific situations which may be functional in obtaining certain goals or end states" (Verplanken, Aarts, & van Knippenberg, 1997, p. 540). An individual's "past behavior guides their future responses" and diverts them from adopting less known courses of action. Habit has been conceptualized in myriad of ways such as a goal oriented automatic behavior, a past behavior or a non-conscious activation (Limayem, Hirt, & Cheung, 2007, p. 710). There is, however, a general agreement that habit formation requires a certain amount of repetition, a satisfactory experience and a stable context (Limayem et al., 2007). The presence of similar cues, e.g. the habit of checking email, when one sees a computer in a room, characterizes a stable context. For this study, we argue that researchers who have existing green research habits were sufficiently satisfied with the practices for them to repeat the practices. Furthermore, under the stable context of being green, researchers whose existing habits promote being green are likely to have the intention to adopt green research practices using Web 2.0. Hence:

Hypothesis 8: A researcher's existing research habits significantly influence their intention towards the use of green research practices.

## METHODOLOGY

### Survey Sample

We used an online survey to collect the data. Major advantages of online surveys are low financial resource implications, short response time, and the ability to load data directly to the data analysis software (Ilieva, Baron, & Healey, 2002). We adopted a diversified but focused sample of 500 U.S. researchers from a mailing list and sent email invitations. Participants clicked on a link in the email to take them to the survey site. At the beginning and in the middle of the survey we included a definition of Green Research Practices as "Researchers can contribute to the "greening" movement by changing their practices in several ways such as reducing the amount of paper generated in printing, reducing travel, and conducting research using online research portals. Collectively we call these 'Green Research Practices'.

Our response rate was 44.6% and resulted in a total of 224 data points. Out of these 223 were suitable for the analysis. We captured demographic data on gender (male = 1 and female = 2); age (using a six point range scale from younger than 30 to older than 70); job title (Professor to doctoral student); discipline (Arts and Humanities, Business, Clinical Medicine, Engineering, Life Sciences, Natural Sciences and Social Sciences); and research experience (a six point range scale from less than one year to more than 20 years). A summary of description of the sample is provided in Table 2.

Female researchers represented fifty-seven percent of the sample. The majority of the respondents (36%) were from the field of Social Sciences. Clinical Medicine, Life Sciences and Natural Sciences disciplines each had between 10-15% of the respondents. Close to half of the respondents (47%) had been a researcher for 1-7 years, about one fourth (24%) had 7-10 years of research experience, and over twenty five percent had been doing research for over ten years. Forty-five percent of the respondents were between the ages of 31-40; close to a quarter (23%) were between the ages of 41-50 years. Sixty-three percent of the respondents were Assistant Professors.

### Measures

The items used in the study are provided in the Appendix section and are examined below:

*Existing Research Practices:* Questions, created for this survey, focused on printing and

*Table 2. Descriptive statistics of data sample (rounded off percentages)*

| | | |
|---|---|---|
| Gender | Female | 57% |
| | Male | 43% |
| Age | 31-40 | 45% |
| | 41-50 | 23% |
| | >50 | 32% |
| Researcher experience | 1-7 years | 47% |
| | 7-10 years | 24% |
| | >10 years | 29% |
| Job Title | Assistant Professor | 63% |
| | Associate Professor | 10% |
| | Professor | 8% |
| Research Discipline | Arts and Humanities | 11% |
| | Business | 12% |
| | Clinical Medicine | 4% |
| | Engineering | 5% |
| | Life Science | 14% |
| | Natural Sciences | 12% |
| | Social Sciences | 36% |

reading practices. We asked about printing paper copies of electronic copies (reverse coded), printing copies of drafts (reverse coded) and preferring to read publications online. The anchor points for all questions were 1 = "Never" to 7 = "Always"; higher scores measuring more "green" existing research practices.

*Web 2.0 Experience:* We measured Web 2.0 Experience by creating a question asking how often (1 = "Daily" to 6 = "Not familiar") respondents used six technologies in their research. The technologies (blogs, wikis, RSS News Feeds, Online research management portals, Social Networking Services and Video Sharing) are common Web 2.0 technologies. We reverse coded the answers so that higher scores reflected more experienced Web 2.0 users.

*Environmental Awareness:* We adopted four questions on attitude and four questions on behavior from Lee, 2008. We asked for a degree on agreement (1="Strongly Disagree" to 7="Strongly Agree") on four statements. For example, ""It is essential to promote green living" for attitude and "I usually promote pro-environmental behaviors to my friends" for behavior.

*Deontological evaluation (DE):* We measured deontological evaluation consistent with Chan et al. (2008) and Reidenbach and Robin (1990), but modified it to reflect the subject of this study: *"Considering your own norms and values, how would you evaluate Green Research Practices?"* Three items captured respondents view on this question "not duty-bound to act this way"/"duty-bound to act this way""; not morally right/morally right"; and "not obligated to act this way/obligated to act this way". The anchor points of these items were -3 to +3. We used the composite score derived from these items to represent DE.

*Teleological evaluation (TE):* We adapted Cherry and Fraedrich's (2002) approach to operationalize teleological evaluation. Specifically, we identified several major possible consequences relating to the Green Research Practice, emulating Ajzen and Fishbein's (1980) elicitation procedure. The procedure led to the identification of four major consequences: (1) saving paper; (2) traveling less thus polluting less; (3) conserving forestlands; and (4) being concerned about the environment. For each of these consequences, respondents were then asked to rate the desirability of each consequence on a seven-point item anchored by 1 = "Very Undesirable" and "7 = "Very Desirable." They were then asked to rate the likelihood on a seven-point item anchored by 1 = "Very Unlikely" to 7 = "Very Likely" that Green Research Practices would (1) save paper; (2) reduce travel and thus pollution; (3) conserve forest lands; and (4) overall be good for the environment. We derived a weighted score for each consequence by multiplying its desirability score with its likelihood score. The summated average of all these weighted scores represented TE.

*Green Research Practice Ethical Judgment (EJ):* We adapted a question from previous work (Dabholkar & Kellaris, 1992; Mayo & Marks, 1990), and asked, *"Considering your own norms and values, and the desirability of the estimated outcomes, how would you judge green research practices?"* Four seven-point items (-3 to +3) captured the respondents' replies. The anchor points of these items were "unacceptable/acceptable," "unethical/ethical," "wrong/right," and "bad/good," respectively. EJ represented a composite score derived from these items.

*Intention to Use Green Research Practices:* We modified a previous scale (Chan et al., 2008) by asking respondents to indicate their willingness to perform each of the following behaviors: (1) to pay a nominal amount to move to Green Research Practices; (2) to change my research to follow Green Research Practices, and (3) to advocate for Green Research Practices. We used a seven point scale from 1 = "Very Unwilling" to 7 = "Very willing and averaged the scores to derive a measure of Intention to Use Green Research Practices.

## DATA ANALYSIS AND RESULTS

We tested the hypothesized relationships in this study using structured equation modeling (SEM). This second-generation multivariate technique facilitates testing of the psychometric properties of the scales used to measure a variable, and estimates the parameters of a structural model, i.e., the strength and direction of the relationships among the model variables (Fornell & Larcker, 1981).

We used multiple indicators of latent variables to estimate measurement error and reduce the bias effects of random and systematic errors (Williams & Hazer, 1986). To assess discriminant validity of the measures, i.e., the degree to which items differentiate among constructs or measure distinct concept (Churchill, 1979; Straub, 1989), we examined the correlations between the measures of potentially overlapping constructs. The use of latent variables requires a two-stage analysis (Anderson & Gerbing, 1988). The first stage includes the assessment of the measurement model and the evaluation of the construct independence, while the second stage provides verification for the structural model. Confirmatory factor analysis discriminates the theoretical constructs and validates the operational measures of the constructs.

### Measurement Model

To test the measurement model, we used a confirmatory factor analysis in AMOS 7.0. To assess the model's overall goodness of fit, we utilized four common model fit measures. The overall measurement model had a $\chi^2$/d.f.=2.97; marginally below the three (3) recommended by Bagozzi and Yi, (1988). The goodness-of-fit index (GFI=0.91) and comparative fit index (CFI = 0.96) exceeded the recommended cut-off level of 0.9 (Alwin & Hauser, 1975). The adjusted goodness-of-fit index (AGFI = .87) also exceeded the recommended cut-off level of 0.8 (Bentler, 1990). The root mean square error of approximation (RMSEA =

0.058) was just below the cut-off level of 0.06 as recommended by Browne and Cudeck (1993).

Table 3 summarizes the results of confirmatory factor analysis - the degree to which multiple attempts to measure the same concept are in agreement derived by examining the factor loading within each construct and composite reliability. The factor loading for all items exceeded the recommended level of 0.7, the cutoff number that most researchers use (except for Tele_4 - factor loading of 0.69 which is just below 0.7). We concluded that all composite reliability measures of constructs exceeded the recommended level of 0.7 (Bagozzi

& Yi, 1988). The correlations of potentially overlapping constructs assessed discriminant validity. No pair of measures had correlations exceeding the criterion (0.9 and above), suggested by Hair et al., 1998, implying that multicollinearity was not a concern in this study. To examine further discriminant validity, the shared variance between the factors we contrasted with the average variance extracted of the individual factors (Fornell & Larcker, 1981). This analysis showed that the shared variance between factors was lower than the average variance extracted of the individual factors, which confirmed discriminatory validity

*Table 3. Confirmatory factor analysis*

| Latent Constructs | Items | Factor Loadings | Composite Reliability |
|---|---|---|---|
| Environmental Awareness | EA1 | .950 | .947 |
| | EA2 | .965 | |
| | EA3 | .880 | |
| | EA4 | .823 | |
| Environmental Attitude and Behavior | EAB1 | .836 | .849 |
| | EAB2 | .860 | |
| | EAB3 | .746 | |
| | EAB4 | .723 | |
| Deontological Evaluation | DE1 | .894 | .752 |
| | DE2 | .813 | |
| | DE3 | .820 | |
| Teleological Evaluation | TE1 | .796 | .847 |
| | TE2 | .795 | |
| | TE3 | .896 | |
| | TE4 | .833 | |
| Ethical Judgment | EJ1 | .835 | .946 |
| | EJ2 | .854 | |
| | EJ3 | .960 | |
| | EJ4 | .937 | |
| Intentions | INT1 | .774 | .861 |
| | INT2 | .817 | |
| | INT3 | .830 | |
| Existing Research Practices | ERP1 | .818 | .761 |
| | ERP2 | .672 | |
| | ERP3 | .880 | |

(Campbell & Fiske, 1959). Based on our analyses, we concluded that the measurement model demonstrated adequate reliability, convergent validity, and discriminant validity.

## STRUCTURAL MODEL

Given the satisfactory results in the measurement model, we then examined the structural model to test the relationships among the constructs (Figure 3). The structural model has a chi-square of 262.8 ($\chi^2$/d.f.=1.87). Other fit indexes included the goodness-of-fit index (GFI = 0.922), and comparative fit index (CFI = 0.97). The adjusted goodness-of-fit index (AGFI = .89), and the root mean square error of approximation (RMSEA = 0.051). The combination of these results suggested that the demonstrated measurement model fit the data. To test the structural model, the path coefficient of an exogenous variable delineates the direct effect of that variable on the endogenous variables.

We found support for all of our hypotheses. The relationship between existing research practices and intention was positive, ($\beta = 0.199$, $p < 0.01$), thus supporting H1. Web 2.0 Experience was significantly related to intention ($\beta = 0.146$, $p < 0.01$), supporting H2. Our results supported both parts of H3. The positive direct relationship between Environmental Awareness - attitudes and Deontological Evaluation (DE) was significant ($\beta = 0.346$, $p < 0.001$) as was the relationship between Environmental Awareness behavior and DE ($\beta = 0.151$, $p < 0.01$). H4 and H5a were supported with both DE and Teleological evaluation (TE) having a direct effect on Green Research Practices Ethical Judgment ($\beta = 0.241$, $p < 0.01$) and ($\beta = 0.546$, $p < 0.001$) respectively. H5b and H6 tested the effect of TE and ethical judgment and on intention to use Green Research Practices. Both hypotheses were supported with H5b ($\beta = 0.346$, $p<0.001$) and H6 ($\beta = 0.504$, $p < 0.001$). Altogether, the variables accounted for 61% of the variance in willingness. The demographic variables had no effect in the model.

*Figure 3. Structural model*

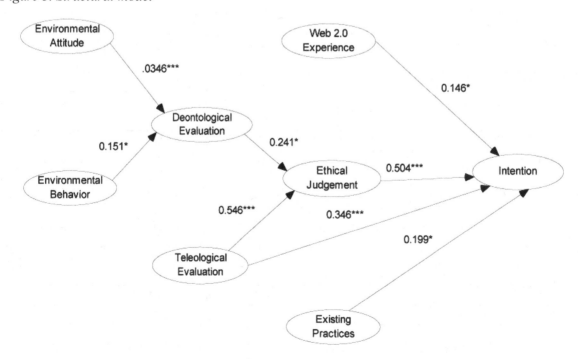

## DISCUSSION

We wanted to examine the factors likely to affect researchers' intentions to use green research practices (called green research practices (GRP) intention). We believed that researchers can contribute to the "greening" movement by changing their practices to conduct research using online research portals (Web 2.0 technology) reducing the amount of paper generated in printing and reducing the carbon footprint by reducing travel. This study made several important contributions.

First, the structural equation model provided insights into the applicability of ethical concepts in a green related context. Specifically, the analyses highlighted that researchers' deontological and teleological evaluations of Green Research Practices directly affect their GRP ethical judgment (i.e., support for H4 and H5a). The analyses also suggested that researchers are more likely to affirm or use their ethical judgment to arrive at their GRP intention (i.e., the coefficient is higher for H5a than H5b), contrary to the study of Chan et al. (2008). Overall, these findings echo a number of important propositions of the H-V theory, and help remind researchers investigating sustainability issues of the potential for applying well-grounded general ethics theories to study eco-friendly practices.

Second, our use of a sample of researchers from many disciplines rather than consumers or organizations, is an important contribution. As researchers, we should also examine our own work practices to see where we might contribute to sustainability. We also linked our study to a particular way of working green, and that is the use of Web 2.0 technology as a way to reduce our paper consumption and decrease our carbon footprint by reducing travel. Additionally, we found, consistent with earlier work (Houghton et al., 2003; Walsh & Bayma, 1997), that usage lags behind attitudes and intentions. Only half the respondents reported using green practices in their current work and most reported not using Web 2.0 technologies in their research. We also found that

environmental awareness behavior had a weaker relationship with deontological evaluation than environmental awareness attitudes (H3). These findings may explain the weaker direct relationship with GRP judgment and DE.

The lag between attitudes/intentions and behaviors might be partially explained by the presence of other "external control factors." Earlier research (Budd & Connaway, 1997; Covi, 2000; Harris & Crane, 2002) highlighted the importance of outside circumstances facilitating or interfering with, the performance of an individual's behavior. Researchers also work within organizations and professional societies which exert influence on their behaviors. Another set of factors influencing technology adoption are individual personality characteristics (Ouadahi, 2008). External factors and individual characteristics together may explain some of the gap between attitudes/intentions and behaviors and is consistent with one aspect of a Kuhnsian model of change that is, affective and normative components are important in understanding any change process (Kuhn, 1970). An important new idea – the use of ICTs by researchers to support green efforts – which may later prevail, is not immediately accepted (Polsby, 1998). Our results thus lend support for the importance of social construction and a lengthy conversion process.

However, the lag between attitudes and behaviors is somewhat of a surprising finding given the demographics of our sample which was young (45% 31-40 years old), relatively new to their professions (47% 1-7 years of experience), and assistant professors (63%). This is the demographic which one might expect to champion changes in research practices (Kuhn, 1970), as they are less established in the research stream. An area for future research is to include sample from a population of graduate students, and newly minted Ph.D. with less vested interests in doing research in the traditional ways.

Our findings show strong support for the mediating role of GRP ethical judgment (H4, H5a and H6) between the two basic moral perspectives (deontological and teleological) and GRP intentions which is consistent with the H-V theory and contrary to previous studies (Chan et al., 2008). Furthermore, our findings showed that teleological evaluations had a stronger relationship with green research practices ethical judgment than deontological evaluation (H4 and H5a). This suggests the need to emphasize the tangible consequences of going green and explicitly link to the "greening" potential of Web 2.0 technologies when encouraging researchers on "growing green."

## Limitations

A major limitation is that our sample is from one country; an international sample would provide robustness. We also did not include personality variables or contextual variables in our model. While survey data is valuable, given the strength of the relationships in our primarily attitudinal/ intentional model, a qualitative study would delve deeper into the apparent gap between attitudes/ intentions and behaviors. Furthermore, we did not examine a wide range of potential green research practices. One of respondents commented that there are many opportunities for recycling, especially in a lab setting, that we did not include.

## CONCLUSION

A general ethics perspective and social psychology literature, within the framework of Kuhn's work on paradigm shifts, offers researchers a way to understand better how their research practices might reduce the carbon footprint through reducing paper and travel by increasing utilization of ICT's. We presented a model of how various factors affected Green Research Practices intention. We empirically tested our hypotheses using a survey of 223 U.S. based researchers. Overall, the findings supported the direct influence of the hypothesized relationships. Our results sug-

gested Existing Research Practices and Web 2.0 Experience directly influenced GRP intention. Environmental Awareness attitudes and behaviors directly influenced Deontological evaluation, but attitudes were a stronger influence than behavior. Deontological evaluation and teleological evaluation positively influenced GRP ethical judgment. Teleological evaluation exerted a stronger influence on ethical judgment than deontological evaluation. There was a direct positive effect of ethical judgment and teleological evaluation on Intention to use GRP. In addition, the findings revealed that researchers' actual behaviors lagged both intentions and technological capability as only half of the respondents reported using green research practices and most did not use Web 2.0 technologies in their research. Academically, these findings provided some encouraging evidence for the application of general ethics theories to examine greening related practices among researchers (an under-studied group). Practically, the findings suggested that a functional approach (i.e., emphasizing the contributions of Web 2.0 technology to GRP) might represent just one effective means to promote GRPs among researchers. However, since our work is another example supporting Kuhn's (1970) proposition that behavior is not connected solely to logic, but is synergistic with choices based on multifarious amalgamations of feelings, thoughts, and norms, we suggest that the adoption of green research practices using ICT's is a socially constructed phenomenon. We hope our study is one among many steps towards more discussion calling into question existing research practices culminating in sufficient critical mass to adopt green research practices.

# REFERENCES

Aarts, H., Verplanken, B., & van Knippenberg, A. (1998). Predicting behavior from actions in the past: Repeated decision making or a matter of habit? *Journal of Applied Social Psychology*, *28*, 1355–1374. doi:10.1111/j.1559-1816.1998.tb01681.x

Ajzen, A. A. (1991). The theory of planned behaivor. *Organizational Behavior and Human Decision Processes*, *50*(2), 179–211. doi:10.1016/0749-5978(91)90020-T

Ajzen, A. A., & Fishbein, M. (1980). *Understanding attitudes and predicting social behavior*. Upper Saddle River, NJ: Prentice-Hall.

Alwin, D. F., & Hauser, R. M. (1975). The decomposition of effects in path analysis. *American Sociological Review*, *40*(1), 37–47. doi:10.2307/2094445

Anandarajan, M., Arinze, B., Govindarajulu, C., & Zaman, M. (2009). *Emerging technologies: Selected technologies holding potential*. Hoboken, NJ: John Wiley & Sons.

Anderson, J. C., & Gerbing, D. W. (1988). Structural equation modeling in practice: A review and recommended two-step approach. *Psychological Bulletin*, *103*(3), 411–423. doi:10.1037/0033-2909.103.3.411

Bagozzi, R. P., & Yi, Y. (1988). On the evaluation of structural equation models. *Journal of the Academy of Marketing Science*, *16*(1), 74–94. doi:10.1007/BF02723327

Bamberg, S., Rolle, D., & Weber, C. (2003). Does habitual car use not lead to more resistance to change of travel mode? *Transportation*, *30*(1), 97–108. doi:10.1023/A:1021282523910

Bentler, P. M. (1990). Comparative fit indexes in structural models. *Psychological Bulletin*, *107*(2), 238–246. doi:10.1037/0033-2909.107.2.238

Boerner, H. (2008). The greening of public corporations. *Corporate Finance Review*, *13*(2), 32–35.

Browne, M. W., & Cudeck, R. (Eds.). (1993). *Alternative ways of assessing model fit*. London, UK: Sage.

Budd, J. M., & Connaway, L. S. (1997). University faculty and networked information: Results of a survey. *Journal of the American Society for Information Science American Society for Information Science*, *48*(9), 348–357. doi:10.1002/(SICI)1097-4571(199709)48:9<843::AID-ASI8>3.0.CO;2-R

Campbell, D. T., & Fiske, D. W. (1959). Convergent and discriminant validation by the multitrait-multimethod matrix. *Psychological Bulletin*, *56*(2), 81–105. doi:10.1037/h0046016

Campesato, O., & Nilson, K. (2010). *Web 2. 0 fundamentals for developers*. Sudbury, MA: Jones & Bartlett Learning.

Chan, R. Y. K., Wong, Y. H., & Leung, T. K. P. (2008). Applying ethical concepts to the study of "Green" consumer behavior: An analysis of chinese consumers' intentions to bring their own shopping bags. *Journal of Business Ethics*, *79*(4), 469–481. doi:10.1007/s10551-007-9410-8

Cherry, J., & Fraedrich, J. (2002). Perceived risk, moral philosophy and marketing ethics: mediating influences on sales managers ethical decision making. *Journal of Business Research*, *55*(12), 951–962. doi:10.1016/S0148-2963(00)00215-0

Churchill, G. A. J. (1979). A paradigm for developing better measures of marketing constructs. *JMR, Journal of Marketing Research*, *16*(1), 64–73. doi:10.2307/3150876

Coleman, D., & Levine, S. (2008). *Collaboration 2.0: Technology and best practices for successful collaboration in a Web 2.0 world*. Silicon Valley, CA: Happy About.

Conner, M., & Armitage, C. J. (1998). Extending the theory of planned behavior: A review and avenues for further research. *Journal of Applied Social Psychology, 28*(15), 1429–1464. doi:10.1111/j.1559-1816.1998.tb01685.x

Covi, L. M. (2000). Debunking the myth of the Nintendo generation: How doctoral students introduce new electronic communication practices into university research. *Journal of the American Society for Information Science American Society for Information Science, 51*(17), 1284–1294. doi:10.1002/1097-4571(2000)9999:9999<::AID-ASI1045>3.0.CO;2-Z

D'Souza, C., Taghian, M., & Khosla, R. (2007). Examination of environmental beliefs and its impact on the influence of price, quality and demographic characteristics with respect to green purchase intention. *Journal of Targeting. Measurement and Analysis for Marketing, 15*(2), 69. doi:10.1057/palgrave.jt.5750039

Dabholkar, P. A., & Kellaris, J. J. (1992). Toward understanding marketing students' ethical judgment of controversial personal selling practices. *Journal of Business Research, 24*(4), 313–329. doi:10.1016/0148-2963(92)90037-C

Daft, R. L. (2009). *Organization theory and design.* Mason, OH: Cengage Learning.

De Kool, D., & Van Wamelen, J. (2008). *Web 2.0: A new basis for e-government?* Paper presented at the 3rd International Conference on Information and Communication Technologies: From Theory to Applications, Damascus, Syria.

Deering, A., Van Hall, A., Jonk, G., & Cook, A. (2008). Internet tools enable organizational transformation from the inside out: the Nokia Siemens Networks case. *Strategy and Leadership, 36*(5), 34–37. doi:10.1108/10878570810902103

Florida, R., & Davison, D. (2001). Gaining from green management: Environmental management systems inside and outside the factory. *California Management Review, 43*(3), 64–84.

Flynn, N. (2006). *Blog rules: A business guide to managing policy, public relations, and legal issues.* New York, NY: AMACOM.

Fornell, C., & Larcker, D. F. (1981). Structural equation models with unobservable variables and measurement error: Algebra and statistics. *JMR, Journal of Marketing Research, 18*(3), 382–388. doi:10.2307/3150980

Harris, L., & Crane, A. (2002). The greening of organizational culture: Management views on the depth, degree and diffusion of change. *Journal of Organizational Change Management, 15*(3), 214–234. doi:10.1108/09534810210429273

Houghton, J. W., Steele, C., & Henty, M. (2003). *Changing research practices in the digital information and communication environment.* Canberra, Australia: Department of Education, Science, and Training.

Houghton, S., & Schmidt, A. (2005). Web-based chat vs. instant messaging: Who wins? *Online, 29*(4), 26.

Hunt, S. D., & Vitell, S. (1986). A general theory of marketing ethics. *Journal of Macromarketing, 8*(1), 5–16. doi:10.1177/027614678600600103

Ilieva, J., Baron, S., & Healey, N. M. (2002). Online surveys in marketing research: Pros and cons. *International Journal of Market Research, 44*(3), 361–387.

Karahanna, E., & Straub, D. W. (1999). Information technology adoption across time: a cross-sectional comparison of pre-adoption and post-adoption beliefs. *Management Information Systems Quarterly, 23*(2), 183–213. doi:10.2307/249751

Lai, L., & Turban, E. (2008). Groups formation and operations in the Web 2.0 environment and social networks. *Group Decision and Negotiation, 17*(5), 387–402. doi:10.1007/s10726-008-9113-2

Limayem, M., Hirt, S. G., & Cheung, C. M. K. (2007). How habit limits the predictive power of intention: The case of information systems continuance. *Management Information Systems Quarterly, 31*(4), 705–737.

Lytras, M. D., Damiani, E., & Ordóñez de Pablos, P. (2008). *Web 2.0: The business model*. New York, NY: Springer.

Manaktola, K., & Jauhari, V. (2007). Exploring consumer attitude and behaviour towards green practices in the lodging industry in India. *International Journal of Contemporary Hospitality Management, 19*(5), 364–377. doi:10.1108/09596110710757534

Mansell, R., Avegerou, C. Q. D., & Silverstone, R. (Eds.). (2009). *The Oxford handbook of information and communication technologies*. Oxford, UK: Oxford University Press. doi:10.1093/oxfordhb/9780199548798.001.0001

Mayo, M. A., & Marks, L. J. (1990). An empirical investigation of a general theory of marketing ethics. *Journal of the Academy of Marketing Science, 18*(2), 163–171. doi:10.1007/BF02726432

McKinnon, C. (2009). Information and governance in a 2.0 world. *Financial Executive, 25*(2), 57–59.

Memery, J., Megicks, P., & Williams, J. (2005). Ethical and social responsibility issues in grocery shopping: a preliminary typology. *Qualitative Market Research, 8*(4), 399–412. doi:10.1108/13522750510619760

Murphy, P., & Lacxnial, G. R. (1981). Marketing ethics: A review with implications for managers, educators and researchers. *Review of Marketing*.

Nickull, D., Governor, J., & Hinchcliffe, D. (2009). *Web 2.0 architectures*. Sebastopol, CA: O'Reilly Media.

O'Reilly, T. (2008). *Web 2.0 and cloud computing*. Retrieved from http://radar.oreilly.com/2008/10/web-20-and-cloud-computing.html

O'Reilly, T. (2005). *What is Web 2.0: Design patterns and business models for the next generation of software*. Retrieved from http://www.oreillynet.com/pub/a/oreilly/tim/news/2005/09/30/what-is-web-20.html

Ouadahi, J. (2008). A qualitative analysis of factors associated with user acceptance and rejection of a new workplace information system in the public sector: A conceptual model. *Canadian Journal of Administrative Sciences, 25*(3), 201–213. doi:10.1002/cjas.65

Peng, Y. S., & Lin, S. S. (2008). Local responsiveness pressure, subsidiary resources, green management adoption and subsidiary's performance: Evidence from Taiwanese manufactures. *Journal of Business Ethics, 79*(1-2), 199–212. doi:10.1007/s10551-007-9382-8

Phau, I., & Ong, D. (2007). An investigation of the effects of environmental claims in promotional messages for clothing brands. *Marketing Intelligence & Planning, 25*(7), 772–788. doi:10.1108/02634500710834214

Preston, P. (2004). *European Union ICT policies: Neglected social and cultural dimensions in the European information society*. Bristol, UK: Intellect Books.

Rallapalli, K. C., & Vitell, S. J. (1998). The influence of norms on ethical judgments and intentions: An empirical study of marketing professionals. *Journal of Business Research, 43*(3), 157–168. doi:10.1016/S0148-2963(97)00221-X

Reidenbach, R. E., & Robin, D. P. (1990). Toward the development of a multi-dimensional scale for improving evaluations of business ethics. *Journal of Business Ethics, 9*(8), 639–653. doi:10.1007/BF00383391

Rogers, E. M. (2003). *The diffusion of innovation.* New York, NY: Free Press.

Shaw, D., & Shiu, E. (2003). Ethics in consumer choice: A multivariate modelling approach. *European Journal of Marketing, 37*(10), 1485–1498. doi:10.1108/03090560310487202

Straub, D. W. (1989). Validating instruments in MIS research. *Management Information Systems Quarterly, 13*(2), 147–169. doi:10.2307/248922

Taylor, S., & Todd, P. (1995). Assessing IT usage: The role of prior experience. *Management Information Systems Quarterly, 19*(4), 561–570. doi:10.2307/249633

UNESCO. (2009). *A global perspective on research and development.* Montreal, QC, Canada: UNESCO Institute for Statistics.

United Nations. (1987). *Report of the world commission on environment and development: General Assembly Resolution 42/187.* Retrieved from http://www.un.org/documents/ga/res/42/ares42-187.htm

Verplanken, B., Aarts, H., & van Knippenberg, A. (1997). Habit information acquisition and the process of making travel mode choices. *European Journal of Social Psychology, 27*(5), 539–560. doi:10.1002/(SICI)1099-0992(199709/10)27:5<539::AID-EJSP831>3.0.CO;2-A

Vincent-Lancrin, S. (2006). What is changing in academic research? Trends and Future Scenarios. *European Journal of Education, 41*(2), 169–202. doi:10.1111/j.1465-3435.2006.00255.x

Walsh, J. P., & Bayma, T. (1997). *Computer networks and scientific work.* Mahwah, NJ: Lawrence Erlbaum.

Williams, L. J., & Hazer, J. T. (1986). Antecedents and consequences of satisfaction and commitment in turnover models: A reanalysis using latent variable structural equation methods. *The Journal of Applied Psychology, 71*(2), 219–231. doi:10.1037/0021-9010.71.2.219

Zhang, Z., Cheung, K.-H., & Townsend, J. P. (2008). Bringing Web 2.0 to bioinformatics. *Briefings in Bioinformatics, 10*(1), 1–10. doi:10.1093/bib/bbn041

Zhu, Q., Sarkis, J., Cordeiro, J. J., & Hung, K. (2008). Firm-level correlates of emergent green supply chain management practices in the Chinese context. *Omega, 36*(4), 577–591. doi:10.1016/j.omega.2006.11.009

## APPENDIX A

### Existing Research Practices

How often do you follow these practices in your research work?

I print paper copies of electronic papers
I select double-sided option when printing
I prefer to read publications online, even when print is available
I print copies of my drafts
I optimize the energy settings for my computer(s) and other devices (e.g. automatic shutoff when not in use)

### Web 2.0 Experiences

How often do you use the following technologies in your research?

Blogs
Wikis
RSS News Feeds
Online research management portals
Social Networking Services
Video Sharing

### Environmental Awareness

Please indicate your degree of agreement with each of the following statements.

Attitude
It is essential to promote green living
It is very important to raise environmental awareness among people
Environmental issues are important to me
It is important to spend money on environmental issues
Behavior
I usually pay more for environmentally friendly products
I usually promote pro-environmental behaviors to my friends
I usually recycle paper, plastic and glass materials
I usually read the label to see if the product is environmentally friendly
Deontological evaluation


*Considering your own norms and values, how would you evaluate Green Research Practices*? (Select the appropriate circle on each scale)*

*Please indicate the degree of **desirability** of the following consequences of Green Research Practices.*

*Please indicate the degree of **likelihood** that Green Research Practices would...*

*Considering your own norms and values and the desirability of the environmental outcomes, how would you judge Green Research Practices?*

*Please indicate your degree of willingness to perform each of the following behaviors.*

*This work was previously published in the International Journal of Social and Organizational Dynamics in IT, Volume 1, Issue 2, edited by Michael B. Knight, pp. 26-45, 2011 by IGI Publishing (an imprint of IGI Global).*

# Compilation of References

Aarseth, E. J. (1997). *Cybertext: Perspectives on ergodic literature*. Baltimore, MD: Johns Hopkins University Press.

Aarts, H., Verplanken, B., & van Knippenberg, A. (1998). Predicting behavior from actions in the past: Repeated decision making or a matter of habit? *Journal of Applied Social Psychology*, 28, 1355–1374. doi:10.1111/j.1559-1816.1998.tb01681.x

ACM. (2010). *Computing curricula*. Retrieved from http://www.acm.org/education/curricula-recommendations

Adler, I., & Kraus, V. (1985). Components of occupational prestige evaluations. *Work & Organizations*, 12, 23–39. doi:10.1177/0730888485012001002

Agarwal, R., & Prasad, J. (1997). The Role of Innovation Characteristics and Perceived Voluntariness in the Acceptance of Information Technologies. *Decision Sciences*, 28(3), 557–582. doi:10.1111/j.1540-5915.1997.tb01322.x

Ahuja, M. K. (2002). Women in the Information Technology Profession: A literature review, synthesis and research agenda. *European Journal of Information Systems*, 11(1), 20–34. doi:10.1057/palgrave/ejis/3000417

Ajzen, A. A. (1991). The theory of planned behaivor. *Organizational Behavior and Human Decision Processes*, 50(2), 179–211. doi:10.1016/0749-5978(91)90020-T

Ajzen, A. A., & Fishbein, M. (1980). *Understanding attitudes and predicting social behavior*. Upper Saddle River, NJ: Prentice-Hall.

Alavi, M., & Leidner, D. E. (2001). Review: Knowledge Management and Knowledge Management Systems: Conceptual Foundations and Research Issues. *Management Information Systems Quarterly*, 25(1), 107–136. doi:10.2307/3250961

Allgeier, A. R. (1974). *The effects of differential amounts of talkativeness on interpersonal judgments*. Unpublished doctoral dissertation, Purdue University, West Lafayette.

Alwin, D. F., & Hauser, R. M. (1975). The decomposition of effects in path analysis. *American Sociological Review*, 40(1), 37–47. doi:10.2307/2094445

Anandarajan, M., Arinze, B., Govindarajulu, C., & Zaman, M. (2009). *Emerging technologies: Selected technologies holding potential*. Hoboken, NJ: John Wiley & Sons.

Anderson, J. C., & Gerbing, D. W. (1988). Structural equation modeling in practice: A review and recommended two-step approach. *Psychological Bulletin*, 103(3), 411–423. doi:10.1037/0033-2909.103.3.411

Ang, S., & Slaughter, S. (2000). The missing context of information technology personnel: A review and future directions for research. In Zmud, R. W. (Ed.), *Framing the domains of IT management: Projecting the future through the past* (pp. 305–327). Cincinnati, OH: Pinnaflex Educational Resources.

Anonymous,. (1995). Equal pay for equal work? Not yet. *Business Communications Review*, 25(5), 29.

Ansari, M. A. (1990). *Managing people at work. Leadership styles and influence strategies*. London, UK: Sage.

Arkin, R. M. (1981). Self-presentation styles. In Tedeschi, J. T. (Ed.), *Impression management theory and social psychology research* (pp. 311–333). New York, NY: Academic Press.

Arkin, R. M., & Oleson, K. C. (1998). Self-handicapping. In Darley, J. M., & Cooper, J. (Eds.), *Attribution and social interaction: The legacy of Edward E. Jones* (pp. 313–347). Washington, DC: American Psychological Association. doi:10.1037/10286-006

Armistead, C., & Meakins, M. (2007). Managing Knowledge in Times of Organisational Change and Restructuring. *Knowledge and Process Management, 14*(1), 15–25. doi:10.1002/kpm.268

Arroyo, E., Selker, T., & Willy, W. (2006). Usability Tool for Analysis of Web Designs Using Mouse Tracks. In *Proceedings of CHI 2006.*

Ashforth, B. E., & Kreiner, G. E. (1999). How can you do it? Dirty work and the challenge of constructing a positive identity. *Academy of Management Review, 24*(3), 413–434. doi:10.2307/259134

Attali, J. (1999). *Labyrinth in culture and society: Pathways to wisdom.* Berkeley, CA: North Atlantic Books.

Baba, M. (1999). Dangerous liaisons: Trust, distrust, and information technology in American work organizations. *Human Organization, 58*(3), 331–346.

Baddeley, A. (1992). Working memory. *Science, 255*(5044), 556–559. doi:10.1126/science.1736359

Badura, V., Read, A. S., Briggs, R. O., & de Vreede, G. J. (2009). Exploring the effects of a convergence intervention on ideation artifacts: A multi-group field study. In *Proceedings of the Americas Conference on Information Systems.*

Bagchi, K., Kirs, P., & Cerveny, R. (2006). Global Software Piracy: Can Economic Factors Alone Explain the Trend? *Communications of the ACM, 49*(6), 70–75. doi:10.1145/1132469.1132470

Bagozzi, R. P., & Yi, Y. (1988). On the evaluation of structural equation models. *Journal of the Academy of Marketing Science, 16*(1), 74–94. doi:10.1007/BF02723327

Bajaj, A. (2000). A Study of Senior Information Systems Managers' Decision Models in Adopting New Computing Architectures. *Journal of the Association for Information Systems, 1,* 4.

Bamberg, S., Rolle, D., & Weber, C. (2003). Does habitual car use not lead to more resistance to change of travel mode? *Transportation, 30*(1), 97–108. doi:10.1023/A:1021282523910

Bandyopadhyay, K., & Fraccastoro, K. A. (2007). The Effect of Culture on User Acceptance of Information Technology. *Communications of the Association for Information Systems, 19,* 522–543.

Banerjee, D., Khalid, A. M., & Sturm, J. E. (2005). Socio-economic development and software piracy. An empirical assessment. *Applied Economics, 37,* 2091–2097. doi:10.1080/00036840500293276

Bansler, J., & Havn, E. (2003). Building Community Knowledge Systems: An Empirical Study of IT-Support for Sharing Best Practices Among Managers. *Knowledge and Process Management, 10*(3), 156–163. doi:10.1002/kpm.178

Barki, H., & Hartwick, J. (2001). Interpersonal conflict and its management in information system development. *Management Information Systems Quarterly, 25*(2), 195–228. doi:10.2307/3250929

Baroudi, J. J., & Igbaria, M. (1995). An Examination of Gender Effects on Career Success of Information Systems Employees. *Journal of Management Information Systems, 11*(3), 181–201.

Barrouillet, P., Bernardin, S., Portrat, S., Vergauwe, E., & Camos, V. (2007). Time and cognitive load in working memory. *Journal of Experimental Psychology. Learning, Memory, and Cognition, 33*(3), 570–585. doi:10.1037/0278-7393.33.3.570

Bashir, S., & Ramay, M. I. (2008). Determinants of Organizational Commitment: A Study of Information Technology Professionals in Pakistan. *Journal of Behavioral and Applied Management, 9*(1), 226–238.

Baumeister, R. F., Heatherton, T. F., & Tice, D. M. (1993). When ego threats lead to self-regulation failure: Negative consequences of high self-esteem. *Journal of Personality and Social Psychology, 64*(1), 141–156. doi:10.1037/0022-3514.64.1.141

Baumgartner, F., & Jones, B. (1993). *Agendas and Instability in American Politics.* Chicago, IL: The University of Chicago Press.

Beasley, R. E., Lomo-David, E., & Seubert, V. R. (2001). Telework and Gender: Implications for the Management of Information Technology Professionals. *Industrial Management & Data Systems, 101*(8/9), 477–482. doi:10.1108/02635570110410663

Becker, G. (1975). *Human capital.* Chicago, IL: University of Chicago Press.

Beckhard, R. (1969). *Organization Development: Strategies and Models*. Reading, MA: Addison-Wesley.

Benjamin, W. (2004). *The arcades project*. Cambridge, MA: Harvard University Press.

Bennis, W. (1966). *Changing organizations*. New York, NY: McGraw-Hill.

Bentler, P. M. (1990). Comparative fit indexes in structural models. *Psychological Bulletin, 107*(2), 238–246. doi:10.1037/0033-2909.107.2.238

Berglas, S., & Jones, E. E. (1978). Drug choice as a self-handicapping strategy in response to noncontingent success. *Journal of Personality and Social Psychology, 36*, 405–417. doi:10.1037/0022-3514.36.4.405

Berman, M. (1982). *All that is solid melts into air: The experience of modernity*. New York, NY: Penguin.

Blascovich, J., Loomis, J., Beall, A. C., Swinth, K. R., Hoyt, C. L., & Bailenson, J. N. (2001). Immersive Virtual Environment Technology as a Methodological Tool for Social Psychology. *Psychological Inquiry*.

Blickle, G. (2003). Convergence of agents' and targets' reports on intra-organizational influence attempts. *European Journal of Psychological Assessment, 19*, 40–53. doi:10.1027//1015-5759.19.1.40

Block, P. (1988). *The empowered manager: Positive political skills at work*. San Francisco, CA: Jossey-Bass.

Bock, G.-W., Zmud, R. W., Kim, Y.-G., & Lee, J.-N. (2005). Behavioral Intention Formation in Knowledge Sharing: Examining the Roles of Extrinsic Motivators, Social-Psychological Forces and Organizational Climate. *Management Information Systems Quarterly, 29*(1), 87–111.

Boehm, B., Grunbacher, P., & Briggs, R. O. (2001). Developing groupware for requirements negotiation: Lessons learned. *IEEE Software, 18*(3), 46–55. doi:10.1109/52.922725

Boerner, H. (2008). The greening of public corporations. *Corporate Finance Review, 13*(2), 32–35.

Bonk, C. J., & Wisher, R. A. (2000). *Applying collaborative and e-learning tools to military distance learning: A research framework*. Arlington, VA: US Army Research Institute for the Behavioral and Social Sciences.

Borges, J. (1998). The library of babel. In Hurley, A. (Ed.), *Collected fictions* (pp. 112–118). New York, NY: Penguin Books.

Bort, J. (2003). Women in Networking. *Network World*. Retrieved from www.nwfusion.com/you/2003/0721salaryside.html

Bostrom, R. (1989). Successful application of communication techniques to improve the systems development process. *Information & Management, 16*, 279–295. doi:10.1016/0378-7206(89)90005-0

Bostrom, R., & Heinen, S. (1977). MIS problems and failures: A socio-technical perspective part 1: The causes. *Management Information Systems Quarterly, 1*, 17–32. doi:10.2307/248710

Brandenburger, A. M., & Nalebuff, B. J. (1997). *Coopetition*. Eschborn, Germany: Riek.

Briggs, R. O., & de Vreede, G. J. (2001). *ThinkLets: A pattern language for collaboration*. Broomfield, CO: GroupSystems Corporation.

Briggs, R. O., de Vreede, G. J., & Massey, A. P. (2008). Introduction to JAIS special issue on collaboration engineering. *Journal of the Association for Information Systems, 10*, 118–120.

Briggs, R. O., de Vreede, G. J., & Nunamaker, J. F. Jr. (2003). Collaboration engineering with ThinkLets to pursue sustained success with group support systems. *Journal of Management Information Systems, 19*(4), 31–64.

Briggs, R. O., Reinig, B. A., & de Vreede, G.-J. (2008). The yield shift theory of satisfaction and its application to the IS/IT domain. *Journal of the Association for Information Systems, 9*, 267–293.

Browne, M. W., & Cudeck, R. (Eds.). (1993). *Alternative ways of assessing model fit*. London, UK: Sage.

Budd, J. M., & Connaway, L. S. (1997). University faculty and networked information: Results of a survey. *Journal of the American Society for Information Science American Society for Information Science, 48*(9), 348–357. doi:10.1002/(SICI)1097-4571(199709)48:9<843::AID-ASI8>3.0.CO;2-R

Bughin, J., & Manyika, J. (2007). How businesses are using Web 2.0: A McKinsey global survey. *The McKinsey Quarterly*, 32–39.

Burton-Jones, A. (2005). *New perspectives on the system usage construct.* Unpublished doctoral dissertation, Georgia State University, Atlanta, GA.

Burton-Jones, A., & Gallivan, M. J. (2007). Toward a deeper understanding of system usage in organizations: A multilevel perspective. *Management Information Systems Quarterly*, *31*(4), 657–279.

Burton-Jones, A., & Straub, D. (2006). Reconceptualizing system usage: An approach and an empirical test. *Information Systems Research*, *17*(3), 228–246. doi:10.1287/isre.1060.0096

Business Software Alliance. (2005a). *Expanding the Frontiers of Our Digital Future: Reducing Software Piracy to Accelerate Global IT Benefits.* Washington, DC: BSA.

Business Software Alliance. (2005b). *Second Annual BSA and IDC Global Software Piracy Study.* Washington, DC: BSA.

Business Software Alliance. (2008). *The Economic Benefits of Lowering PC Software Piracy.* Retrieved June 1, 2009, from http://www.bsa.org/upload/idc-findings_summary.pdf

Business Software Alliance. (2009). *Sixth Annual BSA-IDC Global Software 08 Piracy Study.* Retrieved June 1, 2009, from http://global.bsa.org/globalpiracy2008/studies/globalpiracy2008.pdf

Butler, R. J. (1982). Estimating Wage Discrimination in the Labor Market. *The Journal of Human Resources*, *17*, 606–621. doi:10.2307/145618

Butler, T. (2003). From Data to Knowledge and Back Again: Understanding the Limitations of KMS. *Knowledge and Process Management*, *10*(3), 144–155. doi:10.1002/kpm.180

Byrne, M. D. (2001). ACT-R/PM and Menu Selection: Applying a Cognitive Architecture to HCI. *International Journal of Human-Computer Studies*, *55*, 41–84. doi:10.1006/ijhc.2001.0469

Cameron, B., & Butcher-Powell, L. (2006). Gender Differences Among IT Professionals in Dealing with Change and Skill Set Maintenance. *Interdisciplinary Journal of Information, Knowledge, and Management*, *1*, 152–157.

Campbell, D. T., & Fiske, D. W. (1959). Convergent and discriminant validation by the multitrait-multimethod matrix. *Psychological Bulletin*, *56*(2), 81–105. doi:10.1037/h0046016

Campesato, O., & Nilson, K. (2010). *Web 2. 0 fundamentals for developers.* Sudbury, MA: Jones & Bartlett Learning.

Carroll, J. (2002). Nurture the geek in you. *CA Magazine*, *135*(7), 18.

Carroll, J. M. (2003). *HCI Models, Theories, and Frameworks: Toward a Multidisciplinary Science.* San Francisco, CA: Morgan Kaufmann.

Cawley, J., & Heckman, J. (1999). Meritocracy in America: Wages Within and Across Occupations. *Industrial Relations*, *38*(3), 250–206. doi:10.1111/0019-8676.00130

Chan, R. Y. K., Wong, Y. H., & Leung, T. K. P. (2008). Applying ethical concepts to the study of "Green" consumer behavior: An analysis of chinese consumers' intentions to bring their own shopping bags. *Journal of Business Ethics*, *79*(4), 469–481. doi:10.1007/s10551-007-9410-8

Chapman, G. (1999, September 27). Digital nation: Even if 'geekness' is a disorder, there's no rush to find a cure. *The Los Angeles Times*, p. 1.

Cheng, H. K., Sims, R. R., & Teegen, H. (1997). To purchase or to pirate software: An empirical study. *Journal of Management Information Systems*, *13*(4), 49–60.

Chen, H., Hsu, P., Orwig, R., Hoopes, L., & Nunamaker, J. F. (1994). Automatic concept classification of text from electronic meetings. *Communications of the ACM*, *37*(10), 56–73. doi:10.1145/194313.194322

Chen, P. Y., & Spector, P. E. (1992). Relationships of work stressor with aggression, withdrawal, theft and substance use: An exploratory study. *Journal of Occupational and Organizational Psychology*, *65*, 177–184.

Cherry, J., & Fraedrich, J. (2002). Perceived risk, moral philosophy and marketing ethics: mediating influences on sales managers ethical decision making. *Journal of Business Research*, *55*(12), 951–962. doi:10.1016/S0148-2963(00)00215-0

Chin, W. W. (1998). Issues and opinion on structural equation modeling. *Management Information Systems Quarterly*, *22*, 7–16.

Chin, W. W. (1998). The Partial Least Squares Approach for Structural Equation Modeling. In *Modern Methods for Business Research* (pp. 295–336). Mahwah, NJ: Lawrence Erlbaum Associates.

Chin, W. W. (1998a). Commentary: Issues and opinion on structural equation modeling. *Management Information Systems Quarterly, 22*(1), 7–16.

Chin, W. W. (1998b). The Partial Least Squares approach to structural equation modelling. In Marcoulides, G. A. (Ed.), *Modern methods for business research* (pp. 295–336). Mahwah, NJ: Lawrence Erlbaum.

Chin, W. W., Marcolin, B. L., & Newsted, P. R. (2003). A Partial Least Squares Latent Variable Modeling Approach for Measuring Interaction Effects: Results from a Monte Carlo Simulation, Study and an Electronic-Mail Emotion/Adoption Study. *Information Systems Research, 14*(2), 189–217. doi:10.1287/isre.14.2.189.16018

Chow, G. (1960). Tests of Equality Between Sets of Coefficients in Two Linear Regressions. *Econometrica, 28*, 591–605. doi:10.2307/1910133

Churchill, G. A. J. (1979). A paradigm for developing better measures of marketing constructs. *JMR, Journal of Marketing Research, 16*(1), 64–73. doi:10.2307/3150876

Clair, J. A., Beatty, J. E., & MacLean, T. L. (2005). Out of sight but not out of mind: Managing invisible social identities in the workplace. *Academy of Management Review, 30*, 78–95.

Clarke, D., & Duimering, R. (2006). How Computer Gamers Experience the Game Situation: A Behavioral Study. *ACM Computers in Entertainment, 4*(3), 1–23.

Cohen, P., & Huffman, M. (2007). Working for the Woman? Female Managers and the Gender Wage Gap. *American Sociological Review, 72*, 681–704. doi:10.1177/000312240707200502

Cohen, S. (2001). Welcome to the Girls Club. *InfoWorld, 23*(17), 55–58.

Cole-Gomolski, B. (1998). More Opportunity, Fewer Women in IT. *Computerworld, 32*(45), 4.

Coleman, D., & Levine, S. (2008). *Collaboration 2.0: Technology and best practices for successful collaboration in a Web 2.0 world*. Silicon Valley, CA: Happy About.

Compeau, D. R., & Higgins, C. A. (1995). Application of Social Cognitive Theory to Training for Computer Skills. *Information Systems Research, 6*(2), 118–143. doi:10.1287/isre.6.2.118

Compeau, D. R., Meister, D. B., & Higgins, C. A. (2007). From Prediction to Explanation: Reconceptualizing and Extending the Perceived Characteristics of Innovating. *Journal of the Association for Information Systems, 8*(8), 409–439.

Comrey, A. L. (1973). *A First Course in Factor Analysis*. New York: Academic Press.

Conner, D., & Patterson, R. (1982). Building Commitment to Organizational Change. *Training and Development Journal, 36*(4), 18–30.

Conner, M., & Armitage, C. J. (1998). Extending the theory of planned behavior: A review and avenues for further research. *Journal of Applied Social Psychology, 28*(15), 1429–1464. doi:10.1111/j.1559-1816.1998.tb01685.x

Consortium, C. (2007). *Croquet: Invent the Future*. Retrieved September 14, 2007, from http://www.open-croquet.org/index.php/Main_Page

Cooper, R. B., & Zmud, R. W. (1990). Information Technology Implementation Research: A Technological Infusion Approach. *Management Science, 36*(2), 123–139. doi:10.1287/mnsc.36.2.123

Cotton, J. (1988). On the Decomposition of Wage Differentials. *The Review of Economics and Statistics, 70*(2), 236–243. doi:10.2307/1928307

Couger, J., & Sawicki, R. (1980). *Motivating and Managing Computer Personnel*. New York: Wiley & Sons.

Covi, L. M. (2000). Debunking the myth of the Nintendo generation: How doctoral students introduce new electronic communication practices into university research. *Journal of the American Society for Information Science American Society for Information Science, 51*(17), 1284–1294. doi:10.1002/1097-4571(2000)9999:9999<::AID-ASI1045>3.0.CO;2-Z

Cox, T. (1993). *Cultural diversity in organizations*. San Francisco, CA: Berrett-Kohler.

Crandall, C. S. (2000). Ideology and lay theories of stigma: The justification of stigmatization. In Heatherton, T. F., Kleck, R. E., Hebl, M. R., & Hull, J. G. (Eds.), *The social psychology of stigma* (pp. 126–150). New York, NY: The Guilford Press.

Crandall, C. S., & Moriarty, D. (1995). Physical illness stigma and social rejection. *The British Journal of Social Psychology, 34*, 67–83.

Crawford, C. (1982). *The Art of Computer Game Design: Reflections of a Master Game Designer.* New York: McGraw-Hill.

Crocker, J., & Major, B. (1994). Reactions to stigma: The moderating role of justifications. In M. P. Zanna & J. M. Olson (Eds.), *The Ontario symposium: Vol. 7. The psychology of prejudice* (pp. 289-314). Mahwah, NJ: Lawrence Erlbaum.

Crocker, J., & Major, B. (1989). Social stigma and self-esteem: The self-protective properties of stigma. *Psychological Review, 96*(4), 608–630. doi:10.1037/0033-295X.96.4.608

Crocker, J., Major, B., & Steele, C. (1998). Social stigma. In Gilbert, D. T., Fiske, S. T., & Lindzey, G. (Eds.), *The handbook of social psychology* (4th ed., *Vol. 2*, pp. 504–533). New York, NY: McGraw Hill.

Crocker, J., & Quinn, D. M. (2000). Social stigma and the self: Meanings, situations, and self-esteem. In Heatherton, T. F., Kleck, R. E., Hebl, M. R., & Hull, J. G. (Eds.), *The social psychology of stigma* (pp. 153–183). New York, NY: The Guilford Press.

Crocker, J., & Wolfe, C. T. (2001). Contingencies of self-worth. *Psychological Review, 108*(3), 593–623. doi:10.1037/0033-295X.108.3.593

Cross, R., Liedtka, J., & Weiss, L. (2005). A practical guide to social networks. *Harvard Business Review, 83*(3), 124–132.

Crozier, M. (1973). The problem of power. *Social Research, 40*(2), 211–228.

Crump, B., Logan, K., & McIlroy, A. (2007). Does Gender Still Matter? A Study of the Views of Women in the ICT Industry in New Zealand. *Gender, Work and Organization, 14*(4), 349–370. doi:10.1111/j.1468-0432.2007.00348.x

Csikszentmihalyi, M. (1997). *Finding flow.* New York, NY: Basic Books.

Cukier, W., Shortt, D., & Devine, I. (2002). Gender and Information Technology: Implications of Definitions. *SIGCSE Bulletin, 34*(4), 142. doi:10.1145/820127.820188

Cummings, T. G., & Worley, C. G. (1997). *Organization Development & Change.* Cincinnati, OH: South-Western College Publishing.

Cutrell, E., & Zhiwei, G. *(2007). What Are You Lo*oking For? An Eye-Tracking Study of Information Usage in Web Search. In *Proceedings of CHI 2007,* San Jose, CA.

CyberSmart. (2009). *Web 2.0 tools.* Retrieved from http://cybersmartcurriculum.org/tools/

Dabholkar, P. A., & Kellaris, J. J. (1992). Toward understanding marketing students' ethical judgment of controversial personal selling practices. *Journal of Business Research, 24*(4), 313–329. doi:10.1016/0148-2963(92)90037-C

Dabrander, B., & Edstrom, A. (1977). Successful information system development projects. *Management Science, 24*, 191–199. doi:10.1287/mnsc.24.2.191

Daft, R. L. (1995). *Organization theory and design* (5th ed.). Minneapolis, MN: West Publishing.

Daft, R. L. (1998). *Organization theory and design.* Cincinnati, OH: South-Western College Publishing.

Daft, R. L. (2009). *Organization theory and design.* Mason, OH: Cengage Learning.

Daly, J. A., & McCroskey, J. C. (1975). Occupational choice and desirability as a function of communication apprehension. *Journal of Counseling Psychology, 22*, 309–313. doi:10.1037/h0076748

Daly, J. A., Richmond, V. P., & Leth, S. (1979). Social communicative anxiety and the personnel selection process: Testing the similarity effect in selection decisions. *Human Communication Research, 6*, 18–32. doi:10.1111/j.1468-2958.1979.tb00288.x

*Data Ferret.* (n.d.). Retrieved from http://ferret.bls.census.gov/cgi-bin/ferret

Data Main Page, C. P. S. (n.d.). *Current Population Survey*. Retrieved from http://www.bls.census.gov/cps/cpsmain.htm

Dattero, R., Galup, S., & Quan, J. (2005). Assessing Gender Differences in Software Developers Using the Human Capital Model. *Information Resources Management Journal, 18*(3), 68–87.

Davenport, T. H., & Völpel, S. C. (2001). The rise of knowledge towards attention management. *Library Hi Tech News Incorporating Online and CD Notes, 5*(3), 212–222.

Davidow, W. H., & Malone, M. S. (1992). *The virtual corporation*. New York, NY: Harper-Collins.

Davis, A. J., Badura, V., & de Vreede, G. J. (2008). Understanding methodological differences to study convergence in group support systems sessions. In *Proceedings of the 14th Collaboration Researchers' International Workshop on Groupware*, Omaha, NB.

Davis, A. J., de Vreede, G. J., & Briggs, R. O. (2007). Designing ThinkLets for convergence. In *Proceedings of the 13th Americas Conference on Information Systems*.

Davis, F. D. (1989). Perceived usefulness, perceived ease of use, and user acceptance of information technology. *Management Information Systems Quarterly, 13*(3), 319–340. doi:10.2307/249008

Davis, F., Bagozzi, R. P., & Warshaw, P. R. (1989). User Acceptance of Computer Technology: A Comparison of Two Theoretical Models. *Management Science, 35*(8), 982–1003. doi:10.1287/mnsc.35.8.982

De Boer, M., Van Den Bosch, A. J., & Volberda, H. W. (1999). Managing organizational knowledge integration in the emerging multimedia complex. *Journal of Management Studies, 36*(3), 379–398. doi:10.1111/1467-6486.00141

De Kool, D., & Van Wamelen, J. (2008). *Web 2.0: A new basis for e-government?* Paper presented at the 3rd International Conference on Information and Communication Technologies: From Theory to Applications, Damascus, Syria.

de Vreede, G. J., & Briggs, R. O. (2005). Collaboration engineering: Designing repeatable processes for high-value collaboration tasks. In *Proceedings of the 38th Hawaii International Conference on System Sciences* (p. 17). Washington, DC: IEEE Computer Society.

Deaux, K., & Major, B. (1987). Putting gender into context: An integrative model of gender-related behavior. *Psychological Review, 94*, 369–389. doi:10.1037/0033-295X.94.3.369

Dedrick, J., & West, J. (2004, January 5-8). An Exploratory Study into Open Source Platform Adoption. Paper presented at the 37th Hawaii International Conference on System Sciences, Waikoloa, HI.

Deering, A., Van Hall, A., Jonk, G., & Cook, A. (2008). Internet tools enable organizational transformation from the inside out: the Nokia Siemens Networks case. *Strategy and Leadership, 36*(5), 34–37. doi:10.1108/10878570810902103

DeLone, W. H., & McLean, E. R. (1992). Information systems success: The quest for the dependent variable. *Information Systems Research, 3*(1), 60–95. doi:10.1287/isre.3.1.60

DeLone, W. H., & McLean, E. R. (2003). The DeLone and McLean model of information systems success: A ten-year update. *Journal of Management Information Systems, 19*(4), 9–30.

den Hengst, M., & de Vreede, G. J. (2004). Collaborate business process engineering: A decade of lessons from the field. *Journal of Management Information Systems, 20*, 85–113.

Denning, P. J., & Yaholkovsky, P. (2008). Getting to "we". *Communications of the ACM, 51*(4), 19–24. doi:10.1145/1330311.1330316

Dennis, A. R., Hayes, G. S., & Daniels, R. M., Jr., (Eds.). (1994). *Proceedings of the Twenty-Seventh Annual Hawaii International Conference on System Sciences*. Washington, DC: IEEE Computer Society.

Denyer, D., & Tranfield, D. (2006). Using qualitative research synthesis to build an actionable knowledge base. *Management Decision, 44*(2), 213–227. doi:10.1108/00251740610650201

Diehl, M., & Stroebe, W. (1987). Productivity loss in brainstorming groups: Toward the solution of a riddle. *Journal of Personality and Social Psychology, 53*(3), 497–509. doi:10.1037/0022-3514.53.3.497

Diehl, M., & Stroebe, W. (1991). Productivity loss in idea-generation groups: Tracking down the blocking effect. *Journal of Personality and Social Psychology, 61*, 392–403. doi:10.1037/0022-3514.61.3.392

Doob, P. R. (1990). *The idea of the labyrinth: From classical antiquity through the middle ages*. Ithaca, NY: Cornell University Press.

Dosier, L., Case, T., & Key, B. (1988). How managers influence subordinates: An empirical study of downward influence tactics. *Leadership & Organization Development Studies Journal, 9*(5), 22–31. doi:10.1108/eb053645

Dourish, P., & Bellotti, V. (1992). Awareness and coordination in shared workspaces. In *Proceedings of the ACM Conference on Computer-Supported Cooperative Work* (pp. 177- 114). New York, NY: ACM Press.

Dovidio, J. F., Major, B., & Crocker, J. (2000). Stigma: Introduction and overview. In Heatherton, T. F., Kleck, R. E., Hebl, M. R., & Hull, J. G. (Eds.), *The social psychology of stigma* (pp. 1–28). New York, NY: The Guilford Press.

D'Souza, C., Taghian, M., & Khosla, R. (2007). Examination of environmental beliefs and its impact on the influence of price, quality and demographic characteristics with respect to green purchase intention. *Journal of Targeting. Measurement and Analysis for Marketing, 15*(2), 69. doi:10.1057/palgrave.jt.5750039

Dubin, S. S. (1990). Maintaining competence through updating. In Willis, S. L., & Dubin, S. S. (Eds.), *Maintaining professional competence* (pp. 44–48). San Francisco, CA: Jossey-Bass.

Duchowski, A. (2002). A Breadth-First Survey of Eye-Tracking Applications. *Behavior Research Methods, Instruments, & Computers, 34*(4), 455–470.

Dugan, S. (2001). Confronting the geek within. *InfoWorld, 23*(20), 66–68.

Du, H. S., & Wagner, C. (2006). Weblog success: Exploring the role of technology. *International Journal of Human-Computer Studies, 64*(9), 789–798. doi:10.1016/j.ijhcs.2006.04.002

Duivenvoorde, G. P. J., Kolfschoten, G. L., Briggs, R. O., & de Vreede, G.-J. (2009). Towards an instrument to measure successfulness of collaborative effort from a participant perspective. In *Proceedings of the 42nd Hawaii International Conference on Systems Sciences*, Big Island, HI (pp. 1-9).

Dunlop, J. T. (1984). *Dispute resolution: Negotiation and consensus building*. Dover, MA: Auburn House.

Dyck, J., Pinelle, D., Brown, B., & Gutwin, C. (2003). Learning From Games: HCI Design Innovations in Entertainment Software. In *Proceedings of the Graphics Interface*, Halifax, Nova Scotia, Canada.

Earls, A. R. (1995). Unequal Opportunity. *Computerworld, 29*(36), 70.

Easton, G. K., George, J. F., Nunamaker, J. F. Jr, & Pendergast, M. O. (1990). Using two different electronic meeting system tools for the same task: An experimental comparison. *Journal of Management Information Systems, 7*(1), 85–101.

Efimova, L., & Grudin, J. (2007). Crossing boundaries: A case study of employee blogging. In *Proceedings of the 40th Hawaii International Conference on System Sciences*.

Eisenhardt, K. M. (1989). Building theories from case study research. *Academy of Management Review, 14*(4), 532–550.

Elron, E., & Vigoda-Gadot, E. (2006). Influence and political processes in cyberspace: The case of global virtual teams. *International Journal of Cross Cultural Management, 6*(3), 295–317. doi:10.1177/1470595806070636

Emerson, R. E. (1962). Power-dependence relations. *American Sociological Review, 27*, 31–41. doi:10.2307/2089716

Falbe, C. M., & Yukl, G. (1992). Consequences for managers of using single influence tactics and combinations of tactics. *Academy of Management Journal, 35*, 638–652. doi:10.2307/256490

Farina, A., Holland, C. H., & Ring, K. (1966). The role of stigma and set in interpersonal attraction. *Journal of Abnormal Psychology, 71*, 421–428. doi:10.1037/h0020306

Fedor, D. B., Caldwell, S., & Herold, D. M. (2006). The effects of organizational changes on employee commitment: A multilevel investigation. *Personnel Psychology*, *59*(1), 1–29. doi:10.1111/j.1744-6570.2006.00852.x

Ferdinand, T. N. (1966). On the obsolescence of scientists and engineers. *American Scientist*, *54*, 46–56.

Ferris, G. R., & Kacmar, K. M. (1992). Perceptions of organizational politics. *Journal of Management*, *18*, 93–116. doi:10.1177/014920639201800107

Ferris, G. R., Treadway, D. C., Perrewé, P. L., Brouer, R. L., Douglas, C., & Lux, S. (2007). Political skill in organizations. *Journal of Management*, *33*(3), 290–320. doi:10.1177/0149206307300813

Ferris, G., Hochwarter, W., Douglas, C., Blass, F., Kolodinsky, R., & Treadway, D. (2002). Social influence processes in organizations and human resources systems. In Ferris, G., & Marmocchio, J. J. (Eds.), *Research in personnel and human resources management* (*Vol. 21*, pp. 65–127). Amsterdam, The Netherlands: Elsevier.

Finholt, T., & Sproull, L. S. (1990). Electronic Groups at Work. *Organization Science*, *1*(1), 42–70. doi:10.1287/orsc.1.1.41

Fiske, S. T., & Ruscher, J. B. (1993). Negative interdependence and prejudice: Whence the affect? In Mackie, D. M., & Hamilton, D. L. (Eds.), *Affect, cognition, and stereotyping: Interactive processes in group perception* (pp. 239–268). San Diego, CA: Academic Press.

Fitzpatrick, G. (1998). *The Locales Framework: Understanding and Designing for Cooperative Work*. Brisbane, Australia: University of Queensland.

Fjermestad, J. (1998). An integrated framework for group support systems. *Journal of Organizational Computing and Electronic Commerce*, *8*(2), 83–107. doi:10.1207/s15327744joce0802_1

Fjermestad, J., & Hiltz, S. R. (1999). An assessment of group support systems experimental research: Methodology and results. *Journal of Management Information Systems*, *15*(3), 7–149.

Fjermestad, J., & Hiltz, S. R. (2001). Group support systems: A descriptive evaluation of case and field studies. *Journal of Management Information Systems*, *17*(3), 113–157.

Florida, R., & Davison, D. (2001). Gaining from green management: Environmental management systems inside and outside the factory. *California Management Review*, *43*(3), 64–84.

Flynn, N. (2006). *Blog rules: A business guide to managing policy, public relations, and legal issues*. New York, NY: AMACOM.

Fornell, C., & Larcker, D. (1981). Evaluating Structural Equation Models with Unobservable Variables and Measurement Error. *JMR, Journal of Marketing Research*, *18*(1), 399–350. doi:10.2307/3151312

Fornell, C., & Larcker, D. F. (1981). Evaluating structural equation models with observable variables and measurement error. *JMR, Journal of Marketing Research*, *18*, 39–50. doi:10.2307/3151312

Foucault, M. (1986). *Death and the labyrinth*. New York, NY: Doubleday and Co.

Fox, S., & Spector, P. E. (1999). A model of work frustration-aggression. *Journal of Organizational Behavior*, *20*, 915–931. doi:10.1002/(SICI)1099-1379(199911)20:6<915::AID-JOB918>3.0.CO;2-6

Frable, D., Blackstone, T., & Sherbaum, C. (1990). Marginal and mindful: Deviants in social interaction. *Journal of Personality and Social Psychology*, *59*, 140–149. doi:10.1037/0022-3514.59.1.140

Franz, C. R., & Robey, D. (1984). An investigation of user-led system design: Rational and political perspectives. *Communications of the ACM*, *27*, 1202–1209. doi:10.1145/2135.2138

Frappaolo, C., & Capshaw, S. (1999). Knowledge Management Software: Capturing the Essence of Know-How and Innovation. *Information Management Journal*, *33*(3), 44–48.

Freidson, E. (1966). Disability as social deviance. In Sussam, M. B. (Ed.), *Sociology and rehabilitation*. Washington, DC: American Sociological Association.

French, J. R. P., & Raven, B. (1959). The bases of social power. In Cartwright, D. (Ed.), *Studies in social power*. Ann Arbor, MI: University of Michigan.

Fried, I. (2000). *Cruise line seeks geeks for Perl diving.* Retrieved from http://news.cnet.com/Cruise-line-seeks-geeks-for-Perl-diving/2100-1040_3-244435.html

Fruhling, A., & de Vreede, G.-J. (2006). Collaborative usability testing to facilitate stakeholder involvement. In Biffl, S., Aurum, A., Boehm, B., Erdogmus, H., & Grünbacher, P. (Eds.), *Value-based software engineering* (pp. 201–223). Berlin, Germany: Springer-Verlag. doi:10.1007/3-540-29263-2_10

Gandz, J., & Murray, V. V. (1980). The experience of work place politics. *Academy of Management Journal, 23*(2), 237–251. doi:10.2307/255429

Garrison, D. R., Anderson, T., & Archer, W. (1999). Critical inquiry in a text-based environment: Computer conferencing in higher education. *The Internet and Higher Education, 2*(2-3), 87–105. doi:10.1016/S1096-7516(00)00016-6

Garrison, D. R., Cleveland-Innes, M., & Fung, T. (2004). Student role adjustment in online communities of inquiry: Model and instrument validation. *Journal of Asynchronous Learning Networks, 8*(2), 61–74.

Geek 2 Geek. (2010). *Welcome to Geek 2 Geek.* Retrieved from http://www.gk2gk.com

Gefen, D. (2003). Unidimensional validity: An explanation and example. *Communication of the AIS, 12*(2), 23–47.

Gefen, D., & Straub, D. (2005). A practical guide to factorial validity using PLS-GRAPH: Tutorial and annotated example. *Communication of the AIS, 16*, 91–109.

Gefen, D., Straub, D., & Boudreau, M. C. (2000). Structural equation modeling and regression: Guidelines for research practice. *Communications of the Association for Information Systems, 4*, 1–78.

Gersick, C. (1991). Revolutionary Change Theories: A Multilevel Exploration of the Punctuated Equilibrium Paradigm. *Academy of Management Review, 16*(1), 10–36.

Giddens, A. (1984). *The constitution of society: Outline of the theory of structuration.* Cambridge, UK: John Polity.

Giles, H., Coupland, J., & Coupland, N. (1991). *Contexts of accommodation: Developments in applied sociolinguistics. Studies in emotional and social interaction.* Cambridge, UK: Cambridge University Press. doi:10.1017/CBO9780511663673

Giles, H., & Johnson, P. (1981). The role of language in intergroup relations. In Turner, J. C., & Giles, H. (Eds.), *Intergroup behavior* (pp. 199–243). Oxford, UK: Blackwell.

Giles, H., Mulac, A., Bradac, J. J., & Johnson, P. (1987). Speech accommodation theory: The first decade and beyond. In Mclaughlin, C. M. (Ed.), *Communication yearbook* (*Vol. 10*, pp. 13–48). Newbury Park, CA: Sage.

Gilroy, K. (2001). *Collaborative e-learning: The right approach.* ArsDigita Systems Journal.

Ginzberg, M., & Baroudi, J. (1988). MIS Careers - A Theoretical Perspective. *Communications of the ACM, 31*(5), 586–594. doi:10.1145/42411.42422

Glass, R. (2000). On personal technical obsolescence. *Communications of the ACM, 43*, 15–17. doi:10.1145/341852.341872

Glen, P. (2003). *Leading geeks: How to manage and lead people who deliver technology.* San Francisco, CA: Jossey-Bass.

Glynn, M. A. (1994). Effects of work task cues and play task cues on information-processing, judgment, and motivation. *The Journal of Applied Psychology, 79*, 34–45. doi:10.1037/0021-9010.79.1.34

Goffman, E. (1963). *Stigma: Notes on the management of spoiled identity.* Upper Saddle River, NJ: Prentice Hall.

Goggins, S., Laffey, J., & Tsai, I.-C. (2007). Cooperation and Groupness: Community Formation in Small online Collaborative Groups. In *Proceedings of the ACM Group Conference 2007*, Sanibel Island, FL.

Goldberg, J. H., Stimson, M. J., Lewenstein, M., Scott, N., & Wichansky, A. M. (2002). Eye Tracking in Web Search Tasks: Design Implications. In *Proceedings of the ETRA 2002*, New Orleans, LA.

Goldman, S. L., Nagel, R. N., & Preiss, K. (1995). *Agile competitors and virtual organizations: Strategies for enriching the customer.* New York, NY: Van Nostrand Reinhold.

Gopal, R. D., & Sanders, G. L. (1997). Preventive and deterrent controls for software piracy. *Journal of Management Information Systems, 13*(4), 29–48.

Gopal, R. D., & Sanders, G. L. (1998). International Software Piracy: Analysis of Key Issues and Impacts. *Information Systems Research*, *9*(4), 380–397. doi:10.1287/isre.9.4.380

Gopal, R. D., & Sanders, G. L. (2000). Global Software Piracy: You Can't Get Blood Out of a Turnip. *Communications of the ACM*, *43*(9), 83–89. doi:10.1145/348941.349002

Gould, S., & Eldredge, N. (1977). Punctuated equilibria: the tempo and mode of evolution reconsidered. *Paleobiology*, *3*(2), 115–151.

Graham, W. K. (1977). Acceptance of ideas generated through individual and group brainstorming. *The Journal of Social Psychology*, *101*(2), 231–234. doi:10.1080/00224545.1977.9924013

Grant, R. M. (1996a). Prospering in dynamically-competitive environments: Organizational capability as knowledge integration. *Organization Science*, *7*, 375–387. doi:10.1287/orsc.7.4.375

Grant, R. M.. (199b6). Toward a knowledge-based theory of the firm. *Strategic Management Journal*, *17*, 109–122.

Greogor, S. (2006). The nature of theory in information systems. *Management Information Systems Quarterly*, *30*(3), 611–642.

Grossman, L. (2007). *The Man in the Mask*. Technoculture.

Grudin, J. (1994). Eight Challenges for Developers. *Communications of the ACM*, *37*, 92–116. doi:10.1145/175222.175230

Guan, Z., Lee, S., Cuddihy, E., & Ramey, J. (2006). The Validity of the Stimulated Retrospective Think-Aloud Method as Measured by Eye Tracking. In *Proceedings of chi 2006*, Montreal, Canada.

Gumm, D. C. (2006). Distribution dimensions in software development projects: A taxonomy. *IEEE Software*, *23*(5), 45–51. doi:10.1109/MS.2006.122

Hair, J. F. Jr, Anderson, R. E., Tatham, R. L., & Black, W. C. (1995). *Multivariate data analysis with readings* (4th ed.). Upper Saddle River, NJ: Prentice Hall.

Hair, J. F. Jr, Anderson, R. E., Tatham, R. L., & Black, W. C. (2004). *Multivariate Data Analysis* (4th ed.). Upper Saddle River, NJ: Prentice Hall.

Hammersley, M. (2001). On "systematic" reviews of research literatures: A 'narrative' response to Evans & Benfield. *British Educational Research Journal*, *27*(5), 543–664. doi:10.1080/01411920120095726

Hanover Research Council. (2009). *Current and future classroom and online technologies utilized in higher education*. Retrieved from http://www.hanoverresearch.com

Hansen, M. (1999). The search-transfer problem: The role of weak ties in sharing knowledge across organization subunits. *Administrative Science Quarterly*, *44*(1), 82–111. doi:10.2307/2667032

Harris, L., & Crane, A. (2002). The greening of organizational culture: Management views on the depth, degree and diffusion of change. *Journal of Organizational Change Management*, *15*(3), 214–234. doi:10.1108/09534810210429273

Harter, S. (1986). Processes underlying the construction, maintenance, and enhancement of the self-concept in children. In Suls, J., & Greenwald, A. G. (Eds.), *Psychological perspectives on the self* (Vol. 3, pp. 136–182). Mahwah, NJ: Lawrence Erlbaum.

Haslam, S. A. (2001). *Psychology in organizations: The social identity approach*. Thousand Oaks, CA: Sage.

Hebl, M. R. (1997). *Nonstigmatized individuals' reactions to the acknowledgment and valuation of a stigma by physically disabled and overweight individuals*. Unpublished doctoral dissertation, Dartmouth College, Hanover.

Hebl, M. R., Tickle, J., & Heatherton, T. F. (2000). Awkward moments in interactions between nonstigmatized and stigmatized individuals. In Heatherton, T. F., Kleck, R. E., Hebl, M. R., & Hull, J. G. (Eds.), *The social psychology of stigma* (pp. 275–306). New York, NY: The Guilford Press.

Hemenway, K. (1995). Human Nature and the Glass Ceiling in Industry. *Communications of the ACM*, *38*(1), 55–62. doi:10.1145/204865.204878

Herek, G. M. (1996). Why tell if you are not asked? Self disclosure, intergroup contact, and heterosexuals' attitudes toward lesbians and gay men. In Herek, G. M., Jobe, J. B., & Carney, R. M. (Eds.), *Out in force: Sexual orientation and the military* (pp. 197–225). Chicago, IL: The University of Chicago Press.

Herring, S. C., Scheidt, L. A., Bonus, S., & Wright, E. (2005). Weblogs as a bridging genre. *Information Technology & People*, *18*(2), 142–171. doi:10.1108/09593840510601513

Herscovitch, L., & Meyer, J. (2002). Commitment to organizational change: extension of a three-component model. *The Journal of Applied Psychology*, *87*(3), 474–487. doi:10.1037/0021-9010.87.3.474

Heywood, J. (1987). Wage Discrimination and Market Structure. *Journal of Post Keynesian Economics*, *9*(4), 617–628.

Heywood, J. S., & Nezlek, G. (1993). The Gender Wage Gap among Software Workers: Trends over the Last Two Decades. *Social Science Quarterly*, *74*(3), 603–613.

Hiltz, S. R., & Turoff, M. (2005). Education goes digital: The evolution of online learning and the revolution in higher education. *Communications of the ACM*, *48*(10), 59–64. doi:10.1145/1089107.1089139

Hirschheim, R., & Newman, M. (1991). Symbolism and information systems development: Myth, metaphor, and magic. *Information Systems Research*, *2*(1), 29–62. doi:10.1287/isre.2.1.29

Hochschild, A. R. (1983). *The managed heart: Commercialization of human feeling*. Berkeley, CA: University of California Press.

Hogg, M. A., & Terry, D. J. (2000). Social identity and self-categorization processes in organizational contexts. *Academy of Management Review*, *25*, 121–140. doi:10.2307/259266

Holm, J., Lahteenmaki, S., Salmela, H., Suomi, R., Suominen, A., & Viljanen, M. (2002). Best practices of ICT workforce management – a comparable research initiative in Finland. *Journal of European Industrial Training*, *26*(7), 333–341. doi:10.1108/03090590210432688

Houghton, J. W., Steele, C., & Henty, M. (2003). *Changing research practices in the digital information and communication environment*. Canberra, Australia: Department of Education, Science, and Training.

Houghton, S., & Schmidt, A. (2005). Web-based chat vs. instant messaging: Who wins? *Online*, *29*(4), 26.

Hsieh, J. J. P.-A., Rai, A., & Keil, M. (2008). Understanding Digital Inequality: Comparing Continued Use Behavioral Models of the Socio-Economically Advantaged and Disadvantaged. *Management Information Systems Quarterly*, *32*(1), 97–126.

Hughes, E. C. (1994). *On work, race, and the sociological imagination*. Chicago, IL: The University of Chicago Press.

Hulland, J. (1999). Use of partial least squares (pls) in strategic management research: A review of four recent studies. *Strategic Management Journal*, *20*, 195–204. doi:10.1002/(SICI)1097-0266(199902)20:2<195::AID-SMJ13>3.0.CO;2-7

Hu, M.-C., Zheng, C., & Lamond, D. (2007). Recruitment and retention of ICT skills among MNCs in Taiwan. *Chinese Management Studies*, *1*(2), 78–92. doi:10.1108/17506140710757991

Hunt, S. D., & Vitell, S. (1986). A general theory of marketing ethics. *Journal of Macromarketing*, *8*(1), 5–16. doi:10.1177/027614678600600103

Huxham, C., & Beech, N. (2008). Inter-organizational power. In Cropper, S., Ebers, M., Huxham, C., & Ring, P. S. (Eds.), *The handbook of inter-organizational relations* (pp. 555–579). Oxford, UK: Oxford University Press. doi:10.1093/oxfordhb/9780199282944.003.0021

Ibarra, H. (1999). Provisional selves: Experimenting with image and identity in professional adaptation. *Administrative Science Quarterly*, *44*, 764–791. doi:10.2307/2667055

Igbaria, M., & Chidambaram, L. (1997). The Impact of Gender on Career Success of Information Systems Professionals A Human Capital Perspective. *Information Technology & People*, *10*(1), 63. doi:10.1108/09593849710166165

Igbaria, M., Parasuraman, S., & Greenhaus, J. H. (1997). Status Report on Women and Men in the IT Workplace. *Information Systems Management, 14*(3), 44–53. doi:10.1080/10580539708907059

Igbaria, M., Pavri, F., & Huff, S. (1989). Microcomputer Applications: An Empirical Look at Usage. *Information & Management, 16*, 187–196. doi:10.1016/0378-7206(89)90036-0

Ilieva, J., Baron, S., & Healey, N. M. (2002). Online surveys in marketing research: Pros and cons. *International Journal of Market Research, 44*(3), 361–387.

Information Technology Association of America. (1998). Task force. Image of the information technology (IT) professions. *From myth to reality: Changing the image of information technology*. Retrieved from http://www.itaa.org/

Innes, J. E., & Booher, D. E. (1999). Consensus building and complex adaptive systems. *Journal of the American Planning Association. American Planning Association, 65*(4), 412–423. doi:10.1080/01944369908976071

Int@J. (2007). Information Technology Association-Jordan. *IT Industry Statistics*. Retrieved from http://www.intaj.net/sites/default/files/IT_Industry_Statistics_2007.pdf

International Business Machines Corporation. (2008). *IBM Global CEO Study 2008*. Retrieved June 15, 2009, from http://www.ibm.com/ibm/ideasfromibm/us/ceo/20080505/

Ip, K. F. R., & Wagner, C. (2008). Weblogging: A study of social computing and its impact on organizations. *Decision Support Systems, 45*(2), 242–250. doi:10.1016/j.dss.2007.02.004

Isaacs, E. (1995). Gender Discrimination in the Workplace: A Literature Review. *Communications of the ACM, 38*(1), 58–59. doi:10.1145/204865.384262

Iverson, R. D. (1996). Employee acceptance of organizational change: the role of organizational commitment. *International Journal of Human Resource Management, 7*(1), 122–149. doi:10.1080/09585199600000121

Ives, B., Hamilton, S., & Davis, G. B. (1980). A framework for research in computer-based management information systems. *Management Science, 26*(9), 911–934. doi:10.1287/mnsc.26.9.910

Iyamu, T., & Adelakun, O. (2008). The impact of non-technical factors on information technology strategy and e-business. In *Proceedings of the 12th Pacific Asia Conference on Information Systems* (pp. 1214-1222).

Iyamu, T., & Roode, D. (2010). The use of structuration and actor network theory for analysis: A case study of a financial institution in South Africa. *International Journal of Actor-Network Theory and Technological Innovation, 2*(1), 1–26. doi:10.4018/jantti.2010071601

Jackson, A., Yates, J., & Orlikowski, W. (2007). Corporate blogging: Building community through persistent digital talk. In *Proceedings of the 40th Hawaii International Conference on System Sciences* (p. 80).

Jacobsen, J. (2007). *The Economics of Gender* (3rd ed.). Victoria, Australia: Blackwell Publishing.

Janneck, M. (2009). Designing for social awareness of co-operative activities. In *Proceedings of the 5th International Conference on Web Information Systems* (pp. 463-470).

Janneck, M., & Staar, H. (2010, January). Virtual micropolitics: Informal tactics of influence and power in inter-organizational networks. In *Proceedings of the 43th Annual Hawaii International Conference on System Sciences* (p. 10). Washington, DC: IEEE Computer Society.

Janneck, M., & Finck, M. (2006). Making the community a hospitable place—identity, strong bounds, and self-organisation in web-based communities. *International Journal of Web Based Communities, 2*(4), 458–473. doi:10.1504/IJWBC.2006.011770

Jasperson, S., Carter, P. E., & Zmud, R. W. (2005). A comprehensive conceptualization of post-adoptive behaviours associated with information technology enabled work systems. *Management Information Systems Quarterly, 29*(3), 525–557.

Jones, E. E., Farina, A., Hastorf, A. H., Markus, H., Miller, D. T., & Scott, R. A. (1984). *Social stigma: The psychology of marked relationships*. New York, NY: Freeman.

Jones, M. (1999). Structuration theory. In Currie, W. L., & Galliers, R. D. (Eds.), *Rethinking management information systems* (pp. 103–134). Oxford, UK: Oxford University Press.

Jordan Investment Board (JIB). (2006). *Information communication technology sector*. Retrieved from http://www.jordaninvestment.com/

Joseph, D., & Ang, S. (2001, December). The threat-rigidity model of professional obsolescence and its impact on occupational mobility of IT professionals. In *Proceedings of the Twenty-Second International Conference on Information Systems*, New Orleans, LA.

Joseph, D., Boh, W. F., Ang, S., & Slaughter, S. (Forthcoming). Careers of the information technology workforce: An analysis of career sequences, mobility and objective career success. *Management Information Systems Quarterly*.

Joseph, D., Ng, K. M., Koh, S. K. C., & Ang, S. (2007). Turnover of information technology professionals: A narrative review, meta-analytic structural equation modeling, and model development. *Management Information Systems Quarterly*, *31*, 547–577.

Joshi, K. D., Sarker, S., & Sarker, S. (2007). Knowledge transfer within information systems development teams: Examining the role of knowledge source attributes. *Decision Support Systems*, *43*, 322–335. doi:10.1016/j.dss.2006.10.003

Just, M. A., & Carpenter, P. A. (1980). A Theory of Reading: From Eye Fixations to Comprehension. *Psychological Review*, *87*, 329–354. doi:10.1037/0033-295X.87.4.329

Kaiser, C., & Miller, C. T. (2000). *Reacting to impending discriminations: Compensation for prejudice and attributions to discrimination*. Unpublished doctoral dissertation, University of Vermont, Burlington.

Kankanhalli, A., Tan, B. C. Y., & Wei, K.-K. (2005). Contributing Knowledge to Electronic Knowledge Repositories: An Empirical Investigation. *Management Information Systems Quarterly*, *29*(1), 113–143.

Kaptelinin, V., & Czerwinski. (Eds.). (2007). *Beyond the Desktop Metaphor: Designing Integrated Digital Work Environments*. Boston: MIT Press.

Karahanna, E., & Straub, D. W. (1999). Information technology adoption across time: a cross-sectional comparison of pre-adoption and post-adoption beliefs. *Management Information Systems Quarterly*, *23*(2), 183–213. doi:10.2307/249751

Karahanna, E., Straub, D. W. Jr, & Chervany, N. L. (1999). Information Technology Adoption Across Time: A Cross-Sectional Comparison of Pre-Adoption and Post-Adoption Beliefs. *Management Information Systems Quarterly*, *23*(2), 183–213. doi:10.2307/249751

Karn, K. S. (2006). Eye Tracking for Usability testing, You've Got to Know Your Strengths and Weaknesses. In *Proceedings of CHI 2006.*

Karn, K. S., Ellis, S., & Juliano, C. (1999). The Hunt for Usability: Tracking Eye Movements. In *Proceedings of CHI 1999.*

Keen, P. (1981). Information systems and organizational change. *Communications of the ACM*, *24*, 24–33. doi:10.1145/358527.358543

Keisler, S., & Cummings, J. N. (2002). What do We Know About Proximity and Distance in Work Groups? A Legacy of Research. In Hinds, P., & Kiesler, S. (Eds.), *Distributed Work* (pp. 57–111). Cambridge, MA: MIT Press.

Kelleher, T. (2008). Organizational contingencies, organizational blogs and public relations practitioner stance toward publics. *Public Relations Review*, *34*(3), 300–303. doi:10.1016/j.pubrev.2008.05.003

Kelley, R., & Caplan, J. (1993). How bell labs creates start performers. *Harvard Business Review*, *71*, 128–139.

Kern, H. (2000). *Through the labyrinth: Designs and meanings over 5,000 years*. New York, NY: Prestel.

King, W. (2007). Keynote paper: Knowledge Management: A Systems Perspective. *International Journal of Business Systems and Research*, *1*(1).

Kipnis, D., Schmidt, S. M., & Wilkinson, I. (1980). Intra-organizational influence tactics: Explorations in getting one's way. *The Journal of Applied Psychology*, *65*, 440–452. doi:10.1037/0021-9010.65.4.440

Klawe, M., & Leveson, N. (1995). Women in Computing: Where are we now? *Communications of the ACM*, *38*(1), 29–32. doi:10.1145/204865.204874

Kline, K. J., & Kozlowski, S. W. J. (2000). *Multilevel theory, research and methods in organizations*. San Francisco, CA: Jossey-Bass.

Kock, N. (2000). Benefits for virtual organizations from distributed groups. *Communications of the ACM, 43*(11), 107–112. doi:10.1145/353360.353372

Kolfschoten, G. L., & Santanen, E. L. (2007). Reconceptualizing generate thinkLets: The role of the modifier. In *Proceedings of the 40th Annual Hawaii International Conference on System Sciences* (p. 16). Washington, DC: IEEE Computer Society.

Kosonen, M., Henttonen, K., & Ellonen, K.-H. (2007). Weblogs and internal communication in a corporate environment: A case from the ICT industry. *International Journal of Knowledge and Learning, 3*(4-5), 437–459. doi:10.1504/IJKL.2007.016704

Kotter, J. (1995). Leading Change: Why Transformation Efforts Fail. *Harvard Business Review, 73*(2), 59–67.

Kozlowski, S. W. J., & Farr, J. L. (1988). An integrative model of updating and performance. *Human Performance, 1*, 5–29. doi:10.1207/s15327043hup0101_1

Kozlowski, S. W. J., & Hults, B. M. (1987). An exploration of climates for technical updating and performance. *Personnel Psychology, 40*, 539–563. doi:10.1111/j.1744-6570.1987.tb00614.x

Krackhardt, D., & Hanson, J. R. (1993). Informal networks: The company behind the charts. *Harvard Business Review, 71*, 104–111.

Kraft, P. (1984). *Programmers and Managers: The Routinization of Computer Programming in the United States*. New York: Springer Verlag.

Krippendorf, K. (1980). *Content analysis. An introduction to its methodology*. Thousand Oaks, CA: Sage.

Kroeger, B. (2003). *Passing: When people can't be who they are*. New York, NY: Public Affairs.

Kübler-Ross, E. (1969). *On Death and Dying*. New York, NY: Touchstone.

Lacey, T. A., & Wright, B. (2009). Occupational employment projections to 2018. *Monthly Labor Review, 132*, 82–123.

Lai, L., & Turban, E. (2008). Groups formation and operations in the Web 2.0 environment and social networks. *Group Decision and Negotiation, 17*(5), 387–402. doi:10.1007/s10726-008-9113-2

Landis, J. R., & Koch, G. G. (1977). The measurement of observer agreement for categorical data. *Biometrics, 33*(1), 159–174. doi:10.2307/2529310

Larson, J. (2007). Out of the Video Arcade, into the Office: Where Computer Games Can Lead Productivity Software. *Interaction*, 18–22. doi:10.1145/1189976.1189992

Lawrence, P. R., & Lorsch, J. W. (1967). *Organization and environment: managing differentiation and integration*. Cambridge, MA: Harvard University Press.

Leary, K. (1999). Passing, posing, and "keeping it real.". *Constellations (Oxford, England), 6*, 85–96. doi:10.1111/1467-8675.00122

Lederer, L., & Sethi, V. (1988). The implementation of strategic information systems planning methodologies. *Management Information Systems Quarterly, 12*(3), 445–461. doi:10.2307/249212

Lee, D. M. S., Trauth, E. M., & Farwell, D. (1995). Critical skills and knowledge requirements of IS professionals - a joint academic-industry investigation. *Management Information Systems Quarterly, 19*, 313–340. doi:10.2307/249598

Lee, Y., Kozar, K. A., & Larsen, K. R. T. (2003). The Technology Acceptance Model: Past, Present, and Future. *Communications of the Association for Information Systems, 12*, 752–780.

Leonard, B. (2001). Female IT Contractors Earn More Than Male Counterparts. *HRMagazine, 46*(5), 29.

Levine, J. M., & McBurney, D. H. (1977). Causes and consequences of effluvia: Body odor awareness and controllability as determinants of interpersonal evaluation. *Personality and Social Psychology Bulletin, 3*, 442–445.

Levine, J. M., & Moreland, R. L. (1991). Culture and socialization in work groups. In Resnick, L. B., Levine, J. M., & Teasley, S. D. (Eds.), *Perspectives on socially shared cognition* (pp. 257–279). Washington, DC: American Psychological Association. doi:10.1037/10096-011

Lewin, K. (1946). Research on Minority Problems. *Technology Review*, *48*(3), 163–190.

Lewin, K. (1951). *Field theory in social science: Selected theoretical papers*. New York, NY: Harper and Row.

Li, D., Babcock, J., & Parkhurst, D. J. (2006). openEyes: A Low-Cost Head-Mounted Eye-Tracking Solution. In *Proceedings of the ETRA 2006*.

Limayem, M., & Hirt, S. G. (2003). Force of Habit and Information Systems Usage: Theory and Initial Validation. *Journal of the Association for Information Systems*, *4*, 65–97.

Limayem, M., Hirt, S. G., & Cheung, C. M. K. (2007). How habit limits the predictive power of intention: The case of information systems continuance. *Management Information Systems Quarterly*, *31*(4), 705–737.

Lindgren, H. C. (1967). Brainstorming and the facilitation of creativity expressed in drawing. *Perceptual and Motor Skills*, *24*(2), 350.

Lind, M., & Zmud, R. (1991). The influence of a convergence in understanding between technology providers and users on information technology innovativeness. *Organization Science*, *2*, 195–217. doi:10.1287/orsc.2.2.195

Link, B. G., & Phelan, J. C. (2001). Conceptualizing stigma. *Annual Review of Psychology*, *27*, 363–385.

Linnett, B. J., Fries Duvall, K. E., & Powelson, L. H. (1997). *Software Platform Having a Real World Interface with Animated Characters*. Hoboken, NJ: Microsoft Corporation.

Liu, J., & Wilson, D. (2001). Developing Women in a Digital World. *Women in Management Review*, *16*(7/8), 405–416. doi:10.1108/09649420110411701

Loogma, K., Umarik, M., & Vilu, R. (2004). Identification-flexibility dilemma of IT specialists. *Career Development International*, *9*(3), 323–348. doi:10.1108/13620430410535878

Luftman, J., & Ben-Zvi, T. (2010). Key issues for IT executives 2009: Difficult economy's impact on IT. *MIS Quarterly Executives*, *9*(1).

Lu, Y., Quan, J., & Cao, X. (2009). The Perceived Attributes of Wi-Fi Technology and the Diffusion Gap among University Faculty Members: A Case Study. *Communications of the Association for Information Systems*, *24*, 69–88.

Lytras, M. D., Damiani, E., & Ordóñez de Pablos, P. (2008). *Web 2.0: The business model*. New York, NY: Springer.

Lyytinen, K., & Rose, G. M. (2003). The Disruptive Nature of Information Technology Innovations: The Case of Internet Computing in Systems Development Organizations. *Management Information Systems Quarterly*, *27*(4), 557–595.

MacInnis, P. (2003). The Gender Gap. *Computing Canada*, *29*(11), 26.

Mainemelis, C., & Ronson, S. (2006). Ideas are born in fields of play: Towards a theory of play and creativity in organizational settings. *Research in Organizational Behavior*, *27*, 81–131. doi:10.1016/S0191-3085(06)27003-5

Majchrzak, A. (2009). Comment: Where is the theory in Wikis? *Management Information Systems Quarterly*, *33*(1), 18–20.

Major, B., & Crocker, J. (1993). Social stigma: The consequences of attributional ambiguity. In Mackie, D. M., & Hamilton, D. L. (Eds.), *Affect, cognition, and stereotyping: Interactive processes in group perception* (pp. 345–370). San Diego, CA: Academic Press.

Manaktola, K., & Jauhari, V. (2007). Exploring consumer attitude and behaviour towards green practices in the lodging industry in India. *International Journal of Contemporary Hospitality Management*, *19*(5), 364–377. doi:10.1108/09596110710757534

Manfred, E. (2000). Selling teens on IT. *Computerworld*, *34*(46), 82–83.

Mansell, R., Avegerou, C. Q. D., & Silverstone, R. (Eds.). (2009). *The Oxford handbook of information and communication technologies*. Oxford, UK: Oxford University Press. doi:10.1093/oxfordhb/9780199548798.001.0001

Marks, M. A., Zaccaro, S. J., & Matthieu, J. E. (2000). Performance implications of leader briefings and team-interaction for team adaptation to novel environments. *The Journal of Applied Psychology*, *85*(6), 971–986. doi:10.1037/0021-9010.85.6.971

Markus, M. L. (1983). Power, Politics, and MIS Implementation. *Communications of the ACM, 26*(6), 430–444. doi:10.1145/358141.358148

Markus, M. L., & Robey, D. (1988). Information technology and organizational change: Causal structure in theory and research. *Management Science, 34*(5), 583–598. doi:10.1287/mnsc.34.5.583

Martin, J., Feldmann, M. S., Hatch, M. J., & Sitkin, S. B. (1983). The uniqueness paradox in organizational stories. *Administrative Science Quarterly, 28*(3), 438–453. doi:10.2307/2392251

Mathieu, J., & Zajac, D. (1990). A review and meta-analysis of the antecedents, correlates, and consequences of organizational commitment. *Psychological Bulletin, 108*(2), 171–194. doi:10.1037/0033-2909.108.2.171

Mayo, M. A., & Marks, L. J. (1990). An empirical investigation of a general theory of marketing ethics. *Journal of the Academy of Marketing Science, 18*(2), 163–171. doi:10.1007/BF02726432

McAfee, A. P. (2006). Enterprise 2.0: The dawn of emergent collaboration. *MIT Sloan Management Review, 47*(3), 21–28.

McCroskey, J. C., & Richmond, V. P. (1976). The effects of communication apprehension on the perception of peers. *Western Speech Communication Journal, 40*, 14–21.

McCroskey, J. C., & Richmond, V. P. (1987). Willingness to communicate. In McCroskey, J. C., & Daly, J. A. (Eds.), *Personality and interpersonal communication* (pp. 129–156). Newbury Park, CA: Sage.

McCullough, D. W. (2004). *The unending mystery: A journey through labyrinths and mazes.* New York, NY: Pantheon Books.

McDonald, J., & Thornton, R. (2007). Do New Male and Female College Graduates Receive Unequal Pay? *The Journal of Human Resources, 42*(1), 32–48.

McKinnon, C. (2009). Information and governance in a 2.0 world. *Financial Executive, 25*(2), 57–59.

McNamara, C. (2006). *Field Guide to Consulting and Organizational Development.* Minneapolis, MN: Authenticity Consulting LLC.

Mechanic, D. (1962). Source of power in lower participants in complex organizations. *Administrative Science Quarterly, 7*, 349–364. doi:10.2307/2390947

Memery, J., Megicks, P., & Williams, J. (2005). Ethical and social responsibility issues in grocery shopping: a preliminary typology. *Qualitative Market Research, 8*(4), 399–412. doi:10.1108/13522750510619760

Menezes, J. (1999). Pay Rates Reveal IT's Gender Gap. *Computing Canada, 25*(31), 11–12.

Meservy, T. O., Helquist, J., Deokar, A. V., & Kruse, J. (2009). Enhancing e-learning using artifact-based collaboration. In *Proceedings of the 15th Americas Conference on Information Systems*, San Francisco, CA.

Meyer, J. P., & Herscovitch, L. (2001). Commitment in the workpace toward a general model. *Human Resource Management Review, 11*, 299–326. doi:10.1016/S1053-4822(00)00053-X

Meyer, J., & Allen, N. (1991). A three-component conceptualization of organizational commitment. *Human Resource Management Review, 1*(1), 61–89. doi:10.1016/1053-4822(91)90011-Z

Meyer, J., & Allen, N. (1997). *Commitment in the Workplace: Theory, Research, and Application.* Thousand Oaks, CA: Sage.

Miles, M. B., & Huberman, A. (1994). *Qualitative data analysis: An expanded sourcebook.* Thousand Oaks, CA: Sage.

Miller, C. T., & Major, B. (2000). Coping with stigma and prejudice. In T. F. Heatherton, R. E. Kleck, M. R. Hebl, & J. G. Hull (Eds.), *The social psychology of stigma* (pp. 243-272). New York, NY: The Guilford Press. Milton, L. P. (2003). An identity perspective on the propensity of high-tech talent to unionize. *Journal of Labor Research, 24*, 31-53.

Mintzberg, H. (1983). *Power in and around organizations.* Upper Saddle River, NJ: Prentice Hall.

Mintzberg, H. (2000). *The rise and fall of strategic planning.* Upper Saddle River, NJ: Prentice Hall.

Mitchell, T. (1992). Orientalism and the exhibitionary order. In Dirks, N. B. (Ed.), *Colonialism and culture* (pp. 289–317). Ann Arbor, MI: University of Michigan Press.

Mitchell, T. R., Dowling, P. J., Kabanoff, B. V., & Larson, J. R. (1988). *People in organizations: An introduction to organizational behaviour in Australia.* Sydney, Australia: McGraw-Hill.

Mithas, S., & Krishnan, M. S. (2008). Human capital and institutional effects in the compensation of information technology professionals in the United States. *Management Science, 54,* 415–428. doi:10.1287/mnsc.1070.0778

Mohr, L. B. (1982). *Explaining organizational behaviour.* San Francisco, CA: Jossey-Bass.

Mohtashami, M., Marlowe, T., Kirova, V., & Deek, F. P. (2006). Risk Management for Collaborative Software Development. *Information Systems Management,* 20–30. doi:10.1201/1078.10580530/46352.23.4.20060901/95109.3

Montgomery, M. (1986). *An introduction to language and society.* London, UK: Routledge. doi:10.4324/9780203312032

Montgomery, M., & Powell, I. (2003). Does an Advanced Degree Reduce the Gender Wage Gap? Evidence From MBAs. *Industrial Relations, 42*(3), 396–418. doi:10.1111/1468-232X.00297

Moore, R. J., Gathman, E. C. H., Ducheneaut, N., & Nickell, E. (2007). Coordinating Joint Activity in Avatar-Mediated Interaction. In *Proceedings of the CHI 2007,* San Jose, CA.

Moore, G. C., & Benbasat, I. (1991). Development of an Instrument to Measure the Perceptions of Adopting an Information Technology Innovation. *Information Systems Research, 2*(3), 192–222. doi:10.1287/isre.2.3.192

Moores, T. T., & Chang, J. C. J. (2006). Ethical decision making in software piracy: Initial development and test of a four-component model. *Management Information Systems Quarterly, 30*(1), 167–180.

Morse, G. (2008). Conversation - Wikipedia founder Jimmy Wales on making the most of company wikis. *Harvard Business Review, 86*(4), 26.

Mowday, R. (1998). Reflections on the study and relevance of organizational commitment. *Human Resource Management Review, 8*(4), 387–401. doi:10.1016/S1053-4822(99)00006-6

Muri, R. M., Cazzoli, D., Nyffeler, T., & Pflugshaupt, T. (2009). Visual exploration pattern in hemineglect. *Psychological Research, 73*(2), 147–157. doi:10.1007/s00426-008-0204-0

Murphy, P., & Lacxnial, G. R. (1981). Marketing ethics: A review with implications for managers, educators and researchers. *Review of Marketing.*

Mutula, S. M., & Van Brakel, P. (2007). ICT skills readiness for the emerging global digital economy among small businesses in developing countries - Case study of Botswana. *Library Hi Tech, 25*(2), 231–245. doi:10.1108/07378830710754992

Myers, M. D. (1997). Qualitative research in information systems. *Management Information Systems Quarterly, 21*(2), 241–242. doi:10.2307/249422

Nardi, B., & Harris, J. (2006). Strangers and Friends: Collaborative Play in World of Warcraft. In *Proceedings of CSCW '06,* Banff, Alberta, Canada.

Nardi, B. A., Schiano, D. J., Gumbrecht, M., & Swartz, L. (2004). Why we blog. *Communications of the ACM, 47*(12), 41–46. doi:10.1145/1035134.1035163

Nelson, K. M., & Cooprider, J. G. (1996). The contribution of shared knowledge to IS group performance. *Management Information Systems Quarterly, 20*(4), 409–432. doi:10.2307/249562

Nelson, R. R. (1991). Educational needs as perceived by IS and end-user personnel: A survey of knowledge and skill requirements. *Management Information Systems Quarterly, 15,* 503–525. doi:10.2307/249454

Neuberg, S. L. (1994). Expectancy-confirmation processes in stereotype-tinged social encounters: The moderating role of social goals. In Zanna, M. P., & Olson, J. M. (Eds.), *The psychology of prejudice: The Ontario symposium* (*Vol. 7,* pp. 103–130). Mahwah, NJ: Lawrence Erlbaum.

Neuberg, S. L., Smith, D. M., & Asher, T. (2000). Why people stigmatize: Toward a biocultural framework. In Heatherton, T. F., Kleck, R. E., Hebl, M. R., & Hull, J. G. (Eds.), *The social psychology of stigma* (pp. 31–61). New York, NY: The Guilford Press.

Neumark, D. (1999). Wage Differentials by Race and Sex: The roles of Taste Discrimination and Labor Market Information. *Industrial Relations, 38*(3), 414–445. doi:10.1111/0019-8676.00135

Nickull, D., Governor, J., & Hinchcliffe, D. (2009). *Web 2.0 architectures*. Sebastopol, CA: O'Reilly Media.

Noble, C., & Mokwa, M. (1999). Implementing marketing strategies: developing and testing a managerial theory. *Journal of Marketing, 63*(4), 57–73. doi:10.2307/1251974

Noonan, M., Corcoran, M., & Courant, P. (2005). Pay Differences Among the Highly Trained: Cohort Differences in the Sex Gap in Lawyers' Earnings. *Social Forces, 84*(2), 853–872. doi:10.1353/sof.2006.0021

Noor, K. (2008). Case study: A strategic research methodology. *American Journal of Applied Sciences, 5*(11), 1602–1604. doi:10.3844/ajassp.2008.1602.1604

Nordhaugh, O. (1993). *Human capital in organizations: Competence, training and learning*. Oslo, Norway: Scandinavian University Press.

Northcraft, G. B. (1981). *The perception of disability*. Unpublished doctoral dissertation, Stanford University, Stanford.

O' Reilly, T. (2008). *Web 2.0 and cloud computing*. Retrieved from http://radar.oreilly.com/2008/10/web-20-and-cloud-computing.html

O'Reilly, T. (2005). *What is Web 2.0: Design patterns and business models for the next generation of software*. Retrieved from http://www.oreillynet.com/pub/a/oreilly/tim/news/2005/09/30/what-is-web-20.html

O'Reilly, T. (2007). What Is Web 2.0: Design patterns and business models for the next generation of software. *Communications & Strategies, 65*(1), 17–37.

Oaxaca, R. (1973). Male-Female Wage Differentials in Urban Labor Markets. *International Economic Review, 14*, 693–709. doi:10.2307/2525981

Ojala, M. (2004). *Weaving weblogs into knowledge sharing and dissemination*. Nord I&D, Knowledge and Change.

Orcutt, J. D. (1976). Ideological variations in the structure of deviant types: A multivariate comparison of alcoholism and heroin addiction. *Social Forces, 55*, 419–437. doi:10.2307/2576233

Organization for Economic Co-operation and Development. (2008). *The OECD. OECD Media Relations*. Retrieved June 1, 2009, from http://www.oecd.org

Orlikowski, W. (1992). The duality of technology: Rethinking the concept of technology in organizations. *Organization Science, 3*(3), 398–427. doi:10.1287/orsc.3.3.398

Orlikowski, W. J. (2000). Using technology and constituting structures: A practice lens for studying technology in organizations. *Organization Science, 11*(4), 404–428. doi:10.1287/orsc.11.4.404.14600

Osborn, A. (1963). *Applied imagination: Principles and procedures of creative problem solving* (Rev. ed., *Vol. 3*). New York, NY: Scribner.

Ouadahi, J. (2008). A qualitative analysis of factors associated with user acceptance and rejection of a new workplace information system in the public sector: A conceptual model. *Canadian Journal of Administrative Sciences, 25*(3), 201–213. doi:10.1002/cjas.65

Paiva, A., Andersson, G., Hook, K., Mourao, D., Costa, M., & Martinho, C. (2002). SenToy in Fantasy A: Designing an Affective Sympathetic Interface to a Computer Game. *Personal and Ubiquitous Computing, 6*, 378–389. doi:10.1007/s007790200043

Panteli, N., Stack, J., & Ramsay, H. (2001). Gender Patterns in Computing Work in the late 1990s. *New Technology, Work and Employment, 16*(1), 3. doi:10.1111/1468-005X.00073

Parker, D. (2003). Revenge of the nerds. *Australian CPA, 73*(4), 32.

Pavlou, P. A., & Fygenson, M. (2006). Understanding and Predicting Electronic Commerce Adoption: An Extension of the Theory of Planned Behavior. *Management Information Systems Quarterly, 30*(1), 115–143.

Pazy, A. (1990). The threat of professional obsolescence - how do professionals at different career stages experience IT and cope with IT. *Human Resource Management, 29*, 251–269. doi:10.1002/hrm.3930290303

Pazy, A. (1994). Cognitive schemata of professional obsolescence. *Human Relations, 47*, 1167–1199. doi:10.1177/001872679404701002

Pazy, A. (1996). Concept and career-stage differentiation in obsolescence research. *Journal of Organizational Behavior, 17*, 59–78. doi:10.1002/(SICI)1099-1379(199601)17:1<59::AID-JOB735>3.0.CO;2-8

Peace, A. G., Galletta, D. F., & Thong, J. Y. L. (2003). Software piracy in the workplace: A model and empirical test. *Journal of Management Information Systems*, *20*(1), 153–177.

Peng, Y. S., & Lin, S. S. (2008). Local responsiveness pressure, subsidiary resources, green management adoption and subsidiary's performance: Evidence from Taiwanese manufactures. *Journal of Business Ethics*, *79*(1-2), 199–212. doi:10.1007/s10551-007-9382-8

Pentland, B. T. (1999). Building process theory with narrative: From description to explanation. *Academy of Management Review*, *24*(4), 711–724.

Perlman, D., & Takacs, G. (1990). The ten stages of change. *Nursing Management*, *21*(4), 33–38. doi:10.1097/00006247-199004000-00010

Peterson, B., Major, B., Cozarelli, C., & Crocker, J. (1988). *The social construction of gender differences in values.* Paper presented at the Annual Meeting of the Eastern Psychological Association, Buffalo, NY.

Petter, S., DeLone, W., & McLean, E. (2008). Measuring information systems success: Models, dimensions, measures, and interrelationships. *European Journal of Information Systems*, *17*(3), 236–263. doi:10.1057/ejis.2008.15

Pfeffer, J. (1992). *Management with power.* Boston, MA: Harvard Business School Press.

Phau, I., & Ong, D. (2007). An investigation of the effects of environmental claims in promotional messages for clothing brands. *Marketing Intelligence & Planning*, *25*(7), 772–788. doi:10.1108/02634500710834214

Pinto, J. K., & Millet, I. (1999). *Successful information system implementation: The human side.* Newtown Square, PA: Project Management Institute.

Pitt, J., Kamara, L., Sergot, M., & Artikis, A. (2005). Formalization of a voting protocol for virtual organizations. In *Proceedings of the Fourth International Joint Conference on Autonomous Agents and Multiagent Systems* (pp. 373-380). New York, NY: ACM Press.

Plouffe, C. R., Hulland, J. S., & Vandenbosch, M. (2001). Research Report: Richness Versus Parsimony in Modeling Technology Adoption Decisions - Understanding Merchant Adoption of a Smart Card-Based Payment System. *Information Systems Research*, *12*(2), 208–222. doi:10.1287/isre.12.2.208.9697

Png, I. P. L. (2010). On the Reliability of Software Piracy Statistics. In *Proceedings of the 43rd Hawaii International Conference on Systems Sciences,* Los Alamitos, CA. Washington, DC: IEEE Computer Society Press.

Poesio, M. (1995). Semantic ambiguity and perceived ambiguity. In van Deemter, K., & Peters, S. (Eds.), *Semantic ambiguity and underspecification* (pp. 1–47). Stanford, CA: Center for the Study of Language and Information.

Poole, M., & Van de Ven, A. (2004). *Handbook of Organizational Change and Innovation.* New York, NY: Oxford University Press.

Porras, J., & Robertson, P. (1987). Organizational development theory: A typology and evaluation. In Woodman, R. W., & Pasmore, W. A. (Eds.), *Research in Organizational Change and Development* (*Vol. 1*, pp. 1–57). Greenwich, CT: JAI Press.

Porter, M., Schwab, K., Martin, X., & Lopez-Claros, A. (2005). *The global competitiveness report 2004-2005.* Retrieved from https://members.weforum.org/pdf/Global_Competitiveness_Reports/GCR05_Video_Transcript.pdf

Potosky, D., & Ramakrishna, H. V. (2002). The moderating role of updating climate perceptions in the relationship between goal orientation, self-efficacy, and job performance. *Human Performance*, *15*, 275–297. doi:10.1207/S15327043HUP1503_03

Pozzebon, M., & Pinsonneault, A. (2001, June 27-29). Structuration theory in the IS field: An assessment of research strategies. In *Proceedings of the 9th European Conference on Information Systems*, Bled, Slovenia (pp. 205 -217).

Preston, P. (2004). *European Union ICT policies: Neglected social and cultural dimensions in the European information society.* Bristol, UK: Intellect Books.

Pryor, J. B., Reeder, G. D., Yeadon, C., & Hesson-McInnis, M. (2004). A dual-process model of reactions to perceived stigma. *Journal of Personality and Social Psychology*, *87*(4), 436–452. doi:10.1037/0022-3514.87.4.436

Queensland Government Chief Information Office. (2009). *Queensland government ICT skills framework*. Retrieved from http://www.psc.qld.gov.au

Rallapalli, K. C., & Vitell, S. J. (1998). The influence of norms on ethical judgments and intentions: An empirical study of marketing professionals. *Journal of Business Research*, *43*(3), 157–168. doi:10.1016/S0148-2963(97)00221-X

Ramiller, N. C., & Pentland, B. T. (2009). Management implications in information system research: The untold story. *Journal of Management Information Systems*, *10*(6), 474–495.

Rapeepisarn, K., Wong, K. W., Fung, C. C., & Depickere, A. (2006). Similarities and Differences Between "Learn Through Play" and "Edutainment". In *Proceedings of the 3rd Australasian conference on Interactive entertainment IE '06*.

Reich, B. H., & Benbasat, I. (2000). Factors That Influence the Social Dimension of Alignment Between Business and Information Technology Objectives. *Management Information Systems Quarterly*, *24*(1), 81–113. doi:10.2307/3250980

Reich, B. H., & Kaarst-Brown, M. L. (1999). Seeding the line: Understanding the transition from IT to non-IT careers. *Management Information Systems Quarterly*, *23*, 337–364. doi:10.2307/249467

Reich, B. H., & Kaarst-Brown, M. L. (2003). Creating social and intellectual capital through IT career transitions. *The Journal of Strategic Information Systems*, *12*, 91–109. doi:10.1016/S0963-8687(03)00017-9

Reidenbach, R. E., & Robin, D. P. (1990). Toward the development of a multi-dimensional scale for improving evaluations of business ethics. *Journal of Business Ethics*, *9*(8), 639–653. doi:10.1007/BF00383391

Reimann, R. (2001). Lesbian mothers at work. In Bernstein, M., & Reimann, R. (Eds.), *Queer families, queer politics: Challenging culture and the state* (pp. 254–271). New York, NY: Columbia University Press.

Reinig, B. A. (2003). Toward an understanding of satisfaction with the process and outcomes of teamwork. *Journal of Management Information Systems*, *19*(4), 65–83.

Reinig, B. A., Briggs, R. O., & Nunamaker, J. F. Jr. (2007). On the measurement of ideation quality. *Journal of Management Information Systems*, *23*(4), 143–161. doi:10.2753/MIS0742-1222230407

Richmond, V. P., & Roach, K. D. (1992). Willingness to communicate and employee success in U.S. organizations. *Journal of Applied Communication Research*, 95–115. doi:10.1080/00909889209365321

Riemenschneider, C. K., Hardgrave, B. C., & Davis, F. (2002). Explaining Software Developer Acceptance of Methodologies: A Comparison of Five Theoretical Models. *IEEE Transactions on Software Engineering*, *28*(12), 1135–1145. doi:10.1109/TSE.2002.1158287

Ringle, C. M., Wende, S., & Will, A. (2005). *SmartPLS (2.0 beta ed.)*. Hamburg, Germany: University of Hamburg. Retrieved from http://www.smartpls.de

Ringle, C. M., Wende, S., & Will, A. (2005). *SmartPLS (Version 2.0 beta)*. Hamburg, Germany: University of Hamburg.

Rittenbruch, M., Kahler, H., & Cremers, A. B. (1998). Supporting cooperation in a virtual organization. In *Proceedings of the International Conference on Information Systems* (pp. 30-38).

Rogers, E. M. (1962). *Diffusion of Innovations* (4th ed.). New York: The Free Press.

Rogers, E. M. (2003). *The diffusion of innovation*. New York, NY: Free Press.

Rollings, A., & Adams, E. (2003). *Andrew Rollings and Ernest Adams on Game Design*. New Riders.

Roode, J. D. (1993). Implications for teaching of a process-based research framework for information systems. In *Proceedings of the 8th Annual Conference of the International Academy for Information Management*, Orlando, FL.

Rose, J., & Hackney, R. (2002). Towards a structurational theory of information systems: a substantive case analysis. In *Proceedings of the 36th Hawaii International Conference on System Sciences* (Vol. 8, p. 258).

Rose, M. (1969). *Computers, managers, and society.* New York, NY: Penguin.

Rosenau, J. N. (1962). Consensus-building in the American National Community: Some hypotheses and some supporting data. *The Journal of Politics, 24*(4), 639–661. doi:10.2307/2128039

Rosser, S. (2003). Women are Underrepresented in Science and Engineering Faculties. *Academe,* 25–28.

Roth, D. F., & Stolba, C. (1999). *Women's Figures.* Washington, DC: AEI Press.

Rowlands, B. (2005). Grounded in practice: Using interpretive research to build theory. *Electronic Journal of Business Research Methodology, 3*(1), 81–92.

Rusbult, C. E., Farrell, D., Rogers, G., & Mainouss, A. G. III. (1988). Impact of exchange variables on exit, voice, loyalty, and neglect: An integrative model of responses to declining job satisfaction. *Academy of Management Journal, 31,* 589–599. doi:10.2307/256461

Salancik, G. (1977). Commitment and the control of organizational behavior and belief. In Staw, B., & Salancik, G. (Eds.), *New directions in organizational Behavior* (pp. 1–53). Chicago, IL: St. Clair Press.

Salvucci, D. D., & Goldberg, J. H. (2000). Identifying Fixations and Saccades in Eye-Tracking Protocols. In *Proceedings of the ETRA 2000.*

Santella, A., & DeCarlo, D. (2004). Robust Clustering of Eye Movement Recordings for Quantification of Visual Interest. In *Proceedings of the ETRA 2004.*

Scarbrough, H. (1998). Linking strategy and IT-based innovation: The importance of the "management of expertise". In Galliers, R. D., & Baets, W. R. J. (Eds.), *Information technology and organisational transformation: Innovation for the 21ˢᵗ century organization.* Chichester, UK: John Wiley & Sons.

Schambach, T. P. (1994). *Maintaining professional competence: An evaluation of factors affecting professional obsolescence of information technology professionals.* Unpublished manuscript, Tampa, FL.

Schein, E. (1996). Kurt Lewin's change theory in the field and in the classroom: Notes toward a model of managed learning. *Systems Practice, 9*(1), 27–47. doi:10.1007/BF02173417

Senge, P. (1990). *The Fifth Discipline.* Kent, UK: Century Business.

Shaver, K. (2007). Stay-at-Home Dads Forge New Identities, Roles. *Washington Post,* A01.

Shaw, D., & Shiu, E. (2003). Ethics in consumer choice: A multivariate modelling approach. *European Journal of Marketing, 37*(10), 1485–1498. doi:10.1108/03090560310487202

Sherer, S. A., & Alter, S. (2004). Information system risks and risk factors: Are they mostly about Information Systems. *Communications of the AIS, 14*(2), 36–65.

Shin, S. K., Gopal, R. D., Sanders, G. L., & Whinston, A. B. (2004). Global Software Piracy Revisited. *Communications of the ACM, 47*(1), 103–107. doi:10.1145/962081.962088

Sidorova, A., Evangelopoulos, N., Valacich, J. S., & Ramakrishnan, T. (2008). Uncovering the intellectual core of the information systems discipline. *Management Information Systems Quarterly, 32*(3), 467–482.

Siller, J., Chipman, A., Ferguson, L., & Vann, D. H. (1967). *Attitudes of the nondisabled toward the physically disabled* (Tech. Rep. No. RD-707). New York, NY: New York University School of Education.

Simmers, C. A. (1998). Executive/ board politics in strategic decision making. *Journal of Business and Economic Studies, 4*(1), 37–56.

Simonin, B. L. (1999). Ambiguity and the process of knowledge transfer in strategic alliances. *Strategic Management Journal, 20*(7), 595–623. doi:10.1002/(SICI)1097-0266(199907)20:7<595::AID-SMJ47>3.0.CO;2-5

Singell, L., & Stone, J. (1993). Gender Differences in PhD Economists' Careers. *Western Economic Association International, 11*(4), 95–106.

Sippel, B., & Brodt, S. E. (2008). The psychology of blogging communities: Social identities and knowledge transfer across work-groups. In *Proceedings of the 2nd International AAAI Conference on Weblogs and Social Media.*

Soh, C., & Markus, M. L. (1995). How IT creates business value: A process theory synthesis. In *Proceedings of the Sixteenth International Conference on Information Systems.*

Sohal, A., & Ng, L. (1998). The role and impact of information technology in Australian business. *Journal of Information Technology, 13*(3), 201–217. doi:10.1080/026839698344846

Sorokin, P. A. (1927). *Social mobility.* New York, NY: Harper.

Spector, P. E. (1975). Relationships of organizational frustration with reported behavioral reactions of employees. *The Journal of Applied Psychology, 60,* 635–637. doi:10.1037/h0077157

Spector, P. E. (1978). Organizational frustration: A model and review of the literature. *Personnel Psychology, 31,* 815–829. doi:10.1111/j.1744-6570.1978.tb02125.x

Sri Lanka, I. C. T. Association. (2007). *Rising demand: The increasing demand for IT workers spells a challenging opportunity for the IT industry.* Moratuwa, Sri Lanka: Author.

Staw, B. M., Sandelands, L. E., & Dutton, J. E. (1981). Threat-rigidity effects in organizational behavior: A multilevel analysis. *Administrative Science Quarterly, 26,* 501–524. doi:10.2307/2392337

Steele, C. M., & Aronson, J. (1995). Stereotype threat and intellectual performance of African Americans. *Journal of Personality and Social Psychology, 69,* 797–811. doi:10.1037/0022-3514.69.5.797

Steiner, D. D., & Farr, J. L. (1986). Career goals, organizational reward systems and technical updating in engineers. *Journal of Occupational Psychology, 59,* 13–24. doi:10.1111/j.2044-8325.1986.tb00209.x

Stenross, B., & Kleinman, S. (1989). The highs and lows of emotional labor. *Journal of Contemporary Ethnography, 17*(4), 435–452. doi:10.1177/089124189017004003

Stocker, A., & Tochtermann, K. (2008). Investigating weblogs in small and medium enterprises: An exploratory case study. In *Proceedings of the Workshops on Social Aspects of the Web.*

Straub, D. W. (1989). Validating instruments in MIS research. *Management Information Systems Quarterly, 13*(2), 147–169. doi:10.2307/248922

Straub, D. W., Boudreau, M.-C., & Gefen, D. (2004). Validation guidelines for IS positivist research. *Communications of the AIS, 13*(24), 380–427.

Straub, D. W., & Burton-Jones, A. (2007). Veni, Vidi, Vici: Breaking the TAM Logjam. *Journal of the Association for Information Systems, 8*(4), 223–229.

Straub, D. W., Limayem, M., & Karahanna, E. (1995). Measuring System Usage: Implications for IS Theory Testing. *Management Science, 41*(8), 1328–1342. doi:10.1287/mnsc.41.8.1328

Straub, D., & Limayem, M., & Karahanna-Evastiro. (1995). Measuring system usage: Implications for IS system testing. *Management Science, 41*(8), 1328–1342. doi:10.1287/mnsc.41.8.1328

Struckman, C., & Yammarino, F. (2003). Organizational change: A categorization scheme and response model with readiness factors. *Research in Organizational Change and Development, 14*(1), 1–50. doi:10.1016/S0897-3016(03)14079-7

Sundararajan, A. (2004). Managing digital piracy: Pricing and protection. *Information Systems Research, 15*(3), 287–308. doi:10.1287/isre.1040.0030

Sun, H., & Zhang, P. (2006). Causal Relationships between Perceived Enjoyment and Perceived Ease of Use: An Alternative Approach. *Journal of the Association for Information Systems, 7*(9), 618–645.

Swann, W. B. Jr, & Ely, R. J. (1984). A battle of wills: Self-verification versus behavioral confirmation. *Journal of Personality and Social Psychology, 46,* 1287–1302. doi:10.1037/0022-3514.46.6.1287

Sweller, J., van Merrienboer, J., & Paas, F. (1998). Cognitive architecture and instructional design. *Educational Psychology Review, 10*(3), 251–296. doi:10.1023/A:1022193728205

Sykes, G. M., & Matza, D. (1957). Techniques of neutralization: A theory of delinquency. *American Sociological Review, 22,* 664–670. doi:10.2307/2089195

Szulanski, G. (2000). The process of knowledge transfer: A diachronic analysis of stickiness. *Organizational Behavior and Human Decision Processes, 82*(1), 9–27. doi:10.1006/obhd.2000.2884

Tannen, D. (1994). *Talking from 9 to 5: How women's and men's conversational styles affect who gets heard, who gets credit, and what gets done at work.* New York, NY: William Morrow & Company.

Tarasewich, P., & Fillion, S. (2004). Discount Eye Tracking: The Enhanced Restricted Focus Viewer. In *Proceedings of the Tenth Americas Conference on Information Systems*, New York.

Taylor, S. E., & Brown, J. (1988). Illusion and well-being: Some social psychological contributions to a theory of mental health. *Psychological Bulletin, 103*, 193–210. doi:10.1037/0033-2909.103.2.193

Taylor, S., & Todd, P. (1995). Assessing IT usage: The role of prior experience. *Management Information Systems Quarterly, 19*(4), 561–570. doi:10.2307/249633

Tesser, A., & Campbell, J. (1980). Self-definition: The impact of relative performance and similarity of others. *Social Psychology Quarterly, 43*, 341–347. doi:10.2307/3033737

Tesser, A., & Campbell, J. (1983). Self-definition and self-evaluation maintenance. In Suls, J., & Greenwald, A. G. (Eds.), *Psychological perspectives on the self* (Vol. 2, pp. 1–31). Mahwah, NJ: Lawrence Erlbaum.

The American Heritage Dictionaries. (2000). *American heritage dictionary of the English language* (4th ed.). Boston, MA: Houghton Mifflin.

Thong, J. Y. L., & Yap, C. (1998). Testing an ethical decision-making theory: The case of softlifting. *Journal of Management Information Systems, 15*(1), 213–237.

Thong, J. Y. L., Yap, C.-S., & Raman, K. S. (1996). Top management support, external expertise and information systems implementation in small businesses. *Information Systems Research, 7*(2), 248–267. doi:10.1287/isre.7.2.248

Torraco, R. J. (2005). Writing integrative literature reviews: Guidelines and examples. *Human Resource Development Review, 4*(3), 356–367. doi:10.1177/1534484305278283

Trammell, K. D. S. (2007). Candidate campaign blogs: Directly reaching out to the youth vote. *The American Behavioral Scientist, 50*(9), 1255–1264. doi:10.1177/0002764207300052

Tranfield, D., Denyer, D., & Smart, P. (2003). Towards a methodology for developing evidence-informed management knowledge by means of systematic review. *British Journal of Management, 14*(3), 207–223. doi:10.1111/1467-8551.00375

Transparency International. (2004). *Transparency International Corruption Perceptions Index 2004*. Retrieved September 17, 2007, from http://www.transparency.org/policy_research/surveys_indices/cpi/2004

Traphagan, M., & Griffith, A. (1998). Software Piracy and Global Competitiveness: Report on Global Software Piracy. *International Review of Low Computers, 12*(3), 431–451. doi:10.1080/13600869855298

Trauth, E., & Quesenberry, J. (2006). Are Women an Underserved Community in the Information Technology Profession? In *Proceedings of the Twenty-Seventh International Conference on Information Systems (ICIS)*, Milwaukee, WI (pp. 1757-1770).

Travica, B. (2005). Virtual organization and electronic commerce. *SIGMIS Database, 36*(3), 45–68. doi:10.1145/1080390.1080395

Trevino, L. K., & Webster, J. (1992). Flow in computer-mediated communication: Electronic mail and voice mail evaluation and impacts. *Communication Research, 19*, 539–573. doi:10.1177/009365092019005001

Trice, A. W., & Treacy, M. E. (1988). Utilization as a dependent variable in MIS research. *Database, 19*(3-4), 33–42.

Trimi, S., & Galanxhi-Janaqi, H. (2008). Organisation and employee congruence: A framework for assessing the success of organisational blogs. *International Journal of Information Technology and Management, 7*(2), 120–133. doi:10.1504/IJITM.2008.016600

Truban, E., McLean, E., & Wetherbe, J. (2002). *Information technology for management* (3rd ed.). New York, NY: John Wiley & Sons.

Truman, G. E., & Baroudi, J. J. (1994). Gender Differences in the Information Systems Managerial Ranks: an Assessment of Potential Discriminatory Practices. *Management Information Systems Quarterly, 18*, 129–141. doi:10.2307/249761

Tsai, H. Y., Compeau, D., & Haggerty, N. (2007). Of races to run and battles to be won: Technical skill updating, stress, and coping of IT professionals. *Human Resource Management, 46*, 395–409. doi:10.1002/hrm.20170

Tschohl, J. (2004). Geeks: Train and handle with care! *The Canadian Manager, 29*(3), 24.

Tuckman, B. W. (1965). Developmental Sequence in Small Groups. *Psychological Bulletin, 63*, 384–399. doi:10.1037/h0022100

Turner Parish, J., Cadwallader, S., & Busch, P. (2008). Want to, need to, ought to: employee commitment to organizational change. *Journal of Organizational Change Management, 21*(1), 32–52. doi:10.1108/09534810810847020

Turner, J. C. (1991). *Social influence.* Berkshire, UK: Open University Press.

Turner, K. L., & Makhija, M. V. (2006). The role of organizational controls in managing knowledge. *Academy of Management Review, 31*(1), 197–217.

Twigg, N. (2010). *Celebrate Geek Pride Day 2010.* Retrieved on from http://www.forevergeek.com/2010/05/celebrate_geek_pride_day_2010/

UNESCO. (2009). *A global perspective on research and development.* Montreal, QC, Canada: UNESCO Institute for Statistics.

United Nations. (1987). *Report of the world commission on environment and development: General Assembly Resolution 42/187.* Retrieved from http://www.un.org/documents/ga/res/42/ares42-187.htm

Van de Ven, A. H., & Poole, M. S. (1995). Explaining development and change in organizations. *Academy of Management Review, 20*(3), 510–540.

van der Heijden, H. (2004). User acceptance of hedonic information systems. *Management Information Systems Quarterly, 28*(4), 695–705.

Vann, D. H. (1976). *Personal responsibility, authoritarianism, and treatment of the obese.* Unpublished doctoral dissertation, New York University, New York.

Veel, K. (2003). The irreducibility of space: labyrinths, cities, cyberspace. *Diacritics, 33*(3-4), 151–172. doi:10.1353/dia.2006.0014

Velicer, W. F. (1976). Determining the number of components from the matrix of partial correlations. *Psychometrika, 41*(3), 321–327. doi:10.1007/BF02293557

Venkatesh, V., Brown, S. A., Maruping, L., & Bala, A., Hillol. (2008). Predicting different conceptualizations of system use: The competing roles of behavioral intention, facilitating conditions, and behavioral expectation. *Management Information Systems Quarterly, 32*(3), 483–502.

Venkatesh, V., Davis, F., & Morris, M. G. (2007). Dead or Alive? The Development, Trajectory and Future of Technology Adoption Research. *Journal of the Association for Information Systems, 8*(4), 267–286.

Venkatesh, V., & Morris, M. G. (2000). Why Don't Men Ever Stop to Ask for Directions? Gender, Social Influence, and Their Role in Technology Acceptance and Usage Behavior. *Management Information Systems Quarterly, 24*(1), 115–139. doi:10.2307/3250981

Venkatesh, V., Morris, M. G., Davis, G. B., & Davis, F. D. (2003). User acceptance of information technology: Toward a unified view. *Management Information Systems Quarterly, 27*(3), 425–473.

Vennix, J. A. M., Akkermans, H. A., & Rouwette, E. A. J. A. (1996). Group model-building to facilitate organizational change: An exploratory study. *System Dynamics Review, 12*, 39–58. doi:10.1002/(SICI)1099-1727(199621)12:1<39::AID-SDR94>3.0.CO;2-K

Verplanken, B., Aarts, H., & van Knippenberg, A. (1997). Habit information acquisition and the process of making travel mode choices. *European Journal of Social Psychology, 27*(5), 539–560. doi:10.1002/(SICI)1099-0992(199709/10)27:5<539::AID-EJSP831>3.0.CO;2-A

Vigoda-Gadot, E. (2003). *Developments in organizational politics.* Cheltenham, UK: Edward Elgar.

Vigoda-Gadot, E., & Cohen, A. (2002). Influence tactics and perceptions of organizational politics. A longitudinal study. *Journal of Business Research, 5*, 311–324. doi:10.1016/S0148-2963(00)00134-X

Vigoda-Gadot, E., & Drory, A. (2006). *Handbook of organizational politics.* Cheltenham, UK: Edward Elgar.

Villimez, W. J. (1974). Ability vs. effort: Ideological correlates of occupational grading. *Social Forces, 53*, 45–52. doi:10.2307/2576836

Vincent-Lancrin, S. (2006). What is changing in academic research? Trends and Future Scenarios. *European Journal of Education, 41*(2), 169–202. doi:10.1111/j.1465-3435.2006.00255.x

Von Baeyer, C. L., Sherk, D. L., & Zanna, M. P. (1981). Impression management on the job interview: When the female applicant meets the male (chauvinist) interviewer. *Personality and Social Psychology Bulletin, 7*, 45–51. doi:10.1177/014616728171008

Wadlinger, H. A., & Isaacowitz, D. M. (2006). Positive Mood Broadens Visual Attention to Positive Stimuli. *Motivation and Emotion, 30*, 89–101. doi:10.1007/s11031-006-9021-1

Wagner, C. (2006). Breaking the Knowledge Acquisition Bottleneck Through Conversational Management. *Information Resources Management Journal, 19*(1), 70–83.

Wagner, C., & Bolloju, N. (2005). Supporting Knowledge Management in Organizations with Conversational Technologies: Discussion forums, Weblogs and Wikis. *Journal of Database Management, 16*(2).

Wagner, J. III, & Hollenbeck, J. (1998). *Organizational behavior: Securing competitive advantage* (3rd ed.). Upper Saddle River, NJ: Prentice Hall.

Walsham, G., & Ham, C. K. (1991). Structuration theory and information systems research. *Journal of Applied System Analysis, 17*, 77–85.

Walsham, G., & Waema, T. (1994). Information systems strategy and implementation: A case study of a building society. *ACM Transactions on Information Systems, 12*(2), 159–173. doi:10.1145/196734.196744

Walsh, J. P., & Bayma, T. (1997). *Computer networks and scientific work*. Mahwah, NJ: Lawrence Erlbaum.

Wasko, M. M., & Faraj, S. (2005). Why Should I Share? Examining Social Capital and Knowledge Contribution in Electronic Networks of Practice. *Management Information Systems Quarterly, 29*(1), 35–57.

Wattal, S., Racherla, P., & Mandviwalla, M. (2009). Employee adoption of corporate blogs: A qualitative analysis. In *Proceedings of the Hawaii International Conference on System Sciences*.

Weasenforth, D., Biesenbach-Lucas, S., & Meloni, C. (2002). Realizing constructivist objectives through collaborative technologies: Threaded discussions. *Language Learning & Technology, 6*(3), 58–86.

Webster, J., Trevino, L. K., & Ryan, L. (1993). The dimensionality and correlates of flow in human-computer interactions. *Computers in Human Behavior, 9*, 411–426. doi:10.1016/0747-5632(93)90032-N

Webster, J., & Watson, R. T. (2002). Analyzing the past to prepare for the future: Writing a literature review. *Management Information Systems Quarterly, 26*(2), xiii–xxiii.

Wehmeyer, K., & Riemer, K. (2007). Trust-building potential of coordination roles in virtual organizations. *The Electronic Journal for Virtual Organizations and Networks, 8*, 102–123.

Weick, K. E. (1993). The collapse of sensemaking in organizations: The Mann Gulch disaster. *Administrative Science Quarterly, 38*(4), 628–652. doi:10.2307/2393339

Weiner, B., Perry, R., & Magnusson, J. (1988). An attributional analysis of reactions to stigmas. *Journal of Personality and Social Psychology, 55*, 738–748. doi:10.1037/0022-3514.55.5.738

Weiss, J., & Anderson, D. (2002). CIOs and IT professionals as change agents, risk and stakeholder managers: A field study. In *Proceedings of the 36th Hawaii International Conference on System Sciences*.

White, J., & Dozier, D. M. (1992). Public relations and management decision making. In Grunig, J. E. (Ed.), *Excellence in public relations and communication management* (pp. 51–84). Mahwah, NJ: Lawrence Erlbaum.

Whitten, N. (1995). *Managing software development projects: Formula for success*. New York, NY: John Wiley & Sons.

Wildavsky, A. (1974). *The politics of the budgetary process* (2nd ed.). Boston, MA: Little, Brown.

Wilensky, H. L. (1967). The failure of intelligence: Knowledge and policy in government and industry. In *Proceedings of the Nineteenth Annual Winter Meeting of the Industrial Relations Research Association*.

Williams, L. J., & Hazer, J. T. (1986). Antecedents and consequences of satisfaction and commitment in turnover models: A reanalysis using latent variable structural equation methods. *The Journal of Applied Psychology, 71*(2), 219–231. doi:10.1037/0021-9010.71.2.219

Winch, G., & Schneider, E. (1993). Managing the knowledge-based organization: The case of architectural practice. *Journal of Management Studies, 6*, 923–937. doi:10.1111/j.1467-6486.1993.tb00472.x

Wixom, B. H., & Todd, P. A. (2005). A theoretical integration of user satisfaction and technology acceptance. *Information Systems Research*, *16*(1), 85–103. doi:10.1287/isre.1050.0042

Wloszczyna, S., & Oldenburg, A. (2003). *Fickle finger of fashion puts 'eek' in 'geek*. Retrieved from.http://www.usatoday.com/tech/news/2003-10-22-geek-chic_x.htm

Wolff, S., & Sydor, K. (1999). Information systems strategy development and implementation: A nursing home perspective. *Journal of Healthcare Information Management*, *13*(1), 2–12.

World Bank. (2007). *Key Development Data and Statistics*. Retrieved July 17, 2007, from www.worldbank.org/data/countrydata/countrydata.html

Yardi, S., Golder, S. A., & Brozozowski, M. J. (2009). Blogging at work and the corporate attention economy. In *Proceedings of the 27th International Conference on Human Factors in Computing Systems*.

Yardi, S., Golder, S. A., & Brzozowski, M. (2008). *The pulse of the corporate blogosphere*. Paper presented at the Computer Supported Collaborative Work Conference.

Yin, K. (2009). *Case study research, design and methods* (2nd ed.). Newbury Park, CA: Sage.

YouTube. (2001). SHRM commercial version 1. Retrieved from.http://www.youtube.com/watch?v=Now74xATro4&NR=1

YouTube. (2009). *Barclays: fake*. Retrieved from http://www.youtube.com/watch?v=-N-Htse4sPI

Yukl, G., & Falbe, C. M. (1990). Influence tactics and objectives in upward, downward and lateral influence attempts. *The Journal of Applied Psychology*, *75*(2), 132–140. doi:10.1037/0021-9010.75.2.132

Zhang, Z., Cheung, K.-H., & Townsend, J. P. (2008). Bringing Web 2.0 to bioinformatics. *Briefings in Bioinformatics*, *10*(1), 1–10. doi:10.1093/bib/bbn041

Zhu, Q., Sarkis, J., Cordeiro, J. J., & Hung, K. (2008). Firm-level correlates of emergent green supply chain management practices in the Chinese context. *Omega*, *36*(4), 577–591. doi:10.1016/j.omega.2006.11.009

# About the Contributors

**Dawn Medlin** is the Chairperson and Professor of Computer Information Systems in the John A. Walker College of Business. Dawn also serves as Co-Chair of the Center for Applied Research on Emerging Technologies. Her teaching, research, and consulting activities have primarily been in the areas of security, health care information systems, webpage development and design, and the interaction between computers and people. Dr. Medlin is very active in research activities and she has published her research in journals such as the *Journal of Computer Information Systems, International Journal of Information Security and Privacy, Journal of Information Technology Research, Journal of Information Privacy and Security, Information Systems Security: the (ISC)2 Journal,* as well as other national and international publications. Additionally, she had completed several funded research projects and served in several capabilities of leadership to many professional organizations. Dr. Medlin taught in Angers, France as a Visiting Professor in 2007, and has been an invited lecturer in Ethiopia and Taiwan. Before joining ASU she owned a Business/Marketing company and worked in the IT field for more than 10 years.

\* \* \*

**Salem Al-Agtash** got his PhD in electrical engineering from the University of Colorado at Boulder in 1998. He served as a department chair (2001 – 2003) and a managing director (2003-2005) at Yamouk University and a dean (2005 – 2009) at the German-Jordanian University. Dr. Al-Agtash is currently an associate professor of computer engineering at Yarmouk University and a senior advisor on ICT and Technology to the Arab States Research and Education Network GmbH and to the Arab Organization for Quality Assurance in Education. He has worked on several research and international development projects, mainly with the World bank, European Commission, JIKA, and USAID. He has been very active in developing relevant and quality ICT educational programs, strengthening tri-partite links between university, private sector and government, and building international cooperation in education, mainly in Europe. His research interests are in the areas of electricity industry, agent based systems, software engineering, and education management.

**Murugan Anandarajan**, Ph.D., is a Professor of Management Information Systems in the Department of Management at Drexel University. His current research interests include Artificial Intelligence-based classification, artificial life, and Internet usage. His research has appeared in journals such as Behavior and Information Technology, Computers and Operations Research, Decision Sciences, Industrial Data Management Systems, Information and Management, International Journal of Information Management,

Journal of Management Information Systems, Journal of Global Information Systems, Journal of International Business Studies, and the Omega-International Journal of Management Science among others.

**Soon Ang** (PhD Minnesota), Goh Tjoei Kok chaired professor in management, heads the Division of Strategy, Management and Organization at the Nanyang Technological University (NTU) in Singapore. She is current senior editor of MIS *Quarterly, and past senior editor of Information Systems Research (ISR),* and *Journal of the Association for Information Systems.* She publishes extensively in *Management Science, MIS Quarterly, ISR, Organization Science, Communications of the ACM, Academy of Management Journal, Journal of Applied Psychology,* etc. She has won Best Paper awards in SIGMIS, HICCS, and Academy of Management. Soon Ang is recognized world authority in Cultural Intelligence (CQ), global leadership, and outsourcing. She was recently awarded the Public Administrative Medal (Silver) from the President of the Republic of Singapore; the Distinguished Leadership Award for International Alumni from the University of Minnesota; and the Nanyang Award for Research and Innovation, the highest recognition on outstanding research given by NTU.

**John Conway** teaches English and writing online for The Art Institute of Pittsburgh. His dissertation in English literature at The University of South Carolina, "American Labyrinths: Cultural Explorations of Identity and Place" is a study of the labyrinth as a trope in American literature, film, and the culture at large. The project attempts to reconcile the modern prevalence of the sign with its mythical foundation and its genealogy within the Western tradition.

**Gerald DeHondt** is an Assistant Professor in the School of Computing and Information Systems at Grand Valley State University. Prior to his current role, he worked for Compuware Corporation providing consulting services to Fortune 500 companies. While at Compuware, he held increasingly responsible positions as a Programmer/Analyst, Quality Assurance Manager, Network Architect, Enterprise Architect, and as a Project Manager guiding delivery of high-value projects. Dr. DeHondt has taught courses at the Graduate and Undergraduate level in Information Systems Strategy, Project Management, Information Security, Systems Analysis and Design, and Network Architecture. His research interests include Offshore Outsourcing of Systems Development and Agile Software Development Methodologies. He has a number of journal publications and his research has appeared at various national conferences, including the Decision Sciences Institute (DSI), the Americas Conference on Information Systems (AMCIS), the Conference on Information Systems Applied Research (CONISAR), and the Hawaii International Conference on System Sciences (HICSS).

**Amit V. Deokar** is an Assistant Professor of Information Systems in the College of Business and Information Systems at Dakota State University. His recent research interests are in business process management, collaboration processes and technologies, decision support systems, knowledge management, and healthcare informatics. He has published several conference publications, journal articles, and book chapters in these areas. He holds a BE in Mechanical Engineering from V.J. Technological Institute, Mumbai, a MS in Industrial Engineering from the University of Arizona, and a PhD in Management Information Systems from the University of Arizona. He is a member of AIS, ACM, and AAAI, and is currently serving as the President-elect of MWAIS.

**Sean P. Goggins** is an Assistant Professor in the College of Information Science and Technology at Drexel University in Philadelphia, PA, where he teaches courses in human-computer interaction, collaborative software design, software engineering and technology management. Dr. Goggins' current research interests include management of distributed work teams, collaborative information behavior and social computing. Dr. Goggins has 15 years of experience designing and implementing cutting edge collaborative software at Fortune 500, Global 50 and technology startup companies. Dr. Goggins may be reached at outdoors@acm.org

**Jesus Guajardo**, MD is an Assistant Professor at University of Texas Health Science Center San Antonio.. Dr. Guajardo also holds a Masters in Health Professions from the University of Ilinois at Chicago, and is a PhD candidate at the School of Information Science and Learning Technology at the University of Missouri-Columbia.

**Joel Helquist** is an assistant professor of accounting at Utah Valley University. Dr. Helquist graduated with a Ph.D. in Business Management with an emphasis in Management Information Systems from the University of Arizona. Prior to completing his Ph.D., Dr. Helquist worked as a risk management consultant for Arthur Andersen, LLP and KPMG, LLP in Seattle, Washington. His research interests are primarily focused around risk management and processes and technologies to support collaboration.

**Andrea J. Hester** is an Assistant Professor in Computer Management and Information Systems in the School of Business, Southern Illinois University Edwardsville. Her primary teaching area is information systems for business emphasizing both concepts and applications. Andrea's research interests focus on social and organizational aspects of technology use, Knowledge Management and Knowledge Management Systems, Innovative Technology Diffusion, and Wiki Technology. She has published work in proceedings of national conferences including ICIS, AMCIS and HICSS.

**Tiko Iyamu** is a professor of information systems at the Tshwane University of Technology, Pretoria, South Africa. He also serves as a professor extraordinaire at the department of computer science, University of the Western Cape, South Africa. Before taken fulltime appointment in academic, he held several positions in both public and private organisations. He was Chief Architect of the City of Cape Town; and Head of Architecture & Governance at a South Africa telecommunication company. His research interests include Mobile Computing, Enterprise Architecture, Information Technology Strategy; and focuses on Actor Network Theory (ANT) and Structuration Theory (ST). Iyamu is author of numerous peer-reviewed journal and conference proceedings articles. Tiko serves on journal board and conference proceedings committees.

**Monique Janneck** is junior professor for Work and Organizational Psychology at the University of Hamburg, Germany. She studied Psychology and earned a doctorate in Informatics with a thesis on the design of cooperative systems from a communication psychology perspective. Her research focus is on the interplay between human behavior, social structures and technological development: She is interested in the way humans interact with technology, the way theories and findings on human behavior can inform the design of information technology, and the way technology impacts individual, organizational, and social behavior and structures.

**Damien Joseph** is an assistant professor of information technology and management at the Nanyang Technological University (Singapore) where he received his PhD. His research interests are in the management of technology professionals; examining issues relating to their careers, compensation, competencies, culture, and leadership. Damien's research is published in top international journals including *MIS Quarterly, Communications of the ACM* and *Communications of the AIS*. Damien is a regular participant at major international conferences including the International Conference on Information Systems, Academy of Management Meetings, and the Association of Computing Machinery's SIGMIS-CPR Conferences. Damien has extensive consulting experience serving major local and international organizations such as the Center for Creative Leadership (Greensboro, N.C.) on its global leadership studies; Information Technology Management Association (ITMA, Singapore) on its salary benchmarking exercises; International Labor Organization (Geneva) on its World Employment Report 2001; Singapore Airlines; Singapore IT Dispute Resolution Committee, and Singapore Computer Society.

**John Kruse** is a Lead Information Systems Engineer at the MITRE Corporation. Previously, he was the Director of Systems Development at the Center for the Management of Information at the University of Arizona. He received his Ph.D. in Management Information Systems with a minor in Management and Policy from the University of Arizona in 2001. He holds a B.S. in Management Information Systems and an M.B.A. from the University of Wyoming. He has worked extensively with a wide range of educational, governmental and military groups to help develop group processes, software that supports collaborative work and automated means for deception and intent detection.

**Mary Sue Love** is an Associate Professor in the Department of Management and Marketing at Southern Illinois University Edwardsville. She holds a Ph.D. in organizational behavior with minors in social psychology and organizational communication from the University of Missouri, as well as an M.B.A. and a B.B.A. in management and organizational behavior from the University of Missouri - Kansas City. Before returning to school for her Ph.D., Mary Sue worked in the insurance industry, holding positions in underwriting, provider relations, and customer service. She teaches organizational behavior and negotiations. Mary Sue is primarily interested in improving interactions at work and has published articles in the *Journal of Applied Psychology, Career Development International, Communications of the ACM, International Journal of Management Concepts and Philosophy, Journal of Leadership and Organizational Studies, Leadership and Organization Development Journal,* and *Business Horizons*. Mary Sue can be reached at marlove@siue.edu.

**Thomas Meservy** is an Assistant Professor of Management Information Systems at the University of Memphis. He graduated with his PhD in Management from the University of Arizona in 2007. His research interests include software development tools and methodologies, collaboration, and automated understanding of human nonverbal behavior. His dissertation focused on creating and validating systems to augment human capabilities in automatically detecting deception by observing nonverbal behavior. In 2001, Dr. Meservy graduated from Brigham Young University with a B.S. in Management and a Masters of Information Systems Management. Since the late 90's Dr. Meservy has worked as a software developer/engineer for small-medium sized businesses, as well as larger consulting firms. He enjoys systems development and has been an independent consultant advising firms on best practice software development techniques.

**Jo Ellen Moore** is a Professor in the Department of Computer Management and Information Systems at Southern Illinois University Edwardsville. She holds a Ph.D. in organizational behavior and HR management from Indiana University, a master's degree in psychology from Illinois State University, and a B.A. in mathematics from Millikin University. In the corporate environment, Jo Ellen worked as an IT manager, project manager, systems programmer, and applications programmer. She teaches project management in the SIUE curriculum and in workshops offered through the School of Business Executive Education. As a researcher, Jo Ellen is interested in the management of IT professionals and technology. Her work has been published in both academic and applied outlets such as *Information Systems Research, MIS Quarterly, Academy of Management Review, MIS Quarterly Executive, Communications of the ACM, Human Resource Management Review, HR Magazine* and *Cutter Benchmark Review*. Jo Ellen can be reached at joemoor@siue.edu.

**Joi L. Moore** is an Associate Professor in the School of Information Science & Learning Technologies at the University of Missouri where she manages and teaches courses in the Digital Media Curriculum. Dr Moore's current research interests include: analyzing information architecture in Electronic Performance Support Systems and Interactive Learning Environments; usability engineering; and designing user-centered web applications based on Human Computer Interaction and Human Information Behavior.

**George Nezlek** is Associate Professor and Information Systems Program Chairman in the School of Computing and Information Systems at Grand Valley State University. Prior to that, he held a faculty appointment at Loyola University in Chicago, Illinois. While completing his PhD studies at UW – Milwaukee, he managed a software and facilities management consulting practice. He also holds an MBA in Information Systems, and a BA in Economics. Dr. Nezlek's research interests are in the areas of development methodologies, multi-platform computing, intelligent power and computing grid applications, and the application of economic theory to problems in Information Systems. His research has appeared in leading journals and conference proceedings, including CACM and HICSS. His teaching experience covers a broad range of subjects, but his specializations are in Databases and Systems Analysis. He currently serves as a vice-chairman of the Information Technology Interfaces Conference, and is a member of the AITP/EDSIG Advisory Board.

**Robert K. Plice** is an Associate Professor of Management Information Systems in the College of Business Administration at San Diego State University. He obtained his Ph.D. degree from the Graduate School of Management at the University of California, Irvine. His research interests include electronic commerce, the impact of network-centric organizations on firm strategy, the information economics of electronic communications, and the economics of software piracy. He holds MS degrees in business administration and computer science, and a BA degree in economics. Prior to joining SDSU he was active in the computer systems-integration and software industries as a manager, consultant, and engineer.

**Philip Raeth** is a doctoral student at the Institute of Research on Information Systems (IRIS) at the European Business School (EBS) in Wiesbaden/Oestrich-Winkel, Germany. He holds a Master's degree in Business Administration from the EBS. In addition to his academic work, he has worked as a consultant for IBM's Lotus branch. His current research interests include information systems success and information systems adoption. His work has been published in several conference proceedings.

**Bruce A. Reinig** is a Professor and Chair of the Department of Management Information Systems in the College of Business Administration at San Diego State University. He received his Ph.D. in Management Information Systems from the University of Arizona and his B.S. in Marketing from Truman State University. His research interests include the development and evaluation of technologies and work practices to support decision making, computer supported collaborative work, and the protection of intellectual property rights, particularly as it relates to software piracy.

**Matthew Schmidt** is a PhD candidate in the School of Information Science and Learning Technologies at the University of Missouri. He designs, develops and supports technologies to enhance learning and instruction across a multitude of disciplines, including nuclear science, radiation protection, biological anthropology, second language acquisition, architectural archiving, veterinary medicine and social competence instruction for individuals with autism spectrum disorders. His research interests are situated in the intersection of curriculum and technology and focus on how emergent technologies can be best implemented for optimal learning outcomes. He is currently project manager of the iSocial project (http://isocial.missouri.edu).

**Claire A. Simmers**, Ph.D., is a professor of management and department chair at Saint Joseph's University in Philadelphia, PA. She has been at SJU for the past fifteen years and she received her Ph.D. from Drexel University in strategic management. Her current research interests are in the sociotechnical interfaces in the Internet-connected workplace, including the changing workplace, human capital contributions to competitive advantage and strategic decision-making.

**Stefan Smolnik** is an assistant professor of information and knowledge management at the European Business School (EBS) in Wiesbaden/Oestrich-Winkel, Germany. He holds a doctoral degree from University of Paderborn, Germany. Before joining EBS, he worked as a research and teaching assistant at this university's Groupware Competence Center. Stefan Smolnik has done research on the success and performance measurement of information and knowledge management systems, which has included several benchmarking studies. In addition, he is interested in the successful organizational implementation of social media. His work has been published in the Business & Information Systems Engineering journal, the International Journal of Knowledge Management, the Business Process Management Journal, the Proceedings of the Annual International Conference on Information Systems, the Proceedings of the Annual Hawaii International Conference on System Sciences, and the Proceedings of the Annual European Conference on Information Systems.

**Henning Staar** is a research assistant and PhD candidate at the Department of Psychology (Institute for Work and Organizational Psychology) at the University of Hamburg, Germany. He graduated in Psychology and Applied Linguistics. His research interests are on the role of influence and power in working processes, especially in virtual collaboration settings. His research focuses on the measurement of informal political behavior in inter-organizational virtual networks and on the ways informal processes affect network goal achievement.

**Mei Ling Tan** is a doctoral student in management at the Nanyang Technological University (Singapore) where she received her master's degree in business. She is a recipient of the prestigious Nanyang President's Graduate Scholarship. Her research interests include the role of sense of humor, cultural intelligence, and language proficiency in multicultural settings and the integration of diverse workforces. Mei Ling has published on the topics of psychological contracts, cultural intelligence, and global culture capital. She has presented her work at international conferences including the Academy of Management meetings and the International Association of Chinese Management Research Conference.

**Maliha S. Zaman**, MBA, is a doctoral candidate of Management Information Systems in the Department of Management at Drexel University. Her current research interest include electronic government and use of public sector website, the use of technology by Gen Y in the workplace. Her research work has appeared in Computers in Human Behavior and IEEE Transactions on Professional Communication.

# Index

## A

Affective commitment 79-80, 82
Affirmative Action 167
All-Views-Qualitative-Analysis (AVQA) 194, 196
Annual Demographic Supplements (ADS) 34
areas of interest (AOI) 197
artificial wage discrimination 44
Assertiveness 180, 182-183, 185
Association of Information Systems (AIS) 129
average variance extracted (AVE) 25, 100, 149
awareness features 188

## B

Blascovich's theory 198
Blocking and Manipulating 180
boundary spanners 175
Bronze Age petroglyphs 229
Business Services Branch (BSB) 80
Business Software Alliance (BSA) 214

## C

Chief Technology Officer (CTO) 52
Claiming Vacancies 177-178, 180, 182, 185-186
Cognitive presence 91-92, 94-98, 101-103, 105
Cohen's Kappa 117, 176
collaboration community 103
Collaboration Engineering (CE) 109
Collaboration success 91-94, 97-98, 101-103
Community Benefits 135, 137
composite reliability (CR) 100
computer-mediated communication (CMC) 93
convergence 5, 57-59, 61, 63, 66, 71, 91, 108-113, 118-120, 187, 189
corruption perceptions index (CPI) 218
Current Population Survey (CPS) 31-32, 34
cybertext 227, 236-238, 241

## D

Daedalus 229-231, 233, 235
Data warehousing 4
deep structure 77
demographic variables 34, 183, 254
Deontological evaluation (DE) 251, 254
Deontological norms 248-249
digital media and animation (DMA) 10
Disaggregated ideas 111

## E

Ease of Use 138, 143, 147, 150, 153, 155, 157, 195
Embedded technology (ES) 10
Enterprise Resource Planning (ERP) 3
Ethical Judgment (EJ) 252
Executive Committee (Exco) 162-163
eye-tracking (ET) 194, 196

## F

face-to-face (FTF) 91
FastFocus 111-113, 118
favouritism 165, 167-168
flaneur 238-239
FreeBrainstorm 112

## G

gender wage gap 31-34, 38-39, 41-47
generation gap 165
Google Documents 207
green research practices (GRP) 243, 255
gross national income (GNI) 215
Group effectiveness 92, 95-96, 109
group formation 209
group support systems (GSS) 93